FLYER BEWARE

MY FOUR-YEAR ORDEAL IN
A PERUVIAN PRISON

PATRICIA BARONOWSKI-SCHNEIDER

ISBN: 979-8-89079-007-1 (Paperback)
ISBN: 979-8-89079-008-8 (Ebook)

TABLE OF CONTENTS

CHAPTER 1

It's a beautiful world we live in—Niagara Falls, the Eiffel Tower, Cancun, Jamaica, and so on. There are so many tourist attractions with so much beauty in the world. If you're like me, your bucket list is to travel the world and take in all its glorious sites, just like in the movie *The Bucket List*. That, too, was one of my goals in life: to travel around the world and see all of its beauty. I used to tease my husband because he never had a passport. He used to tell me, "There's plenty of beauty in the USA to see. You don't need to travel abroad to see things." That may be, but I always wanted to venture to faraway places to see the beauty around the world.

While I didn't have the money to travel the whole world, it still was something I yearned for. I had traveled before, and one year, I was able to take my kids to Cancun, Mexico. It was such a joy to me. We had a great time and toured around all the sights the city had to offer, taking it all in. I also went to London for business once, but sadly did not have enough time to travel to Paris from there. Still, I managed to tour around London one day to take in all the sites. I also had clients around the world, from countries like Ireland, Germany, and Europe. They customarily traveled to the USA since their businesses were listed on the New York Stock Exchange. This meant that they would come here because their shareholders were here, which did not leave me the opportunity to travel there to see them.

Besides, in the world of cyber business, all it took was the click of my mouse to market all my client's accounts to the entire world. Nowadays, the whole world is online; it is nestled somewhere between all the laptops, computers, iPads, smartphones, and so on. The internet makes navigating all aspects of business fast and easy. While being face-to-face is always good, it just isn't as necessary in business as much as it used to be. One can have video chats on Skype, WhatsApp, etc., making travel less of a necessity.

I still loved exploring the world, anyway, whether it was via television, the internet, or books. When I would watch movies or look at videos and see all the beauty of the world, I would imagine myself exploring it. I always believed in the old idea, "One can always dream, right?"

I know movies and such often make some places look more exorbitant than they actually are. Movie props and cinematography can really enhance visuals in a stunning way, but nonetheless, it still gave my appetite a taste for parts untraveled.

The irony is, when we yearn to travel, we research the various places and see the beautiful highlights, but rarely do we ever see the bad stuff front and center. The tourist places show you the resorts. And there's a good reason why they do. In essence, the responsibility of resorts is to provide a one-stop-shop to see the beauty of the country with curated tours to show you the sites. You never really know what lies under the truth about countries.

For example, when my kids and I toured Cancun, we stayed at a beautiful resort and went with tour guides to see the sites. One of the tour guides took my kids and me on a little excursion to show us how the locals live. He said, "It is a third-world country, and maybe it would help your kids to have more appreciation of life back home." It was interesting to see ten people living in a tiny wooden home with animals all around, clothes hanging all over the place, chickens and roosters racing everywhere, etc.

When we wanted to venture off and explore on our own one night, we walked along the beach and down some local streets. You could see the streets getting darker and scarier as we ventured away from the resort. In the local town, we were approached by people trying to sell us drugs. At that point, I made a quick U-turn and ventured back to the resort with the kids since we started to feel unsafe, and rightfully so.

I'm not saying New York, my hometown, is any better, but as a Native New Yorker, I learned street smarts and how to recognize trouble. Tourists, of course, don't always know how to notice those things and can get victimized as well. As beautiful as it is, the world is sadly also full of very evil people with agendas that are not always in line with decent people.

I am sadly shocked by how many evil people there are in the world. I had stopped watching the news for some time because it was so depressing. I lived through 9/11 in New York, where suicide bombers flew airplanes through the Twin Towers, killing themselves and thousands of innocent victims. It was a horror to live through, yet I was not even one who lost a loved one that day. Friends, yes, but not a loved one myself. A coworker of mine lost her husband, who she had just recently married. I also saw an interview of a woman who was two months pregnant and lost her husband that day. I couldn't even fathom how she'd endure the rest of her pregnancy, give birth to their child, and explain later why the child's dad was not there. Back then, I remember watching the news and seeing the televised interviews of families and friends who lost people that day. It was so depressing. Why would someone do that? From what I read, it was for the religious beliefs they had.

I also read the story about the hijackers and the guys who took over, flew the airplanes, and crashed them. It was not something that happened quickly on a whim one day. Instead, it was a carefully planned and calculated operation. These men lived in the United States for a while and learned their way around things. They had girlfriends, jobs, and what could otherwise be called a "normal" life. They got their pilot licenses in Florida after training for a few months. It was all carefully planned out and executed in the exact way they had intended.

I remember running to my kids' schools that day to make sure they were safe and sound. Their school ended up being closed for five days straight because of the massive scale of devastation that went on at the time.

One day shortly after this, I took my daughter to work with me. We were walking toward the Port Authority, which is a big bus/train station and a key point to various states across the USA, and saw people running toward us in droves and then running back to where we came from, away from the station. In fear, we turned and started to run with them since we had no idea what they were running from. Someone shouted that there was a rumor of a bomb at the Port Authority, so everyone was running away from it.

My daughter, who was only eight years old then, ran with me while crying, "Mommy, why are they doing this to us?" Those words went right through me, as it was a question that I could not answer. While they may have had religious reasons as their purpose, it still made no sense to me how one could just take so many innocent lives like that.

This was not something new, really. Going back to before I was even born, the world had endured wars for various reasons, the likes of WWI, WW2, the Vietnam War, the Gulf War, and more. While countries may disagree on various topics, the men and women in the military go to battle on behalf of their respective countries and risk their lives to win a war, which is, in essence, one country winning a battle to get its way. The "winner" is just the one that gets to set the terms.

I was never a very political person. I never really followed politics and wars. But with several of my family and friends in the military, it still always scared me that they may one day be sent off to war and never return home.

When my son was in high school, I remember the military trying to convince the seniors to sign up for the military by enticing them with offers. "We'll pay for your college, and you'll get benefits. Think of how proud everyone will be of you to represent your country." I was furious about that. My baby boy was becoming a man, and instead of allowing him to make that decision on his own, they went to schools and tried to convince them to sign up with their persuasion. To me, they were painting a rosy picture of joining the military instead of telling the truth. They never said, "You'll be away from your friends and family for a few years while we train you for war, and we may or may not send you to the front lines of war. You may never see your family again if you get killed while trying to fight over something you may or may not even agree with." Once you signed the papers, that was it. They owned you. But saying that would turn away potential recruits, which, of course, they did not want to do. I was glad my son did not sign anything.

Be it countries or the people living within them, evil knows no bounds. You can take one away but there will always be additional means of evil in the world. I went to Mexico for a business meeting once, and my client had their driver pick me up at the airport. He said that under no circumstance should I get in any other car, as it was not safe. While I was waiting in the airport, a couple came up and silently whispered to me, telling me to hide my watch. They said I was being watched by thieves. I was shocked and immediately hid my watch.

The driver eventually came and drove me to my hotel. I called my client and was told that the driver would take me to their office the next day. I thought I would then spend the day browsing around but was advised not to leave the hotel as it was not safe. I was told I could get mugged, raped, or even killed. Since my client was a local there, I had to trust his judgment. Later in the trip, I was told that taxis there would often spot a tourist and would not take them to their destination. Instead, they would take a detour, rob them, and then throw them out of the taxi. It is scary how evil people can be. I allowed my client's driver to take me to my meetings, then back to the airport, and made it home safe and sound.

While I could sit and say, "How could a country be like that to tourists?" the US, sadly, has its own share of criminals and scammers as well. The only difference here is that I am not customarily a target. That's not to say that I was never scammed or robbed there, either though. As a teenager, I fell victim to card games on Broadway, people selling me counterfeit items, having my jewelry and cell phone stolen, etc.

One day, I remember going to take the train to school. While in the station, a man ran up to me, snatched the 14-karat gold chains off my neck, and ran off. I was devastated. Not only did he scratch my neck and rip my shirt in the process, one of the chains he snatched off me belonged to my stepfather. He had just given it to me, and it meant a lot to me. I felt like a failure once it was snatched away from me.

The crazy part of this story was that I was with a fellow classmate of mine as we headed to school. I figured the thief was most likely planning to pawn the jewelry at a local pawnshop. And so, I decided I would go looking for it. I didn't care that I would have to pay to get it back at a pawnshop. It was sentimental to me.

My classmate and I ventured off on the train toward 42nd Street in Manhattan, where a few local pawnshops were located back then. As my luck would have it, we got picked up by the police for truancy (cutting school) just as we were leaving the train station. Back then, in all my sixteen years of being on God's green earth, I had never once heard of or seen truancy police before in my life. But apparently, as we had just witnessed, they existed, and they picked up the two of us when all we wanted to do was search for the jewelry that was just stolen right off my neck a few short hours prior.

My mother and the school knew about my whereabouts, so it was a complete waste of my time. But still, we were made to go through the whole rigmarole of being taken into a van with other truant individuals. They drove the van with us and took us to a location where we sat for hours. Then they called our parents and school to tell them they caught us cutting school. To their surprise, they were informed that both our parents and the school knew. They asked them to release us both, which they did hours later, with still no jewelry on us.

That is just an example of how the US has its share of bad people, too, just like every other country. It never ceased to amaze me how people could be so cruel to others.

One time, my family's apartment got robbed. The thieves broke into our place after climbing down the fire escape and breaking our window. We were on the top floor of the building, so sadly, they chose our apartment to rob. They took all our jewelry and everything of value. We were a middle-class family with three children and not much to rob. And yet, despite this, thieves seemed to only care about *their* needs and wants. They could care less about the effect their actions would have on us. What if what they stole was for our rent? What if we were evicted if we didn't have the money to pay it? What if it was for a lifesaving operation or medical care for our family? Sadly, bad people truly don't care, nor do they even think about how their actions affect others. They just don't care. I know this firsthand for many reasons, but I will talk first about my early experience.

CHAPTER 2

I dated several losers in my time, unfortunately, but one stands out as the bigger loser. To give a little background, I was a single mom of two small children who were young at the time. I was also training to become a licensed skydiver. It all started when I participated in a tandem skydive once, fell immensely in love with the sport, and wanted to train to be licensed to be able to travel around and skydive my heart out.

It was during my time as a skydiver that I met a fellow skydiver at a drop zone, and we started dating. He "palled" around with a female skydiver but told me they were just friends, and she never once questioned me about him and me hanging out, so I assumed it was true. From then on, we dated at the drop zone, and he even came and visited me at my apartment and met my kids. He also had two children that were my kids' age. They lived with their mom in Pennsylvania for the most part, but he got them for visitation every other weekend.

We dated for a while and then went on a vacation to Las Vegas, just the two of us. Unfortunately, we had gotten into a fight because he wanted to get married in Las Vegas that weekend. I had never been married before, and my kids and family were not with me, so I did not want to do that. He did not want to take no for an answer and was beyond relentless and would not stop until I agreed. I had never been in that type of persistent situation before and was unsure how to handle it. I did love him but did not feel right about having my marriage on the sneak, away from my kids and my family, but he was very conniving.

We got married in Las Vegas, but luckily, it was not an Elvis Presley wedding. It was at a chapel and was over in ten minutes. It was not at all what I ever expected my first marriage to be like. It was done now, so I had to accept that. The flight home was quiet, and my stomach was in knots. I didn't know how on earth I'd explain this to my family. We agreed not to tell them at first; that made it easier. But I knew I had to eventually tell my kids and family that I was married.

After two or three weeks, I finally broke down and told my family. They were beyond shocked and sad, but luckily for me, they didn't harass me about it. My mother threw a party for me, and we celebrated. Sadly, that was the beginning of the end of what was good. As with the 9/11 terrorists and all other evil people in the world, my husband's true colors began to surface.

My life with this man soon took a turn for the absolute worst. We returned from Las Vegas as a married couple. I then bought a house in Pennsylvania, which was his neck of the woods. Due to his extreme persistence, the house was in my name only. It was only afterward that I found out his credit was horrific. He couldn't get credit, and trying to put him on the mortgage would have made the price skyrocket, so it went in my name only. He wasn't working either, so that was another problem. I bought the house, and then we moved into it. That's when the nightmare started.

This man became extremely abusive the moment we shared space. Not only was he physically abusive, but he also leveled mental and verbal abuse as well. I did not know where to turn. I had been a very hard worker, a single mom of two kids. All in all, I was a very responsible and professional person. Now, I was living in hell and scared to tell my family that this was happening. It was bad enough that I got married on the sneak; now I was living in Pennsylvania, and all of this was happening. Luckily, he never touched my children *yet*. But I was determined never to allow that to happen. They were my pride and joy. I'd risk my life for my kids. I would never ever allow someone to touch them or abuse them.

Well, this man, besides abusing me, also wound up robbing me blind. He went from stealing every penny I had in my bank, including all the money I had saved up for my kids from their Baptisms, births, birthdays, etc. Since we were married, he managed to swindle his way into all my things. He maxed out every one of my credit cards, robbed all my money, wrote out checks from my bank account, bounced checks all over the place, selling all of my belongings, including laptops, cell phones, jewelry, etc. This went on for a year and was a living hell for me. He called me all day long while I was at work, picked me up at work each day, drove me home from Manhattan to Pennsylvania, then drove me back to work again in the morning to start the whole nightmare over again.

It was a never-ending cycle. It was so hard to be free from this man. I couldn't take it, but I couldn't just leave either. My kids were in school in Pennsylvania now, with me working in Manhattan. It was not easy to just leave.

I remember him leaving one day while my kids were with family for the weekend. He not only took out wires from my car so that I could not escape even if I wanted to, but he nailed the windows and door to the house closed from the outside, so I could not escape. It truly was hell on Earth. The last straw was once when he grabbed my son—who was 15 years old at the time—by the shirt and yelled at him. In my heart, I knew this was a sign that his next step would be to hit my son. That's where I drew the line. The next day, I called my older sister, who came to my rescue. She met me, and we managed to drive back to Pennsylvania—after he dropped me off at work—to get a restraining order, gather my belongings, pick up my kids, and flee.

It was not as easy as that, though. He continued to stalk me, harass me, torment me, write bounced checks in my name, etc. It was insane. He had zero regard for the law or the restraining order I had on him. I later found out that he also somehow managed to forge my signature on another account that he put in both our names and wrote out thousands of dollars in phony checks from that account while putting my telephone number on it. He also remembered my PayPal login info and tied it to this bank account. Then he went around small local airports and claimed to be an airline GPS salesman and told Cessna pilots that he could sell them a $20,000 airplane GPS for $10,000. Several people were interested. They then PayPal-ed him money to my account, unbeknownst to me, which he then withdrew himself and mailed each person a rock in the mail. I only knew this when my telephone started ringing off the hook from people demanding their money back from me since it was *my*

PayPal they sent the money to. Sadly, I had to borrow $40k from my mom to pay these people back. This was money *he* stole from them, yet he tied *me* to it.

I, a single mom of two children, was doing my best to raise my two amazing children and teach them to be good people. I raised them with zero child support and was on the run from this man, with no money to my name, debt up to my eyeballs thanks to him, and with no home to live in. Lucky for me, I was fortunate enough to have a sister who allowed me and my kids to stay with her until I figured something out.

Just thinking about all this makes me feel exasperated. He ruined my credit, put my house into foreclosure before setting it on fire, maxed out every single credit card I had, and robbed every penny from my kids and me. How can someone be so cruel?

Well, as I later found out, people like him have a habit of doing unspeakable things like this, and they rarely stop. I was not his first victim by any means. He was in jail prior for bounced checks. He was married before and abused his exes, too. The biggest kicker was the woman he was palling around at the skydiving drop zone, who he said was just a friend, was in a relationship with him! He conned her into believing that he got a job as a truck driver and was on the road. I learned later that he maxed out all of *her* credit cards and bank accounts also, as well as his last wife's, too.

It took me about a year and a half to escape him. He stalked me relentlessly. I was back in Manhattan with my kids trying to pick back up the pieces of my life. He even went so far as to tattoo a naked photo of me on his back that said, *Larry and Patty together forever*. This was *after* I left him. It was insane.

Sadly, I wish I could say it was a one–time thing, but I later learned that he *also* stole someone else's identity, purchased an RV, and traveled around the USA, still scamming people. He went on to meet another woman in Arizona who also had two children, one of whom was autistic, and he also convinced her to marry him in Las Vegas. After that, he started the cycle of abuse and did the exact same things to her. He maxed out her credit cards, destroyed for condominium, and stole all her things. It got so bad that she had to eventually leave and move in with her parents.

I still can't wrap my head around this. How can people be so heartless? The man whose identity he stole said it was a nightmare. It took that person over a decade to straighten out their finances because of that mess. Yet, did Larry care? Nope! Did he care how he ruined my life and all the other women's? Nope! And did he care how he robbed us of all of our money and belongings while we were single parents with kids, and we had no place to live nor any idea how we'd feed ourselves or our kids? Nope!

From the get-go, his only concern was himself, sadly, not even *his* kids. In fact, he even went so far as to steal *his son's* identity! Since his credit was shot, he made an ID with his photo and his son's name. Then, he started getting credit cards registered and maxed them all out. I couldn't even think of doing such horrific things to people or ruining their lives in such a way, let alone my children. But I guess that's the difference between a good person and a bad/evil one. Good people consider their actions and their effects on others. Someone with a conscience and a good heart would never hurt someone or cause them pain and heartache the way some people do.

There are different breeds of bad people out there, like the people who robbed our home, stealing all our money and belongings, the man who snatched my jewelry off of my neck on my way to school, or the countless men and women like my ex-husband, who torment and torture people, in front of kids no less. I must wonder, where are their hearts? Do they even have them? Do they have a conscience? What about the men and women who commit rape? Not only is that a horrible crime and abuse of control and power, but the emotional effects it causes to the victims are effects they may never recover from. Do the rapists care? Apparently not. What causes someone to do such a thing? Mental illness seems to be the usual suspect, yet that is only one suggested reason. What about other reasons? Some people, sadly, enjoy hurting and harming others. Some people truly do not care *at all* about anyone other than themselves. The world we live in can be truly evil sometimes.

I've learned that many people rob and steal to get money and acquire belongings that may not have otherwise come their way. Does that make it right? Of course not. But at least one can try and understand why someone would do what they did, like my ex, for example. He robbed everyone he encountered. The ironic part was that he was an extremely smart man with a photographic memory. A brain like that could have gotten a variety of jobs, made lots of money, and lived a good life. Instead, he chose to rob people and have more than he could have ever needed. It never seemed to end, no matter how much money he had. It never seemed to be enough. It's something that's beyond my understanding. I mean, there is help for people in need, such as food stamps, public assistance, public housing, and welfare. But some people want more than the basics that public assistance provides. For these people, public assistance can be readily substituted with scams, lies, and robbery. Does that make it right? Of course not. Does that stop people from doing this? Sadly, no.

What makes people do such things that are obviously wrong? What makes people step on others to get what they want, despite how it may affect them? How and why do people do what they do to others, often causing harm and heartache? These are questions I have been trying to understand for quite some time, but even more so these past four and a half years.

Why? Well, let me explain in as best detail as I can.

CHAPTER 3

As I mentioned, I was a licensed skydiver. I had been jumping for fifteen years. As the perfectionist I am, I trained and trained to be the best skydiver I could be. I also became an instructor to teach others how to skydive safely and enjoy the sport as I did. I was passionate about skydiving. It was one of my biggest passions, and I enjoyed it immensely. I jumped for nine months a year, every day that I could. I truly loved it.

One September day in 2015, I was skydiving and was accidentally hit in the head while in freefall at 5,000 feet. The hit knocked me out cold, and I was hurling toward the earth at 175 miles per hour. Lucky for me, in my parachute, I had what was called an AAD, which is an automatic activation device. If you are falling at a certain speed at a certain altitude, an AAD is designed to detect that something is wrong and automatically deploy your parachute.

In my case, I was unconscious and falling at a freefall speed below my deploying altitude, so my AAD picked up on it and deployed my parachute automatically. However, I remained unconscious while under my canopy. The wind blew me into a tree, where I landed, still unconscious, stuck in the tree. I was eventually cut free and airlifted to a hospital. I had a broken back, neck, and throat and was functioning at the mental capability of a five-year-old.

Doctors could not say if I would recover, how long it would take, and how much of my brain would go back to normal—if at all. They said that the brain is one organ that they did not fully understand to the extent of predicting such answers. I was communicating with people at the hospital eventually—but only to the level of a five-year-old. I was given a circle and asked to draw a clock on it, meaning I had to place the numbers 1 through 12 and two hands. This was to determine my brain functionality. I was told later that I drew two eyes and a mouth, and then I turned on SpongeBob cartoons on the TV. Yet, other times, they would ask me, for example, if it was cold outside, what would I wear? I would answer with, "You would wear a shearling jacket."

I have been told that the brain works like a file cabinet; it holds the things you have learned, seen, heard, etc. Maybe a shearling jacket was something I had seen in a magazine at some point in my life or on television. It just happened to be the answer to that question at that point. It didn't mean I knew what I was saying, though, since I'd go right back to answering other questions strangely.

Apparently, on the bulletin board in my room where doctors posted my information for other doctors, I would argue with my husband that I was updating my Facebook status on it. He managed to get it on video and showed me after the fact. I was convinced in my state of mind that the TV remote was my tool to update my Facebook on the board. I was annoyed that no one believed me. It seemed at that time that my mind was acting on autopilot, talking about my experiences and things that I had done. I was not actually doing them, but my brain was, in a sense, scrambled. It was not differentiating the differences.

PHOTOS OF ME IN THE HOSPITAL AFTER THE SKYDIVING ACCIDENT

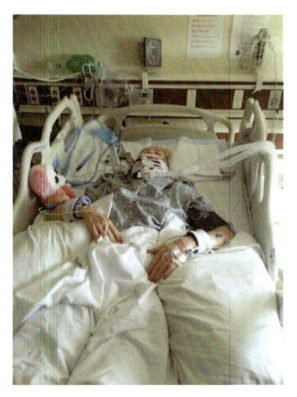

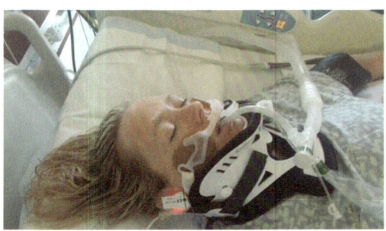

This went on for the month that I was in the hospital, but then I had to be released to outpatient therapy since, health-wise, there was nothing more they could do for me. The hospital performed surgery on my neck and put a metal bracket in it to prevent paralysis if anything shifted. I also had a chest and back brace to wear for my broken back, and my throat had fused and healed. So, physically, I was getting back to normal. However, mentally, I was not there yet.

I remember now that when I first got home, I was still unsure of the television channels. My brain remembered channels from where I lived in Manhattan with my kids over a decade prior. I was having a hard time, struggling to understand why my favorite shows were not on these channels. Then I thought we did not have certain channels, and I was trying to order them through the television remote control. It is strange how my mind was functioning. At the time, I did not catch on to any of this, but years later, I remember bits and pieces.

I still have zero memory of the day of the accident or the entire day before. I have no memory of the entire month in the hospital and only sporadic memory of the two to three months of my first being home. Some of it is hit or miss. Some things I remember, and other things I cannot remember at all. I remember being told not to jump right back into work, to only start one or two hours a day. I had been working since I was 12 years old and never had all day to myself with nothing to do. I was completely lost. I tried watching TV, but it seemed that during the day, it was either reality TV or soap operas, neither of which I enjoy, so I was lost. When I sat in front of my computer, I felt at home. I had been working from a computer for decades, so it was normal to my mind when I worked. I felt back to normal, in my mind, anyway. Sadly, my work productivity was not the same, but I did not catch on to that, and my husband seemed more relieved to see me in what he thought was back to normal. Therefore, he did not catch on to or pay as much attention to the quirks and differences in me. My mother had caught on to them and kept telling me that she wanted me to see a doctor. Unfortunately, I just kept blowing it off since, in my head, I thought I was back to normal. I didn't see the problem, sadly.

For starters, I hired a man called Eric* from Croatia. I hired him from an online agency called Upwork.com. It used to be called Odesk.com but then became Upwork. On Upwork, you can hire people from around the world for a variety of jobs. It gave a good opportunity to hire people who did not charge top dollar, as was always the case in New York. What's more, it gave you a chance to get global experiences.

What I liked most about a recruitment model like this was that you paid your employees through Upwork, not directly. Of course, this led me to believe that Upwork screened all employees to validate them and their work. This gave me the false hope that even if everything went sour, I wouldn't end up losing my money. I hired Eric to help grow my company and bring in more business. I thought I could hire people to help run the company, and I would work a little less and spend more time with my kids and family. Eric worked for a while and sadly wasn't bringing in any new business or work.

Soon after, he introduced me to a woman named Lisa Parker* from Connecticut. We had several telephone calls and group video calls on Skype. She also sent me her resume and various documents confirming her identity. She assured me that she knew everyone in the business, and she was beyond confident that she could help me grow my company. I agreed to hire her for one month to see how it went. We had many chats on the phone via Skype, video conferencing, and emails. She told me about her two children, her boyfriend, who was supposedly a prince in a foreign country, and all sorts of her supposed success. Unfortunately, I believed Eric about how good she was since I really didn't know her.

After the first month, she asked me if I could lend her $40,000. I was beyond shocked and asked Eric what was up with that. He just assured me that it was a legitimate request and that she was good for the money. She then signed a contract with me, and I wired her the money.

That $40k turned into another $30k, then $50k, and then another $50k. All told it ballooned up to a hefty $170k in total. Each time she would sign a new contract, and sadly, Eric assured me that it was legitimate and that she was good for the money. Sadly, before the accident, I would have seen every red flag here, yet after it—I didn't. Every time I questioned it, Eric assured me it was fine, so I believed him and went along with it.

At one point, I ran out of money to give. In fact, the first $120k was my firm's money, and the last $50k wasn't even mine to give. We hosted a conference each year, and the presenters at the conference paid a fee that covered the expenses for the venue. I lent her *that* money only because she promised it **all** back to me that very weekend, which never happened. After the accident, my brain was still not functioning at full capacity enough to recognize these problems or see the red flags that would have been crystal clear to me prior. I also did not see the magnitude of the situation to raise awareness among my family.

All of this brought me into major debt. Eric then introduced me to a loaner, who assured me that he could repay me the money to get things back to normal. Again, I was in a state of not seeing the red flags. I did not shy away when the loaner told me I had to fill out an application with all my personal details, a copy of my passport, plus $5,000 as a deposit.

Obviously, that loan never came to fruition. Eric again introduced me to not one but *two* more loan bearers, all asking for the same. That was another $15k I was out, with no loan in sight. In hindsight, I clearly see the red flags and how no legitimate lender would ever ask for a deposit upfront, but I just hadn't recovered enough to recognize all of this.

At that point, I was out $170k, my last $50k, and the $15k the loaners took from me. How was I supposed to pay for the conference? I had lent Lisa that money, money that wasn't all technically mine to lend, only because she had promised it back to me *that* weekend. Obviously, that never happened. She took the money and never gave me a dime back.

You can imagine my surprise when I found out that the money was not wired to her directly. Instead, it was wired to other people as per her instructions, all out of the US. I was stuck. I had the hotel demanding their payment for the conference and did not have the money to pay them. I was crying, and my sister mentioned something to my mother. I never discussed what happened, partly due to my embarrassment but also because I was not seeing it for its true magnitude. My mom lent me the money. This money was not only supposed to pay back the hotel but also to help purchase a mobile home for my daughter.

CHAPTER 4

My daughter had just given birth to my very first granddaughter, who was my pride and joy. I was so in love with the precious angel. Coupled with this, my daughter's boyfriend also had custody of his other two children from a previous relationship, so I purchased a mobile home for her that was only about twenty minutes from my home to move them closer to me so that I could help her with the children and be there for her and my grandbaby, to watch her grow, and be a part of her life.

I paid for the trailer, and the next day, I was introduced to Timothy Streaks*, another man out of Texas, introduced to me by guess who? Of course, Eric! Timothy claimed to own an actual business, an OTC company. He stated that he was cash-poor but artist-painting rich, but dollar-poor at the moment. He sent me a presentation about his business and everything. Like all the others, he had asked me to loan him $30k for a project and signed a contract that I would get back $300k in exchange for my loan in two weeks. I was extremely hesitant by this time, after constantly having all my money disappearing, especially since I could not afford to lose the conference money again. He assured me he would guarantee it back to me in ten days and that he was good for it. Unfortunately, I sent him the money. Dare I say it? I never got the money back.

Desperate is an understatement of how I was feeling at that point. Again, with all these scammers, how could people be so cruel? Even Lisa Parker was nothing more than a thief! I wound up coming in contact with other individuals that *she* had scammed. One man and his fiancée had loaned her thousands of dollars, and his elderly mother had as well. In fact, he had even taken money from his 401k to loan her $50k, and none of them ever got any of their money back, either.

I made Google posts about these scammers, trying to prevent future unsuspecting victims from falling prey to them. Due to my posts, I had been contacted by others who had been scammed. It seemed with the world of cyberspace and digital communication, there seemed to be no safe place. I was even contacted twice by people claiming to be in London, working for a bank, claiming to be someone in charge of a case of a deceased person who had hundreds of thousands of dollars in an account with no next of kin. They would tell me that if I partnered with them, they'd give me half of the money in the account as the supposed next of kin.

These people had letterhead documents, telephone numbers, and email addresses, all pretending to be someone they were not. They used pretend lawyers. It all seemed real, yet it was completely fake. The scam is to get you to pay some pretend taxes or processing fees, ranging anywhere from $150k or more, all with the promise of $500k or more in the end. Of course, if you send the money, you never receive a dime. I was approached by this scam twice. In fact, I was later contacted by an individual on my business email who told me that someone, probably one of these same scammers, had made up an email address, patriciabaronowski@gmail.com, and pretended to be *me* trying to scam people. It was never-ending. I tried contacting Google to report the phony email, but sadly, it took a little over four years before the email was taken down. No one had ever responded to me or acknowledged my emails. I just kept checking it. Lord only knows how many people that email scammed throughout that time, too. It was a sick game that these scammers played with innocent people's lives. It truly is sickening.

It seemed either the world was being taken over by scammers, or sadly, I was on the target list for every scammer on Earth. I had even responded to an email from a company that stated they were in Asia but needed a US presence to assist them with communicating with their US and Canadian clients and inspecting orders for them. I researched them, and they had a full-blown website showcasing all of their products and how you could order online, etc. It looked like a Macy's website.

I signed a business contract and was told they would pay $5,000 a month and send me products to inspect and then ship to the buyer with the pre-printed label with postage already paid for. It seemed self-explanatory to me. Within a week, I was sent an email with a tracking number for the first package I was being sent to inspect. I was shocked when the package came to me but in someone else's name. My husband got the UPS package and asked who the person was. I opened the package to find a G-string pair of women's panties.

It was strange. The package came to me to inspect and then to send with the pre-printed label, which was under a different name. Something didn't seem right with it. The name on it was the same as on the packing slip in the package. But again, it was not the same name of who I was to send it to. I researched the name, found a telephone number, and called it. I spoke to an elderly man and wanted to confirm that he purchased this. He explained that he did not purchase anything and was unaware of the company and that the credit card on the shipping label belonged to his son. He also never had heard the name of the person I was supposed to ship it to.

I told him to report his credit card as stolen. I told him about this company and sent him the website, job post, and contract they gave me. I also mailed everything to him and advised him to contact the police. I assume the panties were a trial to see if I would comply, and if I did, then I would get bigger items such as computers, television, etc. I am assuming that at the end of the day, it would appear as if I stole someone's credit cards and was ordering all these things for myself and shipping them home since that's how they had appeared. Luckily, I nipped that scam in the bud.

Did it end there? I wish! I got another email from a company again, claiming they needed someone in the US to handle their communication and collections with the US and Canadian clients. I would supposedly get paid $5,000 a month. I thought that was okay, so I agreed. I then got a check in the mail made out to my business for $80,000, which looked like a normal check from a reputable company using a regular bank. The check was double-endorsed and looked very real. I deposited into my business account and was asked to then wire the $80,000 to them.

I had wanted to talk to my accountant first, though. Besides, I wanted to make sure the check cleared. Although it looked like a legitimate business check, I wanted to run it by my accountant to make sure I wouldn't get stuck having to pay taxes on money that wasn't mine. During this time, I was still getting daily emails asking me to send the money to them. After three days, I was surprised to learn that the check had cleared.

Upon discovering this, I transferred the $80,000 into my savings account to not mix it with my business money. I had planned on sending them the $80k the next day, right after my accountant answered me. Well, after the fourth day, before I could send them the $80k, I was informed that the check had bounced. As it turned out, it was a fake check.

This caused trouble with me and my business account because I had moved the $80,000 into my savings account when it looked like it cleared. So, now my account was negative $80,000, and it appeared that I was trying to scam the bank out of money. The bank's legal team had gotten involved. I had to sign a ton of papers, have them notarized, and explain what happened. I was required to provide them with all the information on this scam business and who did it. Can you imagine what would have happened if I had sent $80,000? The outcome would certainly be me being separated from my money. These scammers were relentless.

My nerves were shot from all the stress and scams I was now involved in without even knowing about them. I often felt like I could not understand why I was saved from my skydiving accident, only to wind up on every scammer's target list. I was losing money left, right, and center while feeling like such a failure. It felt like it would only be a moment before I came across the next scammer.

Lo and behold, that day wasn't too far off. I got introduced to Michael Braham, now by Eric S. He started a group chat on Skype between us three. Michael told me he worked for the IMF (International Monetary Fund) and that he was retiring soon. He said he had put together a business growth program and that Eric had highly recommended me. He said Eric had told him about all the scams that I had fallen for (I am sure, excluding the fact that every scammer came from him) and that he felt bad for me and wanted to help me.

Michael said this program was for entrepreneurs, and only a select group of people were selected and could participate. Eric had apparently told him how much money I had lost to scams (which he obviously knew very well since they all came about from *him*; for all I knew, he was getting a nice commission from it all). I was told that this IMF program consisted of debt consolidating and funding to grow your business.

I initially thought, *Wow, debt consolidation. I have $150,000 in debt from my daughter's college tuition loan that I could clear away. And the business funding would allow me to hire people to help run and grow my business while I spend more time with my new grandbaby.*

Naturally, I was very excited at the prospect. If this one was what it claimed to be, it could really help me out. Unlike the other times, Michael had also sent me a copy of his passport, so I could verify who he was.

I was fully aware of IMF, as they are a huge global institution. I called and left many, many messages trying to verify this program and even this Michael Braham. Sadly, not one person got back to me. All I had to go on was, again, Eric's word. Sadly, my brain, which was slowly trying to recover, was still not yet up to par.

I have a friend who works for the FBI. I had sent her a copy of the passport Michael gave me to ask if there was any way to see if the passport was good or if it was stolen or forged in any way. I had first-hand experience with this when my identity was stolen, and I had to report *my* passport as stolen, as advised by the passport agency. The person was using my passport, pretending to be me, and scamming others. They're also the ones who were using patriciabaronowsk@gmail.com.

My FBI contact pointed out three obvious mistakes with Michael's passport. They were very obvious to her, of course, just not to me. I guess, to normal people, you would have seen it also, but I, sadly, was still in brain-recovery mode.

I immediately wrote to Michael (I'll call him MB from here on to make it easier) and cc'd Eric, pointing out the three fraudulent errors with the passport and chastising him for trying to scam me. He stated that he was shocked that I would accuse him of trying to scam me and that he would never try to do anything like that in a million years. When I asked him to explain the phony passport, he told me that his passport had been stolen too. He explained that he hadn't realized that the passport he sent me was the bogus one the scammers had used. He then stated that I was immediately ejected from the IMF program and that I had now missed the opportunity of a lifetime. He stated that all he wanted to do was help me, and yet I just slapped him in the face with my accusation.

We had been chatting online via Skype and email for a few months, and I felt bad. We talked about business, family, etc. I told him about my kids, new grandbaby, husband, business, etc. He told me his wife had passed away, and so had his twin brother. He stated that his son was running a business selling clothing. I felt bad about accusing him, but having fallen for so many scams recently, who could blame me? Plus, he was writing to me from a Gmail account and @representative.com email, not an IMF-designated email. I could not find his name on the IMF website, but it is a huge firm, which made it next to impossible for me to find anything without help from the institution. Besides, MB had an answer for everything. I had even asked if he could video chat via Skype instead of just text. He stated his cell did not have camera capability. While I could say, "Who doesn't have a camera on their phone?" I could also say that I know many elderly people who still use old-fashioned phones that do not have the capability, so it was a tough call.

He had cut off all communication for the next three months, around the holidays. As the new year approached in 2017, I sent an email out to my entire email contact list wishing them a happy and healthy New Year with wonderful wishes for each. What I had forgotten was that MB was also on the email list. He responded by thanking me and expressed again how I had missed the opportunity of a lifetime. He stated that he never asked me for anything—not a penny—and all he wanted to do was help me, but instead, I attacked him and accused him of trying to scam me.

I apologized to MB and said that it was unfortunate, and I hoped he would have seen my concern after all I had been through. He stated that he did but wished I had just asked him instead of accusing him. I apologized again.

The next day, MB asked me if I still had my passport. I stated that I did. He said he had a change of heart with me and wanted to put me back into the program. I asked if he had retired yet, as he had said he was. He stated that his replacement was his friend and that he could reenlist me in the program. I didn't know what to think or say. No one had replied to me from IMF, and Eric kept assuring me, "He's never asked for anything—no money or anything. He's not scramming you."

That was true; he never asked for any money. What did I have to lose? If it was legitimate, I would eliminate all the debts for the college tuition and all my credit cards. I could grow my business and spend more time with my kids, grandkids, and family. What did I have to lose? He stated that I would have to fly to Peru to meet with the US IMF representative there, who was meeting with all the American people to be enlisted into the program.

I was told that once I was in Peru, he would email me the IMF documents I would have to sign and attach my photos. He had me bring thirteen passport photos, all of which would be attached to the documents when I was there. We had agreed for me to come in March. I brought both of my passports with me since I wasn't sure how it all worked with my getting a new one. I wasn't sure if all the information was in the system yet. There was no difference between them, anyway. They contained my same name and the same information. It's just that one was canceled, and the other was new.

I had informed MB that I needed to be home by March 31st since that was my birthday, and the next day, April 1st, was to be my grandbaby's Baptism. There was no way I was missing that. MB had sent me my itinerary, which had me arriving in Lima, Peru, staying at a hotel, then leaving for Hong Kong a week later, where I was supposed to be initiated into the program. The flight was not direct, but from Peru to Madrid to Doha to Hong Kong.

While waiting for my flight to Peru in JFK, I Googled the hotel, and it was in what appeared to be a bad neighborhood and looked pretty shady. I then found myself a nicer-looking hotel in a safer-looking location in Miraflores. MB Skyped me to confirm my arrival, and I told him about my new hotel. He threw a fit and told me that IMF had its own rules and that if I would not follow their rules and program, then I might as well just go home. I was shocked. I told him I would follow the program, but I just switched hotels because this one looked safer. He didn't sound happy, but he let it go. The next day he emailed me the forms, and I had to ask the front desk to print out two copies of them for me. The form was on IMF letterhead and had me fill in my personal information, beneficiary information, and all of my banking information, which was supposed to be for the business funding.

Before even stepping foot off the plane in Peru, MB asked me if I had an offshore bank account or an HSBC account, which I did not. He said I would need an account where I could deposit $500k, but I could open up an HSBC account when I arrived in Hong Kong since that account would accept such a deposit. I actually went and opened up a plain/generic HSBC account before flying to Peru. I thought it would speed up opening a business bank account in HSBC when I got to Hong Kong since the bank would now have all of my information in their system now.

I sat at the hotel for several days, waiting for this "IMF representative" to meet me to collect the papers. The internet was not good in the hotel room, so I spent my days in the hotel lobby, in their waiting room, trying to work from my laptop while waiting for someone to arrive. I panicked, knowing that there was no way I would make it to Hong Kong and back in time for my granddaughter's Baptism, since many days were passing and no one was showing up to collect these papers. During the day, I managed to walk to a few local stores and buy souvenirs for my family, but I never ventured far for fear of missing the IMF representative. One day, MB told me the representative was not coming that day. Since I was there, I figured I might as well spend the day exploring Lima, Peru. I would have liked to have seen Machu Picchu, but that was several hours away, and I did not have enough spare time. Instead, I toured around Lima with a tour group and took tons of photos to share with my friends and family. After that, I was still waiting for the IMF representative, who was not coming. I knew for sure that if I waited any longer, I would not make it back in time for the Baptism, and I had told MB from the start that was not optional. I would not miss my grandbaby's Baptism. When I realized I would not make it if I waited any longer, I booked my flight back home.

MB was not happy when I told him, and he kept telling me not to go. He said if I missed the Baptism, it would be okay because I'd be coming back a changed person who could help my whole family and have a wonderful life. I told him absolutely not. I would not miss the Baptism; I had told him that from the start, and he told me the process would be fast. Instead, I sat for a full week in the hotel lobby, and no one showed up. I couldn't wait any longer and left.

CHAPTER 5

I arrived back in New York on March 31st—my birthday. I was too tired to go out with friends to celebrate my birthday and just worked that day instead. The next day was the Baptism, and I was delighted that I made it back for that. The event was glorious, and the baby was truly a princess that day. I had written to MB that I was very disappointed with how the ordeal had turned out. It was extremely disorganized, and I waited so many days for nothing. He told me that there were over 200 American people in Peru for this program. But I still wished that it had progressed and not sent me home empty-handed, as I had different expectations based on his original explanation of my initiation into the program that he explained to me before I went to Peru.

MB wanted me to fly back again the day after the Baptism. I couldn't do that because I had a few work things and a vacation planned to fly to Florida to visit family. At this point, I assumed I would be going straight to Hong Kong. But he said, "No, back to Peru." I asked, "What? Why?" to which he replied, "Because you didn't sign the attendance sheet."

What? The hotel could verify that I was there. My flights confirmed I was there. Going back to Peru just to sign an attendance sheet seemed silly to me. But he told me, "You don't work for IMF. They have their own rules and procedures, and you must follow them." He then booked a new itinerary for me for April 20, 2017, again. It was the same situation. It had me flying to Peru, staying at the hotel they chose, then meeting their representative, giving them the papers, then flying from Peru-Madrid-Doha-Hong Kong—to be initiated into the program. Then, I would open a business HSBC account, have the program funding wired into the account and then fly home. He had the itinerary for seven days in Peru but told me that was just a formality, that I would probably only be there for three days.

I stayed at the hotel they chose, which was only ten minutes from the airport. It was in a very bad neighborhood. In fact, on my first night there, we heard someone getting mugged outside the hotel. The police department was two blocks away, but no police ever came, which was strange. I worked from the hotel again, waiting for the IMF representative to show up this time. For the first three days, no one showed up. On the fourth night, I was in my room when the receptionist phoned me and said, "Someone is here to collect papers from you."

Finally! I went downstairs and found a Nigerian man chatting with the front desk staff in Spanish. I don't speak or understand Spanish, so I had no idea what they were saying or talking about. I went down with my papers, and he walked into the next room with me, which was a small office waiting area.

I asked the man if he was the IMF representative, and he nodded. I handed him the papers and secretly snapped a photo of him with the papers. I just wanted proof that I gave him the papers. I did not want to be told I'd have to come back to Peru again since this trip was becoming a real pain. I thought he'd take the papers, I'd sign an attendee sheet, and then be off to Hong Kong.

Instead, he gave me the papers back. I asked why, and he said he'd be back the next day to take me to lunch and would get the papers then. That was odd. I went back to my room while he returned to the front desk and continued talking to the girl in Spanish. He never came the next day but did the day after. He wanted to take me to lunch, but I told him I couldn't go because I had to host a webcast for a client and needed to stay at the hotel. He seemed annoyed, but I couldn't go; work was my priority. I handed the paper to him and, again, secretly snapped a photo of him with the papers as proof that I gave them to him.

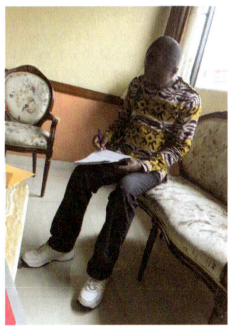

He was supposed to sign them and return them to me, but he took them and said, "I'll email them to you." I didn't know anything about this man other than what MB told me—that he was the IMF representative for US citizens in Peru. I did not know his name or anything. My only connection to him was MB. I saw that he had a cell phone, and I tried to have him message me from the cell so I would have his contact info, but he refused.

Then, he said to me, "The person you are meeting with in HK was supposed to go with you to HK but got called to another meeting. He grabbed his suit and left behind his luggage. He wants you to bring him his luggage to HK."

I asked, "Me? Why me? I thought there were over 200 people in Peru for this program. Why do *I* have to bring it?"

I was told, "He is the representative who is initiating you into the program. It would be a nice gesture for you to bring him his luggage back, and it's the least you could do." I was then told, "You can take all of your stuff out of *your* suitcase and put it into *his* suitcase and throw away your luggage," which I thought was strange.

I said, "What? I *just* bought my luggage right before this trip." He took out his wallet and said, "How much was it? I'll pay you for it." I was surprised. I said, "I don't want the money. I'm not throwing mine away. Why on earth would I do that?" He said, "You are a woman. You shouldn't have to lug around two pieces of luggage." I said, "I'll be fine," and left it at that. So, he took the forms and left. I watched him from the window. He was on his cell phone the minute he left and did not look happy.

I asked MB what the next steps were. I was due to leave Peru for Hong Kong on Friday, April 28 2017. I checked out of the hotel at noon on this date and waited for someone to bring me the luggage and to bring to the airport for my 9 p.m. flight. I waited and waited and kept getting told that they were stuck in traffic. Then at 8 p.m., I got a call from a 000 number, which turned out to be the Nigerian (whom I believed was the IMF representative), telling me to go outside, and that someone was there with the luggage for me. I walked outside, still on the phone, and saw a Hispanic-looking woman standing with a black suitcase. She, too, was on the phone. I wasn't sure if she was who was apparently bringing me the luggage or if she was merely a guest at the hotel. I was expecting the Nigerian IMF representative to bring me the luggage, so I was confused.

While still on the phone with the Nigerian, who was calling me from a blocked number, I walked toward the woman, who was still talking to someone on the phone. I had planned to ask her if she was here for me or if she was a guest at the hotel. But as I approached her, she pointed to the luggage, passed it to me, and then turned and walked away from me. Since I still had the Nigerian on the phone, I had just confirmed that I had it but that I had also just missed my flight. He then told me to go back into the hotel, and he'd book me a new flight for the next day, Saturday.

Since I had already checked out of the hotel earlier that day, I had to ask if they had room for me to check in for another night. It was strange because the woman that the Nigerian had spoken to earlier in Spanish told me that they were fully booked and had no room. Instead, she informed me she had another place for me to stay, but that I'd have to leave all my suitcases behind. What's more, I would have to let her walk me there. I thought that was strange. I did not care to leave my suitcase behind with all my belongings. I had my laptop and personal belongings in there.

I took the luggage that the IMF representative told me to take into the hotel and opened every nook and cranny to inspect it for anything fishy. I even snapped a picture of every part of it and sent all the pictures to Eric to ask his thoughts. The suitcase was old, not new, and it was completely empty. The only thing in there was a large envelope with papers. The envelope was sealed and stapled closed, so all I could do was hold it up to the light to inspect it. Eric told me it was all the IMF papers and was all legitimate. I went over the whole suitcase, snapped pics of everything, and saw nothing. It did appear to me that maybe it was true; someone had to leave in a hurry, grabbed a suit, and left their luggage behind. I also, as always, believed Eric.

I opened my laptop and used Travelocity to search for a hotel. I found what appeared to be a nice one in Miraflores that I could get for $50. I thanked the woman and asked her to call me a taxi to take me to the other hotel, which she did.

As soon as I saw the new hotel, I was very impressed. For one, it had air conditioning (something I had yet to see anywhere else in Peru, having only come across fans that blew around hot air). But apart from that, it also had a Jacuzzi in the bathroom, too. I was totally impressed. I kept my laptop open on the bed that night because the Nigerian had told me that he would be bringing my new airline tickets on Saturday, and I wanted him to know that I was not in that hotel anymore and was instead in Miraflores. MB Skyped me at about 3 a.m. and told me he was emailing me a new itinerary. Sadly, it had my departure on Sunday now. Instead of being a non-stop flight to Hong Kong, as the Nigerian told me, the journey went Peru – Madrid – Doha – Hong Kong once again. It was a two-day trip! I was not happy, but I was told that was the only thing available.

I had only booked one night at this hotel since I thought I'd be leaving on Saturday. In the morning, I had to ask the hotel clerk if I could book another night. She said it was no problem, but I had to pay full price now since the $50 a night was the Travelocity price. I only booked one night and couldn't do it again. The price was now $100 a night, which, to me, was still worth it. The only other down-fall was now I had a full day, Saturday, with nothing to do, so I asked the concierge about tours. They helped me book tours to fill the day.

On Saturday, I visited some churches, cemeteries, the capital, a stadium, a nice park with food vendors, and a water park with waterspouts that lit up in various colors and had a light show when it got dark. I also toured some pyramids, mountains, rivers, and other parks. I ended the tour at a restaurant with dancing performers, buffet-style food of all varieties, and singing and dancing. I was at a table of tourists, the only one by myself, but that was okay. I had a great time and was very impressed by the performers. I had taken so many pictures and remember emailing them to my daughter that night. She said, "I'm so envious of your life!"

I went to sleep that night, excited to be leaving for Hong Kong the next day and being initiated into the IMF program that would ease my financial burdens. I also had clients in Hong Kong, and since I'd never been there before, I was very excited to visit them.

I had to check out of the hotel at 11 a.m. but wasn't leaving for the airport until 3 p.m. I walked around buying souvenirs for my family and then sat in the hotel lobby waiting. I spoke at length with one of the workers of the hotel. He had mentioned that he had a disabled daughter and was working two jobs to pay for her medical equipment and care. He mentioned how the USA had more options for him, but his family couldn't just move there. I gave him my business card and told him to reach out to me. I would see if I could find anyone to put him in touch with to help him. That's all I could do. He then got me a taxi to take me to the airport.

Miraflores was about an hour from the airport, and traffic in Peru was insane. I got to the airport at 3 p.m., just as planned. I had my luggage, the IMF person's luggage, and my carry-on with my laptop. I got out of the taxi, proceeded to the airport, and checked in. In the US, when you're at the airport, they always ask, "Is this your luggage?" and "Did anyone give you anything?"

If I were asked the same questions, I had planned to mention how only the one was mine. But they never asked these kinds of things in Peru. I never put my name on the luggage that wasn't mine, but I *did* check it in. Within seconds I was surrounded by flashes and cameras in my face and police surrounding me. I had no idea what was going on.

"Follow me, please," the police officer said. I asked why and was told to just follow them, with cameras surrounding me. They brought me into a back section of the airport and told me they had reason to believe I was transporting drugs. I thought that was the most absurd thing I'd ever heard. I am a mother, grandmother, wife, business owner, and vegetarian who does not smoke or do drugs. What were they talking about?

I followed them, and they swabbed my luggage, which was fine. However, when they swabbed the IMF guy's luggage, it turned blue, which apparently meant it tested positive for drugs. At this point, I wasn't even thinking about the "how" or "why"; I was more concerned with the "where" since I checked every nook and cranny of the bag and found nothing strange. But based on the fact I was not a drug smuggler, I was not familiar with how mules or smugglers hid their drugs. The police proceeded to take a handsaw and open the luggage casing. I almost fell when that revealed two large bags of cocaine, 2.5 kilos to be exact. I was beyond shocked.

I, of course, was thinking in US terms. I had all my proof of what happened, plus *they* booked my itinerary, so they could investigate it and find out who paid for it. I also had MB's email and Eric's info. At that minute, the Nigerian called my cell from that same 000 number he called me from while I was at the hotel awaiting the luggage.

I told the police, "It's him." They could have let me take the call and set him up or something, but they would not let me. I was totally in a nightmare. I had no idea what was happening. I was in a foreign country and was being arrested for drug smuggling.

This was beyond anything I could have ever expected. A woman called Joanne came from the US Embassy. She took pictures of everything I had—the photos I took of the Nigerian, the emails, the Skype conversations, telephone numbers—all my proof. I told her my friends back home were police, DEA, FBI, etc., and they could all confirm that I was innocent.

She said, "While I believe you, sadly, you are in a foreign country. You will have to do at least three years in prison." What? Three years in prison? How could this be? This whole fiasco took so many hours. On me, I had my laptop, my brand-new iPhone (only ten days used), an iPad and iPod, a Rolex watch, my wedding rings, earrings, bracelet, $2,000 in cash, my credit cards, social security cards, driver's license, etc. The police took everything. Nothing was fast; the whole process took all night. They even had me sign hundreds of papers, all in Spanish, with no translator. Joanne had left, and I was all alone, handcuffed to the chair with cameras still surrounding me.

CHAPTER 6

I was interviewed about what happened, but I did not even know the Nigerian's name. I had no telephone number, no name, only his photo. MB was obviously not MB and was using a phony passport for obvious reasons. MB could have been the Nigerian man for all I knew. None of that made me appear innocent. Yet, it was all true. The Nigerian, when he called, was calling from a number that must've been a computer number, as it only came through as a 0000#. When the airport police were interviewing me, he was calling me. I was told not to answer it. I thought that was strange in that I believed they could have set him up with me, stating that I knew what was in the luggage and did not take it, and if he wanted it back, he'd have to come and pick it up. But I was told not to pick up the phone. In fact, the police then took the phone from me along with everything else of mine.

This whole ordeal started at 3 p.m. on April 30, 2017, and went on until about 2 a.m. The police took all my belongings and documented everything—serial numbers of every bill, every credit card, business card, etc. It went on and on and on. Eventually, I was brought downstairs to the airport lobby again to make my one phone call, with dozens of cameras all in tow. I felt like a complete failure and was also totally embarrassed. Everyone was looking at me to see what was going on since I would have seemed like a celebrity with all the cameras around me, except for the handcuffs.

Punishments & Prisons

The minimum sentence for drug smuggling is six years. Whereas sentences for possession can vary, and can often rely on the discretion and interpretation of your crime by the local police who deal with the case. The judicial system is susceptible to high levels of corruption, therefore becoming involved with the law can have concerning outcomes.

Prisons, like most in South America have a poor reputation for upholding universal standards of human rights. They are often overcrowded, filthy and dominated by internal gangs. Therefore, both prisoners and guards often exploit foreigners with bribes.

Calling my husband had to be the hardest thing I had to do. I don't even know what time it was at this point, but I was originally supposed to call him before my flight to Hong Kong, but since that never happened, now it was *this* call.

The minute I said, "I can't talk long, but I am at the airport. I was asked to take a luggage of—" he had figured it out. And before I could finish the sentence, my husband said, "Nooo," and I had to cut him off.

"It's too late. I did, and apparently, there were drugs in the casing of the suitcase, and I am now arrested." The police made me hang up. I didn't know what to think and felt terrible for dropping a bomb like that on my husband, but what else could I do? I was arrested in a foreign country for a crime I had no idea I was committing.

The police eventually took me in a police car to a medical clinic, I guess to be evaluated. Sadly, I do not speak or understand Spanish, and 99 percent of everyone I dealt with did not speak or understand

English. I remember going to this medical office and having to pee in a cup. Afterward, the doctor tried to tell me that he would examine me. What I understood him to say was that he was going to smack my back; I have no idea if that's what he was saying, but that's what I understood.

"No!" I told him.

My back was broken in the skydiving accident, and I was not about to allow him or anyone to hit my back. He told the police that he could not examine me. We then left and drove to another place, where one of the cops got out of the car and returned around thirty minutes later. I was taken out of the car along with the one bag they allowed me to take.

Here, again, I went through the same info: who I was, why I was there, anything and everything they wanted to know about me. The one cop had to use Google Translate on his phone to communicate with me. By the time we were done, they had me at my first prison called Dirandro. They brought me down a huge set of stairs and into a cell. It was now 7 a.m., and I had not rested since this entire nightmare started—sixteen hours ago. Two other girls there tried to communicate with me, but I was so exhausted that all I could do was climb into the cement bed and close my eyes.

Four hours later, I was woken up to food that was brought in a big spackle-type bucket. The drink was some liquid tied shut in sandwich-sized plastic bags. I am not even sure what the food was, but I watched the other girls. They bit off a corner of the bag and drank that way, squeezing the bag into their mouths. This was so bizarre for me, but I had to follow their lead.

All of this was so out of my element. First, I had never been arrested before in my life. Second, I was in a country where they didn't speak English, and I did not speak Spanish. It felt like a nightmare that I was not waking up from. There were three other women there first, a mother and daughter and another older woman, all Peruvian. They did their best to include me, but the language barrier was too much. My hand charades in trying to explain what I was trying to say only got me so far.

I quickly learned that we were to be taking ice-cold showers; that was definitely not fun. The shower in this place was in a filthy, moldy, and slimy stall with no doors or curtains. I had no shoes or flip-flops, only my sneakers with no laces, so I could not get them wet. With no other options in sight, I resorted to digging out plastic bags from the trash and putting them on my feet, so I could stand in the shower. I didn't even have a towel to dry off and since I thought this was a business trip, I did not have much casual clothes to change into. This was rough.

In this place, I quickly learned how locals got by, and foreigners like me were left out. The security guards there were called INPEs (National Penitentiary Institute of Peru). The way things worked was that men were on one side while women were on the other— think of an "L." The men and women had their sides adjacent to one another, while the smaller section, the bottom of the L, had the INPEs and one television. The guys had a full view of the TV, but the women didn't. So, the Peruvian women were sweet-talking the males and the INPEs. They'd talk them into ordering some real food for them. The INPEs allowed them to make telephone calls, allowed family members to sneak in and see them, and even allowed them out of their cells to sit and watch TV with them. I, of course, was the only one who was never allowed to join those situations since I did not speak Spanish and couldn't communicate. Plus, the police had taken all my money at the arrest, so I had no money for food or phone calls. I literally had nothing. Since I had no money to call my family, I had no idea what was happening or what would happen going forward.

My first day started with my arrival at 7 a.m. when I immediately laid down and fell asleep from stress and exhaustion. I was woken up at about noon to eat. The other women wanted to know who I was and why I was there. I was trying to explain what happened, but it wasn't easy. I was trying to draw what happened to help me communicate. Since they all spoke Spanish, they could chat with each other openly. I was the outcast.

I only happened to have one book to keep me company, but even that didn't last long. I had no blanket, no towel to shower, only one change of clothes, and one pair of sneakers with no shoelaces. Luckily, one girl gave me a big towel that became my blanket for the time being. I literally had all day with nothing to do since I read through the entire book in just a few hours.

By 6 p.m., they were bringing us food again, more liquid in plastic bags, and some slop in the spackle bucket. It seemed everyone was eating in their own Tupperware, which, of course, I did not have. One of the girls kindly gave me one, so I could eat from it.

After supper, the girls managed to sneak back out with the INPEs to watch TV while I read the book, *again..* My mind couldn't even comprehend what was happening to me. I was a business owner and came to Peru for what I was told was a business trip. My beautiful brand-new grandbaby, whose birth I witnessed and who's life I so desperately did not want to miss, was eight months old when I left. I had been there for all her milestones so far. She had just taken her first crawl. I was so excited to be there for it. In fact, three months before coming to Peru, I had helped move my daughter fifteen minutes closer to my home so that I could be there to help her with the baby and watch the little angel grow. Now I was in prison in Peru. How did this happen?

By 9 p.m., the INPEs turned off the lights, and I guess it was time for bed. By 6 a.m., the lights came back on, and we were told to wake up and start cleaning. Clean what? I had no idea. We were given a broom and what I learned was their idea of a mop. It was a towel-like cloth that we were to put over the broom and dampen. That was their mop. We had to sweep our cells and the bathroom. Speaking of the bathroom, the disgusting shower had no curtain, so water got everywhere when you took an ice-cold shower. What's more, the toilet did not flush. You could not flush toilet paper; which I had none of my own anyway, and you needed your own since it was not supplied. We were to fill up a bucket to flush the toilet, which took forever to fill, so when we would take a shower, we'd fill up the bucket with the shower water. I noticed the other girls were washing their clothes in the shower and hanging them up on a line to dry. I had to do the same since I only had one change of clothes.

By day two of this nightmare, I quickly learned that it was the same routine: wake up at 6 a.m. to clean, lunch by noon, dinner by 6:15-ish, and lights out by 9 p.m. I sat alone in a cell throughout the day, reading the same book again. I still could not believe that this was happening to me. Plus, all I could think about was my communication with my family.

The night before my arrest, my daughter had seen my pictures and said she was so envious of my life. I was now envious of *her* life, outside here, back home. For my husband, I had dropped that bomb on his lap on my one phone call from the airport. I knew he had then contacted all my family. How would I even go about finding a lawyer? It wasn't like I was home where I knew people. I couldn't open my laptop and Google lawyers in Peru. I didn't know what to do.

Thank God my family did their research and looked up the US Embassy's website, which had lawyers listed. The first few lawyers they contacted did not speak English, only Spanish, and just demanded money. My family did not feel comfortable with that since they didn't know them and what they were paying for at the time. Then they found Sal Monty. He was on the Embassy's website and was the first English-speaking attorney, so my family was sold. He was someone they could communicate with. I knew none of this at the time, obviously.

On day three, I was put back in handcuffs and a bright orange vest displaying the word *Prisoner* and escorted upstairs to the offices. There, the prosecution asked me tons of questions—again, in Spanish—and had me sign more papers, all in Spanish, with no translator. I had no idea if I even had any rights here to demand an interpreter or refuse to sign. I was in a foreign country with no clue about anything.

After that, I was brought back downstairs again and thrown back into my cell. From there, the drill was the same: I spent all day rereading the one book I had while the other women ate real food, had visits from family and friends, and went out to watch TV with INPEs. I sat all alone all day, not having any clue what was happening, what *would* happen, or what my family was dealing with.

By the fourth day, I was again handcuffed, given my *Prisoner* vest, and brought back upstairs, where I met a man named Sal Monty. He had me sign a form that enabled him to speak to me. He was the lawyer my family had found and hired for me. Once I signed the paper, he was in charge. The prosecutor and anyone else could no longer talk to me or have me sign anything.

He said, "Learn the word *abogado,* which is lawyer in Spanish. That will be a very important word going forward." I could see the look of annoyance on the prosecutor's face since he could no longer get me to sign foreign documents anymore or try to get information from me. I explained to Sal that I did not have many clothes, a towel, flip-flops for the shower, toilet paper, or money. He left and came back with all of this for me. He also handed me S/10, which was ten soles (Peruvian currency). He gave me some coins for a call to try and call my family.

I asked an INPE if I could use a toilet and then make and call. She escorted me to a bathroom and took the roll of toilet paper from me, then proceeded to remove several pieces of it and put them in *her* pocket. I was shocked, but what could I do? I took the roll back and went to the bathroom. After that, she walked me to a pay phone where I was able to call my husband. I could tell by the sound of his voice that he was so happy and relieved to hear from me since it had been several days since that dreaded call from the airport. Before all this, we were together every day since I had a home office. This was the first time I'd been out of touch for many days under these extreme circumstances. He was a nervous wreck. He was relieved to hear my voice and to hear that I was okay, or as okay as one could be under these horrific circumstances. He told me that he and my family spoke with Sal on a group Skype call, and they believed he was the best lawyer for our situation. The US Embassy even listed him on the website, and most importantly, he spoke English.

Charlie, my husband, told me to listen to Sal and follow his lead. Everyone knew I was innocent, but at the end of the day, *I* fell for a scam. Sadly, this was only a year and a half after my accident, and my brain was still not working at full capacity yet. While I was improving day by day, my decision-making was not 100 percent, and that was why I never saw all the red flags that I would have certainly seen before the accident.

I was later informed that these scammers not only purchase medical records of people with brain injuries, dementia, and senility but also buy and sell databases of people who've fallen for scams. I guess their thinking was that if you fell for a scam before, the chances of you falling for one again were greater. Sadly, they were right. The so-called MB even asked me to point him toward any people who had fallen for scams or were conned out of money, stating he only wanted to help people with this program. I passed the IMF information on to people I knew had fallen for some of the same scams as me, but none of them wanted to be a part of it, telling me they thought the act of me telling them was a scam as well. I did reach out to IMF via email and telephone to verify the program, but no one returned my calls or emails. I tried researching the program but could not find anything. Sadly, with nothing else to go off, I believed MB and Eric. Again, if my brain were back to normal, this would never have even been a question. Unfortunately, with it having been less than two years after the accident, I still was not able to recognize it yet, and I fell for it.

I was now in the hands of Sal Monty and at the mercy of Peru. To be honest, Peru was never on my bucket list of places to visit. I knew nothing about Peru other than I was instructed to go there for a business meeting. I later found out that Peru is well known as a major cocaine country. Since I am not a drug user, dealer, or smuggler, I wouldn't know that. I honestly went there solely because I believed MB that I needed to go there for the IMF program because the USA representative was in Peru, initiating over 200 people into their program. We all needed to sign and submit papers and then fly off to Hong Kong to be initiated into the program. I also later found out that this Nigerian cartel knew exactly what they were doing. They were professionals who knew the system, as evidenced by the itinerary they gave me for my flight, even though I later learned that I was never supposed to leave Peru because I was apparently only needed as a scapegoat. They would set me up with the police and then smuggle thousands of kilos of drugs while the police would attack me and countless other victims.

Even the itinerary was orchestrated. My flight route was listed as Peru – Madrid – DOHA – Hong Kong. If the flight was listed as me going back to the US, then the US could have deported me back there, where they would have done an investigation and clearly seen that I was set up and released me. Because this itinerary had me going elsewhere, the US couldn't interfere. They were stuck, and the Nigerians knew it would keep me here. They obviously knew how the system worked, with connections and lots of experience in this arena.

So, back to my cell. I was unsure what would happen, but I was still thinking in terms of the US legal system. I thought that since I finally had a lawyer, he was going to get me out of there. A few days later, I was cuffed again with my *Prisoner* vest and brought back upstairs, but to a different room. Apparently, this was where we would see the judge for the first time; not in a courtroom, as I was used to seeing from jury duty back home, but in a small, crowded office. Sal was there with two other members of his firm, and a young woman acted as my translator. The local team was seated behind me, and I was not allowed to speak to them. This was bizarre.

My translator wasn't very good in that the judge rambled on and on and never stopped to allow her to tell me what he was saying, so every time I tried to say, "What is he saying?" she'd tell me to wait because he was still talking. This went on for about thirty minutes, and I had no idea what was said. I was later told that they were talking about my charge, and the prosecutor said they wanted many years imprisonment for me because I was tied to the drug cartel. Seriously?! I'd think if I was tied up with the cartel, I'd have had more than 2.5 kilos in that luggage. Luckily, Sal got that removed.

Then they said to me that if I pleaded guilty, they would go for a three-year sentence, but if I pleaded innocent, they would fight for fifteen years. I was flabbergasted, and my head was spinning. This could not be happening to me. I had to ask if I could have a moment to talk to my lawyer. The judge agreed, and the prosecutor left the room with him.

With everyone gone, I turned to Sal and said, "I am so confused. I have never been in this situation before. I also don't know you. Have you won cases like mine before? I can't bear the thought of fifteen years in prison, so tell me, what do you think? What does my family think?"

Sal proceeded to say, "Your family does not want you to plead guilty for something you did not do. I believe we have a good case to fight." So, I said, "Okay, well, if my family thinks I should fight this, then let's fight."

After our talk, the judge, prosecutor, and instructor came back in, and I said, "I would like to plead innocent." Via the translator, the judge informed me that I would be remanded to prison for a nine-month investigation. Sal asked if I could do this time via house arrest to continue working. He was immediately told, "No."

The judge asked if I had anything to say. I honestly did not know *what* to say. My head was spinning, my body was numb, and I was beyond shocked. I said, "I have no idea what to say. I am so confused," and that was the end of that. The judge ended it. At this time, I was taken to another section where I had to give all my information. Again, show any scars or tattoos, etc. Sal left and said he'd be communicating with family and would be in touch with me. I was taken back down to the prison. I was there for only a few hours when I was told to pick up my stuff (what stuff?) because I was being moved. I was so dazed and confused.

From there, I was brought up and over and down to another section. It all seemed to be in the same building, but various sections of it, I guess. When I was taken there, I was happy to see two people I knew from the first jail I was in. It was the mother and daughter. This place was one room only, with a very thin mat on the floor where we were *all* expected to sit and sleep.

I could immediately see that the girl and her mom had already made friends with the male INPEs because they had real food all day—yogurt, soda, etc. From what I later found out, if you don't somehow manage to get things, you are on your own; they don't feed you there.

The mother-daughter duo in my cell were kind enough to share their food and blankets with me, which was nice of them. I also had my one piece of luggage with me (whatever crap the police left after taking everything else of any value from me). After the police took all my things, they gave me back my suitcase, which had some clothes, and all of my wires and plugs to my cell phone and laptop, which I no longer had. I also had several travel adapters and converters since I was under the impression that I was going US – Peru – Madrid – DOHA – Hong Kong. I had gotten them to make sure that I was able to plug in all my electronics while traveling. That obviously never happened.

The girl, Anna*, and her mom did not speak English, but through hand gestures and charades, we could semi-communicate. She told me to get rid of my electronic wires, and adapters because the INPEs in this prison would only steal them.

From there, I learned that this prison cell was just another transition spot. This place had men on one side and women on the other, which was different from the first place. If we walked to the front gate, we could go up to the men's section of the cell and see and talk to them (not that I could talk to them or understand what they said). Since I was tall, blonde, white, and non-Peruvian, it seemed everyone was always curious about me. They wondered who I was and why I was there.

The next day, Anna and her mom were taken away, and I was alone again. I was the only woman there—for three days with no food at all. I could not communicate with the INPEs. One male INPE was coming in and out of my section while I was locked into the cell all alone. He took out his cell phone and tried using Google Translate to talk to me. This way, he was able to talk to me all day, asking me who I was, why I was there, and what had happened.

I tried to tell him my story and how I was innocent and from the USA. I told him that the Embassy woman said at the airport that night, "You are in Peru. You will have to do time in jail regardless," which was exactly what this INPE told me via Google Translate.

I was shocked when he said, still using Google Translate, "I will come and visit you in jail. I will be your husband and come see you."

I said, "Umm, I have a husband."

He asked, "Where is he?"

I said, "He's back home in the USA."

To this, he replied, "Well, he's there, and I'm here."

I was shocked. Is this what I would be dealing with? I just said, "No, thank you. I am happily married," to which he laughed.

After he left, I made it a point to pretend to be asleep whenever he passed by again, so I wouldn't have to communicate anymore. If he had tried to open my cell, I would have screamed bloody hell.

I was surprised by a visit from a girl from Sal Monty's office. She brought me food to eat and a soda to drink. Inca Kola was Peru's soda, I noticed. I'd never even heard of it before, but it is made by Coca-Cola and is a yellow soda. I wasn't a fan of it, but I was so hungry and thirsty, having not eaten in three days. She said they had been trying to find out where I was for three days, and even they were given the runaround and not told where I was being held. She brought me more toilet paper and took my luggage back with her since I did not want the prison to take any more of my stuff. I then thanked her for bringing me food, and she was gone.

I did not have many clothes since I thought it was a business trip. Most of what I brought with me were business suits and dresses. Plus, it was spring back home, and it was fall in Peru, so the clothes I had would not help me. I only had about two or three items of clothing, no blanket or shampoo, soap, etc. These were things that the hotel customarily provided, so I didn't travel with them. The woman from Sal's office came the next day, too. They would not let me see her this time, but they did bring me the food she had brought me: a chicken sandwich, cookies, and more Inca Kola.

All day, I was all alone with nothing to do. There were no windows, nothing. There were three cells, one empty, one locked with file cabinets and papers thrown all over, and then there was my cell. I browsed the hall and tried to read all the writing on the walls. The walls were scribbled all over but in Spanish. When I ventured near the front gate, the men tried to talk to me. I had no clue what they were saying, so I'd go back to my cell.

I walked over to the room with all the papers thrown every which way and managed to pull some of them out. They were all in Spanish and several years old, according to the stamped date. But since I had a pen on me, I used the back of the papers and managed to draw a deck of cards and rip the papers to allow me to play solitaire. It is amazing how long a day is when you have nothing to do. I played solitaire many, many times and then was running out of steam.

I was then approached by INPEs again and told to pack up my things and was moved again to the other side of where I was. Again, I had to give all my information: who I was, date of birth, country, etc. I never understood why every place made me do this repeatedly. There seemed to be no system. It had to be a major thing there because I felt I had fingerprinted over 200 documents by that time.

Then they would make me dump out everything I had while going through it to make sure I had nothing I shouldn't have. Again, each prison did the exact same inspection every single day. If I was locked in a cell, how would I have something one day that I didn't have the day before? It made no sense to me, but what could I do? I had to oblige.

After this whole process, I was brought into another cell that had another girl in it. It had one bunk bed, and she was on the bottom, leaving me with the top bunk. I climbed up and laid down. A while later, I heard some strange noise. I peeked over and saw her pumping breast milk into a cup. As always, she spoke no English, but through my charades and limited Spanish, I later learned she had a five-month-old baby. Later that day, her family brought the baby for her to breastfeed. Every time we needed to use the bathroom, we'd have to call an INPE to let us out to use the bathroom since there was none in the cell. It usually took like thirty minutes for someone to let us out, and at night, no one would let us out at all.

The next morning, as always, we were woken up at 6 a.m. We were not let out of the cell until 7 a.m. to use the bathroom and shower. During my first time in this shower, I used Ace, which is for cleaning the toilet. Why? Because I had no soap. Luckily, I did have a bottle of shampoo that Sal had given me. So, I hopped in the shower. In the shower were two bathrooms and two sinks. One for the INPEs, which was clean, and one for prisoners, which was not clean.

In the middle of my shower, I was told to get out immediately. I didn't know what was going on, so I quickly jumped out of the shower and rushed back to the cell to get dressed. In my panic, I left the shampoo in the shower. I thought about going back to get it since there was only me and another girl, and since she wasn't in the bathroom, it would still be there. We had to wait in the cell while the next day shift INPEs came on board. And again, we had to empty out all our stuff while these INPEs went through everything. Once that was done, I asked to go back to the bathroom. I went to grab my shampoo, and it was gone. I quickly asked the INPE what happened to my shampoo, and she looked at me like I had three heads, so it was gone, and I was back to having nothing. This was starting to show me what I was soon to endure daily in prison in Peru.

The girl and I were told to pack that afternoon because we were moving again. We had to sign several papers and were fingerprinted and handcuffed again. Then, we were stuck in the back of what seemed like an ambulance with two-rowed seats. There were others in it already, and as she and I climbed in, the INPE said he wanted to be my husband and visit me in prison. He was at the door directing us all into the vehicle. I tried to avoid any eye contact.

Where were we going now? I had no clue. We drove for a while and picked up more people on the way. Men and women, all hand-cuffed, being transported from one prison to another. We eventually arrived at yet another Callao jail. Some other people were dropped off along the way, and the rest of us were all dropped off at this place. I was delighted to see Anna again, but she was with about ten other women. When I arrived, Anna greeted me. There were no more beds, so the newcomers had to put foam pads on the floor to sleep. Once we picked a spot to sit/sleep, we were all taken to the doctor.

I forgot to mention previously that I had my migraine medicine with me from the USA. I always traveled with it, "just in case." I had always had vicious migraines, yet miraculously did not have any after my accident. But knowing how bad they were, I kept my medicine on hand in case they ever came about. I also had Zzzquil with me, which I used to sleep with since I had crazy insomnia. The routine thus far, for every prison I'd gone to, was they would initially take my medicine/pills upon arrival, but then, I assume, since they didn't know what exactly they were since it was all in English (and not even meds they have in Peru), they would give them all back to me. Well, it was the same process at prison number four. The doctor there, as well as every other person of authority I had seen thus far, didn't speak nor understand any English, and I didn't understand any Spanish. Just like before, this had all been more of a nightmare. The doctor was trying to ask what my meds were for, but we couldn't communicate. From what I could understand, it was typical. The doc would hold on to them, but if I needed any, I was to go to him. I was going each night for the Zzzquil, but sadly, since I was only expecting to be traveling for a short time, I did not have too much with me.

We were brought to another room with who I believed was a dentist and someone who inspected us for scars, tattoos, etc. When I went to the dentist, he tried to put a wooden popsicle stick into my mouth. Still, having seen about ten different people all going through before me and only seeing the one wooden stick in his hand with no others around, I would not let him put it in my mouth. One can only assume that it was in other people's mouths prior, so I refused. He did not seem happy and mumbled a lot of stuff to the INPEs, but I kept saying no.

Eventually, I was brought to another room with tons of other men and women being evaluated and processed. It always seemed like a big fiasco because I knew little to no Spanish. That night, new people were brought into the cell, and Anna and several of those women left.

One of the newcomers was apparently a lesbian. As I was lying on my foam on the floor, she came and laid on top of me and said, "I am going to kiss you."

I was initially delighted that it was in broken English, but then, I thought, *Oh no. Is this what my prison experience is going to be like?*

I replied, "Kiss me where? Here?" and pointed to my cheek.

She admired my reply, laughed, and kissed my hand. She did not speak much English, but we became friends after that initial experience. There were two older women and three younger women, all brought in new. The older women smelled like body odor and had long hair under their arms. It was hard to smell good in this place, even for me. Sal's office provided me with only a small stick of deodorant when they brought me toilet paper and soap.

I also met another girl from Mexico. She spoke no English, but through our charades, we communicated. She gave me a Tupperware bowl, which I later learned was a necessity if I chose to eat. She also tried to tell me that if we ever wound up in the same prison, she'd share her food with me since her family was sending her some. That was nice of her to think of me.

I guess people started to complain about the two older women's body odor because they asked to borrow deodorant from me. Me? I wasn't from there, where my family could bring me more, and I only had one roll-on deodorant. I was not about to pass it on to share and give back to me. They did not have much, and I assumed they were poor. Why everyone looked at me as if I had everything was beyond my understanding. I had very little of anything myself. I later learned that this is how Peruvians view Americans, like walking ATMs.

We stayed at this transitional place for a few days, with people leaving and new people coming. I was taken away one day, handcuffed, and thrown into a car that was brought to Interpol. All I knew of Interpol was what I'd seen on TV. I was always a fan of NCIS, and Interpol was frequently mentioned. This place was very busy, with tons of people coming through for whatever reason, not tons of workers, but it reminded me of going to the DMV for something. There were lots of people waiting their turn. I was the only one handcuffed, though. It was so embarrassing, but what could I do? It also was not very professional looking. I would imagine Interpol HQ to look like an FBI agency or someplace since they are a highly powerful organization. I expected it to be much more professional looking, but I guess in a third-world country, it was as good as it would get. Here, again, I was fingerprinted, photographed, and documented. Again, I was surprised that I was the only one brought to Interpol. I later learned that everyone goes through that. Perhaps they were repeat offenders and already in the system? I don't know.

The next day, we were all woken up and had to clean, as usual. Then, that day, INPEs came in and had us empty out all our stuff, where they inspected everything—such a silly daily routine. We were all locked in one room all day. No TV, no nothing. What could we possibly have done differently from the night before? This was the typical daily routine of all the places I had been.

I was not too happy to see how many cockroaches there were at that place. I am not a fan of roaches, and they were everywhere. They were on the walls, the floors, and any other nook and cranny they could find. I could not get away from them. While I knew very little Spanish, *cucarachas* was a word I knew all too well. I would scream, "Cucarachas!" when I saw them climbing the walls right by my head. The other girls found that funny.

That afternoon, we were all inspected again. This time, the INPEs took my pen. Apparently, it was not something we were allowed to have. They also cut the hood off my hooded sweater. For some reason, we were not allowed hoods either. If that wasn't enough, they also wanted to take the neck pillow that I had bought from the airport and was now my sleep pillow when I rolled it up. It was red velvet on the outside, and apparently, red and black were not colors that were allowed. I asked if I could just take the red cover off but keep the cushiony material for a pillow, and they said okay. We were all put into buses and transported, along with many other men and women, to various jails. I was not sure where I'd wind up.

Several other women from this past prison were dropped off at various places. One of the older women who asked me for deodorant wound up in Santa Monica with me. This was my fifth prison. The girl who was pumping breast milk in the third place came with me, and the girl who was a lesbian. I recognized others from transition places and people I hadn't seen before. These women were now with me in this new place or dropped off at other prisons. Anna was here, which I was happy about. She also had a bunch of people from place number four in her group.

Anna set me up in a bed, and I asked her, "Is this it now, or are we moving again?" I mean, this was the fifth jail I was moved to, which was getting silly. Each time we went to someplace new, the whole process would start all over again. All our things were thoroughly examined, we were frisked from head to toe, and we had to go to see their medical office. I was surprised to see cats roaming around. I sat down to pet one. People kept telling me not to pet them, that they were dirty, but the cat seemed okay to me. Besides, I love animals.

We were not seen by an actual doctor but by nurses. They took us each in, one by one, asked us questions I did not understand, and had us sign a form showing they saw us. As always, they took my Zzzquil and migraine medicine and gave me one of each to go to sleep. Then, we went back to the room. At least there was a TV there. It was in Spanish, but it was something. Lights were turned off at 9 p.m. We were then off to sleep since we couldn't do anything else. I noticed a few women were washing their clothes and hanging them on lines made of string to dry.

The next day, we were woken up at 6 a.m. and given brooms and a broom with a towel and a hole where the stick went through. Again, their version of a mop. We were instructed to go to one section and sweep and mop and then do the same in our room. Besides this, we also had to scrub down the bathroom. I was surprised that the lesbian managed to get a cigarette from someone. She had friends there. I later realized that many of the prisoners were repeat offenders.

While we newcomers were not allowed to go anywhere, Anna and the others, who had been there two days prior, were allowed to go somewhere else. I don't know where that was, but Anna had told me she would buy me a bag since my plastic garbage bag with my stuff had ripped open and my things were falling out. She also promised to get me a pen and a brush since the INPEs took my plastic brush, too. I gave her soles, and she came back that afternoon with everything she said she would. I was happy to be able to put my stuff now in a zip-up bag and have a pen back, where I could write my family. I had asked to use the phone, but it wasn't until several hours later that they let me use the pay phone for five minutes. I called my husband, who was happy to hear my voice and know I was surviving. He told me that Sal was in constant contact with them and that he was working on things. My call was quick, and then I was sent back to the room.

Many of the fellow prisoners are Quechuan - The Quechua people today are not a single ethnic group, but rather several indigenous groups scattered throughout South America, such as the Q'ero and the Wankas in Peru, the Kichwas and Otavalos in Ecuador, the Ingas in Colombia, and the Kallawaya in Bolivia.

Inside some of the various prisons I endured.

CHAPTER 7

I'll describe what the usual routine was. At 6 a.m., the INPEs would blow their whistles, and we'd all have to form a line for what was called *quenta,* where they read off everyone's name from a list to make sure we were all still there. Daily, quenta was 6 a.m., 6 p.m., and 9 p.m. Breakfast was called *desayuno,* and that came daily around 8 a.m. It was usually what they called Quaker, which was a watered-down, what-appeared-to-be oatmeal, but with no oats. I'm told it was soy, also. I'd normally have to pull strands of hair out of it every day. As gross as it was, I had no choice if I chose to eat. One day, our lunch was a bowl of soup. I thought that was okay. They'd send the food in a huge pot, and we were to use a plastic jug (*jarra*) to take our food.

All things considered, the food was all good until I saw actual chicken feet. I'm sure it is an acquired taste, but the women seemed to love it. I, on the other hand, was completely grossed out. I did not eat lunch that day.

Anna and some of the girls who arrived with her had all gone out that day; I did not know where. The rest of us newbies had to stay inside and watch TV. It was all in Spanish and appeared to be shows they were all familiar with. I just wrote letters to my family and tried to watch TV, even though I had no idea what was being said. It was strange. Around 2:30, one of the INPEs called me and handed me a foam food container. I had no idea what it was or why she was handing it to me, so I just took it and said, "*Gracias.*" When I went to my bed, I opened it and found four chicken bones and five or six French fries inside. I had no idea where it came from and wondered why this INPE called me out to hand me her garbage. I threw it away.

Around 4 p.m., all the girls returned, and it was quenta again. I later learned that Wednesday, Saturday, and Sunday were visitor days. It was Wednesday that day. Anna had a visit from her mom, who was arrested with her. She was apparently walking with her daughter Anna and cutting through the airport on a detour (or so she thought). Her mother had no idea that Anna had drugs in the bag. As you would expect, they were caught. However, her mother convinced the judge that she had no clue about it, and they let her go. I'd learned a lot throughout my ordeal, but it seemed Peruvians got much better treatment than foreigners.

Her mom remembered me, and as she was visiting her daughter, she had sent me food. That night, Anna asked if I got the food that her mom had sent me. It turned out that was the foam container I was supposed to get. That INPE ate it all and gave me the garbage to throw away! What freaking nerve! Such was the beginning of my life in prison in a foreign, third-world country.

Anna and the girls with her group were told to pack up that night because they were going to be leaving. That night, I asked the doctor/nurses for my medicine. When I got it, the INPE tried to ask me what it was for. I tried to use my charades to show that it was to sleep. Then, she proceeded to try and tell me that she didn't sleep and wanted some. Ugh! This whole mess kept getting crazier and crazier. This wasn't the same INPE who stole my food. It seems INPEs changed and rotated shifts constantly.

At 9 p.m., the lights went out, and it was time for bed again. The Zzzquil helped me fall asleep, which was a tremendous help. I had no clue where Anna and the others went, and I was told that this fifth place would be my home now. Was I going to be transferred again? I had no idea.

Thursday and Friday came and went. The same routine: 6 a.m. wake-up, so-called mops were given to us to clean with, then back inside for breakfast and a dirty ice-cold shower. Then nothing but watching TV, sleeping, writing, and resting until around 12:30–1:00 pm when lunch would come. Thank God the girl from Mexico had given me a Tupperware container or I'd have no way to eat. Lunch was also something with rice and potatoes. Here they ate heart, lungs, and kidneys, so with me being a vegetarian, I was finding it hard to eat.

Breakfast always had only two rolls. They were small rolls, but at least they would help fill me up. After lunch, we went back to nothing else to do. I'd ask to make a call, but if the INPEs didn't ignore me, they'd make me wait hours before even acknowledging me. I was trying to ask the INPE if I could use the phone, but she seemed not to understand what I was saying.

A little while later, a girl came over to our room gate and asked me in English, "What do you need from the INPE?"

I was quick. "You speak English?"

The first English prisoner I had met so far. I was so relieved. She wasn't extremely friendly, but she was nice. She said "Yes" and asked what I wanted.

The girl was named Tina*, and the INPE called her because she said she had no idea what I was asking for. I told the girl I wanted to use the phone and how glad I was to find another English-speaking person. She said the prison was all Peruvians, but there were about four to five other English-speaking people from Africa, Holland, Thailand, the USA, etc. She also said that a few English women came every Sunday for Bible study, and all English-speaking people sat with them to study the Bible. I was happy to hear that, but then she left. I'd later learn that she was already there for seven years on a nine-year sentence, which was why she was sort of icy. She just did her thing to pass the time until her nine-year sentence was complete.

I managed to call my husband again to say hi. He was relieved to hear from me. I wanted to call my mom, sister, kids, and others, but what would I say? I was so embarrassed by this whole mess. How could I face them? Yes, this was not something I intentionally did, but I *still* fell for a ridiculous scam and was now a prisoner in a third-world foreign country.

Plus, there was my business. I ran everything and had been in this line of work for over thirty-three years. My sister was working with me, but she never understood the work to the extent I did. Now she was trying to run the show, to keep my business running. No one had any of my login info, usernames, passwords, etc., for all my personal and business logins. They were all doing their best to try and figure out how to handle everything back home. I ran all the banking, personal, and business issues. Now my husband and sisters had to figure out how to pick up where I left off. I know I left a big mess back home, but it was never intentional. Never in a billion years would I have expected this to happen.

Eric was emailing me, apparently, checking to see if I made it out of Peru. My sister, who was handling my business emails, stopped replying to him. She did this because we were now convinced that he was part of the scam, as he was part of every other scam I encountered after my accident and after hiring him. My sister had initially told him that I got arrested and that there were drugs in the suitcase the so-called IMF representative gave me.

Eric played it off as shock and pretended to be helpful, but we later realized nothing mattered. I was in jail in Peru, and absolutely nothing would change that. I did not call my family for a little while but called my husband. He was so scared for me, so it was good for him to hear my voice. We talked for five minutes, but I was still clueless. He had all sorts of questions, like "Where exactly are you?"

and "How long will you be there?" This was now my fifth home in this mess. When was I going to stop being moved? I had no idea.

Saturday came, and we were told to pack up again. As I packed what little I possessed, my mind raced with thoughts like, *Are they moving me again? I thought this was my new and final home in this mess. Now, we are moving to a sixth place? All in only a few weeks? This is getting ridiculous!*

I packed up with all but two of the girls in the room who had come after us. We were told to remove the crappy foam from the beds and take it with us. Huh? I was so confused. So now I had to take this foam and my bag, and we had to carry it to the other side of the prison. Apparently, we were in a holding place while they processed us into the system and decided where we'd go. There were three buildings called *pabellons* that were divided into one, two, and three floors. I was moved to 2B and placed in a small room with three bunk beds that were all full. That meant I got the floor! I'm told Pabellon 1A's ground floor was where moms with babies up to age three went, and 1B and 1C were others mostly there for four years or more. There was no 2A, only 2B and 2C, where we all went, and 3A mainly was elderly, sick, and disabled folks, while 3B and 3C were the troublemakers.

I quickly realized just how overcrowded this prison was—my *sixth* home. The room was small, with three bunk beds, so my twin-size foam took up the whole floor. I was quickly informed that the other six women in the room did not want me to put the "bed"

down until 9 p.m. I was to get up at 6 a.m. and pick the foam off the floor so they had room to move about.

Everyone had a bed with enough room under it to keep their belongings. I, on the other hand, had nothing. I had my bag on the floor near the door and could only put my foam down for sleeping. Not to mention sleeping on the floor meant sleeping next to water bugs, mice, rats, etc., crawling all over me.

This prison was 99 percent Peruvians. There were two women from Thailand—all for TID, which I was told was Peru's term for drug trafficking—*traffico illicito de drogas*. Two women were from the USA; one was in for TID, and the other was in for counterfeiting money. Another was from Holland; she had a fifteen-year sentence. All told, there were only six English-speaking people among the hundreds of women there, all in different pabellons. I was at least glad there was someone I could talk to since I'd spent weeks being moved all over and unable to communicate with anyone. I was always the room's newcomer and couldn't communicate at all.

This prison had many rooms, all with one to three bunk beds and a big room at the end called "the Salon." That room had a TV for everyone to watch together, and it had over one hundred and sixty people in it. There were bunk beds everywhere, and it was a noisy and messy room due to it being crowded and being the TV room. I learned that people there were not neat and didn't have manners. They would eat and drop their food and garbage right where they were, whether they were in the room or walking; it made no difference to them. They'd also fart and pick their noses right in front of you and think nothing of it. If I was talking to someone, it was not uncommon for someone else to cut right in front of me with their back to me and start talking to the person I was talking to. They'd think nothing of it and would do it constantly, with zero manners. Yet, this seemed to be the norm. I couldn't take it personally since they all did it even to one another. This, indeed, would take a lot of getting used to.

The bathroom was all the way down the hall and had four toilets, four showers, and three big sinks. I had to learn the system here. One sink was for laundry, one was for dishes, and the smallest was for washing your hands or brushing your teeth. Plus, with four toilets, four showers, and over four hundred people, you can imagine what it was like.

After the 6 a.m. wake-up, trying to get into a toilet or shower was a fiasco. To top it off, on my first morning there, I waited in line, assuming we were all just waiting for "the next available shower." Nope, I learned you had to pick which shower you wanted and then find out who the last one was in "that line" and then say *atras tu yo,* meaning "I'm after you." So, since I did not do that, I was waiting for nothing. Plus, peeing right after waking up was difficult since I had to wait forever for an available toilet. And I learned about the various sinks after trying to brush my teeth in an available spot, only to be told, "No!" I obviously had a lot to learn here, and with such a language barrier, this was not easy. Tina and the woman from Holland and USA were in other pabellons. I only had the two girls from Thailand in my pabellon but in different rooms. Finding someone to translate for me was difficult.

Due to the bathrooms being down the hall, this prison did not lock us into our rooms but instead locked us into our floor. We were not allowed to walk into each pabellon or to various floors unless our room was there. Otherwise, you could only go to pabellons 1, 2, or 3 to the entrance of each floor and ask someone to get whoever you needed from that pabellon or floor. How do I know this? Well, as I was new and still learning my way around, I had left my pabellon (2B) as newbies were instructed to go downstairs and sweep. We had to do this for our first six months. Anyway, this was all still new to me. As I went to return, I lost my bearings and wasn't sure which pabellon I was in. I apparently walked into Pabellon 1 and tried to walk in the direction of where my new room was. Tina approached me, since this was her pabellon, and told me that I could not just walk around. I was so lost and confused. I apologized, went back downstairs, and tried to backtrack to find where I was. When I went back up to 2B, people were mopping the hallway and yelling at me as I walked where they were cleaning. What the fuck? I had to go downstairs to sweep, and even that had a line waiting for one of the six brooms. I could only go back upstairs when I was done sweeping since they had my name on a list with all the others. And if I didn't do it, I'm sure I'd be in trouble somehow. If that coincided with the time they were mopping upstairs, how was that my fault?

Then, I heard someone yelling, "*Desayuno!*" which meant breakfast. Two women had a rolling cart with a big metal pot of Quaker, and they went from room to room. We had to get in line outside our room with our Tupperware for them to give us "breakfast." They took forever to make their way down halls to over four hundred people. Then another person came down yelling, "*Pan!*" which is their word for bread, or breakfast rolls. Two per person, and yes, they count it meticulously.

Sometimes, it would come with either an orange, a platano, some jelly-type thing, one piece of cheese, or three olives, which they called *aceitunas* (three olives per person). However, we only got one of these sides per day, and it varied from day to day. By the time this was done, INPEs were blowing whistles like crazy.

I asked, "What's that for?"

It was quenta. We had to make our beds (in my case, put up my foam and fold my blanket) and make sure everything was put away and presentable. Then we had to form a line in the hall.

The line went according to room and beds and corresponded to the list the INPEs had. I stood where I was directed to as the INPE did quenta, which after breakfast, they would shout, "*Buenos dias!*" We were to reply with the same. Then they shouted, "*Attencion de la lista!*" To this, we would have to call "Attencion!"

I felt like this was the military. You weren't allowed to wear what they felt were pajamas as they thought it was disrespectful. Seriously? An INPE is a security guard. They don't carry guns. But apparently, there was a massive ego kick going on. They'd walk down the halls and pop their heads into rooms. If a bed was not made to their liking, they'd raise hell and have you remake it. It was all so crazy.

After that, we were to go downstairs. Saturday and Sunday happened to be visitor days; as luck would have it, the English Bible study women were in. I was approached by an English-speaking girl, who brought me to the group, where I met Annie* and Marge*, the two English-speaking women from the Bible study and the other English-speaking women in this prison; these were all the English-speaking women. This was overwhelming for me, but I was happy to be around people I could communicate with.

I met Viola*, the woman from Holland with a fifteen-year sentence. She'd already been there thirteen years when I got there, so she knew the place well. She took me under her wing, even though we were in different pabellons. She told me that if I wanted to write a note for my family, Annie and Marge would email it to them. That was great. So, I quickly wrote to my family, since I had not yet called them, only my husband. I got introduced to Marge and Annie and explained my story. They were volunteers from Canada and Europe and visited the women in prison to study the Bible. They also brought in things that women might need, such as toilet paper, deodorant, shampoo, toothpaste, etc. They would bring lunch for the group, nothing fancy, but maybe half a sandwich or crackers and cheese. Either way, it was a nice gesture, and the group looked forward to their visits. They also brought the girls English books, Bibles, and spiritual daily reading material. They welcomed me to the group, and I agreed to meet with them when they visited each week. I am a Catholic, but truth be told, I was not practicing as I could be.

After their departure, I got to talk to Viola. She told me about Santa Monica, the prison I was in, regarding what to expect, how things work, and how the INPEs were not big fans of foreigners. They felt that we came to their country to commit a crime, so we were not good people. Yes, many knew what they were doing and got caught knowing the consequences, but that was not the case for *all* of us. I, for one, certainly did not go to Peru to commit a crime. I had no clue that I was set up. To be honest, I knew nothing about Peru other than knowing that I had to get there for a business meeting.

The next day, I was called by the INPEs to go to one side, where they handed me a bag of some of my clothes. I was trying to ask where these came from, but there was a language issue again. Then they pointed to another room where a man and woman waved to me, and the INPE said, "Abogado," which is "lawyer."

I assumed they were from Sal's office, but they would not let me talk directly to them for whatever reason. I guessed Sal's office tried to send me whatever they thought I'd need from my luggage, but sadly my clothes were for spring, whereas it was fall here. I did not have warm clothes in my luggage. I was not expecting to be in Peru for long, only passing through. Plus, I only had work clothes except for two to three casual outfits.

In this prison, they had one pay phone for each pabellon, and everyone got five minutes. Well, I learned in time that I got five minutes, but sadly had to wait while countless Peruvian women got three to four phone calls. It did not take long for me to see that I was treated differently, and the fact that I did not speak Spanish, I guess they saw it to their advantage. I surely couldn't tell on someone. No one in authority spoke English. With hundreds of women in a building and everyone getting five minutes for one call and only one call a day (yet not for Peruvians, I saw), this was hard. We were not allowed out of our caged floor until after quenta at 9 a.m. and then had to go back after 6 p.m. quenta. So that left eight hours with twelve calls per hour; it was hit or miss. There was a woman who sat on the phone every day with a list; she put your name down, and you were not allowed to leave until your call. If you left, she'd take your name off. That's how I saw Peruvians getting on/off the line to make several calls, but what could I do?

There was a pay phone up on our floor with the same procedure, someone with a list, but for whatever reason, the upstairs phone would not allow me to dial international, so downstairs was my only option. I later discovered a secret: the "C" pabellon had a phone that hardly anyone used. Every pabellon has what they call a *delegado*. In prison, she played the same role played by a headmistress at college, someone who oversaw things and who'd try and help you if you had a problem. Well, the delegado for S/I would let you use *that* phone in a pabellon that was not mine. So, since not everyone knew about that, I had that as an option, as long as I kept it quiet. She wasn't supposed to do that, but I later learned how Peruvians would do anything and everything they could for money, whether it's allowed or not. There was never a fear of, "What if the INPE catches you?"

For S/1, INPEs tended to never see anything. Welcome to my life in a Peruvian prison.

I spent my first few days not knowing what to do. Upstairs, the television was in Spanish. Many girls worked, so they were not around. If they didn't work, they all hung out with each other, but I could not communicate with them since we didn't speak the same language. Viola didn't work, but after thirteen years, she had her routine, and I still pestered her all day, begging her to translate for me. She was very helpful to me, yet at times, I know I was a real pain in her butt with constantly needing her help. Since I was a vegetarian, she told me I could ask the doctor to sign off on vegetarian meals. I thought that was great. Of course, I needed her help with translating.

Back home, I ate no red meat but did eat chicken. I was told here, "No." Either I had to eat all meat or none, so I had to choose none at all. The only time they gave a special meal was lunch. I had to drop my Tupperware off with my name and pabellon number in the morning, and I would have to pick it up at lunchtime. I suppose many others were getting special diet food for various medical needs. The crazy part was where the food was cooked and prepared, which was also where I had to drop off my Tupperware. It was full of pigeons. I do not doubt that these pigeons had pooped in our food on numerous occasions, but there was nothing I could do about it. I was in prison in a third-world country that genuinely didn't care about my issues, thoughts, or complaints.

My vegetarian meals became a joke to me. Every day it was the same: rice, potato, and a hard-boiled egg—every single day. On a few occasions, I tried to crack open the hard-boiled egg, only to find out it was a raw egg. I had no way to cook it, so apparently, they just forgot to boil it, but as always, what could I do about it? Nothing. Back home, we usually eat rice *or* potatoes—not both. Here, both were the norm. Even the KFC in the mall served chicken with rice and French fries. I had nothing to eat every day. I couldn't eat that same meal every single day.

I also had terrible stomach issues. Back home, I ate fruits, vegetables, and fibrous food daily and was fine. Here, they fed me carbs only. In my first seven days, I had not gone to the bathroom. They should have brought me to a hospital, but they just kept giving me pills. I do not know what the pills were, but they did nothing for me.

Finally, a woman named Cynthia, from the USA who fell for a scam like me, gave me some fiber from Peru called "Salvador Triple." She told me to mix it with liquid yogurt and drink/eat it. That seemed to do the trick for me. That wouldn't last me forever, so what could I do? They had a section where people made real meals and things you could buy. It was called Gastronomia. They made salad also.

This would get pricy fast, and I was obviously not working and couldn't keep asking my family to send me money. As it was, I was asking them to send me money for calling cards, plus I quickly learned that prisons here were not free. You had to pay for the slop they fed you, the cleaning of the halls, the lights, the water, etc. It was very apparent that prison was a business to Peru. Inmates had to pay to be in prison and work when there. Plus, you could make food, shoes, clothes, bags, etc., all work available to inmates. Yet, as typical with any corrupt country, whatever you sold, the prison took a commission. It's truly a disgrace.

Sal, my lawyer, had asked his junior associate, Rebecca* to visit briefly on Wednesdays, the visit days, and to bring me fruits, veggies, yogurt, and fiber. That was indeed a blessing. I'll never forget the first day Rebecca came with the bags; when she arrived, she was white as a ghost—completely distraught. I asked if she was okay. She said that she was just thoroughly frisked in the worst way she'd ever been. She was in shock. Sadly, she got a taste of what I was dealing with daily. I was very grateful for all she had brought me. She quickly realized how bad the INPEs were with me.

Peruvians were allowed to come in with plenty of bags for people, no problems at all, yet they constantly stopped Rebecca with whatever she was trying to bring me. First, they told her she was only allowed one bag or four apples, and she constantly told them, "Show me where it says that!"

They couldn't, of course, since it was not an actual rule. It was happening every Wednesday, so Viola advised me to get a prescription for the fruits and veggies since I needed them for my stomach, and it would help her bring the bags in. So, I had to see the prison doctor with Viola and ask for monthly prescriptions for fruits and vegetables. How silly was that! But I had to do it to help Rebecca—to help me.

I was also told that I'd need to see the prison psychiatrist. Viola was not around, so I had to see him alone. As usual, he spoke no English, and I spoke no Spanish, so there was no actual examination or conversation. All I knew was that I was suddenly put on 2.5 milligrams of clonazepam and fluoxetine. I did not know what these pills were or what they were for, but I was told I needed to take them. Being alone in a foreign prison, I did as I was told. I later found out these pills were for bipolar disorder and depression—neither of which I had ever been diagnosed with in my life. How did he come up with that diagnosis? Did he know just by looking at me? We never spoke to one another, so I was dealing with this. I was also told that clonazepam is like Clonipan in the US, but they usually prescribe 0.5 milligrams, whereas I was taking 2.5 milligrams there. I would have to stand in a line at 8 a.m. after quenta every morning to wait for my fluoxetine pill since I'd have to be given one capsule every morning, wait my turn, and take it in front of them. That way, they made sure I took it.

To be honest, I didn't feel any different with this medication. At 4 p.m. I'd have to go back in line for the clonazepam and follow the same procedure, taking it in front of them. I am told they give these pills to many people to make them zombies so they are out of sight and out of mind. I'd take the pill at 4 p.m. and would be fine, then 6 p.m. was quenta, and by 7 p.m., I'd be sound asleep, two hours and lights out. Everyone was all around me, talking, yelling, etc., but I heard nothing with this medicine. I also realized that I was being robbed blind every night also. They saw I was getting bags of food every Wednesday, and on Thursday, they were helping themselves to my stuff as I was knocked out every night. I am usually not a deep sleeper, but I was in such a deep sleep with this medicine.

I learned very quickly that nothing was safe. You needed to keep your money and anything of value with you at all times. One of my roommates gave me a little money holder that went around my neck.

That was to be always with me. Anyone who left their money or anything in their bed or off themselves would find it disappearing in a flash. It happened all the time. As much as I was annoyed by being robbed, I had no way to prove who it was, and the women were still nice to me. I started to accept that they weren't intentionally trying to harm me. They had no money or means of getting necessities such as toilet paper or food, so they stole it whenever they saw it. They'd steal my oranges, make orange juice, and then offer me some juice. I knew it was my oranges, but how would I prove it, and who could I tell in English? I learned they were good people but did what they were accustomed to doing to survive. I did not hold them responsible for their actions since, being in a corrupt third-world country, this was the only way of living they knew.

Pictures of the outside view of the Santa Monica prison rooms

Pictures showing how crowded Santa Monica is

Me working in CUNA (the daycare)

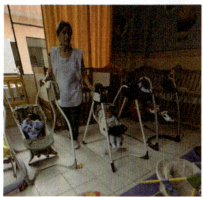

This is the Nigerian scammer. He is holding the so-called-IMF papers with my passport photo attached to them, pretending to be an IMF representative. This exact photo was later seen in the hands of the airport police, waiting for my arrival when I thought I was flying to Hong Kong for the IMF program. Coincidence? Not at all. They are all corrupt. This is the fake passport that MB gave me, pretending to be him. Sadly, my brain was not well enough to catch on to this scam at the time.

This is the same Nigerian (so-called-IMF representative) again pretending to be an IMF representative signing the forms. You can see the photos I took of the luggage he gave me. I took a ton of pictures and shared them with Eric asking if he thought this was normal or legitimate, and of course, he assured me it was. Why? Well, considering he introduced me to every scammer I ever encountered, I can only assume that he is in on the scams and probably gets a commission from them all.

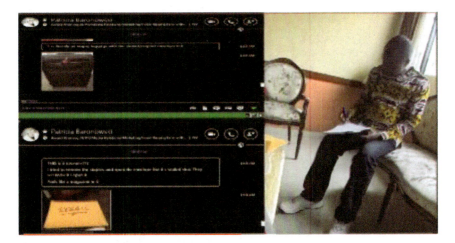

You can see how dirty and crowded these prisons were

CHAPTER 8

As my family and husband were going through all my emails to figure things out, they saw all the scams that I had fallen for, even before the MB one that had landed me in prison. I had so much medical proof of my brain injury back home. I spent one whole month in the hospital, which I have zero memory of to this day. I also have no reconciliation of the days following my release to home and only a sporadic memory of the first few months being home. Even when my memory was returning, it was not completely 100 percent. The doctors told my family that it may or may not return to what it was; if it did, no one could guess how long it would take or to what extent it would return. No one could know that; all anyone could do was wait. My medical documents helped prove that since my accident, I could not decipher right from wrong in this scam. Yes, I was caught in the airport in Peru with drugs in a suitcase checked in by me, but I was unaware that I was lured there for a scam, and my brain did not see the red flags in what I was asked to do.

That said, Sandy* immediately had me evaluated by Dr. Ladd, a top forensic psychiatrist in Peru. He came to Santa Monica with a translator and did a comprehensive examination for an entire week, one to two hours per day. I answered everything honestly. I was still relatively new to being in prison. This whole situation was all new to me, but I answered as honestly as possible since I was not lying. After the weeklong examination, he also conducted an SIRS II exam, which I found out later was a verbal lie detector test to determine if I was lying and/or faking my injury. I passed the exams with flying colors, and Dr. Ladd's determination coincided with doctors back home. I suffered a brain injury due to my accident and could not decipher right from wrong.

This was all presented to the court, and as I later found out, Peru does not do *anything* fast. As I've come to know, prison is a business in Peru. I was paying to be in prison. We all were. We had to pay for the water, lights, food, etc., and now my family was paying for legal fees, ironically in US dollars. (The US dollar was three and a half to four times Peru's local currency.) Why would Peru want to send us home? They keep prisoners in jail for extreme amounts of time, and their justice system made no sense to me. It seemed as if anyone caught with .5 kilograms of cocaine was allowed to go home. They considered that personal use, which was bizarre. But one to ten kilos is an automatic six- to eight-year sentence usually. If they could stick you with more time, they would always try. Ironically, you could murder someone or rob a bank and get out in less time than someone with a kilo of drugs. It's nuts.

Well, I spent my first month there completely bored; I called my family when I could. My letter to my family, sent via the Bible study woman, helped break the ice. No one hated me or was mad at me. Instead, they were all worried about me.

In fact, my mom was the one paying Sandy since I had lost so much money due to all the scams. I'm told at the onset she had asked Sandy how much this would cost, to which Sandy said, "I've never seen it go above 120 thousand US dollars." Hearing that, my mom signed on for it. Sadly, if there's one thing we've learned now, it's that I do not seem to fall under the category of the norm.

Talking to my mom was a joy. I had everyone's telephone numbers programmed into my cell phone because it was hard to remember them. Luckily, I knew my husband's, my kids', my sisters', and my mom's cell numbers. My mom was worried sick. No mom wants their babies in trouble, no matter what age, and one of her babies who was in a different country did not make it any easier.

I don't know what I would have done if it was one of my kids. Probably the same as my mom. I'd hire who I thought was the best lawyer I could find from the country and probably one recommended on the US Embassy's website. That's exactly what my mom did. She told me to stay strong and that she hired Sandy, who felt confident we had a strong case. Sadly, none of us had any experience in this situation or any information about Peru. We had an American mentality and thought this was a no-brainer because of the ample proof of everything. Sadly, we later learned that Peru is not the USA, and our way of processing and legal investigation are *nonexistent* in Peru.

I only had five minutes with the call, so I had to end it, but it was good for us to talk. I think we both needed it. I did not know how I'd talk to my kids. I did my best to raise them right and to stay out of trouble. Yet now, their mom was in jail in Peru for drug trafficking. Of course, they and anyone who knew me knew I was innocent, but I was away from them now, even my precious granddaughter, despite being so attached to her. She was only eight and a half months old when this happened and had taken her first crawl a week before, and I was so excited to witness it. Now, how long would I be here? What more would I miss? Only time would tell.

After my first month of reading books, walking in circles, pestering Franny* and just thinking all day about how sucky my life was, I realized I needed to do something. Working here was making shoes, crocheting, sewing, pocketbooks, or clothes—none of these I knew how to do because I had worked on computers my whole life. To avoid boredom, I had someone teach me how to crochet. My first project was trying to make a scarf, which was a complete comedy show. The woman instructing me kept taking it apart repeatedly since I kept messing it up. After so many times of this, I stopped asking her to help me correct whatever I was doing wrong. The result was a scarf that was so zig-zagged that it looked like a slithering snake. But I didn't care. It was my first real attempt at crocheting, plus it helped me pass the time. I quickly realized crocheting wasn't the best option for me working, and I didn't know how to do anything else. Sadly, no one could teach me other skills with the language barrier.

There were several babies in this prison. Pregnant women and women with babies could keep their babies with them in prison until the baby was three years old. Then, the baby must go home to the family. Franny told me there was a daycare in prison called CUNA where the babies went all day without their moms since they were working. It was initially Monday to Friday from 9 a.m. to noon. I would need to find a mom who needed a babysitter. Even though you'd technically be watching *all* the kids, you'd be hired and paid for by a particular mom who hired you for the day.

Franny and I stood outside Pabellon 1A and asked all the moms if they needed a babysitter that day. A woman named Sonia* agreed to let me watch her one-month-old. She was such a precious little angel. She had the cutest dimples and was such a happy baby. CUNA ran for babies 0–6 months, 6–12 months, 1–2 years, and then 2–3 years old. Inga*, Sonia's baby, was obviously in the 0–6-month-old room. I went to work, and there were about six other 0–6-month-olds in the room. The room consisted of cribs, swings, rocking seats with toys and mobiles, and a mat where we could play with the babies.

I truly bonded with Inga. She filled the massive void I was feeling from my missing granddaughter. I played with her every day; even after CUNA, we bonded. I called her my Peruvian granddaughter. She, too, had taken her first crawl steps. I was so excited every morning that I'd go downstairs for my morning fluoxetine from "Topico" and then stand at the gate waiting for Sonia and Inga for CUNA. Inga would start searching for me, and I would hide. The moment she'd spot me, her dimples would shine bright, and she'd light up my day. Some days, the INPEs would have no problem with me going to work; other days, it was a hassle, and we'd have to get the director of CUNA to come and tell them I was working there to get them to allow me to come outside. That was a typical day for me, a foreigner, in a Peruvian jail with different INPEs each day.

Babies at six months and older are at the age where they absorb everything like sponges. Unlike the parents, they understood me just fine. Their moms and everyone else spoke to them in Spanish, but I spoke in English, and they responded. It was great and made my time in Santa Monica as lively as possible.

I admired the director of the prison CUNA's work. As a marketing professional, I saw how hard she worked. She had several high-end people come in and view CUNA. She'd have me sing to the babies "Twinkle, Twinkle, Little Star," the ABCs, and other nursery rhymes in English so the visitors could see how hard she was working on teaching the babies English. We'd take the babies every morning, play with them, push them in the baby swings, change diapers, etc. At certain hours of the day, the moms would come to breastfeed, and then I'd burp the babies and have them nap. Then by noon, the moms would come to get their babies. With the director's effort, she eventually got CUNA to be 9–12:30 then 2–4:30, and that was a big help to the women who worked since work was the same hours. Technically, you'd make S/4 for the a.m. and then S/4 for the p.m. shift. For me, Sonia did not have to pay me.

I enjoyed doing it, and no other mom ever paid me. It was always some excuse, so I worked for free, but it kept me sane. After about six months, the director of CUNA had the entire CUNA renovated, and then it became a state-run program. The prison girls who were employed by them would be working for CUNA but be paid for by Peru. Unlike all other work there (Taller), where you'd have to pay to work, in CUNA, you didn't. And Peru was paying S/250 a month for CUNA Mas (the new name). This would have been great, except, as is always the case in my life, *I* could not qualify for this because it only applies to Peruvians. Then I was told that it only applied to babysitters taking care of babies 6 months to 3 years old and not those taking care of 0–6-month-olds, so I was back to not being paid. I tried to move to 6–12 months so I would fall within this regime. But I was rejected since I didn't speak Spanish. That meant I was back to taking care of 0–6-month-olds and still not being paid. I did look on the bright side because it helped me pass time. I latched on to Inga on weekends and after CUNA for the one and a half hours before the 6 p.m. quenta when we had to go up to our rooms for the day. I also played with her on Saturdays while her mom worked, and on Sundays, Sonia would invite me out for her visit, where I sat with her family. We couldn't communicate since her family spoke no English, but we had Inga in common, so it was all good.

I watched many pregnant moms come through prison and after they gave birth, the babies went to CUNA during the day. I watched babies as early as two weeks old. It was such a joy to be with newborns. I tried to make their prison sentence as joyful as I could. It was remarkable that they could be with their moms. You always want to share the joy with your family. They could give you a break with the newborn, not just once or twice a week on visitor days, but it was what it was. I remember as Inga was growing, I got to share so many of her first milestones.

One day, I had a few soles and brought a fruit shake from Gastronomia (where they sell food for prisoners and visitors that you buy on your own). It was actually pretty good. I tried to give some to Inga to try (she was about 9 months old), and she drank from a straw for the first time. She drank half my shake, which was pretty funny and incredible, seeing how smart she was. I even watched her roll over for the first time, crawl for the first time, take her first step, and more. She truly was filling the void of my Punpkin Munkin (the nickname I had for my granddaughter back home).

Aside from CUNA, I did not have much of anything else fun to do. The prison was 95 percent Peruvians who spoke and understood no English. The English women were either working or had their routines. The INPEs were not friendly, and the TV was all in Spanish, so unless I walked around in circles, which I did on countless occasions to pass the time, there wasn't much else to do.

One day, I had a toothache. To help with that, Franny told me that there was a dentist at the prison. I went there, and they gave me five days of injections. That seemed to be their routine; they would either drug you up or give you injections. God knows what was in those injections. Because I had no other choice, I got five days of injections, and when I went and saw the dentist, she gave me an injection in my gum. I assumed she would fill my cavity. Imagine my surprise: I blinked, and she had a tooth in her hand.

I asked, "Is that mine?" pointing at myself. She replied, "*Si.*" What the fuck? Thank God it was the tooth near the back and not one of my front teeth. After four years of braces, if she'd pulled one of my front teeth, I would have had a fit. Not to mention, there were no X-ray machines. I know from experience that sometimes you might think that you have a cavity in one tooth, but after an X-ray, they see the issue is in a nearby tooth. You only feel the pain in that area due to where the nerve is. I could only hope that she got the right tooth and that I wouldn't need another tooth pulled later.

Another time, I was walking with Inga, who had fallen asleep in my arms. Not surprisingly, someone had spilled Quaker all over the floor, which I could not see due to Inga being in my line of vision. The next thing I knew, I was flat on the ground. It was something out of a cartoon. My motherly instinct apparently kicked in, and I used my elbow to shield Inga's head from impact, but it woke her up. I must've not known what happened. I hit my head in the same place where my back and neck were broken in my skydiving accident. My head took a hard hit that day and knocked me unconscious for a moment. I was in agony when I realized what had happened and then immediately yelled, "Where's Inga?" Two women had picked her up when she was crying, and Sonia brought me to the doctor. They didn't do anything other than give me three days of injections. I was told Inga needed a tranquilizer to sleep that night. The sudden sleep to falling had scared her, understandably so.

This prison also had a church I went to every Sunday. Of course, it was in Spanish, but I knew God understood my prayers and confessions. Weekly, I made confessions and went for communion. One day, as I was going to church, the INPE working that day would not let me go. Again, me being the foreigner, I was singled out. From what I could understand, the INPE would not let me go because I was not appropriately dressed. I was in fucking prison! What did they expect from me, to wear a gown? I had capri pants below my knees, a short-sleeved shirt, and sneakers. I was presentable. Several Peruvian women went to church in short shorts and tank tops; they had no trouble at all. Yet I, the American, was forbidden to go. I snuck out past her and ran my butt off to the church (with the INPE racing behind me). When we got to the church, one of the nuns was there. The INPE was trying to tell her that I had to leave, that I was not dressed well enough, while I stood there seeing Peruvian girls wearing shorts where you could see the cracks in their asses. I chimed in with my Spanglish and said my clothes were being washed, so the nun told the INPE to leave me there, and it was okay.

After church, when I had to go back to the gate, I asked the other INPE what the other INPE's name was. She was confused as to why I asked but told me. I then said, "Gracias, me telefono me Embajada, no problemo," and walked away. In English, that meant, "Thanks, I'll call my Embassy, no problem." I know the prisons were very afraid when someone said they would contact their Embassy. Sadly, I can confirm that the US Embassy does nothing to assist Americans in prison. Other embassies visited their prisoners regularly. They brought them money, food, clothes, toiletries, and anything they needed. The US Embassy does absolutely nothing. But regardless, it jolted a little fear into the INPE, and that was all I needed.

I was in Santa Monica for five months without a visit from the US Embassy. I finally called them, and then they came. Whenever the prison calls your name for a visit, whoever it is—a visitor, a lawyer, the Embassy—they charge S/1. Every other embassy pays the S/1 for us, *except* the US Embassy. One, two, or three Americans—it didn't matter. We *all* had to pay our S/1 for being called. It was nuts. The visits lasted sixty seconds and were the same routine questions: "Anything new with your case? Anything you want to tell us? Okay, bye." And that was it.

I had told them about the clonazepam and fluoxetine that I was put on for no reason. They just said, "We'll make a note of that," and did absolutely nothing at all about it. I told them about the dentist pulling my tooth, about me not being allowed to go to church, about the CUNA issues with not allowing me to work for money, about me having no clothes, limited money, lunch, not having my cholesterol medication, and so much more. Did they help me? Ha! Not a chance. But the INPE was still frightened when I said I'd contact them.

Also, whenever the US Embassy comes, they ask if you need to update their form, which states who they are allowed to give information to, such as family, friends, media, the government, etc. I had filled out the form many times, authorizing them to give anyone information about me. I hoped that someone might be able to help me. Ironically, whenever someone *did* request any information or update on me, they would say the same boilerplate response: "We're in constant contact with Patricia and her lawyer. We are not authorized to provide any information at this time."

The funny thing was that they were not in constant contact with me *at all*. I had authorized everyone on the forms multiple times, but sadly, they were useless. They issued the same replies repeatedly. If they even looked at my file, they'd see that the forms were authorized multiple times. Even when I was first arrested, I had no blanket, toilet paper, towel, flip-flops, money for a call—nothing. Did the Embassy help me or bring me anything? Not at all. They never even visited to see how I was doing. It was a disgrace. As Americans, we all believe that if, God forbid, we ever run into trouble in a foreign country, we'd at least have the Embassy assisting us. I am proof, along with other Americans I've met, that this is not the case. In the USA, I pay taxes. My tax money should assist me in times of need. Then the US state department contacts the US Embassy, yet all they say is, "We're not allowed to interfere with the laws of another country."

How is assisting us interfering with the law? If we asked for necessities like toilet paper, we'd be told, "We do not have a budget to assist," or some other snarky comment.

There was another Christian group that came to the prison. They were called Emaus. They held a three-day retreat when I first arrived in Santa Monica. They had a sign-up sheet and only accepted 100 women. I was told initially that since I did not understand Spanish, it would be best to do the retreat another time. I blew it off after that and never gave it a second thought. A few weeks later, I was called to join the retreat. I thought they had me confused with someone else. But miraculously, I was somehow accepted into the retreat.

It was three days out in the visitor area and one hour a day in the church. They even fed us and gave us snacks and soda. I was fortunate enough to have one of the ladies of Emaus translate for me. It wasn't a Mass or anything like that. It was a time when everyone shared their stories about why they were in prison and how faith had helped them in their life journey. At one point in the retreat, we were asked to write ourselves a letter from God and give it to them. I did not know what to say. I had no clue why I was in this mess and why God had let me get scammed. Now that I think about it, and as strange as it may sound, several signs pointed to that.

But sadly, I did not see them as signs at the time. For example, first, MB stopped communicating with me when I pointed out the phony passport he provided. (Sadly, later, he had excuses for it that I fell for.) Then I had to cut my March trip short in Peru due to my granddaughter's Baptism. Was that another sign? MB had also wanted me to turn right around and come back the day after the Baptism, but I declined due to a preplanned vacation.

On my way to the airport in April, I lost my cell phone and almost missed my flight because I was trying to find an open store to replace my phone. Then on the April trip, I noticed something on the IMF forms he had me complete, which stated that I had to pay a processing fee. I tried reaching MB via Skype to verify this, but he did not answer me. I thought that was a scam, so I booked my flight back home. A few hours later, MB replied and said to ignore that. Throughout the ordeal, he said, "We have never once asked you for money. That is not our way. We solely want to help you, which is why I have enlisted you into this program. Disregard where it asks for fees. I have already waived them for you." And again, I believed him. So, it almost seemed in hindsight that something or someone was trying to deter me along the way, but I was too naive to notice.

So how does one write a note to God? I wrote that God caused my accident to slow me down and allow me to spend more time with my family. Unfortunately, since my terrible accident, I had gone back to working sixteen hours a day. I had not appreciated the gift of life that God gave me. Because of that, I did not grow closer to him or slow down to see that my family was standing by me. God had taken care of me, and I should have trusted him to continue taking care of me instead of thinking outside the box and joining some program that no one had even heard of.

Now, he wanted me to strengthen my faith, learn to trust him, and stop thinking that I had to take care of everyone, as this situation had proven that they could and would survive without my help. It showed me that all people want is me in their lives—safe and sound. Emaus took the letters and gave us a nice send-off after.

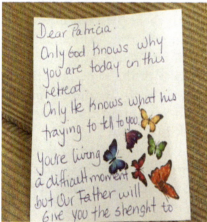

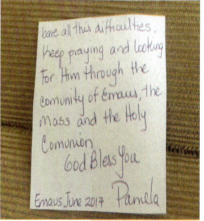

On the second day, I think Peru's food and/or water got the best of me. Halfway through the second day, I was throwing up, had diarrhea, and felt horrible. After Emaus, I went up to the pabellon, and while I was still sleeping on the floor, and they did not want my bed on the floor until *after* 9 p.m., I stood my ground. I needed to lie down. It was 5 p.m., and while they were not happy about it, they would survive. I wasn't sure if I'd make it back to Emaus for that final day, but luckily, I woke up much better. I realized then that I could no longer eat much of the local food; my stomach couldn't handle it.

I wear glasses for reading only and see fine without them. At 50 years old, I knew that my eyesight was getting worse. I could see, but it is blurry when I try to read unless I hold the material far away from me. One day, they told me an eye doctor was coming in for anyone who needed to have their eyes checked. Of course, it was not free, but I only had one pair of glasses with me, and they were scratched and falling apart. I went to the doctor, with a translator, and showed them my glasses, and they performed an exam. I then picked out a pretty pair of glasses that cost me S/300.

About three weeks later, they returned with my glasses, and I couldn't believe it. They were like magnifying glasses. I had to get a translator to ask what the heck had happened. They said these glasses were for walking around. I was frustrated and told them again that I saw fine walking around and that I needed *reading* glasses, not to mention if I walked around with those glasses, I'd probably fall. What kind of exam did they even do? So, they huffed, took the glasses back, and said they'd be back in two weeks with the correct ones. Well, they returned in two weeks with the same prescription again. I saw no change. I realized it wasn't worth arguing anymore. I just took the glasses, thanked them, and left. It wasn't worth arguing about for S/300 which was only like USD$75.

Another thing I found, considering the corruption in Peru, was that a visitor could pay an INPE to bring anything in, even things not allowed, such as perfume, drugs, cell phones, knives, etc. The INPE would also note what room it was going to. A few INPEs also sold Avon. We could purchase things such as makeup and perfume, which were not allowed for some reason. I think they were afraid it would cause trouble if someone used a lighter with perfume.

So, someone either paid to sneak stuff in *or* paid an INPE to order Avon. But the stuff you got wasn't a guarantee. The INPEs could then raid your room and take it all back. I had personally seen this happen on multiple occasions where they'd sell all the stuff and then they raided the rooms, took it back and then sold it to some-one else. It was so stupid. There were other days, totally unexpected, where the INPE would do morning quenta, and we would leave the pabellon briefly, as always, until quenta was over, when we could return.

But on these days, as we left the pabellon, we were all surrounded by about twenty-five male guards. We were told to sit on the floor and wait while they raided everyone's room. They looked to see if people had knives, scissors, perfume, drugs, or anything else they shouldn't have. This was called *requisa* when they raided the rooms. They were like tornados. They threw everything off our beds and emptied everything out—bags, clothes, etc. When all was said and done, by the time you got back to your room, it was as if a tornado swept and threw everything all over. Everything was thrown everywhere, and you had to figure out what was yours, separate everyone's stuff, and then neatly put it all back into place.

The craziest part was no matter how often they caught people with stuff—such as drugs, phones, knives, perfumes, etc.—they didn't question the corrupt INPEs. With as much security as visitors went through to enter, the fact that anything made it through must stem from somewhere, right? That's right, the INPEs! Yet no one looked at them. I know even when my lawyers would visit me and bring fruits, veggies, or snacks, the INPEs would tear apart the bags right in my face and take things they wanted. They knew we could not do anything about it. They'd go through cookies or chocolates and take what they wanted. Everyone knew it wasn't worth complaining or arguing because you were not going to win. That was prison life in Peru—insane.

Another funny story about chocolates— well, not really funny, but another story on how chocolate ranked there—occurred when I was advised by Sal Monty* that the aunt of one of his employees was a nurse at the jail, and if I ever needed something, I could go to her. Well, to be honest, I hardly ever saw her. She was not the nurse who gave me fluoxetine or clonazepam. I assume that she only worked a few days a week or in a different spot. I saw her randomly, just not all the time. The one nurse who was the usual one to give me the daily medicine called "Topico" and "Tratamiento" was nice. She also trusted me and could tell that I was not someone who was going to sell the medicine or abuse it. I was and am an honest person.

She started to give me several pills at a time, so I wouldn't have to go and stand in an hour-long line every day, twice a day. I was not allowed to tell anyone since she was not supposed to be doing it. I never asked her to, but I did appreciate it. For her kindness, I'd buy her a fruit salad or something to snack on every now and then. A few times, after my lawyers had brought me my fruit and snacks, I'd drop in and give her some snacks, too. Once, I gave her some chocolates that Rebecca had brought in for me; she was so happy. She never asked me for anything, but I wanted to show my appreciation. Plus, with the language barrier, it was my way of saying thank you.

Anyway, one day the nurse, the aunt of an employee for Sal Monty, was here, and I tried to say hello, and she was rude and completely dismissed me. I thought to myself, *What the hell?* I mentioned it to Sal on the phone. I guess he asked his employee to find out what happened. She explained that she was with a client one day, and I had stormed in on her. She said I was making all sorts of demands and embarrassing her in front of her client and that she was done with me. I told Sal that everything about that was off because it was *not* in me to barge in and demand anything, and we didn't even speak a common language, so how on earth could I have made demands that didn't go over her head? Sal Monty asked me to ignore her even though it bugged me. The next time I saw her, I tried in my best Spanish to apologize, "*Permisso, lo siento mucho. Nunca quise causar ningún problema. No estoy seguro de lo que hice, pero lamento mucho haberte molestado de alguna manera.*" I wasn't sure what exactly I was saying, but I was trying my best to apologize with the help of charades. After trying my best, she said, "*No está bien. No hay ningún problema. ¿Tienes chocolate?*"

There was the answer right there. I hadn't done anything to her, but there it was: she wanted chocolates! Apparently, she had seen me give the other woman chocolates and was annoyed that I didn't give her any. Unbelievable! I went and got her some chocolates and then just stayed clear of them all. I did not want to continue with these stupid games.

As bad as my situation was, I could never live in Peru. Their justice system made no sense to me, and they do nothing fast. Even with the language barrier, I was able to communicate with people as best I could. In Peru, you get less jail time for murder than for drugs. Can you believe that? Drugs of 1–5 kilograms are an automatic seven-year sentence, yet murder is only five years. Plus, with benefits, you can be released after completing one-third of your sentence. A fellow inmate had killed her two children and chopped up their bodies. She was sentenced to five years and got released in under three. Yet someone with drugs had no such privileges.

On top of that, with Peru being all about money, they also charge you hefty fines for your release, and if you can't pay your fine, you must stay and finish your complete sentence. One girl's fine was S/25k; that's a lot of money. Obviously, she couldn't afford to pay it, so she had to stay and do all her time. It's S/25k and what they call a *dias multa* fine. Hers was counted as three hundred days at S/7 per day. That's an *additional* S/2,100. So, she could go for what they call "expulsion." This is where you petition for one-third of your time and pay your fines. If you don't pay, you stay and do all your time. Most prisoners do not have money, which is why they are in jail. These scammers prey on their desperation for money.

I met a wonderful woman in Santa Monica who was married and had five children. Apparently, her husband had been arrested and was doing time in prison, but I don't know what for. She had moved out of Peru to be with her mother so she could help her with the kids while her husband served time. After his release, she moved back to Peru to be with him and decided to open a beauty salon with her mother. She had just purchased the location and equipment when she was arrested. She kept asking *why* she was being arrested, and they said, "We believe that you knew what your husband was doing, so we're arresting you, too." She said, "That is ridiculous. I had no idea what he was doing. Plus, he's already served and completed his time." Apparently, they didn't care and arrested her for six years and six months, tearing her away from her family and five kids, and a newly purchased business. How could a justice system do that?

Another woman got caught smuggling drugs. She was Peruvian but spoke English. She had five kids and said she was raising them alone and had no money, so she tried to smuggle drugs into Africa to make money. Unfortunately, she got caught and served six years in prison in Africa. After her time, she was released and sent back home to Peru. She said she had learned her lesson. Of course, over time, people know your story. She said she had told a neighbor about her past. Well, her neighbor got arrested for having drugs, and when they asked her who gave them to her, she knew of Michelle's* past, so she said she got the drugs from her. She knew the police would buy that story since she was imprisoned for drugs before. In Peru, that was all it took—no questions asked. They arrested Michelle with no investigation and no evidence—nothing. If someone says they got drugs from you, that's all they want to hear. Michelle swore that she was innocent and that the girl lied, but it didn't matter. She was sentenced again to six years and eight months in prison in Peru.

This other Peruvian woman had four kids, between the ages of eight and eighteen. She was visiting her brother's home when the police raided it and found drugs. She said she knew nothing about that and that she was visiting family. Apparently, it did not matter. They both got sentenced to six years and eight years. The 18-year-old was now in charge of being a "mom" to all the kids.

Inga's mom's story was similar to mine. She happened to be with a friend who said she had to make a pit stop at the airport. The girl got busted with drugs in a bag. Lena said she had no idea about any of that. It was not *her* bag. The police even raided Lena's home and found nothing at all—zero evidence. Again, it didn't matter. I don't know how much drugs were in the bag, but Lena got sentenced to nine years for a crime she did not commit. I honestly could never live in Peru because of how insanely ridiculous their justice system is—no investigations, no formality, no real justice, and more. In the USA, if you are in prison and there is a death in your family, they will allow you to attend the funeral and pay your respects if you are handcuffed and escorted by police. Not in Peru.

I know many people whose parents passed away while in prison. I was friends with a Peruvian girl whose dad had just passed away, and they didn't let her attend the funeral. They tell you that they passed, and that's it. Another girl from the USA had a newborn baby girl back home when she was arrested. Her daughter was killed back home. Can you even imagine? It's bad enough that you are arrested and serving time in a foreign country, but then you hear your first and only baby died? You would think they'd allow her to go home for the funeral. Peru and the USA have an extradition treaty. If she had attended the funeral, the USA wouldn't have kept her there, and she'd have been escorted back to Peru. But nope, Peru doesn't care. They told her everyone must deal with it.

Another thing I saw that was strange is that I know there is a Census back home. No one takes it seriously. I don't remember ever filling out a census form from the mail. In Peru, it's not something sent in the mail; it's a door-to-door visit that they take seriously. They even came to the prison and went through every person to check them off a list. This prison, again, was mostly Peruvian. There were hundreds of women there. By the time they went through every single one on the list and then got to me, it was hours later. All the INPEs had to change shifts to rush home for their census. It was strange to me.

We were also given pills for pesticides every 4–6 months. Apparently, there are things in the water there—the water we shower in, wash our clothes in, wash our fruits and veggies in, and brush our teeth in. We were ingesting it, and since it was not good for us, pesticide pills were their answer. Also, not sure if it was from the food, the water, the climate, or what, but my hair, which was already thin, was falling out badly. I saw the same with everyone. I'm not sure how true this was, but Viola said that they put something in the water to alleviate sexual urges so that the lesbians would not run rampant. I don't know if that was true. But after a year, others also went to the medical officers about their hair falling out. Their answer? The prison started putting people on birth control pills to prevent their hair from falling out. It was not to prevent pregnancy but for their hair. I did not go that route; I just dealt with the hair issues. I'm in menopause anyway and did not want anything interfering with that. Aside from the constant injections and medication, they also always gave out pesticide pills, three flu injections in one year, and injections for hepatitis and sexually transmitted diseases. I never knew what they injected me with, only that I needed to get them along with everyone else.

I was becoming more and more of a hoarder. I did not want to have more cavities and risk more teeth being pulled out. I brushed my teeth several times a day at home, flossed, etc. In prison, I was brushing my teeth in water with pesticides and whatever their local toothpaste was. I did not have dental floss, so I took the string from my clothes and used that as dental floss. The string would always break, but I made it a habit to take care of my teeth to not have any more pulled out. Also, whenever my soap would start dwindling, and I had to open a new soap, I'd save the little piece of the tiny soap. As this happened repeatedly, I'd have several small pieces to merge to make a new soap—survival of the fittest. I was doing whatever I had to do to survive. Rebecca didn't always bring me the money my family sent her for me. She was already bringing me fruits and veggies, and I hated pestering her to bring other things. I know Sal Monty had instructed her to bring me a Spanish/English dictionary. Sadly, it was stolen from me quickly. Rebecca then brought me another one. That, too, was stolen. She brought me four in total, and they were all stolen from me, so I didn't ask for anymore and always felt terrible whenever I had to ask for anything. I just tried to make the best of whatever I had.

We also had a microwave oven that we were only allowed to use at delegated times, like the phones, all via a list. We were allowed to use it after the 6 p.m. quenta. The salon, the room I was now in, was in the back end of the hallway, so when everyone went through quenta, they immediately got in the microwave line to heat up whatever food they may have had or that a visitor had brought them. By the time I got through quenta and got to the line, I already had thirty people before me. If you calculate, that's five minutes allowed per person, and by the time it was my turn, two and a half hours had already passed. Once, I waited one and a half hours and then just ate my food cold. I'd never do that again.

As with everything in Peru, there was a price. Whenever they called a meeting with the delegado and prisoners, it was called a "reunion." Back home, reunion meant something completely different. Anyway, they called a reunion several times for things such as telling everyone that we all had to pay S/3 per person to have the microwave fixed, or S/5 to have the television fixed, or S/5 to replace the paper used on the bulletin board in the hall that had announcements and schedules. I never got to use the microwave, the television was all in Spanish, and the bulletin board contained things I did not understand, so why was *I* expected to pay anything?

But as always, that was a useless fight—more of the crap I had to deal with here. Apparently, Americans were seen as walking ATMs. Yes, the US dollar was worth almost four times more, but did they not realize that I was not working? And even with Lena, I was never being paid for watching her baby, and my family was now paying a fortune in US dollars to Sal Monty for my defense. Plus, we were paying for Rebecca to bring me fruits, veggies, and yogurt every week. It's not like we were millionaires with a never-ending supply of money. My mom was 72 years old and was using all her hard-earned money to pay Sal Monty to try and bring me home. But apparently, no one cared.

Even downstairs, where they had a little shack where you could purchase things you needed, *I* always seemed to be charged more than everyone else. I was American and didn't speak the language. Calling cards for the telephone should have been S/10. Toilet paper, fruits, deodorant, or anything else was always a higher fee for me. Eventually, Lena, Inga's mother, caught on to what was happening to me and would always grab my hand and bring me back to where I bought things and demand that they refund what they had stolen from me. Like I always said, while I might not have gotten paid for watching the baby, I didn't want to get paid since I did it out of the goodness of my heart, and she paid me back in many other loving ways. She always invited me to sit with her family and eat when they visited. She always stuck up for me when she saw someone taking advantage of me. She often had food left over from her visits and would set up a table for us to eat together, which was always better than *pila,* the name of the prison food. Even during my first Christmas there, we were allowed back downstairs after quenta to sit with our friends and eat dinner together on Christmas Eve. Lena invited me to her table, and I got to spend my first Christmas Eve with her, her other friends, and Inga. It truly made a very sucky situation a tiny bit better. She always felt bad for me, knowing my situation, being away from my family, kids, grandbaby, etc. She knew that Inga always cheered me up, and I was grateful for them both.

Sal Monty kept confusing her with another woman named Mitchy. He told my family to talk to me and tell me to stay away from her because she was trouble, and she spent time in prison in Africa and had other kids, etc. My husband kept telling me this, and I kept trying to explain that Inga was her only child, and she'd never been to Africa. Sal was confusing her with someone else, but my family was far away and only had Sal Monty's word to go by. And since my brain was not deciphering right from wrong, they chose to believe Sal Monty over me, but I knew he had the wrong girl. I just stopped fighting it and said, "Okay, I'll keep away from her," even though I didn't. She was nothing but good, and Inga was innocent, so I continued. I was doing nothing wrong, so I felt I had nothing to worry about either way.

CHAPTER 9

I discovered that my mother had fallen over the Christmas holiday and shattered her hip. No one wanted to tell me and upset me since being away from everyone over the holidays was terrible enough. I had no idea. Whenever I tried to call her and got her voicemail, I assumed she was busy, yet she was in the hospital having surgery to repair her shattered hip and then physical therapy. She was upset about missing my calls, yet she had bigger things to deal with.

Months and months went by with zero movement in my case. I'd later learn that this was typical in Peru. My family and I kept thinking in terms of US justice, yet Peru is completely different, and sadly, there was no US support for me. I spent my first winter in prison in Peru with little to no warm clothes. Even when people gave me clothes to wear, they were so much smaller than me. So, I would wear high-water pants. I had one warm sweater from home, but the prison cut off my hood because hoods were not allowed. Viola crocheted me a hat, so I had that to wear. The summer in Peru is January through March, which is the opposite of the USA.

In December, I had gotten my very first visit. My husband had come to visit me with our dear skydiving friend. Gerry felt bad for my husband and bought him the trip. I hadn't seen anyone since my arrest in April, and Gerry had not intended to visit me in prison since he bought the trip for my husband. I'd known Gerry for several years while skydiving, so he was my friend, and I wanted to thank him. It was such a joy seeing them both. It had been eight months! Sadly, they only had one day to visit for a few short hours, but I relished every minute. My family had wanted to come and visit me all along, but they thought I would be home months ago. Sal Monty had advised them not to visit for fear that if other prisoners saw that I had a visitor from the USA, they'd assume that we were wealthy, which would cause trouble for me, so my family, against their wishes, held off. I did not expect them to travel to South America to come and visit, but I did appreciate seeing Charlie* and Gerry. It broke my heart when they had to leave.

I got called by an INPE one day to go to a room. I followed her and was greeted by three men. They were DEA officers with the Embassy. One spoke English and asked questions about the Spanish woman who had brought me the suitcase at the hotel. I did not have my laptop, phone, etc. He asked me their names, number, location, and more. How he expected me to have this, I did not know. When I couldn't give him anything, he said, "Well, if you refuse to help us, then good luck, we're leaving." I said, "I have nothing here. Annie from the Embassy, who you say you work for, took photos of everything: emails, numbers, photos, etc." Suddenly, this man showed me a photo of the Nigerian and one of the women. I said, "That's them. How did you get these?" he said, "We had them under surveillance." What surprised me was that *if* they were under surveillance and had already gotten this close to them, why were they free, and why was I in jail?

I told him Annie had everything, plus the itinerary was paid for by someone responsible for this. If they traced it down, they'd find them, trace the email and telephone number they contacted me from. He said, "Okay." I then asked him for his business card, and he would not give me one. I said I had a right to know who I was talking to. He held up this card but would not give it to me, so I quickly took out my pen and wrote it down—his name was Jerry Coleman*. I gave him my husband and Sal Monty's information and told him they could provide proof of everything, as they had everything from my emails, Skype, and everything else. He said he'd reach out to them and left. He never did reach out to my lawyer or family.

I left and waited for my turn with the phone. I called Sal Monty and Charlie and told them what happened and gave them Jerry Coleman's telephone number. I knew Jerry wouldn't call them, so best that *they* call *him*. My husband called him and recorded the call. He explained the whole story and all the proof he had. Jerry said, "I believe her. I am running off to a meeting. I'll mention all of this. I have no problem going to battle for someone innocent. I'll see what I can do!" Sadly, he never did anything. I guess he thought I could hand him this Nigerian on a silver platter, and since I couldn't, he had no use for me. As I said, they had them on camera. Why didn't they arrest them? Why did they arrest me instead? I had no clue who he was, only that he was the US representative for IMF, or at least that's what I was originally told. The only explanation I could come to was that Jerry was in on the whole scam and was doing his due diligence in meeting me to check it off his list of duties.

Meanwhile, he never did plan to pursue the Nigerian Drug Cartel since he was one of the corrupt ones in the scam. Sadly, I'd never know since no one planned to stop this from continuing. The Nigerian Drug Cartel worked with the corrupt police and all other corrupt players. Because of this, the US looks the other way, saying, "The crime happened in another country, so we're not wasting our police dollars investigating something that didn't even happen *here*." Peru loves arresting Americans because we help support the country just by being there, so it was a corrupt merry-go-round that I was on. This nightmare never wanted to end.

My Punpkin Munkin back home was only eight and a half months old when I took this trip to Peru. My whole world was shattered dreadfully that day, April 30, 2017, at 3 p.m., when I went to Peru's Jorge Chavez International Airport. It truly was a tough pill to swallow. How could this happen to me? How could these scammers ruin my life like this? It was not only me. I later learned that 290 Americans throughout South America were targeted in America and victimized. Yet, these scammers went about their day, not caring about the damage they inflicted. MB had told me to make the trip a vacation and to take all my family with me. Can you imagine? All of us would be imprisoned in Peru—my granddaughter, too! We'd all lose our jobs, homes foreclosed, etc., yet these scammers do not care. Another big scam is a love scam, where people find so-called love online. They constantly chat with people who claim to be someone else, and they tell people that they deserve nothing but the best. These scammers target older people who've fallen for scams before, are in debt, suffered brain injuries, or have dementia or serenity.

Sadly, we are easy targets for them. An FBI friend told me that these scammers purchase medical records in the USA and target us.

That's how the 74-year-old woman from the USA, a fellow prisoner, got targeted. She was a retired nurse and lived alone and met someone online who said they'd pay for a nice vacation for her. He then told her that his daughter lived in Peru and that he'd love for her to meet her, which she did. Then the girl said, "I bought my dad a pair of pants. Would you be kind enough to bring them back to the USA for him when you see him in person?" So, she agreed. She said that the dogs were all over her suitcase when she entered the airport. She didn't understand why. There was a kilo of cocaine soaked into the pants. She was arrested and then incarcerated for six years and eight months.

She had to sell her house to have money to pay for a lawyer to defend her case. She still had to endure two years before her lawyer could have her released on a humanitarian clause. She was okay but pretended not to recognize people, so they said she was senile and got released on the clause. While that might have been great, she no longer had a house to return to and had to move in with her sisters to another state. Did the scammers care? Nope, not at all. I was surprised she was released on this clause, but I was still here with a provable brain injury. Such is my life, unfortunately.

The airport video of my arrest was on local news in Peru many times. You'd think that hundreds of kilos of drugs were in that bag instead of 2.5. I didn't understand how or why it was on the news as often as it was. It also made it onto a show called *Locked Up Abroad*, run by National Geographic. I'd never seen the show, but several of my friends watched it and saw me on it a few times. The IMF forms MB sent me had me affix several passport photos of myself throughout the documents. The airport video clearly shows that I was set up because that was the *exact* photo being passed around by the police in the airport. Now explain to me how a photo of this Nigerian man holding forms with this exact photo attached to it is in the hands of the police at the airport before I ever even got there. How did they get that photo? This Nigerian Drug Cartel may have paid off the police and the DEA, who had them on surveillance—who knows?

But obviously, the photo being passed around by the police in the airport came from the Nigerian who was still free.

Then you see me get out of the taxi, and the police point to me and say to one another, "There she is, in the white shirt and black pants. Get her!" As I walked into the airport, I was surrounded by police; even when they opened both pieces of luggage, mine was okay, but the one the Nigerian and woman gave me was empty. When they swabbed it, it turned blue, which then tested positive for drugs. I'm later told this is what these cartels do. They set up innocent victims like me with the police to get caught with under three kilos of drugs while they sneak others through with hundreds of kilos without getting caught. They pay for our trip, they pay off the police, and in the end, they make a fortune. It's a win-win for them and total devastation to us. It's sickening and something I'd never known in a million years happened daily in the world.

If you had told me this happened and that I'd fall for such a scam, I'd say you were nuts. I am a successful business owner, mom, grandma, wife, daughter, and more. I am *not* a drug smuggler, and I would have definitely not been a scapegoat for such a scam. Well, that is no longer the case. There I was, a prisoner in Peru, having fallen for the exact scam, still recovering from a brain injury. I didn't recognize the scam as it was happening—even the scams that I fell for in the US.

Well, there were several scams that I fell for after my accident, but two of them happened to me in the USA, as sick as it is. I can see why these scammers do what they do. Why? Because they can get away with it. Let's take Lisa Parker* for example. She was the woman I was referred to by Eric. She was based in Connecticut, talked a good game, and I believed her. We even had Skype video chats, and the woman on the video was the same one in the passport. She had scammed me out of $150k. I later discovered that I was not the only person she had scammed out of money.

Since she's based in the USA, I went to my local police station. And because this happened from my home office, I thought this was the way to get help. The local police told me that if I was dumb enough to fall for her scams, then shame on me. Can you believe that? It was $150k in total—not mere pennies! Again, if it weren't for my brain injury, I would never have fallen for it in the first place. I was furious with the police and said there must be something we could do. She was in Connecticut, and that was verifiable. The police officer told me about a Federal website (https://www.usa.gov/stop-scams-frauds) where you could report scams, and they would follow up with it if warranted. That was it? I left and went home to report this and all my proof online. The website was generic. Once you input all the information, upload your proof, and click enter, the page refreshes. You didn't even get a thank you or any acknowledgment for completing it. Honestly, I did it again since I wasn't sure I did it right. I got the same result—so bizarre.

I then reported the three loan scammers, all introduced to me by Eric. Each loan scammer would tell me that I'd have to pay a filing fee, anywhere from $5k–$10k, all paid either by Western Union or by bank wire. I never got any loan. But I had their emails, telephone numbers, Western Union, and banking information, so I submitted it all to the website with the same no-confirmation ending.

Last, there was the Timothy Streaks scam. He was based in Texas. I researched him and found no information. His partner, Aaron, had sent me documents and a PowerPoint presentation talking about his OTC business and stated, "I am materially rich, but dollar poor." He apparently had an art business and stated that he needed a $30k loan to complete a deal and that I'd get it back in ten days—another contract that did nothing for me. Ten days came and went with no refund. He promised me $300k in exchange for the $30k. I figured that would get me out of all debt the prior scams got me in, but instead, it just added to it. Then he asked for another $15k and said he'd refund me $30k for that loan. He said the deal he was waiting for did not go through and that this $15k would wrap it up.

I was hesitant about it, but as all the scammers do, he promised it back to me in two weeks. Well, it's been over five years and nothing. My sister researched him and found his photo on an FBI website that warns people not to send him any money because he is tied to scams, robbing people of money. Why didn't I get that research result? I researched his name and company and never got anything, yet my sister just googled his name and got that. It's strange how search results are hit or miss in terms of what one gets. Had *I* gotten that result in my search, I would never have fallen for the scam and sent him money *twice,* but unfortunately, I never got it.

So why do these scammers do what they do? Because they can. They know through other scammers' word of mouth that no one will do anything to stop them. Countless other victims I've met say the same thing so far. No matter who you go to for help, they look the other way. They all feel, "You're not that important. You didn't lose billions. What's in it for me? Recognition?" It's the sad reality that we live in, unfortunately.

I hired a lawyer to sue Lisa Parker since I had a contract with her. She lived in a gated community, so every time the lawyer tried to serve her with court papers, she just wouldn't allow the gate people to let them in to serve her, and I was still being charged legal fees, lawyer fees, court fees, processing fees, service fees, and more. I stopped legal proceedings when I was going in circles, incurring fees, and going nowhere. The lawyer told me from the start that I would probably never get my money back from her, but we could at least rattle her cage in court. She had many "business" names, which anyone could do online, and she'd just change the names and email addresses and scam the next unsuspecting person.

One of the loan scammers had even made up a *partricaba-conowski@gmail.com* run by Google. They were using a copy of my passport and pretending to be me scamming people. Sadly, there is no "Google person" to report that to. I had to cancel my passport and report it stolen, as directed by the passport company. I then wrote to every Google company email I could find, telling the story about someone pretending to be me with a Gmail account and scamming people. It's three years later when I write this, and this continues.

Scammers do not care about the damage they cause to the victims' lives. They just know they can get away with what they do. Even my ex-husband, with all the scams he's pulled—robbing people, false identity, abuse, and more—still does it because he can get away with it. It's truly sickening. Yes, he's gotten caught and gone to prison, but the jails are crowded in the US. The justice system says,

"Well, he didn't kill anyone, and we need the room, so let's just give him a slap on the wrist and send him home." That's happened many times, so he knows that he can continue to get away with it, even if he gets caught. So, the USA is not much better, unfortunately.

While still in prison in Santa Monica, after getting my first visit from my husband, my family wanted to visit me. My husband came back a month later with my son. My daughter could not come due to being tied up with her baby, but my son lit up my day when I saw him. I knew that visiting their mom in prison in a foreign country could not be easy, but it meant the world to me to see him and hug him. Unfortunately, men visitors could only visit one day a week for a few hours, and with everyone working back home, I couldn't expect them to stay weeks so I could see them more, so I got to see him and my husband again one time. As always, goodbyes broke my heart. They actually stayed at a woman's hotel. Her name was Tania*, and she was a friend of Sal Monty and had a mansion that she rented out to tourists and visitors. My family had gotten to know her well, and she'd taken them on tours of Peru.

My younger sister came to visit me another time with my husband. It was a nice treat to see her. She's the sister who worked with me, and she told me about how my company was doing. She also asked me why I never told anyone about all the scams and trouble I kept getting into. I told her it was embarrassing, and at the time, I did not realize it was a problem; my brain was getting better little by little, but it still was not good. Even in prison, it was getting better daily, but it still wasn't perfect.

My birthday was coming up on March 31st, and she said she would visit again with my mom for my birthday. In Santa Monica, while women would wait in the never-ending line to visit prisoners, my sister was approached by other visitors who came in with bags of food, fruits, and vegetables. Once inside, they sell it all to other visitors or prisoners. Of course, the prison wants you to buy food already inside since they get money from that, so they don't allow people to sell things. But it didn't stop them from doing it. They'd just sell it on the sneak. In fact, I bought from them myself since it was cheaper than buying from the prison. Since these women had a lot of bags, they asked my sister, who didn't have any bags, to bring in two for them so it didn't look suspicious for them to go in with five or six bags. My sister did it, and when she told my mom about it, my mom had a fit. "Do you not see what happened to your sister? She's in jail for taking a bag from a stranger in Peru! Now you're taking strangers' bags *into* a prison? Don't take anything from anyone!" The damage was already done, and the bags were brought in, but no trouble resulted. *Peru, Peru, Peru* is all I ever would say. The land where you can expect the unexpected because anything can and will happen.

In Peru, they seem to be the kings of holidays. They have more holidays than any place I've ever seen. In fact, the courts semi-shut down the entire month of February for some holidays. I'd been in prison since April 30th and the judge ordered a nine-month investigation; but, months later, they had not done anything, I somehow fell through the cracks throughout February when other parts of the court were running. Apparently, they realized this towards the end of February and notified me that I suddenly had court, which was called *deligencia,* the next day. That was odd. I quickly called Sal Monty to tell him that I was just told that I had deligencia tomorrow. He did not say much, but he was aware that the courts had already missed their deadline and was not okay with that.

I went to court the next day. There, you are handcuffed and stuffed in the back of what looks like a black ambulance. It had one side bench where some people sat, and others stood. We picked up and dropped off other prisoners along the way. This ambulance, like Santa Monica, was full of cockroaches and hot as hell; January, February, and March are summer months in Peru. There are no windows, and they drive like maniacs, so I was sick during the drive. I got to the Callao men's prison courts. It was a small court where everyone sat behind a gated wall. Other people have their court with you. This day, neither Sal Monty nor anyone from his team appeared. When I spoke to him the day before, he told me he'd see me at court, so I was unaware he'd not be coming. The translator asked where my lawyer was, and I said he must be on his way. Everyone was rushing me because deligencia was an all-day ordeal, and no one wanted to wait. The judge said that they'd adjourn if he wasn't there in ten minutes. I didn't know what was happening. After five minutes, they ended court and threw us back into the ambulance.

Typically, we'd leave Santa Monica at 8 a.m. and wouldn't get back until about 8 p.m. We'd leave Callao, drop people off along the way, then go to another prison, get taken out of the ambulance, and be placed into another jail with tons of other women and men. It was dirty and smelly. We'd sit there for hours before being put back into an ambulance and making our way back to Santa Monica. I'd be soaking wet with sweat and starving since you didn't get food. Yet, as always, the Peruvians would sweet-talk the INPEs to bring them food, but *I* got no food. Deligencia was always a horrible all-day ordeal.

I was rescheduled for another court date a week later, and it was the whole deligencia nightmare again. This time at court, the translator was horrible. He didn't translate anything for me. I was trying to guess what was going on. From what I could tell, Louie* was going head-to-head with the prosecutor, but I had no idea what they were talking about. The INPEs sitting with me kept looking shocked and were smiling. I had no idea what was happening, Louie just looked at me once and positively nodded his head, but I didn't know what was happening. As I was walking back to the ambulance with the INPEs, they were trying to tell me, "*Tu abogado muy bueno.*" They said my lawyer was great, and I'd be going home. What? Home? Finally! I thought I'd have been home months ago, not a year later, but at this point, that was music to my ears. Louie apparently told them that they had nine months to do an investigation and had done nothing. He said they had no right to keep me in prison any longer and had to release me.

As my luck would have it, there was a whole crackdown on corruption in the courts at this time. Someone had taped one of the judges making a money deal to let a murderer go. That spread across the media and caused them to investigate many corrupt judges. Well, the one judge who was supposed to sign my release papers got arrested and was sent to jail, so I was in limbo. I now had a new judge, a woman, who was a first-time judge. Sal Monty had filed a habeas corpus on the prior judge, and demanded the new woman judge sign my release papers. She showed him a mile-high stack of documents that were all her case files and said that I was somewhere in the pile, and he'd just have to wait until she got to me. Another court member told her, "He just filed a habeas corpus on the last judge. Are you sure you want to say that?" Having been told that, she signed for my release. I was beyond happy until I phoned my husband, and he broke the bad news to me. When Peru says, "You get freedom," they meant house arrest, and while that would be okay, it meant house arrest in Peru. Peru is not my home! Either way, why was this still going on?

Before this was even agreed to, Charlie and my sister asked Sal Monty at the court if house arrest counted as time served before it was even signed, and Charlie told him, "If it doesn't count, keep her in Santa Monica," but he assured them that it did count. Nine months came and went with nothing happening with the courts, so why was this not over? Well, like everything else, Peru's justice makes no sense. Yes, they were granted a nine-month investigation. It had been eleven months, and nothing happened. Still, they could continue their investigation (which they had yet to start), but I'd be released to a home in Peru due to habeas corpus. I wanted to fall and cry. I could not believe this nightmare was continuing!

My Punpkin Munkin was one-and-a-half years old. I'd been in prison for eleven months, and it was still not over. The courts and prosecutor had done absolutely nothing so far. Meanwhile, my family had run all over, gathering all my medical records back home and having them translated, certified, and sent to Peru. Dr. Ladd conducted his two comprehensive exams on me and submitted his reports, yet the prosecutor had done absolutely nothing, which I am told is typical. My mother and sister were planning to visit me for my birthday, and we were hoping I'd be out of jail by then. We did not want my mom to have to see me in prison.

My husband had to sign and pay for an apartment in Peru for me to go to. One of Sal's clients owned a condominium ten minutes from his office, so he rented it to us. We had to sign a one-year contract. And what seemed to continuously be the case for me, where everyone else was charged S/1,500 a month rent, mine was USD$1,500 a month. That equaled S/5,100 a month. This seemed to be my life in Peru; everyone thought I was walking around as the Bank of America. My name was Money to them, not Patricia apparently, yet I sadly did not have much choice.

The police would have to approve the apartment, and since I was the first American accused of drug smuggling to ever get house arrest, they were unhappy about it. Even though this apartment was a condo in a gated complex with security and cameras at the entrance and a doorman, the police had to come and inspect it; as expected, they did not want to approve it. They said there were kids in the complex, and I was a drug smuggler, they couldn't have me there, etc. Sal had to come and talk some sense into the police and get them to sign off on it. I'm sure, knowing how corrupt the police are, that they wanted an incentive, meaning that Sal would pay them to agree to it, but who knows? I wasn't there, and Sal would never admit to that. All I know is that suddenly, they finally signed off.

Peru prisons are also known for "conveniently" making minor errors in paperwork to drag things on and on and on. I was told at the end of February that I'd be going "home in Peru." I was then told my papers were being processed for *libertad,* which is their term for freedom, but it was mid-March, and I was still there. As usual, they conveniently misspelled my name and made other random mistakes, which kept me there longer. Some prisoners wind up staying over a year longer for this type of idiot nonsense they pull, and without a lawyer to fight their battles, they sit and wait for the corrupt prisons to get around to fixing it. I was hoping to be out and in the apartment for my mother's visit for my birthday, but it didn't look like that was going to happen.

My birthday fell on a Saturday, which was men's visitor day in Santa Monica, and my mom and sister couldn't come and visit until Sunday, which was the women's visitor day. Lena, being the sweetheart she was, threw me a party on my birthday. She invited several friends to a table and brought food, soda, a cake, etc. She also made me an excellent pocketbook by hand. It was such a nice gesture, and I was beyond appreciative. Even the little angel Inga got to share some cake with us. Inga turned one year old three weeks prior, and I got to share her birthday with her and her family. The little baby, my so-called Peruvian granddaughter, was now a year old. She was so precious. The next day, the day after my birthday, my sister and mother came to visit. This was the first time I'd seen my mom since this nightmare started. She was walking with a cane since she had broken her hip only four months prior. Seeing them was fantastic, and I know it broke my mom's heart to see me there, but she stayed strong and made me laugh. All was good, as always, until the good-byes came. Saying goodbye was always hard, but I had no choice. I was still waiting to be released to house arrest.

My mom and sister left for the USA. About three days later, I got told "Libertad." I was so happy; I was finally leaving! I packed up my stuff and was told that the police would drive me to the apartment. When someone got told "Libertad!" everyone would gather around them and cheer for them. As I was leaving with my bags, Inga and Lena came to see me off. Inga had no idea what was happening, just that everyone was yelling and screaming around me. She must have thought something terrible was happening to me, and she was crying so hard and hugging me. It broke my heart. I was sobbing with this angel who wanted to protect me. She was such a doll, but I had to go. Lena had to take her from me. She was still so upset that night, not knowing what happened to me, that Lena had to take her to the doctor to get a tranquilizer to calm her down so she could sleep.

I was told I was leaving but got sent to prevention with no reason or explanation. What the hell? What was going on? I didn't have my Tupperware for food, medicine to sleep, or anything. There were women in prevention already, some bad people who were being punished, and some new people in transition. I had no idea why I was there and when I'd leave. Outside the gate, families were returning babies (yes, families were allowed to take the babies for days or weeks), and lawyers were coming to see their clients. I caught someone's attention and asked them to give Viola a note with my husband's number and a message asking what was happening. I gave her a calling card to call him, which she did. She was able to come back to me and tell me what he said. Having been there for fourteen years, she knew the INPEs well and could get the favor to come and talk to me.

My husband said Sal was working hard. As typical with Peru INPEs, they customarily misspell things—a name, a date of birth—to keep you there longer. Well, that was what happened to me. Sadly, I was in prevention, not in the pabellon. I had limited supplies since I had given everything away to people who needed it, such as clothes, food, shoes, a towel, and everything I had accumulated throughout my thirteen months there. I had expected to go to a furnished apartment that my sister and husband had stocked up for me *with* food just a few days before they came for my birthday. I did not bring anything with me because I wouldn't need it if I went straight to the apartment.

Sadly, this went on for three days: no food, no medicine, nothing. The newcomers were given a broom at 6 a.m. and woken up to go to a section to clean. The INPEs were giving me a broom. I was not new. I was furious and refused to sweep. They motioned for me to sweep the room. *Fine*—but I was not cleaning the whole prison! I had no towel to shower with, but luckily it was still warm out. It was early April, Peru's fall, so it was warm enough for me to shower and air dry before everyone came back from sweeping outside. I'm used to it back home; when it is hot, you don't usually feel it to the extent we did in Peru. Why? Because there is air conditioning everywhere. I'm sure it is different for those working outside or doing manual labor, but working on a computer and being inside all day meant being in the cold air conditioning all summer. We had air conditioning in offices, homes, cars, stores, restaurants, etc. The only real time you feel the heat is when walking to or from your car.

In Peru, the summer was hot as hell. Of course, it was extremely hot with no air conditioning in prison. Even the hotels just had fans, which blew around hot air. All summer long, I was dying. It was sizzling hot, and I was working with the babies, so I was up and down constantly. Even in the pabellon at night, it was hot all the time. I was always taking ice-cold showers, which was our everyday anyway, but in the summer, I was taking several showers a day, not drying off, and leaving my hair soaking wet to drench my back to cool me off. Lena was always yelling, "Patricia, no!" But I was so hot I didn't care. I've always been a sweater, and I needed to cool off.

I later understood why Lena and everyone else was telling me no. I lost my voice because of the cold and wet back. When my husband, mom, and sister had come to visit me, I had a limited voice, but once I was in prevention, I had to shower and air-dry, which only made it worse.

I was still waiting to hear what was happening. I asked the INPE if I could go out of prevention to use the phone and got told, "No!" I asked if I could go to the stand where we could buy necessities. I figured I could buy water and some vegetables for a salad but was again told, "No!" I was furious. Why was I being treated like an animal? Everyone else was allowed to use the phone and buy what they needed, but I wasn't. Since they never understood anything I said due to the language barrier, I mumbled a few choice words at the INPE and stormed back into the room. First, I was told, "Libertad!" yet I was being treated like I murdered their president.

Viola came back to see me the next day and said she was still in contact with my husband, but all he could say was to hang tight. Sal Monty was doing everything he could to correct this and get me out. When Viola came on the second day, the INPE told her that I called her a bitch. I thought that was funny. They always claimed not to understand any English for one year, but *that* she understood. Ha ha. I told Viola it was nothing personal toward her, but she wouldn't let me get food, make a call, or anything else, which was truly messed up. Viola apologized for me because I wasn't apologizing. It was dead wrong how she was treating me.

She brought me some toilet paper and a salad, which was nice. She said she'd continue calling my husband. I had to give her more money to call since the calling card ran out, and I did not have any way of getting a new one. Lena had found out I was still there and sent a message asking if I needed anything or wanted a cucumber. Since I was a kid, I have always loved fruit and would eat cucumbers, skin and all, just as is, with no cutting or peeling. I would bite right into them while holding them like a lollipop. They all thought I was strange and looked at me like I was nuts, but it was what I'd always done. I just asked Lena through a messenger if I could get a phone card and then had Viola convince the INPE to let me use the phone to call my husband to tell him I was there. Sal Monty had already told him, but he was happy to hear my voice.

That afternoon, I was again told, "Libertad!" This time, I had to go to the doctor to sign off on me again. This was their way of saying, "If you are sick or hurt when you get to your destination, it had nothing to do with the prison." The doctor's area was in the prison (whereas I was in prevention at that point), so I got to see everyone again, even Inga. I was happy to see her again. Sadly, everyone was yelling and screaming for joy for me, but she again thought I was being attacked—poor little angel. I got to say one more farewell to Lena.

I didn't have many things with me. Since we didn't have much room in prison, when the weather got warm, I gave Rebecca all my winter stuff and blankets to hold for me. She had all of that in the apartment waiting for me, too. As I said, I didn't have much in Santa Monica originally, but my older sister had sent me some winter clothes when I needed them, and another girl who was given her freedom about two months after my arrival in Santa Monica had given me her blanket. Even when my sister was trying to send me winter clothes, everything shipped had to go through customs, which they'd steal every time. Corruption was rampant in Peru from every angle.

I was put in a police car with my bag and driven to this apartment. It was obviously my first time seeing it. It was a two-bedroom apartment, but I only needed one. The second bedroom would come into play when my family returned to visit a few months later. Actually, my husband came to visit me two months after I got to the apartment, and my older sister came about two months after that for a week. In total, my son, younger sister, older sister, and my mom had come twice, while my husband had come thrice. My mom brought two or three big suitcases of food from the USA each time she came. Seeing everyone in a home environment and not in prison was such a joy. We could watch TV, talk, and more. They could go out and go to stores, but unfortunately, I was not allowed to leave the apartment.

CHAPTER 10

The police were to check on me four times a day at random. During their visits, I would have to sign a book and fingerprint myself. Although they came only once a day, they'd call the house phone randomly to ensure I was there. Outside the complex were video cameras that would show anyone who came or went, so they'd have proof *if* I tried to go anywhere. Since I was told that I was the first American accused of drug trafficking to ever get released to house arrest, I was not about to do anything to jeopardize that. I did not want any more trouble, but I was getting even more depressed. In Santa Monica, I had a job and was around other people. In the apartment, I sat all day and night alone.

I learned that out of all the television channels, only two or three had any shows I would watch, and they showed repeats constantly. I watched *Grey's Anatomy*, and it would come on Monday nights at 7–8, 8–9, 9–10 and 10–11. I watched it one night during the seven o'clock hour while doing a puzzle. My sister had left some puzzles and activities for me at the apartment. When *Grey's Anatomy* came on again, I could have sworn that it was the same episode, but I thought maybe I wasn't paying that much attention since I was also doing the puzzle. Well, from 9–10 and 10–11, the same *Grey's Anatomy* episode played again and again. I couldn't believe what I saw—the same episode played four times in a row! This was typical for the English channels, unfortunately. My sister had loaded Netflix on the laptop she left for me, but I'm not a massive fan of watching TV on the computer. Plus, you needed the internet for that to work. I quickly realized how sucky the internet, phone, and cable were there. It seemed to be down and out of service more often than not. I tried to upload a three-minute video once. Thirteen hours went by, and it still had not been uploaded. Rebecca was constantly calling

"Movistar" for me, which is the carrier for service, but there wasn't much they could do. It was just the service, sadly.

So, what did I do all day long? I did puzzles, browsed the internet when it worked, read books, and did homework for the Bible study course I took with the two volunteer Bible study women who visited us in Santa Monica. Since the women continued to see me after their weekly visit to Santa Monica, that was good, but outside of that, there wasn't much else for me to do there. I spoke very little Spanish, and no one around me spoke English. I did not know anyone besides the Bible study women, Marge and Annie. I used WhatsApp to contact the woman from Emaus to let her know where I was. She was happy to know I was out of prison and in an apartment. After their visit to Santa Monica, she came with the whole Emaus team one evening to say hi. Other than that, there was nothing else to do. I called my family often, but they all had routines and work to do, so I did not want to bother them.

When I first got to the apartment, I called my kids to see how they were and how my Punkin Munkin was. My daughter told me that she had put together a video of pictures for me. She then sent me the video and told me to call her after watching it. I got to see her, her boyfriend, the kids, and my Punkin Munkin, and then I thought it rewound. She was pregnant, in the hospital, and with a newborn. I followed it until I saw the male genitals on the newborn. What was I looking at? Then I realized that the pregnancy pictures were in the new apartment. My daughter had a second baby in January, three months prior. What? I called her back right away, and she was crying. She thought I'd be mad. Of course not. Thanks to this sucky situation, I was mad that I was not there for her. She never needed to be sad. I was happy for her but sad I had missed everything. She had a Cesarean birth, and I felt I should have been there for her to offer support— however I could. But instead, I was stuck in Peru fighting a ridiculous battle. In the USA, they would have done a proper investigation. Even if it took a while, I'd at least be home. Instead, I was thousands of miles away and missing everything. She had a beautiful, big baby boy. He was three months old, and my Punkin Munkin was one year and eight months old; I was missing everything.

My husband was a massive help to my daughter and her new family. It was beneficial to all of them, really. It helped him stay occupied but also filled the void a little for everyone. He was there to help them in my absence, and it also helped him to feel needed. My daughter was even at our house one evening for a BBQ. I tried to video chat with them to see everyone, but I hung up and blamed it on bad connections. While I was so happy to see everyone there having fun, as they should have, it also broke my heart to see everyone without me. My Punkin Munkin was running around. She was a tiny baby the last time I physically saw her, and the new big boy punkin was smiling at everyone. *How could this happen to me?* It was so heartbreaking. My one neighbor at the apartment was pregnant. I never spoke to anyone, but I saw her coming and going from my window and could see she was due any day. As happy as I was for her, I knew she'd be happier if she had her family around her. I got sad thinking about it because now my daughter wouldn't have that, thanks to me and the sucky situation I was put in.

When I first was in the apartment, the toilet was broken. I had to call Sal Monty about it. He had to call a repairman to fix it. They spent about one and a half hours fixing it, then charged me, of course. In the process of them fixing the toilet, they somehow broke the shower rod. After they left, water was leaking from the bathroom, so I had to ask Sal to call them back. They returned and had to repair the leak, which they claimed was coincidental and a new job and charged me again to fix that. I also mentioned the shower rod since it was not mine to break. They apparently had to buy a new one the next day and return to repair that. That was another fee that *I* had to pay despite *my* not breaking it. But at least it was fixed.

The rent in the apartment included the monthly maintenance fee, phone, internet, and cable. The monthly maintenance was only S/75–S/100 a month, and the phone, internet, and cable fees were not that much. So, as with all other bills in Peru, they were making out very well at my expense. It was a nice apartment, but man, was it noisy. I'm told it was typical and nothing to do with the complex.

The neighbors seemed to party constantly; loud music blasted all night, followed by loud laughter and talking. I slept with earplugs, yet I stayed awake for hours hearing everything. Plus, I always heard firecrackers going off. For a third-world country, they surely always found a reason to celebrate and be happy. I was baffled.

Tania, the woman who owned the hotel my family had stayed at during one of their visits before the apartment came into play, had told my husband to call her if I needed anything. I soon realized that I would need groceries since I had no way to go and get them on my own. Tania asked me for a list of things and was kind enough to bring them to me one evening with her boyfriend. I was very grateful. She told me about two other stores where I could order groceries online if ever needed. One was Totus, and the other was called Wong. That made my life a little easier since I always hated pestering people.

Totus was difficult to order from since it did not accept my credit card online, but Wong was easier and I was finally able to order online. The webpage was translated into English (when I had service), so it stated they would deliver the next day. All was great except when they called the apartment to tell me about something, such as being out of stock on something or needing to adjust the order somehow. If I used the online chat on their website, I had to open two browser windows, one for their website and the other for Google Translate. It was always interesting, but it worked; that's all that mattered. I could then order my groceries weekly without having to nag anyone. I also found Inkafarma would deliver if I needed anything. I'd order VicksZzzz to sleep and Pepto Bismol for any stomach issues. I also had to order their version of peroxide and pesticide pills. I'd always have to use the internet to figure out Peru's version of what I needed.

One morning, I was awoken to my bed shaking as if someone was at each corner of the bed jumping up and down. I didn't know what was going on. I sprang up, looked at my watch, which read 4:24 a.m., and ran to the window to see what was happening. From what I could see, everyone was going about their business. I tried to lay back down, but my heart was beating a mile a minute. Apparently, at that hour, many people were awake and getting ready for school and work, but no one seemed concerned about the crazy shaking. I later learned that what I felt was just one of Peru's many earthquakes.

Peru is located on a seismic plate and apparently has many earthquakes. I remember in Santa Monica, we would routinely have earthquake drills. Various circles were drawn on the ground in multiple locations, and whenever we heard the drills, we had to drop everything and run to the circle's center. I assume they felt the circles' locations would prevent us from being crushed if the earthquakes caused the pabellons to collapse. I'd felt random shakes in Santa Monica, but never to the extent I felt that morning. Perhaps it was my location or the magnitude; I don't know. I'm used to earthquakes, as I saw in the original *Superman* the ground opening and swallowing whatever was in its path, but these earthquakes were trembling. They still scared me. We didn't usually have them in New York. Hurricanes, yes, but not tornadoes or earthquakes. Just another thing for me to adjust to, I guess. I'd later learned from Annie the tips for handling earthquakes to ensure one's safety. They were all good to know for future reference.

I also learned that Peru is a super humid country. The humidity index customarily ran 90 to 98 percent. Imagine my surprise when my toothbrush, razor blade, pocketbook, luggage, and clothing were all moldy! I tossed the toothbrush and razor into the garbage and washed everything else, but I needed to buy a dehumidifier. Sal and Rebecca had to assist me. That was another expense—S/990 for a dehumidifier—but it could also dry clothes. The instruction manual was in Spanish, so I had to take pictures of it and email it to Sal. Between him and his wife, they could tell me how to use it. I couldn't believe that with a two-liter tank, I had to get up a few short hours later to empty the tank. I was asleep and heard a noise. It was the dehumidifier making a sound saying that the tank was full. This went on every two or three hours. I only turned the dehumidifier on during the night while I slept. It heated the room with all the moisture being taken out of the air, which was a bonus. Plus, the humming of the machine drowned out much of the noise from outside daily.

Water was always an issue in Peru. Countless times in Santa Monica, we, for whatever reason, had no water. I remember one time I and three others were in the shower, soaped up, only to have the water stop. Everyone had to use buckets of water on their hands to get the soap and shampoo rinsed off. It seemed the people knew the system already and had water buckets on standby. As the newcomer, I had no idea, nor any bucket, so luckily, people lent me some to rinse off.

One day, we were told that the apartment would be without water for a few days. The few days turned into almost two weeks (the first time), and it was during a visit from my mom and sister. The maintenance downstairs had water, so we'd have to wash dishes and fill up a bucket of water to flush the toilet. I again had no bucket, but the maintenance man lent me a bucket to fill. Imagine my surprise when I had a bucket of water for the toilet, and my sister passed by and said, "Oh, look at the tadpoles or whatever they are." What? Tadpoles? Sure enough, I bent down and saw a few little things swimming around in the water. This was the water we used to brush our teeth, shower, make tea/coffee, wash our fruits/vegetables, and more. Gross!

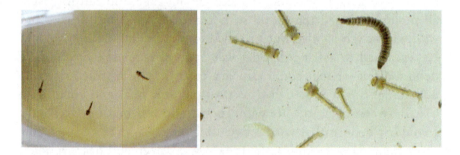

This all explained why they were giving us pesticide pills every six months in prison and why most newcomers initially got sick from the food. I knew from my vacation in Cancun never to drink tap water due to Montezuma's revenge. I was warned about that. This was probably why I got so sick during the Emaus retreat in Santa Monica. However, over time, I think my stomach got used to it.

When my family and husband visited, they often got diarrhea and nausea, so I knew to have Pepto Bismol (Peru's version) on hand. It wasn't from drinking the water, but even from brushing your teeth with it. They'd turn the water in the apartment on for about an hour each evening when everyone in the complex had to quickly shower, wash up, or do whatever they needed. The hot water did not last long, so I told my mom and sister to jump in the shower first since I was used to cold showers by then and could go last.

Throughout my time in the apartment, the water was "out" on several occasions. The people in charge would claim that every tenant needed to pay S/100 to repair something with the system for everyone's water to get back to normal.

I told Sal this, who conveyed it to the apartment's owner. Sal then told me, "They say this every year. Nothing is broken, and they don't fix anything. It's just another play for money." Apparently, this happened several times. It just sucked that it had to happen on a visit from my family the one time, but we survived.

One day, my mom was in the shower while my sister and I were watching TV when we heard a rattling sound.

My sister said, "What the heck is that?"

It went on for about thirty seconds before I told her, "It's just an earthquake."

"What?" she exclaimed.

Apparently I had gotten used to them, but her reaction was the same as the one I had initially. The rattling noise was from the kitchen door.

"Welcome to my life," I told her.

When my mom, sister, or anyone came to visit, they always brought lots of microwaveable food from the US and other things I loved, such as turkey bacon, my Juice Plus shakes, and candy. One of my sisters also made me food she knew I loved. She's a great cook. That was a gene I never got. When family came to visit, they would go to the stores each day and get good food to eat, such as Chinese food, burritos, pizza, vegetarian burgers, etc.

When my mom visited, it became a daily routine where she would take pictures of the menus on her phone, bring them to the apartment, and try to translate them using Google Translate. It was comical. Google Translate was never completely accurate, but it was close enough.

What was strange was that once, my mom had a Chinese menu from back home in her pocketbook. She knew what she wanted and brought the menu to the Chinese restaurant in Peru, yet they didn't understand it. She then had to point to a photo and hope it was what she wanted. Nine times out of ten, it was not. I'd never leave the apartment to go with them. I was not about to get into any more trouble. I stayed inside every day. Besides, I would have random visits by the police and needed to be always there, which I was.

My mom cooked me breakfast every day she was there. It was so much food. She had brought me several packs of turkey bacon from the US, so she'd make me eggs, turkey bacon, toast, or a buttered roll and tea every morning. Then about three hours later, she would go out and come back with several lunches for us to choose from.

Then, for dinner, she'd do the same. Afterward, she went to a place that was apparently across from me and got me several different pastries to choose from. It was so much food. I think she was trying to fatten me up. I did cook dinner, like, once a week. She knew I was a lousy cook, but I think she was trying to save food in the apartment for me for after she left, so she kept bringing us food.

Mom would also go to a nearby casino every day, waiting for the restaurants to open. We never could figure out their hours; they changed daily. Sadly, nothing in Peru made any sense to me.

Surprisingly, my mom was quite lucky at the casino. It made me nervous because, like me, there was no denying she was not Peruvian. We stood out like sore thumbs. If she won at the casino, I was terrified that she would get robbed coming back to the apartment. I didn't even know where she was since I'd never been outside the apartment except in the police car from Santa Monica.

The cop still came daily, and I had to sign in a book four times per day as well as get fingerprinted, which seemed to be such a huge thing in Peru. Since the day of my arrest, throughout Santa Monica and then in the apartment, I must've been fingerprinted thousands of times. My finger was always inked with blue or black. I seriously doubted they even had the technology to verify fingerprints if ever needed, but it seemed to be the norm there.

When my mom and sister came, Marge and Annie from Bible study lent me a queen-size blow-up mattress and blankets. It came in handy since it was a two-bedroom apartment, but there were now three of us. Marge and Annie had been so tremendously helpful. They were volunteers, one from Canada and the other from London. There were other women, too, but Marge and Annie had been the regulars (for me, anyway). Even in Santa Monica, they came weekly. We did Bible courses, and they would bring us necessities if we needed them, such as soap, food, tea, shampoo, deodorant, etc.

Even in the apartment, they visited me every week, bringing me a burrito whenever they came. It became our routine, which I graciously appreciated and looked forward to. We did various studies, but the toughest one was called "Boundaries with People and Situations." It was meant to keep us from being overwhelmed, taken advantage of, and for feeling helpless. Since I've always been someone who has trouble saying no to people, this was definitely going to be a challenge for me, but it was a good study, nonetheless.

My mom and sister left after a three-week visit. Then, my husband returned for a week, my other sister came for a week, and my mother and son came for a visit. Visits were one of the good things about the apartment, plus a warm shower. But other than that, to me, it was solitary confinement. I sat alone every single day. It was depressing beyond words.

I remember fighting with my husband on many occasions. We would talk on the phone, and I would be left feeling depressed. He would snap at me, telling me that I needed to start being more appreciative since I was in an apartment and not in prison anymore. Of course, that was easy for someone to say to me when they were not in my shoes.

In Santa Monica, I had a job and was around other people. This was truly solitary confinement. Visits were great, but I didn't get them all the time. While yes, my husband was suffering in his way, he still left the house every day to go to work. He had neighbors and friends who checked on him all the time. He would go to his friend's or cousin's house, go out on the boat, go out for food, spend time with the kids, the babies, and his family, and play with our dogs. I could do none of this while being far away and stuck there. It was hard for him to understand just how different our suffering was. I went from living in a house with everything I would ever need—a loving home, family, and friends—to being in prison in a country where I didn't speak the language and surrounded by people I could not communicate with. It was roach- and rat-infested, overcrowded, 98 percent humidity every day, dirty, smelly, surrounded by thieves without a clue what was going on or when this nightmare would end. That was my life in Santa Monica when, sadly, my brain was still trying to function to the best of its ability. Overwhelmed is an understatement.

It was a lot—taking ice-cold showers every day, eating the slop they fed us, and being screamed at by INPEs when I had no clue what they were even saying. What little escape I had from it was sitting on upside-down spackle buckets and watching Spanish TV. And then, at the end of the day, I had to go to bed, either on the floor or in an overcrowded room on a metal bunk bed that was so worn down that you had to stuff cardboard under the so-called foam mattress to give it any sturdiness at all—something that did not help the cockroach situation. That was my life in prison, and it couldn't have been any more different from my life back home.

After six months of being in the apartment with no visit from the US Embassy, I called them and asked them to visit me. Six months! When you are arrested, your passport gets confiscated and given to your embassy. When I realized that there was still a scammer using my passport photo in the real world, pretending to be me, and scamming other people—I know this because people emailed me on my business email asking if that really was me—I mentioned this to the American Embassy. I asked them to bring my passport with them so I could deal with that. They quickly told me no; they would not return my passport but would come for a visit. I told my husband about the Embassy's typical lack of assistance. He immediately ran to our local congressman and told him about it.

Congressman Peter King then called the Embassy in Peru and demanded they return my passport to me immediately. The next day, I had both of my passports in hand. It was no secret back home that I was not a criminal. If I were, I would have immediately fled once I had my passport. However, I was not. I had no reason to flee. I was completely innocent and strongly believed that they would see this and let me go. Unfortunately, I did not know anything about Peru—be it their corruption, lack of justice, unfairness, or anything.

Imagine my surprise when Sal Monty called my husband one day and said, "You won't believe this, but I'm watching Patty's laptop being sold on TV right now!"

Apparently, the one judge who sentenced me was seen on video selling many people's belongings on the street. My laptop stood out quite obviously because of the color and name on it, but all my other belongings were sold. I was beyond myself with dismay. My wedding rings and everything were gone. I'm told two other judges were also in prison due to other corrupt acts they were caught in. The one woman judge—who was a first-time judge—found herself in jail for corruption only a few months later after just getting her first job as a judge.

Apparently, it did not take long to corrupt people in Peru. My neighbor had her baby. I never heard a commotion or anything; I just happened to see her out the window with a baby and no pregnant belly anymore. I was happy for her. Seeing the newborn made me miss my granddaughter again. I was there for her birth and every milestone. She was getting big, and I was missing it all. Months passed with absolutely no movement on my case. This seemed strange, but after a whole year, nothing was happening. It seemed to just continue.

Sal believed this was because the prosecutor had no one willing to challenge Dr. Ladd. I was growing weaker in emotion and strength. I had already spent one Christmas and Thanksgiving in the apartment—after spending one of each in Santa Monica—away from my friends and family.

By this time, Sal had a new client, another US citizen, who fell for a scam and was arrested. He was from New Jersey. He was a 75-year-old man who also came here for a program and was asked to bring a bottle of champagne as a souvenir to the so-called representative. The champagne was liquid cocaine, unbeknownst to him.

The man was arrested and sentenced to a five-year-and-eight-month sentence due to his age. His wife came to visit him and see what she could do to assist. Since it was Thanksgiving and both of us would be away from home (obviously), Sal invited her to the apartment and brought turkey, sandwiches, salads, champagne, cake, etc. He helped us have as good of a Thanksgiving as we possibly could under the circumstances. While it still sucked being in this mess, it was a very nice gesture on his part. He tried to make it pleasant for her and me, which was more than Peru had done for either of us. Sal told us it would be our final Thanksgiving there.

After Thanksgiving, with still zero movement on my case, Sal arranged a media interview with Beta-A TV. A media team came to the apartment with video cameras and interviewed me. I was as open and honest as possible and answered all their questions. The goal was to tell my story and hope that the judge or anyone in power saw that I was speaking out about my innocence and how I was still stuck there, missing my family, work, and life.

As what was proven to be typical in Peru, media interviews accomplished nothing. Either no one in authority saw them or they didn't care, so it did nothing for me.

However, that interview was how Ruth* learned about me. She lived in the complex across from me and always wondered, "Who is in that apartment? We see the blinds open, but no one ever leaves."

Then, when she saw the interview and heard my story, her heart broke for me. I was not a criminal. It didn't take much to see and know that I was innocent. Even simply Googling my name, you would see that I was a business owner and had never been in trouble with the law. But Peru didn't care; they just saw me as money.

The ironic part about the Beta-A news story was that it included my airport video arrest and the photo I took of the Nigerian who set me up in Peru. It also included the photos of the IMF forms and all the proof I had.

Coincidentally, a few days after the interview aired, I got a random email from someone who told me to just relax and that all would be okay, how he understood what it was like being away from family. I asked who it was, and he replied, "I am a Peruvian, but not living in Peru now."

He wrote to me saying he had taken a job out of Peru and that he would also be away his family. I asked how he knew of me and asked what triggered him to contact me.

He replied, "I saw you on the news."

I said, "I thought you were not in Peru now. It's a Peruvian news station."

He said, "Yes, but I always check the news of my country online."

I didn't believe that and nowhere on the news did it give my email address. It wouldn't take a rocket scientist to Google *my* name, find my company, and write my company's general email, but this was my work email. My guess was this was MB, who, for all I knew, was probably the Nigerian man in Peru. He likely saw his photo on the Peru news and emailed me to try and lure me into something to throw me back into prison. The only thing that made sense to me was that it was him since we had always communicated through email and Skype. These were all things that made me wonder.

I stopped replying immediately, and he wrote two more times, asking why I stopped replying, but I just ignored it, and he did not write again. He may have thought my emails were being traced or monitored or something. That would have been the case in the US, but in Peru, it was doubtful.

It's funny, but Eric also emailed me randomly, asking, "Hi, are you out of jail?" What were the odds of that? Yet another reason why this all pointed to him being a part of all these scams. I ignored his email, too.

On Thanksgiving, as I talked to the woman Sal brought over, we both understood just how evil these scammers were. They had no heart, no care or concern for who they scammed. Her husband also had fallen for many scams prior to this one. We apparently had that in common, and we were probably on the same scam target list. She told me that he was also a severe diabetic and that the corrupt police were constantly stealing his insulin in prison. Sadly, she could not do anything about it, but she fully understood all I'd been going through. Due to his insulin being stolen, he was losing his eyesight and memory. He had been rushed to the hospital on several occasions because of it. No one in authority cared at all.

I was told many foreigners died in prison, yet their attitude just seemed to be, "Oh well, then you should not have come here to commit a crime." It was nuts.

This unfortunate woman was trying to petition for the humanitarian clause for her husband. But with all the recent corruption on the news with the Justice Department and everyone being arrested like flies, no one wanted to do anything, especially anything that would let foreigners go.

Still, she tried to remain hopeful that the humanitarian clause would work for him, but unfortunately, I had been under arrest longer than her husband. I had seen so many changes and a lack of justice and support for Americans that I was not as optimistic, but I hoped she was right for her husband's sake.

Unfortunately, around Christmas, I was browsing the internet and was on Facebook checking out my daughter's pictures of the grandbabies. I also browsed LinkedIn to send my regular holiday greetings to all my connections. I somehow saw a post about someone stuck in a foreign country and seeking funding to be released. I didn't know this person, but I did donate $10 to help them. Later, I got a reply from someone named Martin Rood, thanking me for my donation and asking about my story.

I explained my story, and he was surprised that, despite everything, I was still willing to help someone else. I mentioned how that has always been my nature. I'd give the shirt off my back if I thought it would help someone. I've always felt that if I could help in any way, I would. Martin then proceeded to tell me how he is the same, and that was how he came to start the fundraiser for the woman and her children. He didn't know her personally, but he came to know her story and wanted to help her. Now, he wanted to help me, too.

I was surprised yet grateful to have found a random caring stranger. He was based in the US and had three young children. We talked, and I educated him on my whole story and even directed him to the Beta-A news story. He thought reaching out to the politicians, celebrities, news stations, and authorities that handle brain injuries would be the way to go. I also connected him with my husband, sisters, and mom since I knew my brain injury caused me to fall for so many scams, and I did not want to fall for more.

Everyone in my family spoke to him. While they were skeptical initially, since it was unusual to find a genuinely nice person, they did their research and found nothing bad about him. I had spent my days and nights researching so many emails for him, and he worked with my husband to put together letters to send out. Martin then followed up with phone calls. We sent out thousands of emails, and he made hundreds of phone calls. Yet, sadly, no one seemed to care. They either all ignored us or simply blew us off. My good friend Lou Reed* helped my husband and me. Lou put my husband in touch with a reporter who did podcasts and agreed to do a podcast with my husband telling our story.

Before doing so, he first wanted to do his due diligence on both me and my husband. He confirmed that we both came up clean. He stated that he even tried to reach out to the man in the DEA in Peru, who believed I was innocent, and told my husband that he would go to bat for me, which of course, he never did. When we called him, the DEA just hung up on him. Welcome to my life.

We had circulated the link to the podcast to the database I had created for Martin, figuring it might be beneficial for people to hear my husband's story about this, plus links to the Beta-A interview, which was me telling the story. But again, it was complete silence. No one replied. It made no sense.

A few days before Christmas, the complex had a celebration where they set up a table downstairs and gave out and accepted chocolate. I didn't understand this tradition, but apparently, someone mentioned me, and the man at the front gate came up and brought me panettone bread and hot chocolate. I was so grateful, yet I did not have anything to give back. But he wasn't looking for anything in return.

At that point, I spent my second Christmas arrested In Peru. In Santa Monica, on Christmas Eve, we got to spend it eating our dinner with friends (fellow inmates), and I spent mine with Lena and Inga. It's not like I was home with family, but at least I was not alone.

I spent my second Christmas alone in the apartment, which I considered solitary confinement. My family would have liked to have been with me, but I was not expecting anyone to travel over Christmas. Plus, they all had other family members to tend to, which I fully understood. I went to sleep early on Christmas Eve because it was a sad day for me. I spoke to my family on the phone, but it still broke my heart not to be there with everyone.

Then, surprisingly, I got a knock at the door. I opened it to find two women who spoke no English, but thanks to Google Translate, I learned that they were neighbors from across the way and had come to bring me Christmas gifts. I was so surprised, yet I obviously had nothing for them, nor could I run to the store and get them something. They didn't stay long but gave me a Peruvian plaque and some honey and tea. I later found out that they had seen the Beta-A

TV and recognized the apartment building. They knew that it was me, the foreigner who never left the apartment and who no one knew anything about. They felt sad for me and wanted to reach out somehow, knowing that I was all alone, and they used Christmas as a perfect segue.

Martin Rood was also working on Christmas, emailing the names of people to research their emails and numbers for him to follow up with. I couldn't believe that he was still focused on helping me. I kept telling him to go and enjoy Christmas with his girls. I truly appreciated his dedication, especially since I was a total stranger, but he had a good heart and wanted to see me home with my family, not stuck in Peru for such nonsense. All my friends felt the same. We had created a website, www.helppettybeesfreedom. On the site, we included all the information and proof: the DEA person's audio stating that even he believed my innocence, the Nigerian photo, a timeline of all of the events that led me to Peru, the podcast interview, the Beta-A interview, the petition, the airport video, and Dr. Ladd's report. We had everything and anything up there, thinking that maybe it would help.

Rather than writing out a long-winded email or adding dozens of attachments, maybe writing a few paragraphs and providing a link to the website with all the information was better. It was worth a shot. All my friends circulated it to anyone we could think of. I continued to send it to President Trump, Obama, Dr. Phil., Dr. Oz, Oprah Winfrey, the Kardashians, and Ellen DeGeneres. I even tried writing to Andrew Yang, who was running against Trump for the presidential election at that time. I thought perhaps if he knew our current president was ignoring a victimized American, if he helped somehow, it would be good publicity for his campaign. The result? Unfortunately, all he did was ignore my letter and only added me to his campaign email list. I was shocked. I even tried writing to Trump on Twitter, which he apparently was an avid user of, but no reply. It truly was a disgrace the lack of support an American got when in trouble abroad. Seems unless you are a celebrity or someone who could help "their" visibility by helping you – they just don't care.

My friend Lou Reed, who helped get the podcast interview, was still trying to find anyone who might listen to our story, but no one seemed to care. I have many friends in the media, yet even *they* were not allowed to cover this story. I was told that the moment drugs were mentioned, no one would cover it. I'm not sure if that was it or what. It just showed the lack of assistance the US provided to one of its own.

As a matter of fact, everyone I knew was circulating this story across Facebook, and ironically, Facebook kept pulling it down and blocking it. I found that very strange. I had seen so much crap on Facebook—porn, derogatory messages, bullying, etc. *That* was allowed, but my story wasn't. I could only shake my head in disbelief.

Before it was pulled, I circulated the story on social media, and one of my daughter's old classmates passed it along to a colleague of hers who lived in my neighborhood back home but was from Peru. She even tried helping and reaching out to anyone she could find but got no results. She, like everyone I knew, felt helpless. A skydiving friend even reached out to a fellow UK skydiver who was living in Peru. He came to visit me at the apartment one day and heard my story. He confided what I'd already known, sadly, which was that there was not much anyone could do for me. He was a good source of emotional support. He said he'd look around to see if he could find anyone of assistance, but it seemed to be like finding a needle in a haystack in Peru.

On one occasion, my neighbor, Ruth, came by with our other neighbor. They brought me crackers and tea. She seemed so sweet and caring. The language barrier was an issue, but we did our best with Google Translate.

My bathroom window in the apartment was high and small, but it seemed to face west and was over water. I had always been such an avid sunrise and sunset lover. As a matter of fact, doing a sunrise skydive had to be one of the most amazing highlights of my skydiving career. I videoed the entire jump, but even the GoPro did not do it justice. It was the most glorious view I'd ever seen.

As bad as my Peru experience had been, the one thing I will give Peru credit for is its gorgeous sunsets. I could not see much, but if I stood on the ledge in the bathroom at sunset, I'd see the sunset behind the other buildings, and it was so beautiful as it lit up the sky.

That became my evening routine, taking pictures of the sunset. A few times, I tried to time-lapse it because it was so gorgeous and colorful that my husband used to think I was photoshopping the color. But I wasn't. It was just gorgeous. So, every single night from the window, I took photos of the sunset in the distance. I also shared the photo with Ruth, and she was blown away by the colors. She had eye problems with her cornea and needed surgery, so staring at the sun or sunset was not something she normally did, so she enjoyed me sharing the pictures with her. We became good friends, and she came over to visit often. She even cooked for me, shared Peruvian fruit, and showed me pictures of her family—all of which I enjoyed.

CHAPTER 11

In Peru, summer lasts January-March. With no air conditioning, it can get swelteringly hot. I had bought a big fan for the bedroom. My sister and husband had bought a fan when they came before my release to house arrest, so I brought another one from Wong online, and they delivered it. I knew it would come in handy for when my mom visited next.

Before buying the fan, I kept the windows open. Well, as extremely afraid of water bugs that I am, words can't describe the panic I experienced one day when I went to get something out of the closet, and a water bug came scooting out between my legs. Normally, I would have run out of the apartment for help, but I obviously could not do that. I was forced to face my fear, find and kill it, and then make sure there were no others. That truly was a test of my strength. I must've thrown every single thing I could find at it to try and kill it. Then, I had to pick it up and throw it away. My knees were weak in fear, but I did it. Phew!

Then, tearing everything apart to make sure there were no more was another daring task, but I did it and found no more. I know there were many roaches in Peru, and they most likely came through the open window, but it was so hot. Ruth had a screen in her window. We could buy window screens back home, but not here, apparently. Ruth had her screen made and had the builder come and visit and make screens for my windows. I was so relieved! I thanked her immensely since that helped a little. No air conditioning was surely something I was not a fan of, but it had been two years of this nightmare for me, and all I could do was roll with it.

My mom and sister came to visit me again. Since I was allowed to go downstairs and sit on one of the benches, I was not "leaving" the complex, and the videos could prove that, too. So, when they came to visit, we'd go after dinner and sit on the bench for an hour or two. My sister even had my mom buy me a selfie stick for my sunset pictures. That was a big joke because I always made fun of people taking selfies with selfie sticks, yet there I was, with my stick. I wasn't taking selfies, though! The apartments were on five floors, and I was on the third floor. We could not go to the roof, but I went with my sister to Ruth's side of the building, and we used a selfie stick to get a different view of the sunset. Wow, that made our experience even better. I was higher up and not looking from a tiny window, so it was even more beautiful. That had become my sunset routine. We sat on the downstairs bench and soaked in the sun and then walked up the stairs on Ruth's side and stopped to say hello to Ruth. We only stayed thirty minutes; I did not need any trouble.

When my mom and sister visited me, they would go for a walk during the day to a local cuisine store to get food. I'd just sit in the apartment and wait for them. In the morning, my mom would make me a king-size breakfast. Then, they would go to food stores that opened at strange hours. Some of them did not open until 2 p.m., so they would occupy themselves until that time. Then they would come back with lunch or sometimes dinner, too. I would sit and wait in the apartment. The difference for me was that without their visit, I was completely alone. It was painfully lonely. If I had someone there every day with whom I could talk and eat, that would have been different.

I usually woke up in the morning and did some exercise. It wasn't much, but back home, I was on the treadmill daily for forty-five minutes, plus I had a gym membership. In Santa Monica, I was doing nothing; I lost all my muscle tone completely and a lot of weight from not really eating much. My mom was determined to fatten me up. She brought so many cakes and pastries for me to eat on top of the king-sized meals she made. I put the weight back on while in the apartment. I enjoyed my visitors and was in a black hole all other days, never knowing what was going on or when this would end. It was beyond discouraging.

I had my selfie stick, a radio, and my sunsets. I was making the best of it however I could. When my family left to return home, it always broke my heart. I truly hated goodbyes; we all did. Leaving me alone again in a foreign country, being arrested for a crime I didn't even know I was committing , and not knowing when or how it would end was hard for all of us. Martin, Warren, and Angel had no success in trying to help. All my friends reached out to whoever they could find, with no results. It was bizarre. We all think in USA terms. These Nigerians knew exactly which country to stick me in, knowing damn well that Peru has no real justice system and is insanely corrupt. They knew that once you were arrested, you would not be returning home anytime soon.

Eventually, as I was nearing one year on house arrest, with zero progress on my case, my family and I were going broke by the day. Unlike in the USA, a lawyer would give you an itemized invoice for whenever they worked for you. In Peru, we were paying a monthly invoice, a flat fee, in American dollars every single month. Plus, since we were paying in a US bank, the invoice also included an 18 percent tax, as Peru charged that tax for the lawyer to withdraw the money. Ironically, the lawyer made *us* pay that fee, even though we were paying him in the bank that he told us to, and *he* was withdrawing it in Peru.

My family was in this for over USD$150K with no end in sight. With our constant complaining, Sal Monty eventually demanded the prosecutor move. I know Sal always said they were not moving because no one wanted to challenge Dr. Ladd. However, that proved to not be the case because they eventually sent a court-appointed psychiatrist to the apartment to evaluate me.

Unlike Dr. Ladd, who spent a full week for a few hours per day evaluating me almost two years prior and conducting the SIRS II test, I had this man two years later, where my brain was healing daily. He came with a translator for a whopping one hour. His exam was not even an exam. He spent thirty minutes asking me basic questions: my name, family, date of birth, occupation, etc., and then thirty minutes talking about my story. I'm not a licensed psychiatrist by any means, but this was the stupidest exam I had ever done. At one point, he took his cell phone out of his chest pocket, did something manually, and then put the phone back into his pocket with the camera staring at me. I am by no means "stupid."

I knew damn well that he was recording me. Back in the USA, you'd have to ask permission to record someone, but again, this was Peru. I had nothing to hide, so I did not care. As before, I answered as honestly as I'd done all along. I cannot say how good the translator was, as I am limited to what I understood, but all I know is that it was the stupidest exam, and I answered as honestly as I always did. The first time he was scheduled to come and examine me, the translator showed up, but the psychiatrist was a no-show. Everything throughout this whole ordeal dragged on and on and on, sadly. Even after the exam, he took forever to provide the court with his analysis. As ridiculous as it was, it was a one-paragraph analysis, but this seemed to be typical.

As we waited for the analysis, I had a deligencia court date. My case seemed to be in the supreme court with three judges. Obviously, I had to be escorted there by the police. As insane as it was, the cop charged me S/110 to drive me to court. They didn't pay them enough to spend *extra* money to go out of their way to the court, so *I* had to pay it. My mom and sister were there for the trial, and our local congressman demanded that the US Embassy show up for support.

I know that did not make them happy, but when Congress said, "Go," they went. All they reiterated to me was that they could not get involved with the law there. Even the Bible study women had asked me if I'd like them to come for support, and I agreed. So, my first trial date consisted of Sal and his team, my mom, my sister, my husband, the US Embassy, Marge, Annie, and me. Sal told me that the judges were impressed by my support, but I don't know how he came to that conclusion in that they seemed totally unfazed by me. In fact, even during the trial, one judge was on his cell phone, and the other was talking to the other judge. None of them were even paying attention to what we were saying or presenting. I've learned, sadly, that this was very typical in Peru.

Since the psychiatrist did not submit his report, Sal asked that the court be rescheduled since the report was important, as my whole defense rested on it. The court was adjourned for ten days. My mom,

PATRICIA BARONOWSKI-SCHNEIDER

sister, and husband obviously could not stay. In the US, a trial was judged by a jury—not here. Here it was three judges, and you needed the majority to win. Yet, none of them were even listening to anything that we said. Besides, I was a foreigner, a major thorn in their side, apparently. Plus, the habeas corpus Sal filed also did not make my name or his welcome.

After court was adjourned, we asked Marge if she could come to the next trial since my family would be gone. Annie would also be gone as she was going back to the UK for three months. We also asked Congress to request that the Embassy come again. Marge, of course, agreed to come, which was heartwarming. I had two police officers who alternated visiting me in the apartment, and the court date fell on the other cop's date. He said that *I* needed to make the arrangement to get us to and from the court. This sorry excuse for a justice system never stopped. How could I get an Uber to drive us when I had no cell signal outside the apartment?

Luckily, Marge came to the rescue when she said she had a driver and would have him take us all. I had to pay another S/110 for it, and poor Marge had to get up early to pick us all up and take us, but she gladly did it.

When we went to court, we learned this was also the date that one of Peru's ex-presidents was being arrested for corruption. Faced with this, he had killed himself. Apparently, traffic was at a standstill, and my lawyer was late because of it. The trial was at 9 a.m., and I was told by one of the judges, "If he is not here in ten minutes, you are using a public defender!"

Oh no, I thought. I did not want that.

I kept trying to reach him, but he was stuck in traffic due to the traffic jam because of the ex-president's fatality. The three judges got wind of that news and were all chatting amongst themselves, so they lost track of time when Louie came in at 9:40.

The psychiatrist still hadn't submitted his report, so things were postponed again. The judge then demanded that the prosecutor get the report by the next date, or they'd be holding the psychiatrist in contempt of court. The trial was adjourned for fourteen days. I was told that while a regular court can go months or even years from hearing to hearing, the trial could not last longer than fourteen days between dates.

Sal Monty still believed that this was because no one wanted to challenge Dr. Ladd, but I wasn't so sure about that. We had even tried reaching out to top medical doctors and Peruvian specialists back home to plead my case and seek their assistance in bringing me back home. But, to do that, they would need to physically evaluate me since they didn't even know me. And it had been two years since my arrest and three and a half years since my accident. So much had changed, obviously. As always, our plans back home fell on deaf ears. No one ever acknowledged our cries for help. I now had fourteen days of walking on pins and needles, not knowing what to expect.

Two weeks went by like this, and once again, I had to pay Marge's driver to get us to court. Marge came again for the support, but no one else. There was no embassy this time. The psych report was finally in and was a whopping one paragraph stating that I was perfectly fine. So much for Sal saying no one wanted to challenge Dr. Ladd.

Surely this psychiatrist certainly had no problem doing it. Not to mention it wasn't even a thorough exam that he conducted, as it was two years after the fact, so I don't even see how they could compare it. Plus, I knew he was recording me. My picture from his phone was in his report. Regardless, he stated that I was totally fine. So, do we continue to fight this? It had been two years with no positive movement for me thus far, plus it was costing us over USD$6,000 a month in legal fees, rent, food, etc. When would this ever end?

The judge told me again, "If you continue to plead innocent, we will go at you for fifteen years *minimum,* but if you plead guilty, we will go for less."

Of course, Sal wanted to challenge it since he was a litigator and wanted to fight. But the thought of spending thirteen more years there killed me, not to mention the judges had already told Louie that they refused to use a brain injury as a defense. Despite my mounting proof, they felt that if they let me go, they'd also have to let countless others go. They would not do that, so my only defense was something they would not even look at, so what was I fighting for?

Since my initial arrest, everyone told me that I was stupid not to plead guilty from the start, that Peru would never let me go free, and that fighting it would only waste time and money. I asked Sal when I first went to the apartment if I should just plead guilty, but he said it was not the time to plead guilty because we needed this fight as our bargaining chip. I was torn.

Do I continue to plead innocent and risk another thirteen years or plead guilty and go for a lesser sentence? I deliberated.

I know Sal wanted me to plead innocent, but I could not bear the thought of thirteen more years away from my family and life back home. The judge adjourned court so I could go to the apartment and think about it. I'd have seven more days before my next court date to decide.

When I got back to the apartment, I called my family and told them everything. Even Charlie felt that now was the time to make a deal, plead guilty, and see what they offered as a sentence. Sal had told me and my family all along that the house arrest counted as time served and that once you were out, they wouldn't send you back into prison.

Well, as seemed to typically be the case, not everything was always as it appeared. Sal and his team came to the apartment to talk about options. Charlie wanted to be on the phone too, but Sal wanted to talk to me with his team privately first. I did not know why so I called Charlie anyway and secretly had Sal on speaker-phone, so Charlie could hear. I had asked Sal if I'd have to go back to prison if I pleaded guilty because that was what Charlie believed.

He told me, no, that once you were out, you were out. Then he translated things to Louie, who was also there with us, and I saw Louie confirm that I would have to go back to prison.

I could see Sal's face turn since he'd have to explain how he messed up. He posed it in a certain way, saying, "Well, what I think might be best here is if you do go back but only for two or three months, and then you are on your way home."

Well, this was certainly not good news, but Sal kept assuring me that the apartment counted as time served, so I had already served two years. Most drug cases were six to eight years, and you only had to serve a third of the time if you paid your fines. So, if that were the case, I'd only have to serve $2^{1/2}$ months in prison.

I only assumed that I'd be going back to Santa Monica and thought that at least I'd get to see Lena and Inga again for $2^{1/2}$ months. We mutually agreed that this was our best option, to plead guilty, serve $2^{1/2}$ more months, and get the heck out of Peru once and for all. I even said I'd burn my passport once I got back to the US—not because I felt anymore that the US was the greatest in the world and I never wanted to leave it, but because it taught me that once you cross international borders, you are on your own with little to no assistance. I'd be afraid to ever leave the US again.

I went back to the court, having to pay for a taxi for me and the cop. Marge came again, but no one else was with her. Louie came to court, but no one else from his team. It was a very fast court. I pled guilty and was told to come back in three days for my sentencing. What? They wouldn't tell me how many years they'd give me for my sentence? I had to sit around for three days waiting to find out. That was insane.

I left the court with the cop and had to pay for a taxi. Each time for court, Marge would take me to the ground floor, where there was a church, and we would pray together. The cop always followed and stayed in the back. We prayed together before the cop and I returned to the apartment. As always, the cop left me at the gate, and I went upstairs. I called my husband and family to tell them how the court session went. They shared my concern about not knowing what my sentence would be. All we could do was wait.

I had hoped the court would have just said, "Time served, and now leave our country and never come back," but I guess that was not the case. I had just gotten groceries delivered to the apartment. Also, about a week ago, my family was here and bought me tons of groceries we could only find in the US, and they filled up my freezer and refrigerator to last me about two months, so now what? This was beyond enough to make anyone negative.

Sal had told us that he'd go to the court and find out what sentence they would give me if I pled guilty. That was important to me because all I was told in court was, "If you plead guilty, the sentence will be less."

But how much less? The way Peru's comical justice system works, you could only apply for what they call "benefits," which is a third of your sentence (only if your sentence is under seven years). Anything above that does not allow you to apply for benefits. This was an important thing I needed to know.

I had tried calling and texting Sal to find out what he heard from the court regarding my sentencing since he told me he was going to do that. He never replied to anything, yet he wrote to my husband, asking him to tell me to stop bothering him as he was with his kids. Was he serious? I was stunned. It was easy for someone not in my position to think that I was a pain, but if they had put themselves in my shoes for just one moment, I guarantee it would be the same.

I would have loved to have been with *my* kids, but unfortunately, I was still stuck in this country due to his incompetence in getting me released. Once I pled guilty, the monthly retainer of $4,500, aka S/20k+ a year, stopped. Therefore, I apparently wasn't an important asset to him anymore, and he couldn't be bothered. Considering he made almost half a million in his money from us and completed nothing other than me going *back* to prison, it was beyond disgusting how his lack of interest suddenly surfaced.

I complained about this, and Rebecca would tell me that I was too negative. Well, back home, I was always the positive one, the glass-half-full person. I always joked because my husband was negative. But sadly, this whole experience—seeing how evil these people were, how corrupt and dysfunctional Peru was—was leaving me rotting at the core and in a foreign third-world country away from my family for two years so far.

Yes, it was beyond enough to make anyone negative. Whenever Rebecca would rant to me about how negative I was being, I would tell her that she got to go home to her family and go out with her boyfriend, and I did not. It was easy to say but not easy to do. You learn from experience, and my experience in Peru was not good or positive in any way, shape, or form.

I now had tons of things in the apartment that I simply refused to leave behind for anyone. I gathered everything over the next two days, packing up what would be mine to go home with and what I would give away. I gave Marge a ton of things she could use for people on parole or other prisoners she visited. I gave her a big fan to keep cool on the hot days, different luggage, as well as my cell phone, computers, credit cards, passport, etc., to hold on for me until I got released.

I also gave her soles to hold on to for me since she visited the prisoners weekly. I could rely on her to bring me soles weekly since my family was not here in Peru, and I couldn't request Rebecca start coming and bringing me things weekly again. I split everything up. I gave my wonderful neighbor Ruth the other fan and some food; I gave the skydiver from the UK a few small things as well. I gave Marge a lot of things that were left and gave things to my neighbor and the baby. I left a bag of canned and boxed goods outside her door, and sadly, I still had to leave some things behind, but not much.

I also removed the screens that Ruth's maintenance man built for the windows and gave them to Ruth to keep, and she gave me paint to paint the walls where the tape was. I had given her and Marge so many of the groceries I had just delivered, a huge pack of tape, paper, towels, detergents, Downey, shampoo, etc.

I was starting to feel furious toward Sal also because, since day one, he told us about all his connections and successes and let us believe that this would be over quickly. Yet, there I was, two years later, going back to jail for something that I was completely innocent of, even *after* Sal said, "Once you're out, you never go back." Despite all that, I was, going *back* to jail! Did Sal ever really have connections, or was Peru's judicial system just jerking him around the same way they were jerking me around? Who knows? I obviously had my doubts.

I packed myself a bag that I intended to bring to prison since I knew all the things I needed—towels, blankets, clothes, shampoo, conditioner, detergent, Downey, and a thermos. These were all things I had asked Marge to buy for me. The next morning, I had to leave bright and early with the cop, and again pay him to drive me. Ruth met me downstairs, where I gave her and the maintenance man all I had left in the apartment, and cried as I said my final goodbye.

Off to court we went for my official sentencing, which I was never given a heads-up on since Sal never replied to me or my family with that one question. Marge met me at the court also as support. I had left the bag I packed for me for the prison in the cop's car. I did not want to bring it into the court. Sal did not show up at court, but Louis and Rebecca did. The court was pretty quick. My sentence was six years and ten months. There was another cop present, apparently ready to just yank me out of there back to prison. I asked if I could go to the cop car to get my bag, and I was told no.

Oh boy! Here I go again.

They let Marge and Rebecca go and take some of my belongings for me, but sadly they only brought me a few things: my blanket, one change of clothes, and not much else. Rebecca said I could not bring in my medicines without any prescription, which had been a fight for me since day one. In the US, if you have your pills in a medicine bottle with your name, that *is* your prescription. In Peru, you buy one pill, two pills, etc., and you get your prescription slip back. The US didn't work that way, so none of my medicine came in, and neither did my thermos or anything else.

I realize we were all being rushed, but I had also packed three to four packs of fiber for my stomach issues, three to four packs of my sleep meds, three to four packs of cholesterol medicine, shampoo, conditioner, toothpaste, deodorant, detergent, towels, clothes, etc. Now what? As surprisingly as it was, I seemed to go back to the same ridiculous transition of jails that I did the very first time! I went to the one that was my second prison two years prior. I spent one day there with the men on one side and women on the other, with women in one cell on the floor. From there, I got moved to the other side, same as before, to the two-bed cell, where I was alone. Here they went through all my stuff.

I had about S/100 in coins because, in Santa Monica, the phones needed coins to call, unlike Ancon, which was a card. Plus, I had soles for myself. They told me I could not bring that with me. What?

It was mine! Who's to say what I could not have? They also took my pocketbook, which was made for me.

Why couldn't I bring that? Because they said I could hang myself on the strap. Seriously? I had a whole year to kill myself, and *now*, it was a concern? I asked them to call my lawyer, and they did. Rebecca came and brought me a sandwich and Tupperware. Then, she took my pocketbook and gave me soles from my money to keep on me for myself. I told her I needed my clothes and stuff from the bag she had from the day at court.

I did not have my pajamas or a change of clothes. She said she would try and get me something. She left, and I had to stay alone in the cell for two days. I remember my first night, around 9 p.m., I had to pee and was trying to call an INPE to let me out to the toilet so I could go to the bathroom, and she brought me a water pitcher. She did not speak English but motioned to tell me that that was to be my toilet for the night. She obviously did not want to be bothered letting me out to pee. I guess her sleep or TV was more important.

Then came the same as before: Every morning, an INPE had to come in and inspect my stuff and then leave me solo again. Deja vu. After two days, I was moved to another prison, the same one from the last time again. Being transferred here was the same as before. I was put in the back of an ambulance with men. I was the only woman. One man had his entire leg in a cast with pins throughout it. Hopping on and off this vehicle couldn't have been pleasant. Plus, the way the Peru roads were with the crazy drivers was not a pleasant ride. People were hanging on to him. I was getting so car sick with their driving. By the time we got to the third prison, I was so nauseous. I tried kneeling down to avoid throwing up but was told to stand up and deal with it.

I got moved to a cell by myself. I remembered this one from the last time, but I was in a different room last time. It was so dirty, smelly, and water-bug infested. I hated it, but what could I do? I slept the first night alone. I had one blanket, no sheets or anything, because they were in the bag I packed for prison, but neither Marge nor Rebecca gave me the sheets.

I used the blanket as a cocoon to keep me off the nastiness on the floor. I remember as I tried to sleep, I had my sneakers on the floor by my head in case I had to go to the toilet in the room. In the dark room, I saw something shimmy past my face. It was a water bug! It was walking and shimmying past my sneakers right by my face. Oh my God! This was not happening again, was it? Yes, it was! Sometime in the middle of the night, a new girl was brought in.

Of course, we did not speak each other's language. I saw that she only had the clothes on her back, nothing else. So as not to have her sleep on the dirty foam, I motioned to her that if she moved her foam close to mine, I could open the blanket, and we could both sleep on top of it, which she did. It was all good until I got cold in the middle of the night! I didn't want to kick her out of the blanket, so I had no choice but to go under it, sleeping on the dirty foam. Of course, with the whole water bug situation, I got no sleep anyway.

The next morning, they woke us both up to clean, telling her to clean outside the cell and me inside. Afterward, she came in to finish up food in a Tupperware that an INPE gave her. I tried to ask what the INPE gave her. I tried to ask where *my* breakfast was, but apparently, as always, I was shit out of luck with me being the foreigner. No food for me. Total Deja vu.

I had a few crackers left from the food Rebecca had brought me in the last prison, so that was my breakfast. Obviously, the girl and I couldn't communicate, so here we went again. We stayed alone that day; the next day, four girls came in. One girl was from Santa Monica, and she remembered me. The other three were sisters, I believe. They were in Santa Monica maximum. The girl from Santa Monica, in my Spanglish and charades, she said she thought I was gone already to my home and told me how big Inga was getting.

I still had no shampoo or soap, so I used some detergent I found by the toilet for cleaning. It was something called Ace, which, in their language, sounded as if they were calling it acid, and they used it to clean the bathroom toilet, but that was what I used to shower with. The three girls were chatting with family through an open grating above. You couldn't see anyone, but you could hear them, so whatever they were talking about to their people on the outside through the grating, an INPE then brought them in food and stuff. It's amazing what S/5 could do for you there.

We stayed all day in the cell and were inspected again, ready to make our next move. The other girls were all going to Santa Monica, but I was told that I was going to Ancon II. What? Not to Santa Monica? How come? This was not at all what I expected, and I knew it would be a problem with Sal and his team because Santa Monica was fifteen minutes from their office, but Ancon II was about two hours each way.

Ironically, Rebecca had said that it would be too far to visit if I went to Ancon, yet Sal was now hopping in airplanes, constantly flying to Madrid for a paying client. Was that what this was about? I was too far! But Madrid was closer? Or was it that I had no more money for him? Was the half a million soles that he took from me and my family not enough?

Before being moved, we again had to go down to a floor—an open floor. It had one chair for a so-called dentist who inspected your teeth and made notes of any missing teeth, caps, fillings, etc. Then we had to stand in front of a so-called medical person who evaluated us. They'd asked me my height and weight, which was where I was faced with another problem. In the US, we use pounds and inches/feet, but in Peru, they use kilograms and centimeters. The doctor was expecting me to do the math and figure it out. Ha! As if! Send me to the US, and this wouldn't be a problem. I was not about to do his work for him. I did not belong here!

The men were also included in this open room, with everyone being examined. I knew some of the men, having been driven here in the back of the ambulance. The man with the leg cast and pins in his leg was there. As everyone was being examined, I heard what sounded like a loud slap at one point. I looked around to try and see what it was but didn't see anything, so I thought I imagined things.

Then, I heard it again. This time, I was able to see where the sound came from. One of the INPEs had one of the male prisoners with him and slapped him hard on the back of his neck. He grabbed him and pushed him, then said something in his ear. It didn't sound pretty. I felt bad for the guy, but this was Peru jail, unfortunately. Nothing could be done about it.

We then had to get fingerprinted. This was absurd. Was this not in some system already from the first time? So stupid. Once again, I went through the exact same process that I went through two years ago. It was silly.

Once this was done, we girls went back to our "room." We were inspected, and our bags were dumped out and looked through again. Then we were split up in terms of where we were going. We'd all be going to different prisons, and I was the only one going to Ancon II, apparently. I later found out that Ancon II was the men's prison with one smaller section for women and where the foreigners were sent. As I went to follow the INPE out, I saw all the men standing in one room facing the wall, all totally naked. I didn't know what to do, but the INPE said, "*Pasa, pasa,*" which meant to go and pass through. One of the men tried to turn and see me, and he was slapped in the ass with a shoe the INPE was holding. Apparently, they were inspected more thoroughly, probably for a good reason.

I was walking out and saw one of the nice INPEs from Santa Monica who spoke a tiny bit of English. I had helped her with her English homework in Santa Monica. She had thought I was home, too. I tried to explain what had happened and what was going on in the few short moments I had.

She shook her head, gave me a kiss on the cheek, then said, "Be careful." I was whisked away and thrown into the back of the ambulance to wait.

All the men were going to Ancon II, and when they saw how many there were, I was moved to the back of the ambulance in the small section towards the back door to sit with the INPE with a gun by the door since I was the only female. It was better since there was a tiny window that prevented me from getting car sickness. I remember going to deligencia in the summer in the back of those vehicles. Not only were they roach-infested, but they were also hot as hell. By the time I'd get to or from the court, you could wring my clothes out from sweat. The backs of those vehicles were so hot, being crammed with twenty people in a vehicle that only had seats for six and being smooshed, no windows, nothing—just HOT.

I remember one day, I was with three other people, and I saw cockroaches, so I stood. The INPE yelled at me to "*sientate!*"

I said, "No, cucarachas," but they could care less what I was saying. They kept yelling for me to sit down. We didn't get back to Santa Monica that day until around 9 p.m. (since the start of our journey at 7 a.m.). I wasn't even going near the bed until I had a shower.

CHAPTER 12

Getting to Ancon II was about a two-hour drive from wherever I was coming from. The INPE with the gun seemed to be a decent man. Obviously, I could not communicate with him, but he was lending his cell phone to all the men in the vehicle so they could call their families and lawyers to let them know which prison they would be at. That was nice of him. He tried to talk to me, but once he realized I could not communicate, I was sure he was sorry that I was in the seat. Oh well, what can you do?

Eventually, we arrived in Ancon II. I noticed we were up in the mountains (at a higher altitude in what looked like a desert). There wasn't anything around at all. In Santa Monica, we were in a city. Here in Ancon II, we seemed to be in the middle of nowhere. I had to endure the typical initial processing all over again. Since I was the only female, I'm sure it was easier for me. I got moved around a little and then went to a room where another female INPE came in with rubber gloves. I thought to myself, *Oh my God, so it's this kind of exam now?* but apparently, she had the rubber gloves on as she went through my bags again.

This is what the rooms looked like in Ancon II

It's crazy how from one place to the next, everyone finds another thing that we were not allowed to have. It was all for them to keep for themselves, unfortunately. After this fiasco, I was passed on to another INPE who walked me down a very long pathway to their doctor's office. I guess it wasn't really a doctor, but a woman who was giving meds to people; it was sort of like how I had to wait in line two times a day in Santa Monica for my meds. This woman took my information while she was giving everyone their meds. She asked me why I was there, among other things. Normally, the language barrier would have ceased all conversation, but thank God, there was a girl from the Philippines to translate for me. The funny part was that as this Philippino girl was translating for me, everyone there could hear her. When she was telling my story, how I went to Santa Monica, then house arrest, then there, one of the prisoners in the line to get her meds chimed in, "House arrest doesn't count!" I was more annoyed by the fact that no one asked her opinion, and why was she listening to our conversation anyway? That pissed me off, but what could I do. I just said to the Philippino girl, "Yes, it does count. My lawyer promised that it did, so what does she even know?"

After this, I was moved to a section where another girl was there with a foam bed. I was then moved on to what they called *Caliboso*, which was what we called Waco in Santa Monica. Not only did they put people who were being punished there, but it was also where they put new people whose paperwork was about to be processed. The girl handed me the foam bed and I was moved into a room, alone in the entire place. It was a pabellon with two bedrooms and two floors and me all by myself.

Then I met the hole in the ground, aka my toilet. How gross. They locked you into the room at night and locked the door to the pabellon. There was a gated window above the sink where the hole in the floor was. A gated semi-window was fitted in the room. The light in the room did not work. The wires were all frayed and sticking out of the ceiling, so light was a privilege they did not plan to give me.

I tried reading the one book I had with the little bit of light from the hall, but it wasn't easy to see, so I didn't read much. I got to Ancon II around 7 p.m., so it had to be about 10 p.m. by then. The foam they gave me smelled like cat pee, which was nasty, but what could I do?

Again, there I was, dealing with a major language barrier and a new prison. None of it was pleasant. I tried to sleep, but of course, that was impossible. I was back in prison—a totally new prison, not knowing what to expect, plus I was terrified of being locked in a dark room alone with water bugs.

If that wasn't enough, there were stray cats that would jump and run across the roof. Hearing the sounds, I had no clue what it was and thought it was rats. I had gotten up to pee in the middle of the night, which was interesting. You literally had to squat over the hole and pee and then get water from the so-called sink to wash it down. They had an empty water jug over the hole.

I realized why. The smell was horrific once I removed the jug to pee. Apparently, it was like a cesspool and was terrible. Trying to squat over this, with my bad knees and back, while doing it quickly was not fun, but here I was. This was now my life again, in prison in Ancon, all for a crime I had no clue I was committing and with zero assistance from the US.

It was a shame that my country would help senior citizens when they were imprisoned abroad for scams, yet I couldn't get any help at all. Even though I wasn't technically a senior citizen, I was still 50 years old, not a child.

At 6 a.m., the door was opened loudly by an INPE. Then I was brought a broom by a *fellow* inmate from inside the pabellon. I later found out that when new prisoners were brought in, they told the pabellon your whole business—where you were from, what you were there for, etc. Then, since the female prisoners were 25 percent Peruvians and 75 percent *extranjeras* (foreigners), the apparent custom was that they would collect things to help you. I didn't know this, obviously.

At 8 a.m., some Spanish prisoners came and asked me for my Tupperware for breakfast, which I now had thanks to Rebecca bringing me one in the transition prison. I gave it to her, and she came back with the typical "Quaker" and two rolls. Around 8:30, two INPEs came in and, as usual, tore apart my bags to see what I had. It was silly, but what could I do besides go with the flow? They left the room door open, but not the pabellon. I could walk out of the room and into an open section surrounded by four walls. But at least I could go out and get air.

It was early May and autumn in Peru, so it was not too hot or cold. Being up in the mountains, though, made the weather very different than Santa Monica. It was chilly and more humid. With the beach and water on the other side of the mountain, it made the air a few degrees cooler. But whenever the sun came out, it was hot regardless. In Santa Monica, the sun was out a lot more often. From June to December, we were lucky if the sun came out once a week.

So, what did I do all day? I could only read the one book I had so many times. I walked around in circles in the open space. I walked so much that by miles, I probably could have been halfway home by then. I laid out on my back, staring at the sky, trying to see the beauty but also asking God why this was happening to me. The tiny bit of cloud that I saw showed me that the air was still. The clouds hardly moved at all. I eventually walked around inside to covertly check out my surroundings. It was empty but also seemed to be a dirty storage place. There were tons of papers, chairs, and Christmas decorations on the second floor. You could also see across to where the other pabellons were. I didn't stay long because I was afraid an INPE would come and I'd be caught snooping around, so I went back down to the ground floor where my room was.

Eventually, two girls came in with a blanket, toothbrush, and toothpaste. One of them spoke English while the other didn't. These girls were told a foreigner from America was there, and they brought me things they thought I could use. I was grateful. I mentioned my book and how I didn't even have a brush for my hair because the INPE took it from me for some idiotic reason. It was plastic, so I don't know what they thought I'd do with it.

These girls only stayed for five minutes and said that they were also prisoners and that the INPEs wouldn't even feed us in Caliboso. Unless someone brought me food, I wouldn't eat. Welcome to Ancon II.

One girl left and came back with a new book for me, in English. I was very happy and grateful. After a while, they left, and I went back to walking around. Around 12:30, the same Spanish woman came and took my Tupperware again for lunch. The food seemed to be different than it was in Santa Monica. I was told it was because the men made the food, not the women like in Santa Monica. So, in Santa Monica, we got salads and different foods. There, no salads and more food. It wasn't technically more *good* food, but more rice, potatoes, soup, etc. At this stage, with my two years of being there, I'd learned to just go with it. There was nothing at all that I could do about it. I had since learned that, so just going with the flow was all I could do.

At 4, she returned to retrieve the Tupperware for dinner. That was different than Santa Monica. In Santa Monica, dinner was around 6:30 or 7. There, it was 4:30. Again, I just had to grin and bear it. At 6 p.m., the INPE came in again to check on me and locked the pabellon door (not that I was allowed to leave anyways). The sun set around 6 anyway, so my walking around wasn't beneficial anyway. With the little hallway light I could get, I tried reading the book the girl had brought me. I could technically sit in the hall and read, but everything was cement and cold and damp, plus not good on my back.

The humidity was killing my back and neck, which were broken in my skydiving accident only four years prior, but again, I just had to grin and bear it as best I could. At 9 p.m., the INPE came in again and locked me into the room for the night. At 6 a.m., it was the same routine—INPE checked in on me, tore apart my bags, etc. The nightmare continued!

I was in Caliboso for a week and had no clue when I'd get out and brought to the pabellon with the other prisoners. Each day I walked around and read. An INPE occasionally would come and try and ask me my story. It was a massive language barrier, of course. Plus, I later found out they blabbed my story to everyone anyway. I did not care. I had absolutely nothing to hide. I tried to tell them why I was there, but at the end of the day, it didn't matter. I was there.

Sal Monty had assured me that I'd only be there for three and a half months before I could start my paperwork for release. They had a law where if you paid your fines and dias multa and served a third of your sentence, they would release you back to your country, and you'd not be allowed back to Peru for ten years.

I did not care. I would never return to Peru. After a few days, one of the INPEs asked me if I needed anything. I was running out of toilet paper. She walked me to what they all called *kiasko*. These were two booths where you could buy things you needed, such as toilet paper, cold foods, shampoo, deodorant, comb, detergent, soap, soda, yogurt, fruits, and veggies. We had the same in Santa Monica, but at least there, you were able to walk around and have access to these essentials all day long.

In Ancon, I was told that each pabellon got ten minutes a day to go out and get what they needed, but only from Monday to Saturday. So, if you forgot something, you'd be shit out of luck until the next day. The INPE took me out there, and I was able to get a liquid yogurt, toilet paper, a cucumber, lotion, and soap to wash my Tupperware. I was glad Rebecca had left me a few soles worth of my money to be able to buy this. Since I was not in Santa Monica now, and with my family all back home, I could not get necessities as often. Luckily, Marge and Annie visited Ancon weekly, the same way they visited Santa Monica weekly.

This was why I had also given Marge S/$10,000 of my money (in soles) to bring me on a weekly basis since my options were limited. As much as that sounds like a lot of money, it really wasn't and was intended to get me through five months at best—$200 a week or $800 a month. I was able to go back to my room with my cucumber and yogurt at least and read the book again.

Two days later, the INPE let me go out to the kiosko again. She asked me if I wanted to see the religion group. I wasn't sure what to expect, but through our communication charades, she brought me over to a group of women. They were Jehovah Witnesses. I am a Catholic and grew up Catholic. But I learned that in a foreign country, especially in prison, you associated with any religion you could.

I've always believed that there is one true God. While we may all practice our faith in different ways, and I may not agree with each one, I believe that if I take a little bit of knowledge from each and pray, whoever the real God is would understand. The same went for the Catholic religion. I may not agree with every aspect of it, but I did agree with some of it and incorporate that into *my* beliefs.

I met another woman there who I thought was part of the Jehovah's Witnesses. I didn't realize that she, too, was a prisoner. The INPE came over and said I was being summoned to the offices of the prison. I guess, after almost ten days, they finally got around to processing my paperwork to officially place me in prison. Since I didn't speak Spanish, they told the other woman to come with me to translate. That's when I realized that she was a prisoner, too.

They handcuffed us both together and brought us down long halls, through the men's part of the prison, until we reached the offices. There they were asking me questions, which the woman, Jenny*, had to translate for me.

They quickly looked at my file and said, "Oh, she was released and arrested again? Okay."

That was *not* the case. Why did no one look at my file? I was never fully released! I tried to explain it for the girl to translate. Whether or not she translated right, I have no idea, but that's all I could do.

They took notes, and at first, they said they'd place me in maximum detention.

Thank God the other woman was there because she said, "Maximum? Why? She's 50 years old. Why maximum?"

He said, "Oh, sorry. I meant minimum," and then made the correction on the paper. Had she not been there, I'd have been placed in maximum.

After that, we left, still handcuffed together. I mentioned how I wished I could call my family. She had an accent that I could not place, and she told me she was from South Africa. She asked the INPE if she could take me to her pabellon quickly to use the phone. The INPE agreed.

Unlike Santa Monica, where you used a calling card or soles, here you had to use a number specific to you (your passport number) that the prison tech registered, and then you had to use codes to place money on the number, which was, in essence, your specific calling card, and the prison tech people would come daily to collect money to recharge your code.

I obviously had none of this, so Jenny allowed me to use a number she gave me to call my husband. He was relieved to hear my voice and, for the most part, that I was okay. He told me again to have patience and that Sal would do everything he could to get me out of there ASAP. I sure hoped so.

After that, I thought I was to be moved into a pabellon, but as was typical, Peru was the slowest moving country ever, so I was sent back to Caliboso. There, I sat again, alone, for about two days. I kept asking questions to the INPEs who came to do quenta each day.

I would ask, "How much longer will I be staying here before I go to a pabellon?"

But with the language barrier and their lack of interest in anything I had to say, I was getting no response.

Finally, at about 5 p.m. one afternoon, the INPE came to move me to a pabellon. I was trying to carry my so-called mattress along with my blanket and bag. It was not easy, but I had no choice. She surely was not about to help me. I was moved to building 3B, which was minimum security for foreigners. I was also moved to the second floor (top floor) all the way at the end of the hall to the last room, number six.

There were only six rooms per floor (twelve rooms in each) for 3B and twelve rooms in maximum, 3A. Each room had four bunk beds (which were cement slabs in the wall, unlike the metal bunk beds we had in Santa Monica). The rooms held eight people, but most rooms only had four people in them, so now I made five.

They put me in the top bed, which sucked since I now had to climb up a metal ladder to crawl into the bed. When I'd be on my knees and lift my head, my head would bang on the ceiling It sucked, but at least I was not in Caliboso anymore.

My room consisted of girls from Mexico, Bolivia, Thailand, and another American girl from Chicago. The girls from America and Thailand spoke English, which was a blessing. At one point, I tried to introduce myself, and the girl from Mexico in the bunk underneath mine told me that since I was tall, we could switch beds. She said she didn't mind the top bed and that it would be easier for me. I thought that was cool, but apparently, that wasn't allowed.

Still, they told me not to worry. The INPEs wouldn't have any clue if we switched beds. They said the INPEs never went into the rooms once they locked us in at night and didn't even come into the rooms in the mornings when they unlocked us at 6 a.m. They just unlocked the big latch on the metal doors each day. I thought that was okay, yet I was shocked that they locked us in the room each night.

In Santa Monica, they locked the floors, but not the rooms, because if we needed to use the bathroom, we could walk to the end of the hall and use it. In Ancon II, we had our hole in the floor, so they didn't care. They just locked us in the room every night.

There were so many earthquakes in Peru that in Santa Monica if an earthquake felt large enough, the INPEs would at least unlatch the gate and have us run to the middle of the courtyard. This was so we would not get crumpled by any falling buildings. Here, in Ancon II, nope. They truly didn't care. I put my blanket on the bottom bed, and she transferred hers to the top. The women also had a curtain that they glued to Velcro strips that attached to the ceiling. This offered them privacy and warmth since it was cold in the mountains, and we were on nothing but cement.

I switched bunks with the Mexican girl, and she glued her curtain to the top bed. We were all set. The INPEs did quenta at 9 p.m. and locked the big metal door with the huge bar through it. I climbed into the bottom bed; my head and nerves were all over the place with this new experience. About twenty minutes later, I got up to pee in the hole in the floor when I heard footsteps coming quickly down the hall. This was odd since everyone would have been locked in their rooms, so it could only be INPEs.

I quickly shook the girl on the top bed, who heard it too, and she immediately jumped into the bottom bed. The INPEs barged into the room and turned on the lights to see whose bed I was in. I was just standing there, and Ruth was in her bed. They were asking me in Spanish what I was doing, and I said I had to pee. They seemed annoyed and told me to pee and then get back into my bed. The English-speaking girls from the US and Thailand said that was strange since they never did that.

I had no clue since I was new. I peed and was assured they wouldn't come back, so we switched beds again.

I couldn't fall asleep. For starters, my mind was racing a mile a minute, but I always struggled with sleep and took over-the-counter meds, which they weren't allowing me to have. About thirty minutes later, I again heard footsteps coming down the hall and immediately jumped up and shook Ruth again. She quickly jumped into the bottom bed again as the INPEs unlocked the door and barged in. I just stood there. I said I was up to pee again, and they seemed annoyed since I was just up to pee thirty minutes prior. Obviously, they didn't know me because I actually do get up repeatedly to pee. But again, I was told to pee and get back into bed.

Everyone kept saying how strange this was. I said I did not want any more trouble than I was already in and that I should just go into the top bed and end this. They kept telling me, "No, no, it's fine. They definitely won't be back again."

Well, about twenty minutes later, I heard footsteps and did the same drill, swatting Ruth to quickly switch beds. The INPEs approached the room and started shining flashlights to see if they'd see us switching beds, but we had already switched fast. Then they barged in and opened the curtains and started to shine flashlights in my face, apparently to see if it was me and if I was awake from having just switched. It truly was ridiculous. On my first day in the pabellon, this was not quite what I was expecting. I told the girls that I was staying in the top bed.

No one could believe that the INPEs did that, so I just figured that since I was new, they wanted to flex their muscles with me to show me that they were in charge and that we couldn't just do whatever we wanted. The funny part is, the INPEs were not real cops—to me, anyway. They didn't carry guns; they were technically just security guards. Back home, they'd be nothing more than a Walmart greeter, yet here they oversaw prisoners. The men carried rifles, but not the women. It was ridiculous to me, but as usual, there was nothing I could do about it. Such began my life in Ancon II.

My next morning was spent getting acquainted with the prison. Unlike Santa Monica, where we could walk around, we couldn't do anything like that at Ancon II. You either worked in "Taller" or stayed inside. Inside consisted of being in your room or downstairs where there was a television or what they called the "patio." This was a space about half the size of a basketball court where the clotheslines hung around. If you washed your clothes, you would then hang them on the clothesline to dry.

Depending on which INPE was working that day, you either got to watch TV or not. Some INPEs let the TV and lights stay on all day, and some shut them off. This made it a very boring day. Just like in Santa Monica, if I spoke and understood Spanish, I could chat with people and mingle all day long, but unfortunately, I could not. Like Santa Monica, Taller (or work) would help pass the time and was also good for your records. Without this prison having a CUNA (childcare), what was I to do?

Lola, who was Peruvian but had moved to America at around the age of eight, was not in my pabellon. But I had seen her at the kiasko. She told me to join the Costura Taller, which was sewing. I told her that I had zero experience with sewing and machines, and it was not really my thing, but she assured me that she'd teach me, and we would enjoy it.

As with everything in Peru, nothing is fast. It usually took six or more months to get into Taller. You had to apply and be evaluated by the psych and doctor. Well, Lola was a pest and got me in Taller in two weeks. Everyone around me warned me to watch out for Lola.

Lola never told me why she was in prison, but the INPEs all talked about your business to people and, I guess, had told her story. Because of this, people were telling me that she had killed her husband and ex-husband and made a fortune from their life insurance and then fled to Peru to hide, got caught, and was waiting for them to extradite her back to the USA since that's where her crime was committed.

She never told me anything, but she seemed like a decent person, so I just assumed they were rumors. Well, it did not take long for her to show me her true colors and prove everyone right. In Costura, they were mostly Peruvian, including women from Columbia, Bolivia, and Mexico. Lola kept telling me that they all hated me because I was American and kept talking about me. I thought that was strange because I didn't even know them, and I am a very friendly person. She spent all day saying, "She's giving you dirty looks; she's talking about you; she said this and that," and I was stunned.

Then, she claimed that they broke her sewing machine because of me being there. She always said everyone steals from her, etc. Then she kept saying that I had to buy material to work. They didn't sell clothing materials; it was only limited to some minor materials for teddy bears, pocketbooks, and such. She had me buying so much material from *her*, and I hadn't made anything. I felt like I was just buying and buying. It had to stop.

She had a bad habit of saying, "I got this for you." When I'd thank her for it, she'd slap on a price tag that was way higher than it should be. To me, that is technically not buying something *for me.*

That was her using me to make money, not buying me a gift. After a few short weeks, I was getting annoyed but didn't say anything because I did not want any trouble. One day, she was nice and talkative; the next, she would be annoyed. It was hard to know how to act around her. Then one day, suddenly, she started being rude and wouldn't acknowledge me.

I couldn't take it anymore and said, "What is your problem with me?"

She threw her hands up in annoyance and made a stupid "Tss" sound.

To that, I replied, "That is the *last time* you do that to me," and picked up my bag and went to the back of the room with everyone else.

Ironically, after that, everyone was super nice to me there. It seemed no one was ever talking about me. It was *her* they didn't like. Since I had cut ties with her, I was no longer on the enemy side. No one ever robbed her or broke her machine. It was silly lies she used all the time. Everyone said she was crazy and ignored her.

Sadly, I learned this was why she did what she did. She harassed me for months, and no one did anything about it, only saying, "That's just Lola. She's crazy. Just ignore her." She wasn't held accountable for anything she did; she was free to pester everyone.

I was told she was originally in the Peruvian pabellon, but even *they* got sick of her crap. One day, they threw a blanket over her face—so she couldn't see who it was—and beat her up. She was then transferred to maximum security on the foreigners' side (my side). She had her own room with empty beds, and everyone in her pabellon said she was trouble. The fact that all rooms fit 8 people and all had a minimum of 4 people in them and up to 8 people in them, and she was by herself in the room, that tells you something about her. Either everyone protested to *not* be with her or even the authorities knew she was trouble and kept her to herself.

I tried to give her the benefit of the doubt, but like I said, it took only one week for her to prove everyone right. She lied constantly and made up stories. She spread rumors that I was talking crap about the people in my room. Luckily, they all knew how she was and recognized that it was bullshit. But what if they hadn't? That would have been difficult for me. She was trying to make trouble for me.

One day, I was waiting in line for something, and she was in line too. Everyone was chatting with friends; she just stood, facing me, and again, I said, "What the hell is your problem?"

She threw her hands up again with her stupid "Tsss" sound, then turned around and proceeded to give me the middle finger behind her head.

I laughed so loud since that was such a childish response. It seems to be her signature response to people. It was so stupid.

When the US Embassy came to visit, she always claimed to be a US citizen and would run out to them. Amazingly, the US Embassy never called *me* when they came, but someone in a Costura told me they were there, so I went out. They visited Lola constantly, but it wasn't a private room, so if you stood by, you could hear what they were saying. That's not to say it was okay to do that. It should have been private anyway since it was no one's business what someone else was saying.

The US Embassy seemed to constantly call down the Peruvian Lola, a girl from Guam, and a girl from Mexico, who was also a US citizen. But when it came to me and another girl from Chicago, both natives of the USA, both born and raised in the country, the US Embassy never called us. It was a disgrace. I endured the same treatment from them while in Santa Monica, too.

The girl from Guam was talking to the Embassy, and Lola stood outside staring at them and listening to their conversation. She was making rude comments and sarcastic noises and even told someone passing by what the girl from Guam was saying. I was so annoyed at her behavior that when the girl from Guam left and Lola sat down, I made it a point to stand, stare, and listen, just like she did. That way, she could see how rude it was. She then spoke to them exclusively in Spanish, knowing I couldn't understand her. It was quite childish.

Once she was done, she left, and I went in. The Embassy told me the same as always: "Hi, I don't have you on my list to see."

Every time they said that, it infuriated me. I told them, "How do you *not* have the two true Americans on your list every time, but you only see foreigners?"

They got annoyed at me whenever I said that because they would usually reply with, "We only see Americans!"

And yet they didn't see the people born and raised there. What a disgrace. I proceeded to tell them my update, but it was useless. They did absolutely nothing for American prisoners. I turned around to leave, and who did I see standing there again? Surprise, surprise, it was Lola.

It was unreal. I just shook my head and walked away.

Her antics didn't stop there, unfortunately. In Costura, I moved to a machine in the back of the room, away from her. But I had to pass her walking back there every time. Each time I passed by her, she'd make her usual "Tsss" or other stupid noises. I eventually tried walking way around her area to avoid passing her since it was annoying.

Another girl came because she was getting married in prison and had someone making her wedding dress. I walked behind her. As we passed Lola's spot and she made her usual childish noises, I didn't say a word, but the girl heard her. I was glad other people saw her harassment, too. But it was a shame that no one stopped her because this was why she did what she did. She even went so far as to move all her stuff to the table behind her so she would stand and turn to stare at me in the back of the room. It was the most idiotic form of harassment, but with no one stopping her, it was whatever it was.

About two weeks later, the US Embassy returned and did not call me as usual. Someone else told me they were there. I went to them and saw that Lola was already talking to them. As she left, I went in and was told, as usual, "I don't have you on the list." This time, I totally lost my cool. I told them how useless they were. I had all my clothes and belongings outside of prison with Marge. I asked if someone could bring them my stuff, if they could bring them in for me since visitors could only bring in 4k worth of things, and since they brought things for others, it would be over their weight quota.

I was freezing my butt off since it was on the top of a mountain off the water, and all my stuff was outside and needed to be brought in. What did the US Embassy tell me? They said, "No. We can't do that."

I said, "I'm not asking you to buy me anything. I already have it. I just need someone to bring it in."

I got told again, "No, we don't do that."

It's insane. Any other country's embassy would bring prisoners toiletries, clothes, blankets, food, etc. The US was the only embassy I saw doing nothing.

They then told me they were supposed to help if we had trouble, and before they could finish the sentence, Lola was there again. I cut her off, pointed to Lola, and said, "Well, there is my number one problem."

Finally, they told one of the US Embassy personnel to go see what she wanted.

They said they could only help with a few small issues. I explained that I had already told them my issues under these ridiculously small categories, yet they did nothing. I told them that they didn't acknowledge anything I told them and how other embassies visited their citizens often, bringing them things, paying their fines and even their airfare home. Yet, the USA came once every six to nine months and brought sample-size (hotel guest size) bottles of shampoo, tiny hotel guest-size soaps, and sample-sized bottles of vitamin C and calcium. That was pathetic. The USA, being such a big and powerful country, did absolutely nothing at all to assist citizens in need. It was a disgrace, and people needed to know this. As I turned to leave, Lola was standing there again. All I could do was say, "Un-fucking believable," and walk away.

With me still trying to get used to my new home, I tried watching TV in the TV room, where people rented DVDs from the prison and watched movies all day. They only had a small number of DVDs. I was told that people had seen the same movies again and again, but most were new to *me*. Many of the movies could be either in English or Spanish and subtitled below in either language. Sadly, for me, they had everything in Spanish constantly, even though some people spoke and understood English. With everyone having been there for so many years, Spanish became everyone's language, which sucked for me.

The one girl in my room was American but also spoke Spanish due to her being there for five years. Whenever she and I spoke in English, the Mexican girl got annoyed because she didn't know what we were saying and thought it was rude for us to talk in English. Seriously? That was my life *every day* in Peru! She didn't like it, but I had to endure this every moment of every day.

Eventually, as I had started working in Costura (sewing) and I was completely new to all of that, a wonderful woman from Columbia named Marita, who had been there for thirteen years, took me under her wing and helped me. Thank God she had patience with me. Lola was originally supposed to be helping me since she spoke English also, but now I was solo in my English, and Marita did her best to explain and instruct me whenever possible.

Now regarding my case, Sal Monty told my family and me from day one that house arrest counted as time served, but once I went back into prison, he told me I would be in and out within a few months thanks to benefits from a certain law of theirs. Bear in mind, this was the same guy that had originally told me repeatedly, "Once you're out, you never go back," and despite it, I was back in prison. I didn't care. I'd never return to Peru again for all the money in the world.

I was told I needed to have a hard copy of my sentence. I had no visit or contact from Sal's office. All we were ever told was to wait; it was not ready yet. The girl from there, who was also English-speaking and had visited with Marge, highly recommended her lawyer get a copy of my sentencing paperwork because it was important that I had a hard copy. Alex*, her lawyer, visited once a week to meet with his clients. She told me to speak with him to get me a copy of it.

Ironically, Alex and another lawyer of many foreigners visited their clients every week or every other week. My lawyer, who charged a monthly fee of over $4,500+, had made a small fortune and never visited me once. I saw Alex during one of his visits with the one girl to translate for me. I could never know if the translations were good or correct since I didn't speak Spanish, but I had no choice but to trust the translators.

When she explained how I needed a copy of my sentencing paperwork, he gave me a blank piece of paper and said I had to sign it permitting him to access my file to get it. I was uncomfortable signing a blank piece of paper since anyone could write anything on it. He could write that I owed him a million dollars, and my signature would be on it. The girl told me not to worry, that it was standard practice, that this was how it worked, and that everyone did it this way. I asked her to confirm that he was just getting a copy of my sentence for me, nothing else, and she said she did and that he understood.

I also gave Alex my sister's telephone number for WhatsApp to send her a copy of it so she could also pass it around to my family. As was typical of Peruvian lawyers here, he was not only asking me for money but also asking for my sister to send him money too. He was asking her to Western Union S/ and asking me at the same time. It was very shady, but from what I was told, it was typical. Alex came with a photograph of my sentence, not a hard copy. He said it was incorrect because it did not include my house arrest and needed to be corrected. This had been the number one question that I had since I got to Ancon II, and my heart sank when he said that.

I had very little faith in Sal by this time and was wondering if this was why he wasn't rushing to give me a copy. I immediately ran to the phone and called him. In Ancon II, when you called, the phone displayed *Unknown,* so he obviously did not know that it was *me* calling, so surprisingly, he picked up.

I said, "Sal Monty, it is Patty. Have you seen my sentence papers yet?"

He told me, "No, they're not ready yet."

I told him, "That's not true. I am holding a copy of them in my hands, and it shows that I've only served eleven months of a six-year, ten-month sentence. It also says that the house arrest doesn't count, and that I still must serve twenty-three more months! I have technically already served eleven months in Santa Monica and thirteen months on house arrest, and now it says the thirteen months were not counted and that I'd have to do thirteen months again in prison. What is going on?"

He told me to relax and not to worry about it and that he'd take care of it. That was easy for him to say but not easy to do.

Alex had said that for S/3,000, he would correct the sentence and process my expulsions, where I would be able to leave in a third of my time, which was supposed to be August if the house arrest counted. It was mid-June, and I was at a standstill.

I told Alex, "Thank you, but Sal Monty is working on it."

There was a bit of back and forth with Sal's office. Once he realized how calls from me showed on his phone, he stopped picking up my calls. Somehow, I was not surprised. He made a fortune off me and my family, but since I pled guilty, I was not paying anymore. So why would he work hard, right? Sal Monty's office, mostly Rebecca, started to tell my family that they were going to the court every other day but were getting a runaround.

A few days later, the clerk showed them the blank paper that I had signed with Alex. He wrote that Sal's office was fired and that he was my new lawyer.

What? I didn't write that. None of that was what I said!

Sal now claimed that this was a major issue, and it ruined his connection in the court, etc. To be honest, I didn't buy any of what he was saying anymore since he had told us nothing but lies.

First, he lied by telling me that my family wanted me to plead innocent and also telling them that *I* wanted to plead innocent, hence beginning the mounting monthly flat fee retainer of over $4.5k, which translated to S/15,300-S/20,00 per month in his local money. Also, my fines were S/8,000, and my dias multa—which is the fine for the food, lights, water, etc.—was for 240 days, with no *amount* listed. Sal said it was S/30 per day. That made S/7,200. So, my fines totaled S/15,200. Everyone else said S/30 per day was insane. It would never be that much; it ranged from S/2-10. We only knew what Sal Monty said since the amount wasn't in the sentence. (Even Alex and Alberto, other Peruvian lawyers who worked with many foreigners said that was incorrect. They said if it didn't state it, it would be S/7 per day.) This was all so new and foreign to us, and all we had to rely on was Sal's word, which was becoming less reliable by the day.

When my mom asked him to help her get her S/60,000 bail money back, he said, "You are not my client. Your daughter is. You'd have to pay me, and I charge 20 percent of the bail."

This made no sense. He had no problem taking the S/60,000 bail from her, but filing to have it returned was an issue. It was extortion.

After he continued to make an issue about being fired, even when I repeatedly confirmed that I never fired him, he just continued to create this whole fictitious scenario. He told me how this was not the USA and that firing a lawyer looked very bad for both parties. I even wrote a letter in English and Spanish. I signed and fingerprinted it, explaining what happened and assuring that Sal was still my lawyer, for him to show the court if it was as big of an issue as he claimed, even though all that he was saying made no sense to me.

My mom had Power of Attorney papers signed in Peru, granting her POA of me, which we had done when I was in the apartment for her to sign some papers for me back home. My mom used the POA papers to fire Alex officially and rehire Sal to ease any problems that he claimed all came about because of this. I still doubted what he was claiming, but what could I do? I didn't know what to think. Another twenty-eight months? Another Christmas? Another birthday? Another New Year's?

He and Rebecca went from "House arrest definitely counts; we've said it a million times!" to saying it was never official; 50 percent of judges accept it, and 50 percent don't! What? That is totally not at all what he'd said all along. Even prior to my being released to house arrest, my husband and sister asked if it counted because if it didn't, they'd leave me in Santa Monica. But Sal Monty assured them that it counted.

Now, conveniently, he was blaming Alex. How could Alex have caused this? Yes, he had no right to fire Sal on my behalf, but what else did he do wrong? The sentence excluded the house arrest prior to Alex, so how could he blame him?

My husband ran back and forth to Peter King's (our congressman) office. They would contact the US Embassy in Peru. Even writing to the Embassy, all the information they got came from Sal. While I appreciated their help, the information was still coming from Sal, who I no longer trusted. Sadly, my family trusted Congress and the Embassy, but I, being on the inside, had different views and opinions.

Sal had stated that he would contact the courts and have it included, not to worry. But I could do nothing but worry, being locked away in prison, beyond my one-third date, with no end in sight. The cop who came to my apartment daily to check on me told us, after the fact, that he even told Sal from the start that house arrest didn't count, so he was confused as to why I was seeking house arrest. Apparently, everyone but me knew that the judges would never let me go, no matter how much we fought or how much proof we had. He was concerned as to why I'd leave prison to sit alone every day when it wouldn't even count as time served.

But Sal told him, "Yes, it counts." So, he didn't push it.

I had to sit every day in a panic about what would happen to me. His story changed so many times I could not keep track anymore. I continued working in Taller, trying my best to make things. The weather, while it was hot summer back home, was winter where I was. Besides, the weather was colder and wetter than in Santa Monica because we were up in the mountains and over the water. I didn't have many warm clothes, so I was actually making sweatpants, sweatshirts, pajamas, and long sleeve shirts with the help of Marita.

I sucked at it, but she was patient and kept helping me. Of course, she wanted perfection because she was teaching. The whole point of working there was making things you could sell to make money. I was just making things for myself because who could I really sell things to? Since it was just for me, I didn't really care how it looked. It wasn't like I ever expected to take these things home with me. I called them my prison clothes and had planned to leave them all behind. But I understood her wanting me to be good at what I was making. She kept saying, "Don't you want to be able to make things for your grandkids?" Shit, once I was home, I would buy things for them.

With Sal constantly saying, "You'll be in and out in two or three months," I had believed that I'd be home soon. Well, the latest news brought me beyond my one-third date where I could petition for benefits, which they called expulsion, where they let you go and drove you straight to the airport in handcuffs, and you were not technically free until the plane took off. But with the judges denying the plan to include the house arrest, now what? Another thirteen months? It would technically be twelve months if I continued working in Taller, but that was another year in prison. My whole thirteen months going stir-crazy alone in the apartment would have been a complete waste!

Sal put together a detailed report requesting it be included and provided samples of cases where it did count. Sadly, it was proof of "Peruvians," and it was many years prior to when laws changed. We were left to wait, and Peru did nothing fast. It was the slowest country I had ever seen, and they didn't care whose life they ruined in the process. I was the first drug case involving an American that ever got house arrest, so there wouldn't be any prior cases to look at. Peru seemed to be very strict on foreigners, trying to set an example to prevent other foreigners from going to Peru to traffic drugs.

Working in Taller – Costura (sewing)

CHAPTER 13

My daughter had her third baby after many hours of labor. I had two granddaughters and a grandson. The newest little angel was named Selena, which I thought was a beautiful name. I was still crushed that I was not there to help my daughter with the three babies, plus her two stepchildren. The whole point of moving her closer to my home was so that I could help her with the kids. But little did I expect that, three months later, I would be arrested in Peru. My husband had stepped in to help her, and my son did as best he could, but I wanted to be there, too.

If there was one thing I learned in Ancon II, it was how many foreigners were scammed. From everyone I met, it seemed we all were part of some scam. The only difference I saw was that some people knew they would be trafficking drugs. The only thing that they didn't know was that they would be scapegoats and get set up to be caught so the real traffickers could sneak in hundreds of kilos while the police came after them. I spoke with people from Thailand, the Philippines, Africa, Holland and Russia who believed they were part of a trafficking ring when they got caught. And yet, they didn't catch on to the fact that they only had one to three kilos worth of cocaine. Did they really believe that someone paid for their trip all the way across the world to traffic 500 grams or a kilo of coke?

Apparently, they believed this. But again, how these scammers could ruin people's lives like this was disgusting.

Like me, not everyone knew they were trafficking drugs. I believed I was there on a business trip. The woman from Arizona believed she was on vacation and only bringing back a pair of pants from her online boyfriend's daughter. It was crazy.

I met another girl from the US whose baby was only six months old and had just learned to roll over. She met someone online who told her he loved her and wanted to treat her to a well-deserved vacation, saying she deserved a break after the baby. This type of "love scam" with trafficking is huge. But normal, everyday people wouldn't know this. Not knowing any better, this woman, too, agreed, and her online boyfriend paid for her vacation to Peru. Then, he gave her a souvenir for her family and provided her with a bigger suitcase to carry the souvenir. Unbeknownst to her, the new suitcase had two kilos of cocaine in it. As expected, she was busted and sent to jail. She, like me, pleaded not guilty and found herself in prison, away from her baby, while they claimed to do an investigation. This was, as I already learned, a farce. They do nothing.

This woman told me how she spoke to the DEA and gave them all her proof, and they said that they would help her. It was all complete deja vu to me. I know I always hated people telling me what to do. But in this instance, I could only give advice. I told her how everyone had told me since day one that I was stupid not to plead guilty from the start and how Peru would never let you go without doing time. I told her how we even had Jerry Coleman, the DEA I met, on a recording saying how he believed that I was innocent and how he was going to help, yet he did nothing at all.

Like I said, the fact that he had the Nigerian and the girl on film, yet only arrested *me*, I was convinced that these scammers had everyone in their back pockets, and Jerry Coleman was just doing his due diligence to say that he visited me, but he'd never do anything to help.

However, the girl listened to me, and I told her to do whatever she wanted. I could only give my experience and opinion. Everyone echoed the same advice to her. She had court again, but rather than her having to endure the same back-of-the-ambulance chaos, they did hers via video from the prison. They told her the same thing they told me: "We will give you one more chance. If you plead innocent again, we will go a minimum of fifteen years, but if you plead guilty, we'll go for less."

She, like me, had no choice but to plead guilty. They gave her three days and then another video chat to sentence her to six years and eight months, which was the typical sentence for most people.

At least, I should say, it seemed typical for people who had a different lawyer. Judges seemed to not like certain lawyers and make the convicts pay the price for that. It was sickening.

She had already served one year in prison, at which, as usual, they did no investigation. She just looked at it as, "Oh well, I only have to serve another year and some months." It was still shocking how innocent people like us had to endure this with zero help from the US.

That woman would be away from her baby for two and a half years while the real criminals roamed free. Even in the US, I have seen countless criminals walking free, my ex-husband being one of them. Yet, people like me and countless others were imprisoned.

Even the a 75-year-old man from New Jersey who was there because he fell for a scam. They imprisoned a severely diabetic man. And if that wasn't bad enough, while insulin was apparently cheaper there than in the USA, the INPEs were stealing his insulin. It caused him to almost lose his eyesight and be continuously disoriented and forgetful. He was sent to the hospital several times, and his family back home was sent the bill. He eventually went into a coma.

The family was trying to have him released on the humanitarian clause. Sadly, no judges wanted to sign it. It was a constant battle trying to get them to acknowledge his issue. It was dirty hospitals and rusty IV needles. They even had a rusted tube in his arm. Sal claimed that he and his team jumped through hoops without results. The man's wife flew to Peru and stayed in the hospital with him. She stayed several weeks. After a week, he came out of the coma, and they immediately sent him back to prison. There, they kept him in the infirmary, not the cell, which he said was worse. They never checked on him and didn't attend to his needs, so he begged his wife to stay. He said her visits at least got them to acknowledge him. Without her, they ignored him.

His son flew to Peru because the wife did not believe he would make it back home. After Sal's team jumped through hoops (so he said), they were able to submit the humanitarian clause. Then they said, "We have four months to review them." Ironically, in four months, he was able to petition for his benefits since he was sentenced to 5.8 years. It seemed that nothing in Peru made any sense at all.

I'd learned more stuff like this from a girl from Texas who was there. She had petitioned for *translado* (being transferred back to your country to do your time) instead of Peru. And when that was taking too long, she petitioned for expulsion since she had already done a third of her 6.8-year sentence. As typical of this screwed-up, evil justice system in Peru, they then acknowledged her translado papers on a Monday, a day before they were supposedly going to acknowledge her expulsion papers.

Sadly, translados didn't happen quickly. By the time they got around to doing the transfer, she had already served six years, four years after filing for expulsion. By the time she was transferred back home to do her time, she only had one month left of her complete sentence.

Another woman from Switzerland had already done a third of her sentence for a kilo of cocaine and petitioned for expulsion. They denied her repeatedly over the course of three years. Each time they deny you, you must wait three months before you can try again. It was nine months before they finally agreed. They had her imprisoned for three years at that point. These were the stupid games the court played, toying with people's lives without any regard.

The power of nature was also evident in my time in Peru. Earthquakes were common. One night, at about 2:45 a.m., we were all woken up by our beds shaking. While I was getting used to these quakes by now, this one went on for some time. We all panicked when it seemed not to want to stop. I believe the news said it was two minutes and eleven seconds long and registered at a 5.7 on the Richter scale. The fact that the beds were cemented into the walls and shook so violently, you knew it was strong. If there is one thing I will give Peru credit for, it is how they build. I guess they are used to the quakes, so the walls and floors are filled with a foam sealant every few feet. This way, they can withstand the swaying so as not to crack and crumble to the ground.

I also learned how powerful the sun and moon are. My husband used to tell me how the moon played a role in the tides of the water. I learned the sun had its role as well. When it was winter, the sun only came out about once a week. I've been told Peru has zero ozone layer, so no wonder it was freezing. It wasn't like cold snow back home, but sitting all day on metal or cement, a more biting frost. But when the sun came out it, it was as hot as a summer's day. It was bizarre.

Well, one day, I was with some other ladies, and we felt another quake. The one girl said, "Oh, cool. The sun will come out."

I thought she was nuts, but sure enough, two hours later, the sun came out. I have no clue how it all tied together, but I saw it happen a few times. Quakes at night didn't bring the sun in the morning, but it was still interesting.

I kept meeting more people who were scammed and pulled away from their families. Some of these women were women who, back home, were doctors, office workers, etc. Everyone assumes everyone is guilty and must pay the price for their crime, yet I'm living proof that we are not all criminals. My husband fights with me that the USA isn't that fast, and I'd have been arrested back home, too, until they did their investigation. Even if it took a while, I'd be *home* while they did so, not stuck in prison in a foreign country.

Peru is the only country that I know where even for a first-time offense, even with only 500 grams of cocaine, everyone gets high sentences—no investigation, no review, nothing. That's it. And what do they teach you in prison? To be a better person? No. They teach you to lie, steal, and survive. People are scammers, conniving, and bribing. During my first four months at Ancon II, I'd been lied to and scammed many times. People were constantly asking to borrow, all with the notion, "You will get it back in two days when my visit comes."

Well, that never happened, sadly. Even Marge from the Bible study told me that certain people were so wonderful and trustworthy, but I later learned the people on the inside are *not* the same people on the outside for a visit. Everyone on the outside (on the patio when a visitor comes) will show you who you want to see and tell you what you want to hear. On the inside, they are real, and it's all "survival of the fittest." I tried to stop being so trusting and learn a word that has always been hard for me: no. I didn't want to make enemies, but enough was enough. I learned that I would never be paid back, so I had to start saying no.

Like I said, prison teaches people to be liars, thieves, and scammers. Believe it or not, people even dated online, through newspapers, and through other people. Just in my first four months in Ancon II, I'd seen someone from the Philippines get married to a Peruvian in prison. Another girl from Lithuania got married in prison to some older man she met through the paper. People posted seeking a companion, and these women called and replied.

I can't speak for the two women who got married since they claimed to love the men. But all the other women I met only used men. The men would visit and give the women food, toiletries, and other supplies. This one girl was 29 years old and had four men providing for her. One was an INPE, and it was not allowed, but in Peru, everything is okay for a price. You pay the INPEs S/5, and they look the other way.

This one man was even 65 years old! He only had two teeth, and the girl was young enough to be his granddaughter. He said he loved her, and once she was out, they would live together. She, of course, agreed, so he could come and bring her stuff. But she told us that she would quickly return to Mexico once she was released. As cruel as it was to be using these men, the fact that a 65-year-old man was visiting a 29-year-old woman was not good either, but I didn't get involved. It wasn't my business. I was also told that many of these men want to hook up with foreigners so that they can get married and leave Peru. I guess it's not easy to just up and leave without a visa.

Girls also met others at Christmas. At Christmas, they had the men and women mingle and sit together at a mutual table from their country. Since there were many foreigners, there were people from all over the world, so you at least got to interact with men and women from your home country. You were not allowed to write or talk or communicate after that. But like always, for a few soles, INPEs looked the other way.

One of the girls had been seeing a man she met at Christmas three years ago from the US. He was Nigerian. They called each other husband and wife even though they were not legally married. He had been there for many years at that point and was well-established. He sent her clothes, food, letters, and more every day. He was not allowed to, but in this corrupt country, that meant nothing. He paid for her lawyer, fines, and more.

On top of being in prison and having to pay for everything, your sentence also included her dias multa fine and the other fine called reparation civil. Her one fine was S/1,000, then dias multa was 180 days at S/3 per day.

This girl's lawyer, who also happened to be Alex, had gotten her reparation civil fine waived, and it said so in her sentence. The expulsion could only be applied when your sentence was one-third complete and your fines were paid. She did not have much money, nor did her family, and the man, her so-called husband, was helping as best he could. She was there for five years and finally paid the lawyer and her dias multa. She only had a six-year sentence and wanted to petition for expulsion. She went to court and was excited and optimistic, but the judge said, "We need you to pay your fine."

She said it was waived and said so in the sentence. The judge shrugged and said, "Too bad. I want it paid, and you only have two weeks to come up with it, or else you'll have to complete your sentence."

She was so depressed and knew she couldn't come up with S/1,000 in two weeks. I agreed to secretly help her with half if the man could come up with the other half, which he did. Of course, there was a Peruvian holiday, as there always was, and Alex came to pay for it in two and a half weeks. He brought it to the court and paid it for her. It had been two and a half months since then, and she was still waiting for a court date to discuss if she could leave. Most people had to do their complete sentences because they didn't have money for their fines to proceed.

As corrupt as Peru is, some of the prisons charge you for a bed. On the men's side, they do that. You sleep on the floor if you don't have S/100 for a bed. You could try and complain to the Embassy, but it's your word against theirs. They would most likely believe them anyway, and the Embassy will say that they cannot get involved with the laws. The only thing all other embassies do, except the US, is provide clothes, food, toiletries, and other supplies to prisoners. I'll never understand why because I pay lots of taxes back home, but yet all they seem to do here is collect a paycheck.

It was really hard to hear when everyone on the outside tells me: "Relax, take it easy, just have patience," or how they tell me, "I heard this or that." I didn't care what they had heard. Life outside was a hundred percent different from inside, and no two jails are the same. I used to get annoyed with my husband because he always spoke to someone who knew this or that, yet they couldn't know what my days were like; they were not around. Only those with me could know. It was a whole other world there. Not even one person in jail could speak for me in Ancon II, Santa Monica, or even Virgen de Fatima.

I continued working in Taller, Costura, sewing, crocheting, and reading a book at night before bed during my four months of being in Ancon II. I was getting used to it and learning the routines. Waking up at 6 a.m., cleaning the room, and showering outside in the ice cold with ice-cold water. Given breakfast anywhere between 8–9 a.m., then Taller, Trabajo anywhere from 9 to 10:30 a.m., then lunch from 12:30 to 2:00 p.m., where lunch was either rice, chicken, potatoes, liver, lungs, etc. Then, from 2 to 4:30, back to Taller, except for visitation days where quenta was at 3:50, then dinner was at 4:30, which was either more rice, soup with chicken feet, an egg and fried potatoes or a greasy tortilla, then quenta again at 6:00, and we were up on our floors for the night. The final quenta was at 9, upon which we were locked in our rooms for the night.

On non-visitor days, quenta was 8–9 a.m. and 6–9 p.m. Sadly, nothing was ever routine or systematic. In fact, one day, I was in Taller working and forgot it was visitation day. When someone else mentioned it, I ran back to the pabellon. They never announced quenta in Taller, and there was no clock, so it was up to you to figure it all out.

Once I got back, the INPE on duty was still doing quenta, but since several of us came two minutes late (even though it was not yet 4:00 p.m. and she still wasn't done yet), she made us go outside and sweep and mop the entire prison for two hours. My sneakers were soaked, and I was filthy, cold, and wet. As with everything else, there was nothing at all that I could do about it. The US Embassy flat-out told me I had no rights, so there I was. What could I do? My only option was to grin and bear it.

In Ancon II, I had to fill out two different solicitudes and then search out the OTT to have my bed transferred to the empty bottom bed. That took three months to happen, but it made my life much easier. Then I filled out a separate solicitude to transfer my psych papers from Santa Monica to Ancon. It was so stupid. You would think they'd get their shit together and do it themselves.

Nope, I had to sit through a few hours every single Friday through group psych sessions, which appeared to me to be the stupidest excuse for psychiatry, but it was all mandatory for "benefits," so I endured it every week, only to constantly be told during quenta, "Your file is not here, so I can't include you in psych quenta."

After three months of constant pressure, the psychiatrist from Santa Monica came and brought my file with her and, with a translator, asked why I was released and got arrested again, only to be back in prison.

It was insane that this was how they all saw me. I had to explain *again* how I was never released "per se." After she left, I assumed I'd be on the psych quenta list for weekly psychiatry (which is needed for benefits, too), but nope. I could never figure them out.

A week before my four months, the psychiatrist came and, with a translator, started a file for me, asking me the same questions as always: my name, date of birth, address, all about my kids, education, jobs, then when we got to how I was married, she started asking what his salary was and about our finances.

I got annoyed and kept asking what on earth my husband's salary had to do with my being in prison. She just said it was on the form and had to be completed. Sadly, that's the story of my life in prison in Peru. I have no doubt that this was all for them to see my financial status and how much they could get from me. Even the translator, who'd been there for six years so far, told me to say that he made less per month than what he actually made because if the judges saw that, they would expect high payouts if I put in a high amount. I provided a low amount but was still annoyed they even asked.

There were so many silly rules and regulations that made no sense to me, yet as the Embassy told me, I had no rights there. All I could do was grin, bear it, and go with the flow. I kept thinking this nightmare would eventually be over. But the big question was, "When?"

In Santa Monica, it was 85 percent Peruvians and a handful of foreigners, yet it was small. Ancon II was a much bigger prison; even the rooms were four times the size of the rooms in Santa Monica. But Santa Monica was overcrowded, whereas Ancon II had fewer women. The salon alone in Santa Monica had over 160 women. There was only 130 women in *total* in Ancon. There were more men but not as many women since it *was* a men's prison.

While I enjoyed the size of the rooms, there was much I was not a fan of. For starters, we had a lot less freedom in Ancon. In Santa Monica, we could walk around all day if we weren't working. Even with work there, once they took quenta, you were free to leave and do whatever you wanted. In Ancon II, we could not. The only place you could go, if not working, was in your room, downstairs into the TV room, or what they called the "patio."

The patio was about half the size of a basketball court. It was also where you washed clothes and hung them up on the clotheslines or used the outside bathrooms that were not holes in the floor. Or showers outside, where there were four showerheads.

In Santa Monica, you could have visitors who did not have to submit a solicitude with a DNI identification number, and you could invite anyone to sit at your table with you and your guests. In Ancon, you had to submit a solicitude for any guest you expected to visit; no solicitude, they would not get in.

We also had something mandatory called *matutino* in Ancon II. This was from Monday, Wednesday, and Friday at 8 a.m. Every room had to take turns in that we had to do something in Spanish, a prayer, a reflection, something to critique, a joke, and something to unite us. It usually lasted 15–20 minutes, and it was mandatory. It was always tough when our room's turn came because I obviously couldn't speak Spanish, so I'd say it in English, and someone else would translate. All of this was mandatory and needed for benefits.

It amazed me how they felt any of this was making us better people. All people did with matutino was copy snippets from the daily newspaper, and the weekly psychiatrist prayed. None of that would ever fly back home, but as usual, what could I do? I endured everything I was supposed to do, all that was mandatory and required, including cleaning, setting up tables and chairs for visitor days, taking them down, and cleaning them in the end. I even sat outside all day in the cold on another visitor day to collect the money for the tables, which each room, again, had to rotate. I did everything.

Annie and Marge had been visiting two other women at Ancon. They had already put in solicitudes, and then I put a solicitude in. Yet, there were numerous occasions when they could not get in after having traveled very far to get to Ancon Il. For whatever silly reason, many times, either one of them or one of their colleagues could not get in. They'd have to wait outside for the one who got into being allowed to leave, which would be four hours later.

As always, nothing ever made sense to me with this whole situation. In Santa Monica, electricity stayed on all the time, and water also, unless, for whatever reason, the water was out, which happened randomly with notice. In Ancon II, it all depended on the INPEs on duty that day. Most days, the TV stayed on, plus the lights and water, unless the water went out, which happened more times than not.

On certain days, some INPEs would turn the lights and water off from 9–12 and then from 2–4. It made no sense to me. Even with the TV, they had rules. It could only play music for the first two hours, then movies, but from 4:30–5:30, it had to be TV, not music. Then, quenta was at 5:50 anyway. I never understood any of it. Both Santa Monica and Ancon II were corrupt in their own ways, allowing in drugs, knives—anything, really—for a fee. The only difference to me was Santa Monica was 99 percent Peruvian women, and Ancon was 25 percent Peruvian women, 50 percent Venezuelan, and 25 percent from other countries.

I came from Taller one day, and there was rumor of a translado. I know they did that in Santa Monica, from time to time, transferring a group of people to other prisons. The rumor was that they wanted to strictly make Ancon a male-only prison and ship the women someplace else. I just got to the bottom bed the previous month and didn't want to move again.

The rumors went rampant, saying that we would all go to Santa Monica, which made no sense to me since Santa Monica was so tiny and overcrowded as it was, so how could they put over 130 more women in there? Then, the rumors were that you'd go back to the prison you came from. Mine would be Santa Monica, many others also, and others to various other prisons. Then the rumor was Peruvians going to Santa Monica and everyone else to a different prison called Virgen de Fatima. Again, expecting to have been released by now and back home, I, of course, panicked. Plus, my psych papers finally arrived in Ancon II after four months. I had also just purchased material for Costura to make pocketbooks and more clothes.

Various women all ignored this, saying that they'd been hearing translado for years now, but it had never happened. While I was relieved and wanted to believe that, it was 50/50 with what was all being said around me. I was still a newbie, but others said they heard the officials saying the paperwork came in. Still, it wasn't signed and could take forty-five days to a year if it would be signed at all. Yet, the director told our delegado that it was only a rumor and not happening, and the INPEs claimed they knew nothing about it, so who knew?

The woman who was instructing me in Costura had been here for thirteen years. She was packing up the materials to give to a *packetera* so as not to lose them. She said *if* it didn't happen, the packetera would bring it back for her. But she wanted it out since when they said, "Go," you picked up your stuff and went. You usually couldn't take tons of bags, especially having no clue where you would be going.

I was confused and had no clue who or what to believe. I had asked Marge if she could take some of my clothes since they were mine and I could only take two bags with me. I didn't want her to take them and put them in her dresser. I wanted her to put them in my luggage, to hold them for me, since if I couldn't take them, they would then just be tossed away. She refused and stated I was a hoarder. It was unfortunate how outsiders just didn't get it. I am not as much of a hoarder as people think, yet unless they are inside the prison, they have no real clue what we go rough.

In the same way, I believed Sal when he said, "You're going home; you'll be going home soon." Yet, there I was, still in prison, three years and four months later, so why would I *not* hold on to things I would need? It's not like if I ran out of things, I could run to the store! Besides, without having family there, I could only rely on what I had whenever Marge came. So, as for being a hoarder, it really was survival of the fittest on the inside.

Marge had been visiting Ancon II for years, yet one day she had earbuds that went to her cell phone. When she went inside, she left her phone in the car as always but totally forgot she had the earbuds around her neck. That was a big no-no in Ancon II. We had earbuds for our radios in Santa Monica, but when I went to Ancon, they cut my earbuds in two, saying they were not allowed. Why? I have no idea. I was told it was because they were afraid you could record things with them.

If they had nothing to hide, why would they be concerned? Because they have way too much nonsense that they don't want people to know about. People have died in prison here, been raped, robbed, etc. They know that Embassies won't get involved with the laws there, and it was always our word against theirs, so we were screwed. When the INPE found the earbuds on Mary, they wouldn't let her in and threatened to call the police on her. They took the earbuds and made her leave.

After two weeks passed, random rumors of us being moved again were spouting, and others said that it wouldn't happen. Well, on September 5, 2019, after I had just started working in Taller, it was announced, "Pack your stuff; you are all being transferred."

To where? We had no idea.

Of course, I was annoyed because I had just bought my monthly material for Costura, and we had just paid S/40 for our dues for working the day prior. Not to mention, I had also just given S/70 to another Peruvian to have her family get my glasses with my eye exam prescription. All I could do was leave work, return to the pabellon, and start packing. When I got there, it seemed everyone there had already heard the news.

Normally, a translado was immediate. You had about twenty minutes to pack up your stuff and leave, but it was a bit different since everyone was being transferred. This all started at 9:30 a.m. on September 5th. I had just washed my sheets, pillowcase, clothes, and towel and hung them on the outside clothesline. Now what? I went to our room and started packing up my stuff into big bags. We were told that we could only bring one or two bags. Well, some female prisoners had been in jail anywhere from two to twenty years, so obviously, they had a lot of stuff. I was envisioning Santa Monica with the tiny rooms where it was so overcrowded with nowhere to put anything.

Even two big bags would be tough in Santa Monica. I had to leave behind so many things. I had just crocheted my first nice sweatshirt; it was big enough to fit me. That had to be left behind. Most of my winter clothes had to be left behind because Marge had refused to take them, and they were big and bulky and took up too much room in the bags. I had a ton of English books that people had given me, which had to be left behind for space.

I knew people who had been there for many years who either knew people on the outside or knew packeteras who they called, and INPEs let them in to take many people's belongings. I, unfortunately, had no one, so if I couldn't bring it, it would be left behind and trashed. I packed two big bags, but a third one with only my blankets, sheets, and pillows. Considering I was only in Ancon for four months, most of it was donated to me. The blanket was donated to me in Santa Monica and made its rounds to the apartment, to Ancon II, and off again to wherever they were sending me next.

As everyone was scrambling to pack everything up and somehow label it all, despite us having almost no markers or tape, we next heard *ricojo,* which meant lunch. Seriously? Apparently so.

Now, where was all our Tupperware? That was a good question. It was 12:30. We were trying to figure out which bag had our

Tupperware in it to eat. Some people found it, and others didn't. We got our food, and I was still praying my clothes on the outside clothesline would dry. When the sun didn't come out, clothes wouldn't dry for several days. In the winter, which we were still in, it was cold, humid, and rainy every day in Ancon. If the sun did come out, it would be hell-hot, and clothes would dry in hours.

Ironically, the sun was coming out. I sat with my friend from Indonesia, Dana. We ate lunch and shook our heads at this mess. She, too, had been in Santa Monica, then Ancon II. She had been in prison for the past eight years and had a lot of supplies. We ate and were waiting to be told when we'd be leaving. We walked around, not knowing what would happen. My sheets and clothes had dried, and my towel was still semi-wet, but I packed it into a plastic bag, assuming we'd leave soon.

I had called my husband right when I left Taller and returned to the pabellon to tell him that I would be moving again, from Ancon II. My husband was dealing with a big hurricane in the US that was due to hit Georgia, where his daughter was in college. It was a big hurricane, and they were evacuating most of the state because of it. He was scared for her and for me as well. I was trying not to waste money on the phone, but I called my whole family to tell them that I'd be moving and didn't know where or when I'd be able to call again.

We all brought our bags to the main floor of the prison pabellon and waited. There were so many bags. Next thing we knew, men were coming in. They were INPEs, but their uniforms read *GOES*. They were taking all our bags. All our bags, for 130 women—which was a lot of bags—were being shipped separately. That was not reassuring since I knew it would all be mixed up and lost. Besides, our foams, the so-called "mattresses," would be going with us, too. That was ridiculous, but what could we do?

Trying to write our names on our mattresses in pen wasn't the best, especially mixed in with 129 other mattresses, but we all did it. Eventually, all our stuff was gone. As time passed, they started calling our names one by one. We had to sign a *Notification De Translado* paper four times and, of course, fingerprint it. It stated your name and where you'd be going.

I was going to Virgen De Fatima de Chorrillos. It seemed we were *all* going to Fatima. I thought maybe what Marita said was true, that we'd be going to Fatima and all the Peruvians would be going to Santa Monica. I had no way to verify since we were in different pabellons. I signed my paper four times, and they gave me a copy, then told me to sit and wait. Everyone was being called up individually. I got called *again* and tried to explain that I had already signed it, but they didn't understand me. I showed them my copy, and they shrugged, telling me to sign again. Typical. No coordination, no system, just sloppy work all around.

I signed and fingerprinted *again,* then continued to wait. We heard ricojo again and knew what that meant: dinnertime. Unreal, but we were glad to be getting food since we all knew that with a transfer, it would be a while before we ate again. We ate, but we had no Tupperware since it was already taken away by the GOES INPEs. We all just ate like the savages that they treated us as. We ate rice and everything with our hands and put the food in napkins since we had no plates. It was just a typical day in the life of being incarcerated in a third-world country.

By 9 p.m., we were exhausted. Between packing and our nerves, we were tired, yet all we could do was wait. I had changed my clothes into summertime clothes since I wasn't sure if we'd be shipped in the back of the ambulance again, and I knew it was hot in there. But at this time of night, I was freezing. We couldn't even lie down since our mattresses and blankets were gone, too. I couldn't change to warmer clothes because all my clothes were gone, too. I remembered that I had three bags of winter clothes in my room that I'd left behind. Since all the rooms were open so people could use the bathrooms, I saw everything was gone when I went up to find my winter clothes. Typical. It was survival of the fittest. People saw warm clothes and took them.

I had also left the two polyester-type blankets given to me to put under the mattress to prevent the mattresses from molding again. I explained how my mattress was moldy and how another

Thai girl who was released had to give me her mattress because the INPE wouldn't let me exchange the cat pee one, so she gave me hers when she was released after nearly seven years. She also gave me the polyester-type blanket, explaining that I needed to keep it under the foam and off the cement to stop it from getting more mold on it. Even *they* were gone. Nothing was left.

Everyone was on the ground floor of the pabellon. They all lay down to sleep on the polyester–type blankets on the floor. I had no blanket or warm clothes, so I was trying to lay next to Dana and share her blanket, but it was just too cold. This ordeal went on until 3 a.m.—many of the girls slept, but I could not—when we were told to get up and get going. They handcuffed us in pairs and loaded us onto various buses. We were exhausted.

I noticed that all of us—Peruvians alike—were going to Fatima. I didn't know much about Fatima, only what others had told me, and they were there five years prior, so was it still the same or different now? I guessed we would see. As we were escorted out of Ancon II into buses, there were video cameras all videoing us. It was bad enough that my airport video of my arrest had been on the news so many times (thirteen that I had seen), Lord only knows how many other times. Now, *this* was being videoed. This was *not* how I wanted to be famous.

We went on the buses, and after about an hour, we were off. People were sitting and standing on the buses. They were crowded, as was typical. I was originally standing, but luckily, a sweet young Venezuelan let me switch so that I could sit. She then sat on the floor. The bus ride was about an hour long. I was told Fatima was about 10–15 minutes from Santa Monica. When we arrived, it was a mess. It was about 5:30 a.m. on Friday. I saw a quick opportunity to call Charlie and tell him where I was and that I had arrived safely. I quickly learned that S/ on the pay phone here only got me about forty seconds on the phone, but at least I got to tell him.

I saw the sun coming into the sky. There were so many of us all being moved around. They took our cuffs off, and then we had to wait for them to call our names. Eventually, they stopped calling names and just had us sign, after which we were moved from room to room. We were fatigued. Then, we were taken to the medical man who just asked us basic 1-2-3 questions to assess if we were on any meds. Ironically, he was the same man from Santa Monica. He remembered me. I stuck out like a sore thumb. I could not blend in, being tall, white, and blonde.

After this, we were put into their patio. There were three Movistar phones and two Claro phones. None of the regular prisoners were there. I imagine they kept them all out due to our transition. We had to sit and wait for hours. They were telling us which pabellons we would be in; A, B, C, D, or E. Everyone from my Ancon pabellon was being moved to Pabellon B. I, on the other hand, was moved to D. Only one English person was moved with me, and it was someone I wasn't the biggest fan of. Why was I not moved with everyone else? They put all the Thai people together, all the Filipinos, but I was outcasted. Unfortunately, this was my life in a Peruvian prison. At least in Santa Monica, there were a few other English-speaking people. There, it was just me and one other and she wound up not even being in my room.

There was one booth that was their kiosko. We hadn't had breakfast. So, I had to buy a banana, an orange, yogurt, and milk. Everything of ours was in our bags, which we did not have. Around 12:30, we saw them bringing us prison food. We obviously did not have our Tupperware, so I had to buy a bowl, plate, and cup from the kiosko. Since we had the phones there, I contacted my husband on the pay phones again. The phone stole S/2 from me, which I later learned was typical. At least I had about two minutes to have a quick chat and say that this prison sucked, but I was there and alive.

We sat all day, waiting for our bags. We were eventually brought up to the pabellons and shown where our rooms and beds were. Luckily, I had a bottom bunk bed. But there were fifteen other women, five of them from Ancon, who I did not like or speak with, and one of whom I never liked but dealt with. None of them spoke English anyway, so I was stuck in a room of sixteen, me being the only English-speaking person.

We were brought back downstairs again to wait. I was freezing since I still had on my summer clothes, and it was winter and cold, and I still did not have my bag to change. By around 6 p.m., they started to allow five people at a time to get our bags, starting with Pabellon A. It took hours because the bags were thrown into a huge room, mixed up, and thrown around. We had to wait for all the other pabellons to go through and find their bags first, then the INPEs had us empty each bag for them to inspect. I thought I was close to getting my bags. They also were allowing us two at a time, but Pabellons A, B, C, then D, and E to look for our mattresses. By the time I got my mattress and bags, it was almost 9 p.m.

I learned that my bags were torn open, and my thermos was missing. What's more, my blankets were filthy from my bag being open and stuff being dragged on the floor. As the INPEs were going through my stuff, their rules, as always, made no sense to me. For example, I had three ramen soups and oatmeal, which they took from me. Why? I have no idea. I had my huge scissors for Taller, which they never took. I was told they would take them if they saw them, but they missed them.

I also had a lot of shampoo sachets with me. The INPE said it was too many and went to take them, and I immediately snapped. I was a foreigner with no family here; I needed everything I had. If I was Peruvian and my family brought me things weekly, it would be different. She eventually put them back in my bag. But this was how INPEs were. Whatever they wanted, they took; case closed. They did it in Santa Monica and Ancon, too. They even did it to visitors. As they'd go through bags from visitors, they'd take whatever they wanted.

Eventually, they were done, and then I had to lug it all up to the pabellon and get organized. The other people in the room were not happy that all of us were now in their room, taking up space, but that was too bad. None of us wanted to be there either. I spent over an hour setting up the bed and unpacking. In Ancon, we had shelves to put our stuff on. In Santa Monica, we had cubes to put our stuff. There, I had a bed and a floor. The girls around me had taken over under the bed space, so they had to move their stuff to make some room for me.

They weren't happy, but neither was I. By the time it was done, one girl told me I could take a shower. I had to shower using a bucket. I quickly learned here in Fatima that we did not have a hole in the floor. We had a bathroom with one shower, one toilet, and three sinks, one for washing dishes, one for personal use, and one for laundry. While that's good, it seemed the water was only on from 6 a.m. to 7 a.m. and then off all day except from 4 p.m. to 7 p.m. After that, it was turned off. Why? As always, I had no idea, but it was annoying. They had huge barrels of water to flush the toilets and shower with buckets when needed. Then, when the water was on, you refilled the barrels.

I showered with the buckets and realized just how much colder the water was. It was so cold that it burned my scalp. The INPEs did quenta the same as Ancon and also locked us into the rooms each night. We were expected to go to bed after quenta at 9 p.m. By the time I went to sleep that night, I was out cold and slept the whole night. The full day and a half prior were totally exhausting.

I later learned that Saturday was men's visitor day and Sunday was women's. The same as Santa Monica but opposite from Ancon. On visitor days, you had to stay in the room all day; you were not allowed downstairs because that was where visitors were. You could only use the phones in the evening before quenta and only buy things you'd need from the kiasko. And only then, too, because after quenta on visitation day, you were up for the day.

Here in Fatima, each Pabellon did not interact. So, everyone I knew from my Ancon room, who were now in A, B, C, and E, I'd never see again, except for Jenny, who was in D with me. For visitors such as Marge and Annie, this was difficult. In Santa Monica, you could see whoever you called. Since we were all in a different spot and it was pabellon specific, she could only see whoever was in a specific Pabellon, not several of us at once. And only one of us, not both.

In our rooms, we were not allowed curtains around our beds for privacy either, unlike Santa Monica and Ancon. The laundry line was also an issue. It was small and locked all day. You could do laundry and hang it up from 6 to 7 a.m.; then, it was locked. After that, it was open again from 4:30 to 5:30, then locked until the next day. The towel I had washed and hung up the Wednesday prior to being told we'd be transferred had to be hastily put in a plastic bag when it wasn't fully dried. By the time I settled in Fatima, it stunk from being damp for two days. I had to wash it in Fatima; it was almost dry. But with them locking the gate, it rained all night again and got soaked and smelly once more. I could not catch a break!

What else had I learned in Fatima? Most Peruvians did not like foreigners. They tended to be rude and had no manners. I saw that even in Santa Monica. They constantly pushed and shoved. I could also wait in line for food, and they would cut right in front of me like I wasn't there. People would leave the line and say, "*Atras tu yo*," meaning, "I am after you."

When the time came, ten people cut in, saying in Spanish that they were there. I once got off the line and said, "Atras tu yo," to the woman in front of me for a whopping one minute while I grabbed my cup. When I got back, the woman tried saying to the woman who was behind me how I was in that spot, and the elderly Peruvian refused to let me back in line. That seemed to work with Peruvians but not foreigners. Also, the food servings were so tiny. Once everyone was served, you could wait in line for seconds. They'd announce *segundo* or *repetir*, which were the words for getting seconds for your food. But when I'd get there, they'd tell me there were no more seconds, yet I'd see Peruvians get them. It truly was a sickening situation. Yet, as always, there was absolutely nothing at all that I could do about it.

The other women spoke Spanish and found out things that I couldn't know. There was a library. By the time the phones stole my money and I got to talk to someone, it was S/6-S/8 for two minutes on the phone; it was absurd. Then there was a TV on our floor with only twelve seats. There were sixteen people per room with five rooms. That meant eighty people in our pabellon with only twelve seats. There were other chairs that belonged to people, but the open seats were twelve. People would claim many seats for friends or leave a blanket or sweater on it to claim it, so after quenta, when the TV came on for the evening, I'd have no seat at all and again be stuck in the room reading. Once I had a seat, yeah! I put my blanket on it and went inside to pee. When I came out, the entire chair was gone, and I found my blank on another chair's back. Of course, no one saw anything. Such was life there, unfortunately.

This was my final prison in Peru – Virgen de Fatima

CHAPTER 14

One morning at quenta, since the INPE left for a moment, the delagado made us all pledge allegiance to Peru's flag and then end it with "Viva Peru!" Unbelievable. I refused to pledge allegiance to their flag. It was bad enough that I was in prison for three US Fourth of July's and could not celebrate *my* country's Independence Day! Then, the prison director came in again to talk to us. She was not a pleasant person, and I had no idea what she was saying. But I was told that she was again telling us how Fatima was not Ancon. We had to suck it up and follow their rules. It was bad enough that they split us all up into different pabellons.

So now, when Marge and Angie came to see us, they'd have to split up. One would go to one pabellon to see one person, and another would go to another pabellon to see another. We had thought that since Jenny and I were in one pabellon, Marge or Annie could call us both out for a visit. On our first visit that day, we discovered this was not the case. They'd only allow the visitor to call one person. That stunk. Annie left and said she'd visit me the following week. Well, the director told us that day that this would not happen. Whoever the visitor saw on the first visit was who they would continue to see. This was absurd! I had already filled out my solicitude for visitors with Margie, Annie, and their colleagues. We were only allowed to put a certain number of people on the list, and once it was submitted, it couldn't be changed for six months.

Well, I didn't put any family on the list and filled it will Margie, Annie, and her peeps. If I couldn't even see two of the people on my list, I was still not allowed to change my list for six months. I was not even in Fatima a full week, and it had already proven to be the biggest nightmare of them all.

One day, I had a surprise visit from the US Embassy, who called for Tania and me by name. The true Americans whose names are never called. They surprised me. They brought another three months' supply of vitamin C, iron, and calcium. They also brought some sort of chocolate protein shake powder (this was a first) and a tiny one-time-use sample of shampoo, conditioner, and soap. Apparently, all embassies were called in to update them on all of us foreigners who were there, so that's why they came. Still, at least they called us and brought in more vitamins. I told them about how I was moved to Pabellon D while all other English people were in other pabellons and how I couldn't communicate with anyone nor understand anything at all. Still, as usual, all I was told was, "I'll make a note of it."

Embassy personnel asked for an update on my case, and I told her how supposedly Sal and Rebecca claimed they were expecting the courts to wait until the next day, Friday, to say whether they would include the house arrest. She said she'd make a note of it and follow up with Sal. I told her how Sal was trying to blame the other lawyer, Alex, for this situation, but I had several lawyers confirm that the problem had nothing to do with Alex. The problem happened before I even left Santa Monica. They all confirmed how Sal was supposed to have the house arrest documented before I left Santa Monica, and he never did, so that was the problem. However, he didn't want to take the blame or any responsibility, only pass the buck. Another lawyer, who specialized in expulsion, had been saying how Sal screwed up, and we had many emails and WhatsApp messages from Sal, all saying how it *definitely counted*. But I was still in prison after my time to file for expulsion, and I was stuck there. Sal said that if the judges didn't all agree and include it, there was nothing we could do, but he would see what happened the next day. Well, as usual, Friday came and went with no reply from the judges.

If that wasn't bad enough, my husband got an email sent to Congress via the US Embassy in Peru stating that if I didn't stop speaking with other lawyers, they couldn't help me anymore. Seriously? I had my husband barking at me about how I needed to stop talking with other lawyers and that the Embassy said this was Alex's fault. My husband swore by this again, and my mom stated how I had to stop talking to other lawyers. I was numb to my furiousness. The Embassy was in Sal's back pocket; the only information Congress ever got was from Sal or the Embassy. It didn't take a rocket scientist to see what was happening. Sal screwed up and tried to back pedal and fix it, and if he couldn't, he truly would never take the blame and only say, "It's because of Alex."

This would again fall on me, where everyone would say, "She should never have contacted another lawyer in the first place."

If Sal had done his job correctly to begin with, I would be going home, not still there trying to fix things. I had been fighting this battle for so long that I felt numb. Sal lied for over two years. He made a fortune from us, and unfortunately, I was paying the price in a country whose justice system is a damn shame. People spent countless years there, innocent people and first-time offenders; it didn't matter. Peru just kept you there to rot in jail since they made money off us.

A fellow inmate in my room was from Chile. She was sentenced to fifteen years for apparently having three kilos of ecstasy that she didn't know was planted in her bag. She was no dummy; she was very educated and wise, yet like me, she was naive and fell for a scam. It was a mistake she was paying for with fifteen years of her life. Fifteen years! She had been there four years and was fighting to be transferred back to Chile, where she would get released. She never had any issues with prison or the police. Other countries looked at that and worked with you to release you. Peru certainly didn't. All I knew was that I no longer had the strength to do another year of prison in Peru.

People all told me I was strong. I was, sure, but my strength was dwindling by the day. The emotional roller coaster I had been on for the past two and a half years had sucked the life out of me. As much as I desperately wanted to be back home with my family, kids, and grandkids, I felt like that option was slowly slipping away from me. If the judges said I had to do another thirteen months in that shithole prison, even after enduring twelve months of a horrific house arrest, I could say, when I was writing this, that I just couldn't do it anymore. I hoped someone eventually stopped these criminals from scamming innocent people and causing us to suffer countless years like this, all for crimes we are not guilty of. I would hope the US would step up and start helping us citizens since I was proof that they didn't do anything. Even the Embassy said that if I didn't stop speaking to other lawyers, they couldn't help me anymore. I found that comical since, to date, they hadn't done anything at all to help me.

I had been in Fatima for two and a half weeks with absolutely no change at all. It was sickening. My husband always hated when I said the expression, "Say what you mean and mean what you say." Well, that is the exact saying that Sal and Rebecca should have learned. They both always said things and then backpedaled from them.

In fact, the previous week, Rebecca told my family that the courts had to review the file by Friday. Six days later, when absolutely nothing had happened, my mom and husband were texting Sal asking for an update and got snippy replies like, *Nothing to report. If I had something to report, I'd tell you. Also, what do you want me to do, knock down the door and put it in front of the judge's face?*

Again, why did Rebecca say they had to review it within six days? We went off what they said, and what they said hadn't been accurate or truthful all along.

It's amazing how his replies were so different from when we were first his clients. He was so sweet and helpful when he was making a fortune off us. Once I pleaded guilty, we stopped paying him, of course, since there was nothing more to fight. And when that happened, he just became unpleasant and downright rude. As I said in Ancon II, he never came to see me even once, while other lawyers traveled several hours each way weekly to see their clients.

When I got to Fatima, he and Rebecca told my family that they'd come to see me since now I was only about a half hour away. It had been two and a half weeks, and there had been no visit at all. My wonderful neighbor from the apartment, Rosa, had come to visit me in Ancon, taking four buses there to see me, but even *she* tried and brought me fruit, snacks, toilet paper, deodorant, etc. In Fatima, she had visited me twice, bringing me money, food, and other supplies. She was truly an angel, and it was a shame how strangers had been more beneficial and kinder to me than my lawyer or embassy. Yet, as always, there was nothing at all I could do about it.

I wrote a note to my family expressing how I appreciated everything they tried to do to help me, but the reality was that they would drive themselves mad since it was obvious there was nothing they could do that would change this situation. I knew they wanted to help me. If it were me on the other side, I would be the same. But if the last two and a half years had proven something, it was that nothing was going to help.

Since that time, Sal has turned out to be the second biggest ultimate scam. All others sucked and robbed me, but the ultimate scam landed me in prison, and Sal turned out to be the ultimate scam finale. He lied since day one, telling my family how I wanted to plead innocent and then telling me that that's what my family wanted me to do, which was a lie. Then, he quoted my mom US/120k and ended up making over S/400k. He told me that we had a good case and felt confident we would win. He raved about all his contacts and connections in the courts. I've yet to see any connections that he had. Then he told me that I was going home, but I was still in Peru. He repeatedly said how house arrest definitely counted.

"Once you're out, you never go back."

This, of course, only worked out for me to be sent back to prison.

Then he said, "It'll only be for two or three months, then I'll have you out."

This time, I only got a copy of my sentence from someone else since he'd yet to give me anything. Even then, it said that the only time that had counted was eleven months in Santa Monica and that the thirteen months of house arrest did *not* count. Even in the apartment, he said it was his client's condo and that they'd rent it to me. Everyone in the condo paid S/1,500 a month, whereas I had to pay $1,500 a month, which translated to S/6,000 a month!

Plus, as depressed as I was for the thirteen months, getting told those lies made it worse. Both Rebecca and Sal constantly said how I had to stop being so negative and how house arrest counted as time served, and how when all was said and done, I'd be grateful to have been in the apartment counting as time served.

They were lies. Obviously, we didn't catch on to them right away. None of us had ever been in this situation before, and we were overwhelmed by what was happening. Not knowing Peru at all, we only had Sal to rely on, and since he was on the Embassy website and spoke English, my family thought he was the best option. Why wouldn't they?

People say to get a second opinion, but when all lawyers only speak Spanish, and they finally found one who spoke English, it was like hitting the jackpot. Plus, Sal was a good salesman. He made sure he told us everything that we wanted to hear. Did he never expect us to ever learn that he was lying? I have no idea. All I know is that the truth always surfaces eventually, and once it did, I was left paying the price for his lies while he made a fortune off my family.

Between Eric, Lisa, Timothy, MB, these loan scammers, Nigerian scammers, Sal, and the US Embassy and all that I'd gone through because of being naive, I hoped they all pay the price for all they'd done to me and everyone else they'd scammed. I could never hurt people the way these people did. I just don't have the heart to ever cause pain like that to anyone, and most of them knew my situation. Sal knew my mom's age yet had no problem taking all her money. MB knew my situation, my new grandbaby, and how I'd been robbed of all my money before, yet he didn't care. It's just sickening how some people could be so heartless; I could never be so cruel to anyone.

My guess was that Sal would drag this on for another year, blaming the situation on the slow courts, and then when one year went by, which would be me serving the one year and one month of house arrest, he'd say, "I got her released," which would again be a BS lie. I was so numb to it all. I'd been in prison for 2 ½ years for a crime I had no idea I was even committing, away from my family, kids, grandkids—two of whom I'd never even met—friends, etc. I potentially had another year ahead, all in a foreign third-world country whose ethics were nonexistent. You literally can't make this stuff up. The previous week, we had no water all evening. People used whatever was saved in the buckets to shower and wash dishes and clothes. Well, that sucked because there was no water to flush waste in the toilets. Very unhygienic. Then by morning, the water was back on, and everyone was refilling the buckets and showering again. And then the water was gone just as quickly again. Someone who'd been there a few years said in the summer, we could go days without water because everyone was using more of it.

As much as it infuriated me, what sucked was that while, yes, it was a third-world country, what was bad was that it didn't have to be. There were so many things that could have been changed and made better, but with so much corruption, it sadly will never change. The hotels I stayed at before prison were cute but had no A/ C, elevators, or anything. The last one I stayed in, the Habitat Hotel, was nice. It had A/ C, a Jacuzzi, elevators, etc., That just proved to me that these things *could be* in Peru. They just chose not to invest in them. Why do that when they could just pocket the money?

It would never get anywhere like this in a country that doesn't think in the future tense, only in the here and now. There were so many things that I saw that could/should be changed or taken into consideration, but apparently, no one thought there. Yet the buildings were constructed with foam inside many sections of the walls and floors to accommodate the numerous earthquakes. They seemed to think long-term for some things, yet not on others. When it came to money, they all just wanted to put it in their pockets and not invest it into something that would benefit them down the road. If you visited certain areas, you'd see poor homes. They are just boxes to live in. Yet, in other sections, there are gorgeous homes. Very fancy, which probably cost a nice penny in Peru. This is where the corrupt people live. Yes, there is corruption everywhere, obviously, but it is evident in Peru. I didn't know this earlier, unfortunately.

Even if you want to play fair, you can't play fair here in a corrupt country. It just doesn't work. Many women spent 10–20 years in prison for not playing the corruption game. While yes, that is sad, it's the way it is in the Peruvian justice system. My family would have paid to get me out of there, but again, who do you pay? It's not like we knew the judges or how to go about it. It's a sick game to play with people's lives, and I was in it, unfortunately.

I was in Fatima a few days shy of one month, with zero movement in my case. Sal and Rebecca supposedly submitted papers to
the court showing proof of how house arrest counted for other people, so he said. As always, we had no way to verify that. There was
another lawyer, Alberto, whom I met in Ancon. He represents many
foreigners and specialized in expulsion. I met Alberto right after the
whole Alex situation. I told him that I didn't need any more trouble.
He said house arrest counted, and Sal screwed up by not having
that written upon my leaving Santa Monica. He went on (with a
translator) to keep telling me how Sal must fight to get it corrected.
I said that I was told that Sal was. He then told me that it sounded
like he was not very good and told me not to wait too long because
Peru would drag this on forever. He said if I wanted to give Sal one
month and if nothing happened, to give him a call to step in. After
four months of nothing happening, Alberto* called me during one of
his weekly visits to the prison, where he met with all his clients. And
by the way, I had yet to be visited by any member of the Sal team.

Alberto had asked what was new, and I just told him how we
were still at a standstill and waiting. He told me my name was still
wrong on my sentencing paper and asked if Sal was working to correct that, too. I had no idea. He said Sal messed up, no one else, not
Alex (who Alberto didn't even like) or me, but Sal. Ironically, that
same day the Embassy came. I never mentioned anything. It was
the typical boilerplate visit, "Hi, anything new with your case? Any
problems? Do you need to update your confidentiality papers on who
we can disclose info to?" They handed us three months' supplies of
calcium, vitamin C, and iron and then left.

During their visit, when they asked me what was new with the
case, I mentioned how other lawyers had told me how Sal screwed
up, and my house arrest was not included, despite Sal constantly
saying that it is definitely counted. That was really all I said. How
ironic that the Embassy wrote to my mom and said that they were
contacted by another lawyer who stated that I contacted him and
asked him to represent me but that he declined because he knew
that I was already being defended and that if I don't stop approaching other lawyers, they will not be able to assist me further. What?

Are they freaking kidding me? I never approached anyone. Alberto approached *me,* and I never asked him to represent me. Since day one, he told me to fire Sal and hire him. Americans are seen as money, and they all want business. I was furious. Not to mention, what exactly had the Embassy done for me? For two and a half years, the only thing they'd done was notarize something for me. They do nothing at all for any Americans abroad. It made me embarrassed to be an American.

Even with the court, it always took our New York congressman's office to contact them. When he did, then they'd act. He told them to return my passport to me. When I asked them myself, they refused outright. Yet when Congress told them to, I had it the next day. When Congress told them to appear at my trial to show support, they showed up despite not appearing happy. It was a disgrace.

I complained to the US Embassy about how the INPE wouldn't let me go to church one day. They wouldn't let me shift around in CUNA where I could work and get paid, problems I was having with other people, how the police took all my wedding rings, my Rolex watch, bracelets, necklaces, MacBook laptop, iPad, brand-new iPhone, iPod, credit cards, $2,000, etc. that they stole it from me since they were seen selling them all. The US Embassy just replied, "Just worry about getting home." Ironically, my sentence only said that all they took from me was twenty-three credit cards, nothing else. And as stupid as that was, I did not have twenty-three credit cards. There was my wallet, library card, social security card, my kids' social security cards, medical card, dental card, and business cards. There were only four credit cards, but none of this was listed as being taken from me. The videos at the airport police station would have shown all this, yet who is checking it? A corrupt country? An embassy that is just as corrupt as they are? It was sickening! I had no more energy to keep fighting with these morons anymore

About two weeks later, Alberto came back and called me down. He asked what was new, among other things. Through a translator, I explained what the Embassy told my mom. He said he never mentioned me at all to them; I assumed so since the Embassy seemed to be in Sal's pocket, plus I said, "Other lawyers also said how Sal has

screwed up." I'm sure this was why they said that. They were pro-
tecting their nest egg. Sickening! I was told all the embassies were
evaluated for corruption, and the US Embassy ranked number one.
Wonderful! More sickening news. I told Alberto to back off because
I had no more strength to fight. He said he was a phone call away
if needed.

I was sitting down eating lunch one day, and suddenly, I felt like
I was freezing, even though it wasn't that cold. I was running a high
fever. I was shivering like crazy. Another girl had a thermometer, so
she put it under my armpit. Their measurement wasn't the same as
I am used to, but I was told it translated to 103.5 degrees. I went
to their "Topico," where they gave me one injection, which was big
enough for a horse. It hurt like hell. They also gave me two pills, but
I had no idea what they were. I went to bed and lay down shivering. I
had crazy diarrhea, too. I always had fruits, veggies, fiber, and yogurt
daily because of stomach issues. Everyone blamed it on that, but I
always eat that stuff and never had a problem before, so it was not
that.

I was lying down all day, feeling like crap. Around 10 p.m., after
the night quenta, I was asleep, and the girl next to me woke me up
to retake my temperature. I was back up to 103.5. The girls were
screaming out the window for the INPEs to come and take me to
Topico again. After thirty minutes, they shouted, "*Embajada!*" which
means "Embassy!" I guess they were saying that if they didn't help
me, I'd tell my embassy. That seemed to scale the INPEs into action.

They eventually came and got me then. The person in Topico
was asleep, so we had to knock to wake her up. She gave me another
pill, some powder that I was to mix in water, which was supposed
to rehydrate me. It tasted like salt water, but I still took it. The
next morning, I felt better, which I was surprised about, but around
12:30, I started with the chills again. My fever was bouncing around
from normal to 103.5. My poop was still total water even though I
hadn't eaten any fruit, veggies, fiber, or yogurt in two days. I even ate
a ton of nuts, which generally would constipate me, yet it did not
affect me.

I was brought back to Topico, where they gave me two more horse-sized needles. Of what? I have no clue. They also gave me two more pills and more hydrating salt stuff to mix with liters of water. It seemed whatever they gave me would help for a few hours and then stop. I had no idea what was helping. In fact, my wonderful neighbor Rosa came to visit me the day right after I limped out of Topico. I was happy. I was shivering, so she wanted me to go back up and lay down. However, she couldn't just leave. Visitors had to wait until they said "*salid*," which was when they were allowed to leave. I did not want to leave her stranded when she was nice enough to visit and bring me fruit, cereal, and snacks. Marge from Bible study was visiting too, so she eventually told me to go up and lay down and that she'd sit with Marge. I was feeling like total crap by then and agreed. I went and laid down, wrapped in blankets.

My temperature was 103.5 again. The girl with the thermometer gave me a plastic Tupperware bowl and told me to pee in it. Since the girl had a blood pressure monitor and thermometer, I thought maybe she had something to test the urine to see what was wrong with me. Since we couldn't communicate, I peed in the bowl. I was lying there, and she came and felt my forehead. Then she said she would wash me down with my pee. What? Was she being serious? I needed a translator. I had one come in, and I sadly heard her right. She said it was true that my urine would help pull the body's infection out. You can't make this stuff up. I had no strength to argue or fight, so I lay there shivering while she dipped a sponge into my pee and wiped it across my legs, arms, neck, and back. I couldn't even shower because 1) There was no water; 2) The water was ice cold, and with my fever, it would be suicide; 3) She said I couldn't.

As before, the fever disappeared for a while but returned again. This time, she took a potato, sliced it up, and soaked the slices in vinegar. This time she put the vinegar potatoes across my forehead and ears and wrapped my head like I was Arabic. Then she said to sleep. It was bad enough I was grossed out from the pee; now I smelled like a salad. By morning, I felt better, so I was in the shower by 5 a.m. before quenta. I wanted all of this off me, as ice-cold as it was. Then after quenta, I went back upstairs to change my sheets and blankets. What a relief. I didn't feel feverish but was still pooping total liquid. I tried taking it easy and lying down all day, but then I got a strange request.

I was called down and told that the prison director was calling. I ran downstairs. She was in Pabellon C, opposite me, where the girl Aley, who was from California, was. The prison director told me I could sit there and chat with her for a while if I wanted. I said okay but I thought this was beyond odd. Why me, of all people? Why did she call me down to go and chat with another English person? I complained about how they put me in a pabellon with the only one other English person who I barely spoke to, and how in my room, I was the only one who had no idea what was going on or being said because I was the only English one. As if she truly cared. Aley told me she just wanted me to have someone to talk to and that she was planning to move me to another pabellon with English speakers but that only twelve of my files came from Ancon II, so she had to wait.

Why did that not surprise us? How the hell could they send only *some* of my files? Or was it because I was only there for four months? All I knew was, as usual, I was stuck in this shithole, and there was absolutely nothing I could do about it. Sal didn't care, the Embassy was useless, so here I sat to rot. Or was the director having me sit with the other girl to chat as her way of feeling me out, to know what my deal was? Did she want to find out more about me? Did she want to hear if I really was a drug smuggler? The majority of caught drug smugglers *did* know what they were doing, but in my case, I did not. I had no idea. I sat there for a few hours.

We played Rummy. She had a few people in her pabellon who remembered me from Santa Monica who came over to talk to me, and I could only smile and nod as usual. Other people were annoyed as to why I was there and saying that I needed to leave, that I'd been there long enough, and Aley told them that the director approved it, so that shut them up, but I'm sure that didn't make me friend worthy either. I didn't even know why I was there, but I played cards. I had nothing to hide, so I spoke to Aley and chatted like normal since she was American. She'd been there 2 ½ years and confirmed how useless the Embassy had been. In Ancon, Tania, who'd been held there five years, another fellow American, always said the same, so when my family got stupid emails or BS notes saying how they were in constant contact with me and all this other crap, they believed them. Yet, I stressed all the time about how I was there. I could tell them facts and how it was pure bullshit! It was hard for them to believe me, yet as I always say, how can we *all* be wrong? Every other American said the exact same thing.

We were told on day one to fill out a form regarding what visitors we wanted on our list and that we couldn't have more than ten names and couldn't change them for six months. You needed full names, your relationship, their DNI, CE, or passport number, and we had one day to submit everything. Since we were in different pabellons now, I had to put all of Marge and Annie's people down since they'd have to split up when visiting. Plus, Rose* and two of her neighbors sometimes alternated visiting with her. I put a bunch of names down and was later told that some of Marge's and Annie's Bible associates weren't even in Peru anymore.

When I spoke with the director through Aley, she told me that I could change it. When ironically, the Embassy did tell my family (after they had the congressman tell them they wanted to speak with them about this) that they are supposed to allow us to change names every two weeks, not every six months, and that if they didn't let me change names, they'd file a complaint on the director. Not that I ever really believed that they would do this; I certainly didn't need any more trouble than I already had. I filled out a solicitude with everyone's names now, leaving no room for any family members because I had to ensure I had all of Marge's and Annie's people and Rosa and her people because they were all local and could help me as opposed to family who may or may not come for many months.

The solicitudes had to be in Spanish, of course, so I had to beg someone to help me. That usually required a fee. The girl there told me to just copy hers on the top and bottom and fill in my info in the middle. The top had the director's name, the prison name, what the solicitude was for, and the date. Then you wrote your name, where you were from, what you were arrested for, and what you wanted. The girl I copied from stated the name, then went on to say we arrived here in Fatima on September 7th. She asked me which pabellon I was in and more. I saw nothing wrong with that. Well, they gave it back to me saying that there were two different dates on it. Seriously? If they had any brains at all and read it, they'd read what it said.

It would obviously need two different dates. How stupid! So, I had to redo the solicitude, which was a long one. I just excluded the part about when I arrived. I didn't have a calendar on hand, and all the days just ran into one another while I was there, so I put September 25th as the date of the second solicitude. They *again* handed it back because it had the wrong date. It should have been the 26th. Were they fucking kidding me? I was still not feeling that great, in their idiotic prison, with no other Americas in my pabellon, and zero help from the lawyer who robbed us blind, and zero help from the US Embassy in Peru, all for a crime I had zero knowledge of. Plus, there was potentially another year now left for my sentence thanks to Sal! It truly sickened me beyond words, and my strength was running out on me faster than I could cope.

When she handed me back the solicitude, I asked, "*Que pa so?*" She pointed to the date and said today was the 26th. I said, "*En serio?*" She said, "Si." I tossed it. I crumpled up the solicitudes and said, "*Oy ve, tu pais muy muy muy estopida todo estopida.*" She was not happy, but I didn't care. She was only the delegado, no one of major importance, but I didn't care who she was. Solicitudes could only be given on certain days, so what if I had someone coming on Saturday or Sunday? They wouldn't be able to come until the next week now. So unbelievably stupid.

They celebrated birthdays once a month for whoever's birthday was that month. There was a Peruvian, that I did not get along with at all. Most Peruvians are tiny. She was huge all around. She was very tall and fat, loud and obnoxious, and took over everything. She was at an advantage because she was Peruvian and could speak the language, but if you are loud and obnoxious, they just let you have your way to shut you up. Not always, but usually. None of this worked for me. Well, that same night, they were celebrating her birthday, which, might I add, wasn't until October and this was September. I could hear the loud and obnoxious music blasting. It was so ridiculous.

Then she had a big cake and gave everyone in the room but me a piece of it. I swear, this nightmare seemed to get worse. Nothing since day one had improved. It only got worse as the days went on.

I did get a few notes from my mom and my son on Wednesday. As I said, my strength was almost empty. It was hard to continue moving forward like this. I wanted to throw my hands in the air and quit, but then I got a beautiful note from my son that melted my heart. It was mostly about how he loved me, missed me, and was proud of me for not giving up. Things like that kept me going because I had previously made up my mind to end it all there. People said that I had to stay strong for my family and kids and to see the grandbabies.

When would this end? It was not a matter of *if*, only *when*. But for me, it just never seemed to end. Another year in this shithole was more than I could bare. I'd already suffered over two years of this, away from everyone, and they were surviving without me, so it would be easy to do at that point. They'd be sad, but they'd get over it, and I'd finally be done with this nightmare. People kept saying, "You're strong. Stay strong." But my strength was at zero. I had never been a suicidal person, but with all I had endured thus far, I had no more strength to go on. I decided to end it all once and for all. I literally planned it all out on what I was going to do and how I was going to do it, but then I got this amazing note from my son. *That* was what gave me the strength to continue. I love both of my kids beyond words and am beyond grateful that, without knowing, he gave me the courage and strength to continue.

I had a bucket that I used to sit on. Within one week of being there, someone obviously either sat on it or stood on it to reach the top bed and broke it, so then I had no bucket to sit on to at least watch TV, and with only twelve chairs and everyone saving them for friends, I would never get a seat. They stole my good plastic knife to cut fruit with. They used my bed as storage. They didn't do this to anyone else's bed, only mine, the gringo. They also threw garbage in and on my bucket. I was constantly throwing it off. It was *my* bucket and not the trash. I got into it with the big one once because I threw the garbage off the bucket and threw it on the floor. It had dirty

Q-tips and all. She threw a fit and told me not to throw garbage near her bed. I was trying to say it was not mine, but she didn't care and yelled for me not to throw it near her bed. What fucking *ever*. I told her she was an asshole and to go to hell. I was done with all the bullshit. I'd been in Fatima for three weeks, and it was three weeks of hell. So yes, the thought of one more full year was more than I could bare.

Well, it didn't stop there; it just keeps getting better! It was Saturday; as always, the water turned off this morning, but I had already taken my shower, so that was good. We just assumed it would come back in like four hours or so. Well, that didn't happen. It stayed off all day and night. Everyone was annoyed. The buckets in the rooms—the ones people used to shower, wash dishes, flush the toilet, and with sixteen people using them—were all gone very fast. Now what? We all just assumed it would come on again at any moment, but that never happened. By about 7 p.m., another lady was using the toilet.

I was the next one in line. She was taking so long, and I had to pee so badly. My stomach was finally feeling better, actually for a full day. I was no longer pooping liquid. Everyone kept telling me to hurry up and go, but I couldn't go through to the bathroom since someone was already in there. Anyway, she came out after twenty minutes, and everyone told *me* to go in. To my surprise, she was pooping liquid too. That was what I encountered when I walked into the bathroom. Since she couldn't flush it, it was gross, but I also knew they'd all think it was me since I'd been sick for the past five days. They knew it because of a translator with the doctor. So now what? I walked out and tried to tell the next in line that it wasn't me, but with the language issue, it was what it was. Then, of course, the big one came in and was annoyed as usual. I could not catch a break.

The water never came on all night, so the night was very long. I had to get up throughout the night to use the already-gross bathroom, along with sixteen others, and we had hoped and assumed that the water would come on at about 5:15 a.m. At 6 a.m., there was still no water. At 6:02, I heard it come on. I grabbed my towel and soap and stuff and went running downstairs to try and grab one of the downstairs showers before any of the other 79 women tried to, assuming that with everyone now rushing to flush toilets, refill buckets, wash the dishes from the last night's dinner, etc., that it would not last long. I damn near got trampled on my way to the shower. I ran as fast as possible, but of course, there was already a line. When I told people back home about it, they heard me, but unless you were physically there, you couldn't understand the savageness of it all. People were told five minutes only for the shower, but as always, no one complained when the Peruvians took 10–15 minutes, only if *I* took more than five minutes.

I took a super-fast shower and eventually called my husband, as I told him I would. Then I had to hang up because they were serving breakfast. I had enough time to phone and grab some food, or I wouldn't be eating. I wondered how they cleaned the pots and everything and cooked all that in only thirty minutes, but I just didn't want to know some things.

I saw everyone filling buckets upon buckets and barrels. I asked, "Why?" I was told that we'd be three days with no water. Were they fucking kidding me? In the past, we had random times of no water for a few hours here and there. In the afternoon, we had many occasions of no water, where they claimed it was a broken something or other. It seemed, in reality, the INPEs would just give water when they wanted because if things were really broken, no one ever came to fix anything. In Ancon, we went many days with no water, but at least they'd give us a few hours to shower and clean our stuff, but three days? What the hell is with this country? That would never happen in the USA!

People were filling up huge barrels for the rooms, then having three people trying to lug them up a set of stairs into each room. Again, unless you were truly here seeing this, I can't do enough justice to explain just how insane it was. I, of course, only had that one bucket. I was left with a small Tupperware, so I waited in line to fill my little Tupperware, at least to brush my teeth and wash a dish. So, of course, everyone looked at me like I was insane. As always, if I were Peruvian and had family there, I'd have had someone who could bring things for these situations, but I didn't.

One day was particularly interesting. The president of Peru was all over the news. I was told it was because he had just dissolved "Congress" due to corruption. While I was impressed that someone finally stood up in trying to fix their severely broken system, I still ask, "Who dissolves their congress out of the blue—in one sweep?" *Yet another unreal thought process. No backup plan. No stand-in team.*

Peru wanted to oust the president, which shows you just how much corruption there was. I was told this could benefit prisoners since corruption was part of what kept prisoners in jail for so long. It's a money-making business for Peru. In Fatima alone, with over 5,000 women who had to pay S/40 a month to work, they made off prisoners a whopping S/200k a month. That was just for work. We also had to pay other dues for cleaning, water, lights, etc. It was a money business to arrest people. Now *if* the dissolved congress helped to release some prisoners, Lord only knows how long that would have taken and who they would have even considered worthy of this.

When I first arrived at Fatima, I was under the impression that the prison controlled the water and picked and chose when we could have some. I was told no, it was when the tank ran out. Well, after one month of my being there, it didn't take a rocket scientist to know that it was a lie. The prison director denied having control over the water. That was a lie; it was too coincidental how every day between 5–6 a.m., the water came on regardless. Every day at exactly the same time? Coincidence? Then one girl mentioned that the INPEs on duty that day were all bitches and nasty. Well, how ironic that this day we had no water all day, too. Ancon did that, too; on days when bitchy and mean INPEs were on duty, we'd have no water or electricity all day. Coincidence? Ha! We actually had water almost consistently the day prior except for two hours. I was surprised how we had water almost all day, which was a first. But like every other day, the water was cut off around 5 p.m. and not put back on until 5:15 a.m. What was the purpose of not giving us water? So we could be dirty and smelly and not be able to wash our dishes or flush our toilets? I mean, that was how they felt we should be punished? Is that what they thought it took to become better people?

That morning, I heard that Congress, which had just dissolved less than twelve hours ago, fired the president and replaced him with some woman. Normal people would say, "How can a congress that was just dissolved fire the president?" But that was Peru, the land of doing whatever you want and getting away with it if you are someone in power! So, this just highlights how corrupt Peru is. They finally had a president willing to stand up and take a stand against their corruption, only to get booted out so that their corrupt people could continue to flourish. I'm not saying the USA and other countries are totally great and not corrupt; corruption is everywhere. It was just blatantly obvious beyond words in Peru.

Yet again, Congress was still a mess. Apparently, the vice president stepped up, and a new congress was in place. Who knew how that would work since it didn't take long for new teams to be corrupt? As I mentioned, one of my judges, a first-time judge, was arrested for corruption only two months after becoming a judge.

Where I was working at that point, it was hard to do in the summer. It was out in the open, sitting at a homemade table (basically a piece of wood on two stands), but out in the open with no shade. Once the sun came out, it would be hellishly hot, and since Peru had no ozone layer, it was rough. I was expecting to have been back home already, not still stuck there with another year ahead of me. Thanks to Sal and his many lies, there I sat.

I had a killer headache one day, so at 9 p.m., after quenta, they sent me down to Topico. Ironically, the same nurse from Santa Monica was there. The docs, nurses, and INPEs rotated between the prisons. As crazy as it was, she was the same INPE, the aunt of someone who worked for Sal. After being in Fatima for a month, I saw her when I went to Topico for headache meds, and what did she say to me? "Patricia, como esta? Chocolate?"

I couldn't believe it. After all this time, she asked me if I had chocolate for her. She could go to the store and buy some, and I couldn't. Did they not get it? It seemed like everyone had their hands out there, no matter which way you looked.

The woman who ran the kiosko in my pabellon seemed to treat foreigners as ATMs. Everything just had to be way more expensive for foreigners than Peruvians. Here, they used deodorant from sachets, where you had to squeeze it on your fingers and then wipe it under your arms. I'd never seen this before going to prison in Peru. I much preferred roll-on.

Well, I noticed the Kiosko woman had a roll-on, so I asked, "Cuanto?"

She said, "S/30."

What? S/30? It shouldn't have been a penny more than S/10! Then there was the bread—wheat bread. She charged me S/9 when it shouldn't have been more than S/4. Two days later, I needed to buy more bread, and it was now S/9.50. I asked why it increased S/0.50 in two days. But all she would just tell me was S/9.50. She also had tiny, tiny peaches. I grabbed three of them, and she said, S/3. So, one sole a piece? For peaches the size of a walnut? It was unreal.

The director was told of the prices she was charging me through Aley and told me through a translator that she expected me to set up the kiosko lady. They'd give me S/ to have me buy stuff, and then they'd approach her, have her give me the S/ back, and fire her. What? So, *I* was expected to be the prison snitch? I had to live there. I didn't need that kind of trouble! Everyone would hate me. She didn't rob Peruvians, and it was mostly Peruvians there. So, the American would be the one snitching on her and getting her fired? I didn't think so.

I refused, which didn't go over well. Sadly, the director was the one in charge, and I hated pissing her off because she could make my life miserable, but I also didn't need to be the target of everyone's rage here, either. It was a no-win situation for me.

I again handed in my solicitude for the corrected visitor list for the third time. It had been over a week, and I still hadn't gotten it back yet, so again I couldn't have anyone come visit until it was processed. Were they jerking me around? Most likely, but as always, there was nothing I could do about it but wait. I was told that all my paperwork hadn't gotten here from Ancon Il. I think this was a massive confusing issue. I was eleven months in Santa Monica, then thirteen months in the apartment where there would be no file, then only four months in Ancon, so my file would only be eleven months from Santa Monica two years ago. My situation was very different from other people, and I don't think they understood, and I had no way to explain it, so as always, I just waited.

Of course, I still heard nothing from Sal. He swore that he never said that house arrest counted, which was pure BS. He told me and everyone else repeatedly that house arrest definitely counted. My husband even had an audio message from him where he said that, not to mention my entire family all had it on emails and heard him say it to them repeatedly. He and his team also said it to *me* constantly. Now he back peddled and said, "It's up to the judge."

Well, that would have been good to know before removing me from Santa Monica since, if I had just stayed in Santa Monica and not completed house arrest, I'd have been home, not still stuck in that mess. Since my mom and husband were on top of him about this, he was just ignoring them. Last we heard, they reviewed whatever proof he supposedly sent them, showing how house arrest counted for all others and asking them to reconsider my case, but that was if he even gave them this to review. Plus, all proof was Peruvians, and I am an American. I already saw how they did not like foreigners.

It'd been one month of me mentioning how the director said house arrest didn't count and how Sal followed that with, "She doesn't count," and me being stuck in Fatima.

I was shocked to get a visit from Sal on Monday. I hadn't seen him in six months, since I went back into prison. When he came, I had told him all my issues and complaints. He never took a single note, so who knew if he'd do anything about any of it. I wasn't optimistic. He tried to say this whole holdup with the courts was because of Alex again, but I nipped it right in the butt. And now he said that I was the first foreigner ever to get house arrest for a drug charge, and that set a precedence that the courts were not happy about, so because of that, they didn't want to do anything to help me. Plus, with how the judges were angry about the habeas corpus and were not looking to make my situation better, it was clear they wanted me to suffer.

My husband stated that we *all* needed to take responsibility for this because we all wanted me out on house arrest. I disagreed. While yes, I wanted out of prison, I thought I'd go home while on house arrest, not still be stuck in Peru. That was never said to me until I was granted house arrest, and my family only agreed to it because Sal assured us that it would still count as time served. Never once did he say anything different.

This entire situation continued to baffle me. I was at work (Taller) and on my way to the bathroom when I was told I needed to follow the llamadora (the person who calls you when you are being sought). I didn't even get to go to the bathroom.

Anyway, without my sweater, backpack, or anything, I was brought over to Pabellon E, where there was an outside group doing some twice-a-week "coaching" crap. It turned out to be a group of counselors. Why I was brought into this? I had no idea. My guess was that they needed to fill seats and wanted a variety of people and nationalities. It, of course, was all in Spanish, so Aley had to translate for me. All I know is it was four hours, and I still had to pee. I didn;t even have my sweater, so I was freezing. At one point, the coaches displayed some motions and then had us act out emotional things: rage, hunger, sadness, shyness, and then being sexy.

Now, why on earth were we in prison being taught to act out rage and be sexy? I had no idea. I was told I'd get a certificate at the end. I knew people who had been incarcerated for some time had a collection of certificates. I was told it looked good in your file, like you actively participated in things that could change you for the better. So, I decided to stick it out. I had no clue what or why this was considered coaching or what this was all about, but if the certificate helped me in any way, I would do it.

The cop who checked on me daily in the apartment, whose daughter spoke English, grew to like me. He knew Sal was screwing me over and how I was scammed into this mess. He knew I was not going to get into any trouble in the apartment, but he did his job and checked on me. He even drove me to a store once when I needed something. The guy felt bad that I was being thrown back in prison, but he lived near Santa Monica and Fatima. He told my family that his wife and daughter would come to visit me..

I did a solicitude to change all the names to include the cop's daughter and wife. The first time, I got the solicitude back and was told to write it neater. I then did it again but was given it back because I put the date of 9/24 and it was 9/25. I thought that was so stupid. Couldn't they just change it? You could only give solicitudes on Tuesdays and Thursdays! I redid it again and waited for two and a half weeks, and I hadn't gotten it back. On Tuesdays, Jenny and her mom came to visit me and were told that they couldn't because they were not on my list. How idiotic was this?

Now they were just fucking with me. It didn't take two and a half weeks to change names. I felt bad that these people brought me toilet paper, tea, apples, oranges, and water, and weren't even allowed in. They were able to leave the bag for me, and ironically, I got it. I would have to see if I could ask someone the next day to help me set up an appointment with the head of security and see if they could add their names. Other people had done it, but as always, what else could I do? I was told I could file a complaint against the director. But was this really the way I wanted to go? I was stuck there, and she was in charge, so I was left thinking, *Do I piss her off more than my being here does?* Never a dull moment.

Well, with a translator, I was able to get an appointment with the head of security. She was willing to add the names of the visitors but questioned why they were not added originally. People told you to add their friends so they could come and bring them in "things." I had to assure her this was not what I was doing. She told me she'd add these people, but "just this one time, I won't do this again!" Either way, it was fine. At least I got them added, as well as Marge and Annie.

Alberto, the lawyer, came in again and called for me. He visited his clients weekly in all the prisons. It was amazing how he visited weekly, as well as Alex. But Sal, on the other hand, who was paid a small fortune, hadn't come to visit at all while I was in Ancon. He came once to visit me in Fatima, only because Congress barked at the Embassy about him not visiting me, so he did. He told me he'd be back. I doubted that.

When Alberto came, he told me that my name was corrected on my sentence but that the judges declined Sal's request to count the house arrest. What? First, it was amazing that Sal wasn't telling us stuff. All he had to say was, "We're going to court every week, but nothing new to report."

Despite this, it took a lawyer who wasn't even my lawyer to tell me how he was full of shit. The judges already answered his request. I couldn't believe my ears. This had been my biggest fear from when I arrived in Ancon and was told repeatedly by everyone how house arrest did not count. I had a sick feeling that Sal lied, and I'd be paying the price. Sure enough, it would be another thirteen more months in prison, I immediately called my mom and husband and left Sal a message stating that, as they originally said, the house arrest did not count.

Sal sent a text an hour later just saying, *We heard from the judges, and they have declined our request.*

If we had not told him we already heard this, I wonder if he'd pull the same BS he pulled in Santa Monica and just dragged this on and on until a year went by. Then, when the year was up (technically the thirteen months of house arrest), he might have just claimed that *he* got me out, which would, of course, be just another one of his many lies.

My husband called Sal a coward and told him that this news deserved a phone call, not a stupid text. Sal had cut them all off. He wouldn't read texts or answer any of their messages, not from my mom or my husband. Of course, he was still blaming Alex, but I was sick of hearing that nonsense already. He refused to take any responsibility, yet this was all *his* doing. I never once begged him to put me on house arrest in Peru—not once. I begged him to go back home to *my* house; *he* was the one who put me in the apartment. My family was only receptive to it because he told us from day one that it would definitely count as time served. Now, after I suffered through thirteen months of depressive solitary confinement in an apartment in Peru where Sal charged me $1,500 a month in rent (compared to everyone else's S/1,500 a month) where I was checked on four times a day by police only to be told that that was not enough suffering, and I had to do thirteen more months in prison.

Despite all this, Sal wanted to blame everyone else and not take any responsibility whatsoever. It was typical of him at this point. He had gotten all he could from us, so he was done. Plus, trying to extort more money from my mom was a complete disgrace. He made a fortune off us. Hiring him had resulted in absolutely nothing at all aside from making the situation worse than it was. He accomplished absolutely nothing at all except robbing us blind, scamming, and lying to us. It resulted in me having to serve another thirteen months for a crime I had no idea I had committed. I was sick to my stomach over it. I hope he burns in hell for this scam.

Since Sal cut off my husband, he wanted to cut off Sal and hire Alberto—the other lawyer. I had been saying for months that I did not trust Sal with his lies, but as with everything, I guess we all had to see this for ourselves. Charlie saw how untrustworthy Sal was. Sadly, I was stuck paying the price. It was so hard with the Bible study with Marge. It was hard for me to understand why God allowed this to happen. I know I fell for the scam and had to pay the price, but I *did* pay the price. I did my time and was just being jerked around in Peru's corrupt system. So, I asked myself, *Why is God not putting an end to this already?* I paid my dues, and I suffered terribly. I was stuck in a country where I didn't speak or understand the language; it was beyond words. My kids and family were all suffering because of this. I was sick and depressed about missing my family, kids, and grandbabies, yet this nightmare just kept continuing. Why?

I even contemplated slicing my wrists on a regular basis. I was honestly just so tired and drained and had no more strength to continue this fight. Yet I begged and pleaded to God to end this once and for all. I felt like my prayers fell on deaf ears. I always read how God did things on his time, not ours, yet I had been a good person, always doing what I could to help people. Still, this nightmare continued, and I sat and wondered why. I don't understand why God continued to allow me to suffer like that, all for something he knew that I had no clue I was doing. It was not right; it wasn't fair. Sal walked free, the scammer MB and those Nigerians walked free, yet I suffered day and night. It was not right.

My husband had been going weekly to Congressman Peter King's office with his good friend. Peter's office had been the only higher power to help us at all. Unfortunately, all he could do was liaise with the Embassy, which dictated the same BS lies that Sal told. Luckily, after a few short months, even he saw this and realized that the Embassy was only talking for Sal and not doing their due justice.

They saw this but also said that I would need the Embassy when the time came for expulsion. This was when the Embassy played a role and worked. While that was all good, my husband said that was not enough. He wanted answers and no longer wanted to rely on any more BS Sal set through the Embassy since it had been nothing but lie after lie. Peter's office was reaching out to Washington, DC, over this. All I ever heard was how the US couldn't interfere with international laws, and my husband wanted answers. He wanted to hear from the courts and not from Sal as to why they were not counting the house arrest. I'm sure Peter's office was tired of my name by now. I hoped they understood our frustrations and need for answers.

Yes, unfortunately, I was found with cocaine in a bag that wasn't mine, but I had done my time, and they were still jerking me around and not allowing me to go home, and we wanted to know why. I wrote a note to Sal that I had reimbursed my mom the S/60,000 bail for house arrest and that he had to pay my fines immediately from that money and then reimburse me the remainder. I doubted he would do this. I have no doubt that this was another one of his scams to steal more money from us, but if I was stuck there another year, there was no reason he couldn't pay these fines and reimburse the rest.

He wanted S/12,000 from my mom, yet after this screwup, he had some nerve. I'm sure pressing corruption charges on him may have been the next step, but we had to see his response to my note first. My mom stated that he would be coming to visit me, but I seriously doubted it, plus I hoped that he didn't. I had zero tolerance for seeing him after his lies, causing me to spend another year in a horrific prison. I don't think it would be a pretty sight if he came here. I truly wanted to spit in his face.

My husband wanted to change lawyers to Alberto, and I felt this move was long overdue. Jenny and her mom were finally able to get in to see me. It was a pleasant surprise; they were sweethearts. They had brought me water, toilet paper, and fruit. The mom didn't know what I ate, so she said she would come the next Sunday with arroz con pollo for me. That was so sweet of them. The mom spoke no English, but Jenny was an excellent translator.

The two of us shared Sal stories. Jenny stated how her father told him from day one how he didn't understand why I was on house arrest when it didn't count, and Sal just assured him that it did. When he and Jenny tried to talk to me, Sal threatened his job, so he backed off. It seemed Sal wanted to keep everyone who could open my eyes to how corrupt he was away from me. Sadly, neither I nor my family caught on to this. We believed Sal because he was a good salesman and told us what we wanted to hear. And with none of us knowing Peru or its justice system, we, unfortunately, had no choice but to believe him, and that bit us in the ass.

I shared my stories of Sal's lies and robbery, which just sickened them. They did not have to come to see me, but they were genuinely good people and nice and knew that I was innocent and were sorry for me having to go through this. But what could we do? They knew one of the INPEs and asked her to keep an eye on me. Every shift, the INPEs changed, but at least when that one was on duty, she would keep an eye on me. That was nice of them.

CHAPTER 15

Buckets—as crazy as this country and prison were—never ceased to amaze me. When I was in Ancon II, they had issues with the water. They once went three weeks without any, and people had to rely on buckets filled with some to shower, wash dishes or clothes, wash down the hole in the floor—which was the toilet—etc.

The girl who got her freedom and left gave me her bucket since I had none. I filled it with water, and it had a lid on it. In Costura, where I worked in Taller, I made a cushion for the top. I made a nice skirt around it and a cushion for the top for me to sit on when I needed a chair.

Well, when we had the translado, where we all got shipped to Fatima, my bucket came with me with no issues. I had no problems at all. But then, after only a week or two in Fatima, I come to the room to find the top broken. I didn't have water in it in Fatima, but I was keeping bottles, yogurt, and little things in it. Besides, I was using the top to sit at night to watch TV since there were only twelve seats and many women. My room was always last at being called to go up for the evening at quenta, to be up for the night, so getting a seat was impossible. I never got one of the twelve seats since forty-five women went before me. So I used my bucket as my seat. Now, I couldn't sit on it. Of course, no one saw anything when I questioned what happened to my seat.

So now I had a broken bucket and no seat. I asked around how I might get a new cover or top to the bucket, but no one knew. Finally, someone told me that I could buy a bucket top from Gastronomia for S/5 (of course). It was a different type of bucket, though, one of the spackle bucket types. I paid S/5 for it and thought it was all settled. Well, silly of me to think that anything there would be that easy. As I went to leave Gastronomia in Taller with my bucket (that was why I had the bucket there), the INPE wouldn't let me leave with it. It was outside, near what they called the Rotunda, a circular section with the INPE desk in the middle of everything, where visitors came through. There was the director's office in one section, psychology in another, etc., so there was a camera above that section.

Well, it must have been a comical sight when the INPE tried to take the bucket from me. We got into a tug of war with it because I refused to give it up. I just paid S/5 for it, so if anything, I wanted my money back. She was telling me that buckets weren't allowed. As usual, why? I had no idea. It made no sense since every room had them to fill up water for toilets, dishes, showers, etc. I was trying to say that I did bring my bucked from Ancon that was allowed in, so what the fuck? Well, after ten minutes of fighting, we put the bucket on my chair in Taller, and I left.

One of my friends there was Peruvian who spoke Quechua and Castellano; the other was Philippino and spoke Spanish and English. They saw what was going on and planned to try to help me get the bucket to the room. They brought me to what is called El Alcaide (which just reminds me of Bin Laden, Al-Queda, but apparently, they are head of the INPEs). My Peruvian friend and the Philippino girl tried telling Alcaide that I needed the bucket because no one let me shower when the water was on and that I needed one to shower. I think they just wanted to make up a story so I could get the bucket, but they did not mean to cause trouble.

Well, that plan backfired. They called in the delegado of the pabellon and questioned why I was being treated unfairly with everyone not letting me shower, etc. The delegado happened to not only be in my room, but she slept in the bed above mine.

It looked like I was running to the head of security complaining about discrimination in my room, which couldn't be further from the truth. I just wanted my bucket to have a seat to watch TV at night. Then, on top of it, somehow, the issue with the kiosko lady came up again, and they brought the lady who ran the kiosko (in front of all of us). They were questioning why she was charging me more S/ than everyone else and if she was robbing me due to discrimination. Ironically, she did charge me more than others, but I did not need more trouble with anyone. This was becoming a bigger issue than I ever imagined. I only wanted the bucket!

The Alcaide chief allowed me to bring the bucket to the room and told the delegado that she was to announce to everyone how it was *my* bucket and mine only and that no one was to touch it, etc. I couldn't believe all this crap over me just wanting to replace the top that someone else broke. I finally had a seat to watch TV at night, TV that I could not understand anyway since I didn't speak the language.

I brought up the bucket and put the skirt around it and just kept it by my bed and left it at that. Suddenly there was the issue with the kiosko lady, who knew nothing about a bucket, only that she was called into El Alcaide's because, apparently, I was complaining about her trying to scam me, which was not at all what happened. I only wanted my bucket.

I obviously could not communicate with her due to the language barrier, but I was trying to get someone to translate to her, "I'm sorry. I had no idea what happened; I only wanted the bucket."

Obviously, it didn't look that way to her. She mentioned that we saw each other every day and questioned why I would start this kind of trouble for her. I couldn't win.

The lady was in Pabellon A, even though her kiosko was in Pabellon D, plus she strolled through Taller, so it didn't take long for that to spread how I was accusing her of robbing me. Fatima was 90 percent Peruvian, and I knew she was charging me more than them. I had seen it constantly, but it was not a fight I planned to have because it wasn't worth the trouble. Well, too late now, apparently. I just couldn't win.

Sal never did come and visit me again, nor did I expect him to. But what exactly did he do for all the money he made?

Absolutely nothing at all, unfortunately. If I did not have him as a lawyer, I'd have been home now. That is a fact. I know with Congress demanding answers, it puts the Embassy in the hot seat. Congress wanted to question Sal because he told the Embassy, who told them that house arrest counted, but we told them not to do that yet. At this point, who knew what more trouble he could make for me while I was still there?

We did want answers as to why the judges denied it. Why did they deny it? If it's because they didn't want to set a precedence or they didn't like Sal or me, that wasn't okay. That was when I was told by the US Congress that the Embassy could step up. We were told to wait two or three weeks for a reply. The Embassy would have to say their Golden Child lied. He did not request it. If that was the case, there wasn't a thing anyone could do about it. But if he *did*, the Embassy would have to inquire from the courts, "Why exactly are you refusing it?"

The Embassy does not like to work. I witnessed that with my own eyes, so now they were in a tough spot.

We know that Sal *did* request it, but he requested it *after the fact* and not before. He should have been at my sentencing and stated it then, but he never even showed up. I fought with my husband the other day over this, where he said that Sal was negotiating this with the judges when the other lawyer, Alex, stepped in, and that was when the judges just said no, it didn't count! I didn't believe that at all, and all we had to go on was what Sal said. I can count on one hand how many times he has been honest.

I know my husband was annoyed with Sal and wanted to go with another lawyer at this point, but it still didn't help the fact that I was stuck here another year, and putting the blame on Alex and not Sal, where the blame belonged, was wrong. It was back to his BS, saying, "I would have had this done already if she didn't go to Alex in the first place."

That was pure BS. This should have all been negotiated *before the fact* and not after. They all thought it was okay to blame me. As I always said, if I intentionally went there to smuggle drugs and got caught, I would have accepted the blame and taken all the crap that I got, but I did not. I went assuming it was a business trip and fell for a scam.

Yes, this trip came only one year after the accident, when my mind was not completely perfect, but it had now been two and a half years after that event. I was improving daily and getting better.

I didn't speak Spanish and couldn't communicate with anyone, so when I did get to call home, it was nice to chat and vent about things. But when I fought, it brought me down even more.

One day I get the strangest scenario. It was after the end of day quenta when we were brought up for the night. We were all watching television when I was approached by an INPE and told to follow her. Why? I had no idea. I followed the INPE, not knowing where I was going. Turns out, I had to go to El Alcaide. I immediately used my Spanglish and said I needed a translator since I didn't know what that was about. They told me they just wanted my lawyer's telephone number, claiming to be old school friends of his. They obviously could have simply checked my file to get that, since his information would have been in it. I gave them his number and they sent me away. Of course, it looked bad for me again to have been called by El Alcaide late in the evening. It made me look like a prison rat or something. My husband and Jenny seemed to think that this was Sal flexing his muscles, showing off, and telling me, "Go ahead and mess with me because I know people inside there that can mess with you right back."

I had no clue what that was about, but how much worse could he possibly have made things?

Jenny and her mom had come again and brought me arroz con pollo, fruits and veggies, water, and toilet paper. They were true gems. They said we were family and that they would stay by my side throughout all of this. Rosa continued to see me weekly, too, bringing me fruit and such. While many people looked at me like a foreigner who came to Peru for trouble— and so I got what I deserved—there *were* good people who cared about victims. Rosa, Jenny, and the family were proof. They didn't have to be nice to me or help me in any way, but they had been angels to me, and I was beyond grateful.

Finally, Sal wrote to my family after Charlie wrote to him and called him several times. My mom told him about the letter (where I said I paid my mom back and how I wanted the fines and the remainder reimbursed to me so as not to have him rob us more by making my mom pay more), but he claimed he never got the email.

It was convenient how he got all the other emails. However, he called saying how he was sorry she felt disappointed and that he did, too. He also said that the house arrest should have counted, but he did not have the final say. Instead, I got, "What other lawyer would have sent someone to see his client weekly and bring her food and necessities?"

Pure BS, mind you. There were other lawyers that visited their clients weekly, bringing them necessities and food. He was not the only one.

This nightmare kept getting worse and did not want to end.

I would think, *Maybe this is God's way of teaching me something.*

I wondered if that was what he was trying to teach me: to appreciate what you have and not what you want. It was hard to know. I fell for a scam in which I believed I was being enlisted in an IMF program for entrepreneurs where they gave funding to help you and your business. Yet I *did* have a successful business.

Instead of appreciating my current situation, I was trying to make it better. My family hired a lawyer who robbed us blind and made my situation worse than what it was and what it would have been without him. Why? What lesson was that? Was it the lesson to follow God and trust that He will see us through this and not put all our faith and trust in some lawyer we didn't even know? Another thing we might never know the answer to.

Then I was bounced from Santa Monica, the apartment, Ancon, and Fatima while on an emotional roller coaster for over two years. At first, it was all:"You're going home soon; we're working on your case every day."

"I have connections with the courts; we have an awesome defense."

"Once you're out, you never go back."

"This will be your last Thanksgiving in Peru. You're going home soon and will never spend another holiday here."

"You only have to go back for two or three more months, and then you will be going home."

The lies went on and on and on, and my emotions went back and forth to such extremes that I was fully drained and had no strength left anymore. I struggled, asking myself, *Why? I am a good person who goes above and beyond to always help others. Why is God doing this to me?*

At that point I had spent twelve months in prison, four months in Ancon, and two so far at Fatima. It was about to be Thanksgiving in two more days. It was my third one away from home.

Back in Taller, it was small inside and so overcrowded. It was hard to work like this, but I was out of the sun, and I was grateful for that. Now, Desiree*, who got us inside, was going back to working in Cosmetología, where she was in Ancon, doing hair. She was trying to get me moved back into Costura in Fatima. One other girl in there, who was from Thailand, came with us from Ancon. She was trying to discourage me from moving into Costura (she was in there herself). She was telling me it would be crowded and boring, yet it was crowded and boring where I already was. I felt she was trying to discourage me from going in there, and I couldn't help but wonder if this was one of the many signs from above that I usually never noticed until after the fact—after it hit me in the booty.

Desiree was the one who got me out of the sun. She had been helping me make bags and purses in Taller, get material and machines and stuff, and she was trying to get back into Cosmetología and get me into Costura. *So, do I follow that lead or listen to the Thai girl in there telling me not to do it? I have no idea. I guess I'll find out soon enough.*

Unfortunately, if I did go to Costura and then found it hard, I could definitely go back to Manualedades after a month. The only problem was that I'd be outside in the sun since I'd lose my inside seat seconds after I left it, and it would be right smack in the middle of the summer.

I hated these situations. So often, I never saw signs until after the fact, and by then, it was too late. I wish God would just tell me instead of playing games like this, but I had to be grateful. As I said, I felt like every time I complained about something, something worse was shown to me.

Everyone was talking about Christmas, even on the television. And, of course, I was sad to be missing yet another Christmas, New Year's, birthday, anniversary, etc. It broke my heart that my grandbabies would be enjoying Christmas, and I wouldn't be there for any of it again. It was hard to be grateful for things in this situation, but I sure was trying.

Perhaps I was meant to see just how little others had and how they struggled every day; where back home, we decorate the houses with lights, drive around in our cars to view all the beautiful homes decorated for Christmas, get tons of gifts for family and friends and have a nice feast together. Maybe I was to see how others were not as fortunate and to appreciate how we are able to do such? I have no idea.

Yes, we were not technically poor, although I did lose a small fortune due to all the scams I fell for after the accident. My mom had lost a fortune on this lying lawyer (which would have been my inheritance, but sadly, all went down the drain in this Peru mess). Plus, there was the money that *I* had lost on this lawyer for the apartment for house arrest.

So, when I get to go back home, am I meant to be poor and lose my business so I can suffer like others? I can't understand what lesson or message I should get from this nightmare. My husband had to handle things on his own while I was away. Yes, I was continuing to help financially with my sister and my business, but it was not the same.

Again, I was just trying to make sense of everything because that was all I could do. When I complained about something, I was shown something worse, but I didn't know. None of this seemed right or fair to me. I was not a criminal; I was not a drug smuggler. In the US, they would have investigated, and I'd have been home ASAP. Yet, in Peru, I was stuck. And thanks to the shady lawyer, I was stuck for another year on top of the two and a half years I'd already spent. I'd already done it. It just sickened me that those scams happened and innocent people like me were made to deal with them, but as usual, there was nothing I could do about it.

Charlie stated we all needed to take some blame and responsibility for this mess. Yes, I fell for the scam, took the bait, and wound up with luggage containing 2.5 kilos of cocaine. My only defense was that this was two and a half years ago, which was only twelve months since my accident, and my brain was still not thinking straight.

It's still not at 100 percent, but it is way better than what it was two and a half years ago. If you asked me to take a random suitcase now, I'd say, "No way," but two and half years ago, I could not see this. The brain repairs daily, so yes, I take full responsibility for what got me into this, but I could only state how I was unaware of what I was doing. I still blame Sal for me not going home until another year later now because he misled us into believing the house arrest definitely counted. He never once said that it was never definite, that it had to unanimously be agreed upon by three judges, one of whom he filed a habeas corpus on. But anyway, enough talking about that because all it does is sicken and infuriate me, and at the end of the day, there was nothing I could do about it.

In Fatima, a girl was rushed to the hospital with kidney failure. Apparently, she had been trying to get to the doctor for two years with no luck, and her kidney failed. To top it off, the pabellon had to donate S/300 for her hospital. Truly ridiculous. Another girl fell and broke her foot. She was told that if she wanted an X-ray, she'd have to go to the hospital and pay S/200, which we again donated. I was told another girl from Thailand had been complaining of bad stomach pain when in Ancon for a little over two years with no care. They filled out solicitudes and embassies (not US, of course) to get her to a hospital, only to find out she had stomach cancer that was so far advanced by that point that she died, and yet she only had five more months to go to complete her sentence and go home. It was sickening how they genuinely didn't care about you there.

I had been in Fatima for three months, trying to get migraine and cholesterol medicine, but with no luck at all. I was told they couldn't give me cholesterol medicine without blood work, which they couldn't do. For the migraine meds, I was originally given meds that I was told were for gout, which I didn't have.

A month later, with me still trying to get meds, I was given meds that I was told were for high blood pressure, which I didn't have. After two months, with no luck, I asked for a prescription for meds I'd ask someone to get for me from the outside. They gave me a prescription for pills that were no longer in existence. They apparently had been off the market for years.

I continued trying to get migraine meds, which was insane. You had to put your name on a list to see the doctor only on Fridays, and then they only accepted two people. So, more often than not, the list was full, and you couldn't get on the list for weeks. And when I did manage to get on the list, for whatever reason, I didn't get called; it was insane. I'd be dead if I had a life-threatening illness and got this treatment.

I had finally gotten a prescription for real migraine meds, three months later, and also a prescription for Centrum Silver one-a-day vitamins since the US Embassy only brought a two-month supply of calcium, iron, and vitamin C. Yet, they only came every 6–12 months, which was ridiculous. I had to ask Marge and Rosa if they could get me the migraine meds and vitamins and bring them to the prison for me. They went to several Inkafarmas and found the migraine meds, but it seemed Centrum was not something they could find there, so I went back to the drawing board for vitamins. Rosa got me a name of vitamins they sold, so it was just a matter of getting me a new prescription. Deja vu!

As Christmas was approaching, they were decorating massively. It was so depressing. I thought I would have been home for the first Christmas after my arrest, yet this would be my third Christmas. After pleading guilty and getting sentenced, I was led to believe that I would be going home on August 10, 2019, not another thirteen months more! So apparently, in Fatima, with the five pabellons A, B, C, D, and E, they had some competition between all in terms of decorating and via a performance. I was originally asked to sing in English, but I felt that if it didn't assist me with my benefits "in a release," then why should I bother? So, I said no. Then Dec 2nd, I heard my name from a group and finally asked what that was about. Apparently, I was put on the list to sing a Christmas song in English. What? The Russian woman was singing along with me in English and everyone else in Spanish. Not only was there a performance, but the prison director, along with several other high-end people from inside and outside, were attending. Plus, the prison psychologists (which you need for "benefits") were all going to each pabellon to inspect and evaluate them all.

We were told that the rooms had to be immaculate, that the beds had to have nothing on them aside from your blanket with a pillow, no clothes or food on anything, and that everything you had had to be under the beds. Well, the beds were small, and we only had half the space under the bed (half for you both in the bunk bed). There was not much room to hold all our clothes, Tupperware, shower baskets, etc. It was summer. Our winter clothes took up space. They didn't care. Most Peruvians sent their seasonal clothes back home to family to store off-season. Who did we extranjeras (foreigners) have? They said that we could put them in a bag with our names and that head of security would store our stuff for us. Yeah right! I didn't trust a soul in this country. I didn't have much, but whatever I did have was all I needed, so I had to smoosh all that I had deep and far under the bed as best I could.

As for me "performing," what on earth would I sing? I hadn't sung Christmas carols in over thirty years! The only song I could remember was Rudolph the Red-Nosed Reindeer. They technically wouldn't understand me anyway if I didn't know all the words, but being the perfectionist I am, I wanted to sing it right. Well, that Thursday night, each group had to stay downstairs to practice after Quenta. My room (#3) was hardly ever getting called upstairs first at 6 p.m. for quenta, so getting a seat for TV (12 seats/80 women in the pabellon) was almost impossible. Yet this night, my pabellon was called up for quenta first, so I luckily got a seat with no problem, only to get told that I had to go back downstairs to practice. It was so silly. I had to sit through two hours of watching them all practice and then a quick five minutes of singing, of which no one understood a word I was saying anyway.

I was told the next day that I, along with a Russian woman and a Peruvian woman, would walk our guests around the "patio" and show them our Christmas decorations. We would explain in our native language what each was—a nativity scene, Christmas gifts, Santa Clause, reindeer, and a Christmas tree. As rude as they were, I could see the disinterest in all I was saying on their faces. Whoever these folks were, they didn't care at all what I was saying because they didn't understand me, but nonetheless, I did as requested and said what each was, even when right in the middle of it, they walked away from me to go eat. Rude is an understatement, but I did it anyway.

After this, we went to the rooms where the director and the entourage group came and went from room to room to inspect. I went to my room along with the others, and as we were standing there waiting, we heard the room before us singing Christmas songs (to impress the group so they could win the contest).

Quickly, they said in Spanish for me to sing the song I was singing in the performance. What? And as this was told to me, the director and her entourage came in. So, there I went, "Rudolph, the red-nosed reindeer, had a very shiny nose." It was insane since they had no idea what I was saying (and with singing, I tried to animate it as best I could), then they glanced around the room and left. Next I was to sing the same song again to the same group of people that I just sang it to downstairs for the actual performance. The director and her entourage were also in front of pabellons A, B, C, D, and E! Oh, brother! So, we all went to Pabellon A, which has the biggest patio, where we sat, according to pabellons.

Each group went up to do their things, then our group, Pabellon D, had to go. A Black Spanish Santa Claus prisoner introduced me to the group as a United States woman in English. I did my best animating Rudolph—*again!* After my stunt, I left it to the rest of them to do their performances. I snuck off the side to my chair since I was never included in the rest of the performance anyway due to the language barrier. When each pabellon finished, the director got up and said some announcements and the psychologist did as well. Then we were finished and ushered back to our respective pabellons for lunch and then worked as if nothing happened. I was just glad that it was all over. That evening, I told the Russian woman I was glad that it was finally over. She also spoke and understood Spanish due to her many years imprisoned in Peru.

She replied to me, "Not quite; we have to do this all over again on Tuesday."

I asked what she was talking about, and she told me that was what the director's announcement was about. We had to redo the entire thing again on Tuesday, and this time some Peru television show would be filming it. This nightmare just did not want to end! I never intended even to be a part of this, yet somehow got thrown into it, and now, not only did I have to endure this whole fiasco once, but now twice. Plus, they'd be filmed doing it!

I was told that it looked good to the director that I was trying to fit in and cooperate (participate in things), yet this was *so* not my life back home! This is not how I ever expected to be "recognized." I had been on the Peru television show *Alerta Aeropuerto*, where they showed people caught at the airport trying to smuggle drugs. It was thirteen times I had known about it. Lord only knows how many actual times in the past nearly three+ years. Thirteen times *I* knew of. I was told it was because I was an American, and it looked good for them to catch Americans. Innocent or not, they didn't care. I've also been on *Locked up Abroad* and *Beta-A* news, where they interviewed me about this whole fiasco when I was still fighting my innocence. This would be my fourth time on TV over this ridiculous mess. Again, this was not how I ever wanted to be showcased.

It was now Friday the 13th, which made this seem even more appropriate.

CHAPTER 16

My one English friend was finally released the day before, 12/20. I was very happy for her. Like me, she was innocent. She was from Mexico, yet she was a US citizen and could attest to how the US Embassy had done nothing to assist. Her situation wasn't a drug accusation, but she still endured six months of imprisonment for a crime she did not commit. She was in Ancon and then moved to Fatima.

On a Sunday women's visit day, 12/22, they had a massive fiesta for all the kids who came to visit their moms/grandma/aunts/etc. I had to stay upstairs all day, as always, because I did not have a visitor. Some of the girls put on Papa Smurf, Smurfette, Elf, and Christmas tree costumes and danced and sang all day for the kids. They had cookies and candies, as usual. I went down only once to use the phone, but it was so loud. They had music blasting and kids everywhere, so it was hard to hear anything on the phone, but it was okay. It looked cute. But of course, with so many Peruvian visitors, they ran out of chairs, so they came and took the chairs upstairs that we used to watch TV.

Christmas Eve was the holiday Peruvians celebrated, whereas, in the US, we celebrated it on the 25th. Well, on the 24th, we were told that people could come and drop off real food for people; no visit, but they could drop off the food in packages. Then we'd have quenta at 6 p.m., but we could eat with our friends, and at 9 p.m., it would be quenta as usual, but within an instant of them turning off the light, they said we could hang out until midnight. They also said that we could go back down after 6 p.m. quenta in groups of five people and use the phone for seven minutes. I was the first person on the line to go down and use the phone, so imagine how annoyed I was when a Mexican girl ran past me and grabbed the one available phone. She was a girl from my room. I told her that was bullshit, and she said, "Extranjera" (foreigner).

So, I replied, "What the fuck? I'm Peruvian."

I got to call my mom, and I could hear that she was sad, so I did my best to cheer her up and tried to sound positive. "Only eight and a half more months, and I'll be home. We can count down soon." But deep down inside, I was equally sad. This was now my third Christmas in Peru, away from my family. My mom wanted to write a WhatsApp message to Sal and tell him how she hoped he felt bad enjoying Christmas while I was rotting in prison for my third one, thanks to him, but she didn't do it. We were just playing nice for the time being and not attacking him the way we all wanted to because we didn't trust that he didn't have some connections to make my life more miserable.

There was no water all Christmas day. We got water the next day. On Thursday, December 26th, they had a semi-party at "Taller." It was only in the afternoon for about an hour, and it involved a ribbon-cutting ceremony of some sort right smack in the middle of where everyone worked. They built a metal section (I wasn't sure what it was for, whether Costura or what, but we all had to donate S/5 for them to buy stuff to make baskets that would be raffled off).

There were guests in for it and cameras, plus the prison director was there. She was the one who was to cut the ribbon and do the raffle. As I've seen before, she seemed to believe that having foreigners there looked good for her, which was why the Russian woman and I were singled out for Christmas too. Well, either it was a total coincidence, or it would look good for the camera, I'll never know, but "Baronowski" was the first name called for the raffle.

I was also chased down beforehand to make sure I had my ticket, so again, coincidence? I doubt it, but we'll never know! Anyway, they called my name. I took my "basket" (which was stuff really put in a cardboard box, no actual basket), shook hands with the director, and smiled for a photo. It contained milk, soup, shampoo, toilet paper, tea, sugar, toothpaste, a toothbrush, gelatin, and crackers. I gave it all away to people who I knew had no visitors there. It was the least

I could do. It was nice to receive a gift to be able to share it with people.

On Friday, I got to go to the doctor and dentist in prison. All I needed was for the doctor to check and see why my right hand and arm kept going numb. A woman from Thailand, who was a doctor in her country, said it was cholesterol and that I'd need to get cholesterol meds. I took meds for that back home, but when I mentioned that to them here in Peru, they apparently didn't care. I mentioned it to the Embassy, how I needed this medication since it was genetically high cholesterol and how my family suffered from heart attacks and such.

My cousin even died of a stroke at age 40, so it was important that I took care of it, but almost three years into this, they didn't care. The Thai woman pushed for me, and I was told that for me to get cholesterol medicine, I'd need to get blood work that would cost me S/50. Unreal.

I said, "No problem," and then got told to come back the following week.

Thank God I was not dealing with a life-or-death situation. Ironically, I had been asking for the cholesterol meds for years now and always got told that they didn't have the capability to do the blood work. The Thai woman told me, "For money, they will do anything." And sure enough, for S/50, they would do it. You couldn't make this stuff up.

I then went to the dentist, and he told me, "No, it's one or the other, not both [dentist and doctor]," which was absurd! I insisted on needing the dentist. I mean, really—I couldn't see a doctor *and* a dentist? Why? Because I wasn't Peruvian?

Before and during my sentence, I got permission to go to a dentist. I had two teeth removed from prior root canals, and now, there was a bridge before and after the gap filling the gap. The bridge was loose. I was told by the outside dentist that the one tooth holding the bridge was almost gone and that they did need to pull the bridge and then do implants. While I would have loved to have done that there, since that was actually a good, decent dentist, and it would certainly have been cheaper for me, I just didn't have time. I had to go to court in five days.

So, I just left and figured I'd deal with it once I got back home and that it would be quick. After my sentence and Sal guaranteeing me that the house arrest counted as time served, he assured me I'd be home in three or four months, at most. I chewed my food on the other side of my mouth and figured I'd deal with the bridge issue once I got home.

Well, now, several months later, it was obviously not the same. Plus, I still had eight more months to go. My gums were swollen, and it hurt to chew on that side, so I had no choice but to go get it taken care of in the prison. The dentist seemed annoyed to have to be working. He gave me an injection, and my face instantly became numb, but I felt my tooth. I tried to tell him this, but he was ignoring me. I tried calling him, saying, "Doctora? Doctora?"

He would just look up and walk away. I was trying to ask him, but all I got in return was ignored, so I gave up. He then tried to do something with my tooth, and obviously, I felt it. He huffed and gave me another injection. *Sorry to have made you do your job; that's what you're here for!*

My face was numb again, but I could still feel my teeth. However, trying to tell him that was pointless since he didn't care. Again, he tried to do something with my tooth and I could feel it. He was telling me, "*tranquila*" (relax) but fuck that. My tooth was not numb at all. He was obviously a sucky dentist.

After grumbling again, he gave me a third injection in the back of my jaw past my molars. After ten minutes, he went in to remove the bridge. It was not easy, but it eventually came out. With it, two screws also came out. The screws were on one side (where my molar was), so whether they were in my jaw or a tooth, I have no idea. I had no way to see or know this since they didn't have X-ray machines here. He eventually pulled out the stump, the smaller of them. But the bigger one, again, I don't know if there was still a stump stuck in there after the bridge came out or if the bridge took it out with it. All I knew was that my mouth was so sore. They didn't stitch anything up or give me antibiotics to prevent infection or anything.

Between the three injections, having the bridge removed (which was either nailed into my jaw or nailed into a tooth stump either yanked or still stuck under in my gum) or removing the one tooth that seemed to be giving me the problem in the first place, I have no idea what they did. All I know is I was sore. My mom told me to rinse it with salt and water to keep it clean, but of course, the kiosko didn't have any salt. It just never ended. I would give it a few days and see how it felt, I guess.

One day, at quenta, the delegado announced that the director of Fatima said that as of Jan 1, there'd be no more smoking. Even the kiosko was no longer allowed to sell cigarettes; if you got caught smoking, you would be sent to Waco (the Hole). I don't smoke, so I didn't care, but wow! How could they do that? There was no law that said that you couldn't smoke. Plus, it was the biggest stress relief for people in that mess. I didn't know how this would work out, but it would be a big mess. As always, what could we do about it? Nothing. This would be interesting.

Well, my tooth had been in agony. I could actually now feel half my molar still in there. Apparently, this crappy dentist, who pulled off the bridge and then pulled out the one tooth that the bridge was attached to, never pulled the molar tooth, to which the screws were attached, so that explained why I had been in agony. The tooth he pulled felt okay, but the back one, with half a tooth still stuck under the gum, was killing me. It had been four days. I went to the doctor as an "emergency" on Saturday evening because I was already out of the medicine the dentist gave me (their version of Tylenol), which wasn't that strong. He'd only given me enough for two days at the most.

The doctor there was not pleasant. The INPE tried to explain that I didn't speak Spanish. From what I understood, she was ranting about how when she went to the US, she had to speak our language, so I just needed to learn hers. Whatever! Then, she asked me if I was allergic to anything. I said penicillin. She laughed and said in Spanish, "How funny would it be if I gave her penicillin since she doesn't understand anyway? Hahaha!"

Little did she know, I did understand! Then she gave me an injection I had no idea about. All she said was that it was not penicillin! Well, that night, my tooth was killing me. Whatever she gave me did absolutely nothing at all for the pain. Luckily, someone else gave me a pain med from the pabellon. That got me through the night. I was still in pain, but not as extreme.

The next day, my tooth was still in agony. I went back to the doctor, and the same woman was there. She was saying, "Oh, well, the injection is twenty-four hours, so I can't give you another." I tried explaining how it did absolutely nothing at all for me anyway. She then gave me two pills and told me to get out. Unreal! I took the two pills immediately; as always, it didn't do much, but it helped a little.

By Monday, I was supposed to be called to the doctors for them to do the blood work for my cholesterol and to find out why my hand kept going numb all day/night. As mentioned, you had to be on a list, which I was. I waited all day to see the doc and planned to also ask for more pain meds and to see when the dentist could look and fix my tooth still. Of course, as usual, I was never called by the doc.

I was told, "He's busy. Maybe tomorrow." It never ends!

So, that night, as an emergency again, the INPE let me go to the doctor again. This time, a different nurse was there (the same nurse from Santa Monica with the chocolate issue). She gave me another injection, told me to come back again tomorrow, and pulled my file out so it would be there immediately. Whatever injection she gave me left a huge hole in my butt, bleeding like crazy. It soaked through two entire cotton balls, my shorts, and my underwear. But, on the flip side, it helped with the pain, so for that, I was grateful. That night I got a seat to watch TV, and all of a sudden, they called me in for a "reunion" group meeting in the room.

As I got up to go to the room, someone threw half a lime on the floor. I slipped on it and fell, scraping my knee. There were such inconsiderate pigs. I brushed myself off and hobbled to my room. I had a sore butt and, now, a sore knee. I was filthy from slipping on the floor. The reunion was for New Year's Eve. We could all (total pabellon) have food brought in from outside for us to eat dinner. It would cost us each S/8.

Apparently, it would be more, but they'd use money from the "pot" from visitors' fees and stuff.

I asked, "But what is the food?"

It was some pork dishes, rice, and salad. I didn't want to pay for pork, which I don't eat, a salad I could make myself, and rice. But if I could get chicken, I would. They grumbled and agreed. Well, later that night, we were told, "Wait, you can't pay the remaining out of the 'pot' because you still have things you have to pay for, for the pabellon." So, now it was two hours later, yelling and screaming.

Now there would be no food. Then, back in the room, one woman complained that someone had gone into her bag and stolen three packs of toilet paper, and another girl said someone stole her yogurt. I, as well as many others, had toilet paper in packs on our beds, and no one seemed to take it. I had yogurt right under my bed, and it was always there. So that Tuesday, New Year's Eve, the psychologists were involved in the missing stuff. Their solution was to lock our door while we were all at work, and they would reopen it once we took a break for lunch or after the day. This was interesting. They tried this in SM, too, and it would take an hour or two for the INPEs to reopen the doors. They were usually busy chatting and didn't want to be interrupted.

New Year's Eve was another shitshow. I didn't get those people. It was another day when people, families, and friends could bring food (no visits, just drop off food). So, the women who fed me and the other women on Christmas Eve fed us again. Her husband dropped off KFC, so that was a nice treat. We got to go down and make another phone call after 6 p.m.

I ran down and called my mom and husband to wish them a Happy New Year. Then, I went back up, and it seemed everyone was all dolled up (in their best prison clothes) in dresses—nothing fancy, but still their best shoes, makeup, etc.

I don't get it. Who are they all dolled up for? One another? It's just plain silly to me. We are locked upstairs, and they feel the need to be pretty. They had music on the TV and were dancing around. Then they gave out hats, whistles, and horns and had a piñata. For real?

They made so much noise, and dancing around the tiny space was ridiculous. So, I lay down in bed and read books. At 9 p.m. quenta, we were told we could stay awake until midnight. (You gotta love being given a bedtime. I was almost 51 years old!) But anyway, I figured I'd stay awake a few moments more to read. But no one else cared because, unlike Christmas Eve, when they nicely asked me if they could turn the lights out, this night, they never even asked.

Instead, they just turned the light out with me in the middle of reading. I could only shake my head. This was the shit I dealt with every day. I lay down to sleep while they left only the bathroom light on and danced to a loud radio. It was so stupid how they acted and looked. But anyway, just another day. By about 10:30, they were winding down and going to sleep.

At midnight, the fireworks went off again. I was up at 5 to shower while everyone else stayed sleeping. I actually called my husband again. We spoke for about forty minutes since no one else was there to use the phones. I tried to be positive that it was now 2020 and I would be home this year.

I could only hope and pray for that to be true. The 75-year-old American man filed his papers in November for his benefits, and we were now on January 1, and he was still there. Where was the embassy to help him? As usual, nowhere. The courts closed the whole month of February, so we were praying he went home in January or it would drag on to March. He was my only hope to see how long it would take him to get out of this ridiculous country, so I guessed how long mine would take.

I had my angel Rosa visit me, and Marge came a bit later, after her trip to Canada, to see her ailing mom. It was a nice New Year's Day to see them both. Rosa brought me chicken and rice, which was a nice treat. Other than that, it was just another day in this shithole.

I got to talk to my daughter, which was cool. I didn't get to talk to her too much because she was always working or busy with the kids. My precious grandbaby, who was eight months old when I got there, was talking to me on the phone. "I'm three years old," she said.

It was awesome to hear her, but it still broke my heart that I was missing all of this. My other grandson's second birthday was next week, and I'd never even met this baby. I wanted this nightmare to end. I could only hope and pray that 2020 was the end.

I finally got called to the dentist. The delegado for the dentist even said to another English/Spanish girl that it was literally like pulling teeth to get him to see me and that if he didn't help me, to tell the INPE, and if I still got no help, then escalate it to "Alcaide."

We waited a good forty minutes, assuming he was with someone. After another half an hour, a girl said, "Let's see," only to find him in there by himself. Really?? Knowing that I'm outside waiting? He just didn't care.

With the girl translating, she told him I still had half a tooth stuck in there. He acted like it was no big deal, just saying that he'd have to pull it. No shit, Sherlock!

He pulled it and again just went about his business, leaving me sitting there.

I looked at the girl and said, "Is he done??"

And she asked and came back a little later.

She said, "Yeah, it was done," so I got up and left.

Again, no stitches, medicine, or injections. It hurt me *so* bad for a week, and obviously, there was nothing I could do about it but wait and hope and pray that there was no infection.

As I mentioned, the one thing prison teaches you is "every man for himself." Since prison, I'd been meeting weekly with Marge and Annie of the Christian faith and the Jehovah's Witness Group. I'm not sure which I believed. I was new to studying with the Jehovah's Witness Group, but I do believe that we all worship one god, yet in semi-different ways. I didn't know which way was right or wrong, but they all shared similar beliefs in some aspects. So, I feel that I can study with both and pick/choose which parts *I* believe in and worship that way, as I believe we are all worshipping the same God.

Well, a lot of the people from Thailand, Indonesia, and the Philippines all got work for the Jehovah's Witness Group. They made book covers (nice ones) for their Bibles and their Watch Tower books, and the Jehovah's Witnesses paid the girls. They sold the books to their people. I was not meeting them to steal work or anything. I was meeting them for purely religious reasons, nothing more.

Well, one woman was able to visit me on Sunday, which was a miracle. She had already visited another girl in Pabellon "B," and despite my solicitude for her to visit, the director told her she was not allowed to see two people at different times, so her first visit to me was shut down. They told her she was not on my list and sent her away. She showed them the solicitude on Sunday and begged to be let in. After the little back and forth, the INPE let her in and took the solicitude.

So, whether or not she would be allowed back in to see me remained unanswered. Every day was different with the different INPEs. But on Sunday, she gave me money to give to the Indonesian girl for her work.

That spread like wildfire, as they all knew that she had come in to visit *me* and not the other girl.

So, of course it went on to, "Who does Patty think she is? She is *my* visitor. What an asshole she is."

How silly. Is God like that? She was only using the group for some financial reasons, yet I was seeing them for spiritual reasons. Besides, as I had initially felt bad, I had to resort to "every man for himself." I hated to be or act that way since that is not at all how I am. But that was how they were.

I got to call my daughter to wish my grandson a happy second birthday. I was happy to get her on the phone. I also talked to my son on Sunday and was happy to get him. It always brightened my day to get to talk to my kids. I talked to my sister and mom too, which was always nice. Thank God the girl told me about the phone code, which only took S/1 off of my calling card, and thank God Annie was able to get me calling cards.

My visitor tried to bring in my vitamins and migraine medicine, yet apparently, the prescription was not stamped. Funny, but there were two different visitors, each with a different prescription, both of which were not stamped. One prescription with medicines came in, and one was not allowed in due to the prescription not being stamped. Yet how did the other one come in with them when that one was not stamped either? *So stupid!* Yet, welcome to my life in a Peruvian prison. I had to wait weeks to get a new prescription, wait for a visitor to come and get the prescription, and then wait another week for the medicine.

The other day I was at lunch from Taller when the Llamadora called me. I asked, "Abogado?" and she said yes. So, I asked Jenny to come with me and translate. As we walked past where the lawyers usually sit, no one was there, which confused me. They said, "Auditorio," which was also where the library was and where we had two coaching sessions. As Jenny tried to come with me, the INPE stopped her. I didn't know why. I said I needed a translator. They just told me, "English," and pushed Jenny away. Then, as I proceeded, there was no lawyer but a room full of people wearing shirts that said *2 Care,* plus the director. I was confused. This apparently was a group of volunteers (sort of like the coaching group), and they came to learn about the prison. They were from Poland, Africa, Europe, etc. So, again, the director calls for *me* to show off her American prisoner.

Most were English-speaking, with only a handful in Spanish. So here was a translator. The director introduced me as "her American prisoner" and said I was there for drug trafficking. The translator said, "This is Patricia from the USA. She's a drug trafficker." I immediately cut him off and said, "Whoa, *whoa!* I'm an *accused* drug trafficker. I'm not a drug trafficker. If you would make that correction, I'll continue. If not, we're done." I could see the director's face drop a little, but I didn't care. They were filming this, and I was tired of being labeled a trafficker when I wasn't. Peru's justice system refused to acknowledge my innocence, so I would not bow down and say, "You're right. I'm a smuggler," because I wasn't!

They asked a few questions and for me to tell the story. I did. Then the director told me to tell them about Fatima. I knew better than to say what I *really* felt about Fatima. I just said how I'd been in Santa Monica, then house arrest, Ancon II, and now Fatima. I was apparently on a tour of Peru's prisons, and how none of them were my idea of a good tour. I said, "Sorry if that's not what she was looking for, but it is what it is." I was being honest, as I'd been since day one.

After the interview, I went back to the pabellon. The 2 Care Group eventually went back to each pabellon to see them. At 2 o'clock, we were sent back to work. Surprisingly, the 2 Care Group then showed up at Taller to check out everyone working. As they passed by my tiny spot, the director said, "You remember Baronowski, right??" Again, highlighting me. I had a few projects that I was working on around me, little purses and the money holders I had made. The one Poland guy had said he wanted one. I tried to just give it to him since we'd only sell it for S/3, which is under $1. And it was really not worth "selling" since it was one of my first projects anyway and was far from good, but he insisted on paying me S/5 for it, which was nice. They eventually left.

I finally got my psych evaluation, seven months after I got to Fatima. It was only two minutes long. I was told as long as I worked, didn't get into trouble, and had no complaints, they couldn't say anything bad. So, it was a few check marks and a favorable review. I didn't care; all I knew was that I needed the psych review for benefits. I had limited psych in SM (nothing for thirteen months in the apartment, nothing for four months in Ancon, and nothing in Fatima for seven months), and none of that in SM counted. Without it, I'd never get released on benefits. So, I was glad this was an official report for my files.

My new lawyer, Alberto, also visited. I got to tell him about the psych report. So, he was happy. He mentioned how Interpol had my passport flagged and that I was not allowed to leave Peru. This was done due to the house arrest. He said this needed to be lifted for me to leave when the time came. He mentioned how Sal should have notified them when I was sentenced and back in prison, but here we were 8 ½ months later, and it still wasn't done. So, he said he'd work on that since we didn't want any more delays when the time came for me to be released. He also mentioned the presidential pardon. I only knew about this because a woman in SM got released on that when I was there, and the girls from Africa and Thailand were also on the list for a presidential pardon. They'd been on the list for seven years so far but hadn't been released. Rumor was that they would release them soon.

Alberto asked if I wanted to sign up for that. My initial question was, "Will this affect or interfere with my September 10th expulsion?"

He said, "No, they are totally separate." *If it comes through sooner, great, I leave sooner, but if it doesn't, no big deal... September 10th, we work on expulsion.* And since Sal technically hadn't been fired, why didn't he tell me this ages ago? As always, I had zero assistance from him. I told Alberto yes, sign me up, then signed papers for him to work on correcting my name on my sentence and to ensure that the prison had my name spelled right because last I saw, Fatima had my name wrong, too, and if the sentence and Fatima's records didn't match, then I didn't leave.

We were crossing our T's and dotting our I's so that when the time came, we wouldn't have any delays. It was sad that for all the money Sal made, he never did any of this. Alberto seemed more on the ball. I asked him if I'd potentially be there another Christmas, and he said, "No, if we start the papers now for September 10th, you definitely won't be here for Christmas." Of course, this bearing in mind that no hiccups came into play, as the prisons were customarily known for. I mentioned Sal's other client from the US, who he filed in November for his expulsion and was still there, mid-January. He said that I would be released in about two to four weeks after we filed. The other girl from Chicago, who just had court last week, got her freedom granted. She was only sentenced to six years and only technically had four more months before her sentence was complete anyway, but I was curious to see how long after her court days she got out of there. She believed two weeks, too, so we'd see.

The prison banned smoking, and the girls had been going crazy trying to find things to smoke. They started smoking tea— Dulce Sueno and Manzanilla. I drank the Dulce Sueno tea every night to help put me to sleep. It was a natural tea, but it made me sleepy. It was the best I could do without my American medicine helping me go to sleep. The INPEs saw them smoking and thought it was marijuana. They said no, they could test it, and that it was Dulce Sueno. They said if they saw them smoking it again, they'd confiscate all the tea and not allow it in anymore. I told the girl that that would screw me since I needed that tea to sleep. Of course, they all thought I was overreacting, but I was just thinking eight months ahead and how I needed this tea and couldn't afford to have these people mess it up. But, as always, every man for himself. I'd just keep my fingers crossed that nothing happened.

They finally put curtains outside above the workspace at work since there were tons of new people in Taller, and they were sitting outside in the scorching sun. I was originally going to move work to "Cuero" because they work on Saturdays also. In contrast, Manuelidades only worked Monday to Friday, but I didn't because I didn't want to sit out in the sun all summer; it would be horrifying. Putting the curtains up was good. It was not technically the curtain per se; it was the material—like the kind they used in football jerseys. It was a light material with little holes throughout it, but they hung them across the top, and the sun didn't come through as much. So, that was good.

They had a lot of those curtains left over. So, they gave them all away for free to all of us in Taller, and we could do whatever we wanted with them. I thought about having someone from Costura make me a tank top and a pair of shorts. I figured that the material was free and lightweight. So, all I had to pay for it was the Costura part. I gave the girl a pair of long-flowing shorts and my tank top to measure and get an idea of what I wanted. She made them, only S/25 for the set, which seemed high to me. I also asked her to make a second set so I could have two. Of course, everyone saw this and wanted to do the same for themselves. *Grrr,* that was stealing my idea, but it was funny. I guess we'd all be going around wearing matching curtains. I'd have to wear it soon and see if it worked the way I hoped it did.

I had got moved again in Taller. I was near a big window that got some air into the Costura room. Costura got moved outside into the metal section, where we had the ribbon cutting before Christmas. There were a lot of women in there, and it was hot. I was contemplating requesting to move to Cuero, which was outside. Since it was now curtained off from the sun and also worked on Saturday (so I was not sitting all day watching TV). While it would be cooler in the summer, my fear was that it would be freezing in the winter. Plus, the 90 percent humidity every day would make everything wet and dirty. Where would I store all my material?

Their winter was not at all like ours back home. (One day, my husband said it was seven degrees back home.) The winter in Peru feels like typical October weather back home. However, at home, we had jackets, hats, gloves, boots, etc., to wear in the cold winter, whereas in prison, we didn't have any of that. Additionally, your body adapts to your environment, so after I'd been there three years, my body was interpreting it as cold. Also, when you were sitting outside all day, not walking or being active, just sitting in only a sweatshirt, it got cold. So, did I move for two to three months or suck it up or deal with it but be semi-warmer in the full winter when everyone else was sitting outside? I decided to suck it up and try to deal with it as best as possible.

Back home, if I was cold, I layered up my clothes. In prison, I didn't have much to layer up with, so I was limited with how many clothes I could put on. And I didn't have many summer clothes and no air conditioning to endure the summer. I guessed I'd just do as I always did—constantly wet my hair in the summer to try and cool off as best I could. They were constantly yelling at me due to my wet hair and making my back all wet. They told me that I'd get pneumonia like this, and this was not a place where I wanted to get sick. But, when it was hot as hell and with no reprieve, wetting my head was the only thing that cooled me off. It was another no-win situation.

Working in manualidades

CHAPTER 17

Randomly, they picked about ten people and moved their beds and rooms again. Luckily, I was not one of them, but I didn't understand why they did this. In four months of my being there, this was the third time I've seen them do this. It appeared to be once a month. The psychiatrist said once, "It's so you don't get too close to people or get too comfortable." How stupid was that? Well, on the one hand, I could see what they mean.

In my room, there had been several occasions where girls became girlfriends, and they snuck into one another's beds at night and did their business. At least in Santa Monica and Ancon, we had curtains around our beds for privacy. In Fatima, we didn't. But I just shut my eyes and minded my business. Yet, they were only changing rooms, not pabellons. People could still have their girlfriends. Some women had been moved all three times. It had to be tough. You had your space and knew everyone's schedule of showers and stuff. To start all over every month was silly. But as always, what did I know? I was just counting down my days. The good thing was that they didn't do a "requista" the previous night, where they barged in and took all your stuff apart, looking for items not allowed. They had done it every other time they moved people around. I was glad about that, at least.

My "compatriota" from the USA had her Delahencia three weeks ago, and they had finally granted her freedom. What was ridiculous was that she was sentenced to six years instead of the 6.8, ironically. In four more months, her sentence would be completed anyway, and they'd have to let her go. They, of course, did not tell her to go sooner because she didn't pay her fines. She finally paid them (well, her boyfriend, who was in Ancon II, whom she met in prison one Christmas, paid the fines for her, and they agreed to let her go). Well, that was three weeks ago, and it didn't make me feel any better in terms of timing. We knew the court closed the whole month of February, but I didn't know if the courts were needed for her at this point, but I was eyeing her situation to see how long it took.

The 75-year-old man from the US was *still* there. He was able to file his papers for expulsion in November. That was 2½ months ago. Sal was his lawyer, and because he was not getting paid to do anything, he was not doing much to help, not that he'd done much anyway. This man pleaded guilty from the start. So, Sal didn't have much to do, unlike with me, where the situation was supposed to be a fight for innocence for something that I never did intentionally. He plead guilty, even though he had no clue he was being set up for a scam. His wife just did not have the money to fight, so they plead guilty from the start.

Sal sent a junior associate to court, which was what Rebecca was when I met her. He messed up a paper or something. This man's wife has been in Peru for several months now, helping her husband as best as possible. She'd finally resorted to going to the court and begging them to see her husband in court to wrap this up. They first told her to come back in two weeks. Then they said they would try and fit him into the court calendar for March or April. That was over four months after his date to file. It was ridiculous. Then when he got a court date, they either agreed or disagreed with allowing him home, then he waited for the paper to go through, which could take anywhere from two weeks to three months.

Sunday was voting in Peru, voting for congressional people. It was a big thing there. If you didn't vote, you got fined heavily. When you sign in to vote, they run your name into a system that tells them all about you. Ironically, the prison director registered and signed in to vote and got arrested for drug trafficking. Her name pulled up, and she was wanted, so she was arrested. The story and her photo were in the Peru newspapers that Monday.

It turned out her name was confused with someone else. It was not her, so she was released. Back home, we could sue the newspapers for running a false story like that or ruining a reputation, but not where we were, I guess. You'd think that this situation humbled her a little, being falsely accused, being arrested, and photographed, etc.

But of course not. Silly of me to think that it would have humbled her. If anything, it's made her worse! Not to mention, we already know how slow Peru is, so how she got released like nothing in one day tells me that she must know someone to push it through fast because anyone else would still be arrested for at least six months.

I was supposed to see the doctor about blood work, too, to find out why my hand kept going numb. A woman prisoner, a doctor in Thailand, said it was a cholesterol problem. Considering how I mentioned this to the prison since day one, with no care at all from them, I was happy to finally be getting blood work done.

Well, that never happened. I never got called, so another week would go by before I could try again. So far, it had been seven months of trying to get to the bottom of my numbing hands.

The blood work finally got done, but it was a month later, and I still had not received the results. Normally an embassy would step in and call the prison to find out what was going on, but I'd already learned that the US Embassy wouldn't do anything at all. When I kept asking about it, the delegado of medical was getting annoyed at me, as if it was my fault that I had to keep asking.

Melanie*, the JW, had to go to the US for family reasons and asked if I needed anything back home that she could bring for me. I could use shorts, tank tops, and bras for summer, which we were now in. Not much, only two of each. So my sister ordered me some from Amazon since it was winter back home, and no shorts could be found anywhere there for the time being. She had them delivered directly to Melanie, and she said she would bring them to me, but as stupid as it is in Fatima, you can't just bring in clothes or anything. You must do a solicitude, which is done only once a month and brought in once a month, and it's the last week of every month.

Well, I'd missed January, so I'd have to do a solicitude for February. It would come at the end of February, and March ended in summer, so this rule was definitely dumb, but as always, there was nothing I could do about it but wait and deal with it. She also bought me Centrum Silver vitamins from the US since they didn't sell them in Peru. Good luck to me getting a new prescription for them. It would be like pulling teeth again.

Speaking of prescriptions, Rosa had bought me a foot cream that I had needed, and not surprisingly, that was the one thing that the INPE wouldn't allow in because it wasn't stamped, even though Melanie was able to bring in the other prescription that also had no stamps. Some INPEs inspected everything, while others didn't. She knew I needed the cream and that it would take a little while to get a new prescription. I had to get a new prescription and give it to Rosa and wait a few weeks for her to come in and bring it, and even then, I had to wait a few more days for it since the INPEs take it with the script and then give it to me three to four days later.

I spoke to my mom, and she told me that she'd completely lost her hearing in one ear and partially in another. My sister said the doctors wanted to do an MRI for fear of a brain tumor since her hearing loss happened in two weeks. I could only pray it was not a tumor and that she and everyone in my family were staying alive and well. I would be crushed if something happened to her or anyone else, even more so if it happened while I was stuck here.

My "Fatima Lena" was such a sweetheart yesterday. During a conversation, I mentioned my birthday, March 31. Well, apparently, she only remembered "31st" so while at work, she got me a pass for a thirty-minute massage in their cosmetología area. It's a place where women work by cutting hair, styling hair, doing nails, massaging, etc. Nothing fancy at all, but it worked for them. I didn't know why she did it, but I was grateful and happy for the massage.

Then she gave me a facial, which she had just received training on, so I thought I was just her guinea pig. Then we broke for lunch, and she told me to go back to her section at 4:00 p.m. Well, the INPE in Taller hadn't done quenta yet at four, so I didn't go there. At 4:15, she came by me and called me over. When I went, she was trying to communicate something to me, but I couldn't understand it until I finally did. She bought me a cake for what she believed was my birthday. It was January 31, and my birthday was March 31, so she was two months early, but I still thought it was so sweet. Then I understood. The massage and facial was her birthday gift to me. Such a heart of gold. I was so happy. Her birthday was the day after mine, on April 1. So I told her she did not have to redo all this in two months, but we could celebrate our birthdays together in two months. It was still such a sweet gesture. I just felt bad that she bought a cake. I had to eat a huge piece, of course. I told her I'd be three times my size by the time I got home.

Peru passed a new law eliminating the fines foreigners had to pay to leave prison. This was great news. My fines totaled S/15k. Other people had similar or less and sometimes more. It was insane because this was the only way many foreigners wound up staying there for many years because they didn't have the money for their fines. One girl had been there for eight years and could have been gone already if she had paid her fines. Another girl sentenced to six years had court three months ago, and the judges told her to pay her fines or do her full sentence. Well, her family didn't have money to pay her fine. So she'd done all she could to come up with the money just to pay her fines a month prior (before the new law), and they then granted her freedom.

It had been one month, and she was still there. She had been waiting for paperwork and immigration to process this so she could leave. Ironically, in three months, she would have completed her sentence. They would have to let her go anyway, so it wasn't like they did her a huge favor. It was all about them making money off us. The 75-year-old man was *still there*, waiting for a court date to request his expulsion. They told him March–April (four to five months after his 1/3 date) just for a freaking court date, even though they had already paid their fines! So good luck with them getting that money back, unfortunately.

I was just told there was an announcement on the radio the previous night that the ex-president from Peru five years ago had petitioned to have all foreigners removed from Peru prisons. Nothing happened. But they announced on the radio recently that it was just passed that all foreigners would be released back to their countries. He was no longer the president, but I was glad it was passed. Let's see how many years later they actually did this. Seeing how all foreigners are money for this corrupt country, I was not optimistic that we'd ever see this in my lifetime.

As we already know, it's all about Peru. Well, the fines that we'd pay to be released also paid for the food we eat (the pila-slop), the water (which we rarely got), electricity, etc. Well, with us not paying fines, it would cost the prisons for us to be there. Plus, a recent news article mentioned how the prisons were 50 to 70 percent overcrowded (which I saw for myself, people sleeping on floors, roaches everywhere). I was told they wanted to do a sweep, have the foreigners sent away, and wanted to make room in the prisons to alleviate the overcrowding. Part of me knew that Peru did nothing fast. So would it happen soon? Who knew? But on the other hand, Peru was all about money, so if it was costing *them* for us to be there, would they want to get rid of us fast?

They had apparently already gone to Santa Monica and Lurigancho to calculate how many foreigners and what countries they were from, so were they in the process? I had no clue. I didn't want to get my hopes up and have them all crushed down as it'd been going on for ten months so far, so I was looking forward to September 10th to start the process for me, and if it happened sooner, that would be an awesome surprise. I didn't know if it meant we would be released to our countries or if they expected us to go to prison in our own countries. The US would laugh at this atrocity, but I was just going along with it.

It'd been over five weeks, and still no blood work results. My Fatima Lena brought me to a man, Charlie, who was supposedly the head of the doctors. HHHe spoke a tiny bit of English, not much, but he tried. He took my name and whatever medical number was assigned to me. Miraculously the delegado of Topico said this afternoon, "Your blood work results came in. You can see the doctor on Friday." A coincidence? Ha! I doubt it. Everything had a price tag, but I was still glad they miraculously surfaced. I was anxious to see what Friday brought.

The other American girl who had court six weeks prior was going home that Friday. That made me feel a little better about the length of time the process took. I was happy for her.

Again, I had gone to work and got told no, not with a tank top on. The INPE said I'd need to put on a shirt with sleeves of some sort. One minute all INPEs didn't care what you wore, but it just took one INPE with a bug up her butt to make life miserable. It was stupid because the shirt stayed on for all but five minutes, then came off because I switched it in Taller, so I'd never know why they insisted on being difficult.

Our kiosko *lady* for weeks hadn't had anything any of us needed. I was told that the kiosko people change every six months, so they don't want to stock up on stuff they'll lose money on, so they didn't stock up. Yet she *did* stock up on the dumbest things. I'd never figure Peru out.

At Taller, you needed to order materials to work with. I ordered from a man named Frank* for five months without a problem. You order one week, and he then brings it the next week. A week ago, I'd ordered material to make bags and got told on a Monday from the senorita (boss) of Cuero that I wouldn't be getting any material because Frank was from Cuero, and so was the material that I ordered, and I was in Manuelidades, so they *suddenly* wouldn't allow it.

What? A translator came with me to talk to the seniorita of Manualidades (*my* boss). From what I got, she wasn't a huge fan of a foreign woman either, and this woman said she'd be leaving soon anyway, so I just used whatever material I already had. I was confused because I needed the material to make the bag, and wasn't that "manual" (Manualidades)? Shockingly I was told no. Manualidades is jewelry and teddy bears; that was it. It wasn't anything you did *manually*! I'd never figure that place out. Not to mention, I'd been making the same stuff for five months with no issues.

My seniorita didn't seem to care what I was working on so long as I was working, so I'd just have someone from Cuero order my stuff as I needed it. Marge came that day as she did every week and commented about the amount of tea bags I had and called me a hoarder (a comment she heard my mom say once). I really wish people could understand what we dealt with and not call me a hoarder. If there was one thing I learned, it was that everything could change at any moment. This was why we needed to keep all that we had because if

I were to run out of things, it wasn't like I could just run to the store and get more.

The foot cream that Rosa got for me was not doing what we thought it would. Crazy how she had to re-buy it for me because it was over a month later, and I still never got it from the INPE. So yes, if I had more than one of something, I kept it. Why? Because you never knew when you'd need something, and from experience with this nightmare, you didn't always know when you'd be able to get it again. But more importantly, the question was *why* I had so many. Well, with twenty-five in a box and me only drinking one tea a night, I was getting a box a week, plus someone in Taller gave me a box, and Jenny gave me a box. The next thing I knew, I had over 100. I told people not to bring me anymore until I got rid of some of them. I didn't need that much, but I didn't ask for over 100 tea bags. I wasn't about to throw them away since I drank one a day, so if that made me a hoarder, it was what it was. I simply had what people gave me and drank one a night.

I went to find out the deal with my blood work and got told that my cholesterol was very high—*no shit, Sherlock.* And it was the doctor's job to ensure I didn't have a stroke. Obviously, they should have put me on meds three years ago when I first told them about my cholesterol and family history of heart conditions. I even told the Embassy that since my Santa Monica days. I needed cholesterol pills due to genetically high cholesterol, but as we already know, talking to them was like talking to myself.

The doctor gave me three different prescription meds plus a prescription for more pills that I was to have someone get me from outside. Back home, I took one pill, but there I was taking seven in total. Plus, I needed to take one a day, so they gave me a one-week supply and a script. Why? Did anything they do ever make any sense? They said I needed to refill the script every month. We already know how difficult getting a script was, plus getting stuff from outside was time-consuming and often impossible. But as always, what could I do?

Again, the INPE wouldn't let us go to work in tank tops. It was the INPE who sat between Pabellons C and D (where we passed through to go to Taller). She was the real bitch. So again, back up to throw on a shirt with a sleeve to wear for five minutes. Then there was a stupid new rule. Between 12:30–1:30 you got locked downstairs at lunchtime because they didn't want you eating in the rooms. That would be fine, but Wednesdays, Saturdays, and Sundays were visitor days when we were not allowed downstairs. So, eating in the rooms on *those days* was okay? Again, they made zero sense to me. How could eating three days a week and not being allowed to eat upstairs four days a week accomplish anything? Plus, as mentioned, it was hot as hell, so sitting outside was pure torture.

When we all complained about being forced to sit out in the sun for an hour, the director said, "If you were outside, you'd be in the sun at the beach, so quit complaining and deal with it." First of all, *I* would not be at the beach. Second, they had zero ozone layer, and that was the prime sun time to force us to sit in. And third, even if it *were* true, if we were at the beach and got hot, we'd go in the water or go home and shower, but as we already knew with the water issues that it wasn't even an option. So again, we just had to suck it up and deal with this idiotic prison's poor excuses for rules.

On my daughter's birthday, I called her in the morning and got her voicemail, which was okay. I said I'd call her later. At that time, only one of three phones was working, one out of three bathrooms was working, and apparently, our breakfast was changed from quaker to coffee because they ran out of gas in the kitchen to cook. Unfucking believable, as always. Considering I don't drink coffee, that meant no breakfast for me.

I asked to see the doctor or nurse, as I was told to get an injection since I felt like I was coming down with the flu that everyone had. Of course, that never happened. I waited all day and nothing. Then at lunchtime, my Fatima Lena came to my pabellon and asked the INPE to let me see the doctor. The INPE then said I could go at 5 p.m. *Okay, fair enough.* I didn't have an appetite for lunch since I wasn't feeling good, so at lunchtime, I just lay down. I got up before work to call my daughter again for her birthday; I actually got her which was nice. I also got to talk to my granddaughter. I told her I'd take her to the zoo when I got home. She was super excited, and

I couldn't wait. It was 2 o'clock now, so I went to hang up to go to work, and this not-so-charming INPE locked the gate and wouldn't let me leave for work. They never called work even though it was 2 p.m., so what the fuck? So, there I stood, and eventually, when a few more girls came, she let us go. *Unreal.* Again, it's amazing how Peruvians get to go—but me being the Gringo was originally shut out.

One of the things that Alberto had me apply for was the presidential pardon. The Arizona woman got released on that, and it was something Sal should have also signed me up for, but of course, he never did. I signed up for it via Alberto, and several other people had signed up over two years ago. This meant they were finally working on it and approving or denying people. The majority that I knew were denied, mostly because of prior convictions, and others had conduct issues. I understood if someone had been there six years so far and got sent to Waco five years ago for a week for a fight, they would deny her this early release over that. She technically only had eight more months until her sentence was complete anyway, but as a law, it was sickening how they acted and their ridiculous laws and rules.

I was curious to see if Alberto submitted my paper on time and what they would tell me. I didn't know if it was simply a matter of them going through the papers in order and I had a way to go or if I was too late or what. I had no clue but would find out eventually. The people who submitted theirs two years ago were still awaiting a reply. The Philippine girl married a Peruvian ex-con in Ancon II right before we were transferred to Ancon. He did his time and was released. She married him in prison. She was accepted. Was it because she married a Peruvian or because they felt she was worthier than all others? More questions we'd never have answers to.

I tried to go to the doctor at 5 as the INPE said, and she told me now, "No, 5:30." Okay. I waited until 5:30, and then I got told, "No, later." What the fuck? So, I waited again. At 5:40, I was able to go—no injection, just more of that intravenous powder for diarrhea, *which I didn't even have!* Such a major language barrier. Ironically, today it was the same woman from the Santa Monica doctor's office, and again, she was asking me for chocolate. It was comical what I had to deal with. I had Kit-Kats, but in Fatima, it wasn't like I could run up and get some and bring them back to her. So, oh well, no chocolates for her again. That was okay. She could complain about me all she wanted; I didn't care anymore. I was finally at the point where everything was getting on my last nerve. It could be my being sick, lack of sleep, or being fed up with all this crap. I felt as if even the voices of some people were getting on my last nerve. The one woman I wasn't a fan of was loud; her voice killed me. Another woman's voice sounded like nails on a chalkboard, like she'd smoked ten packs of cigarettes a day for decades. I don't even know how to describe it, but it was annoying to hear all day.

Another woman in my room was crying, and I felt bad. I wished I could communicate with her better, but with the language barrier, it was rough. She was Peruvian, and from what I understood, she'd been in prison for six years so far for two joints of marijuana and had another year to go. Her son was 12 years old and lived with her dad. She said he was "alone" and needed his mom. She said she called him every day, but it was not the same. He was sad, and she was a mess. She often talked about how Peru's justice system is disgusting, and she was Peruvian. I saw it with Desiree too. Why was the country punishing people to the extent that it did for the stupidest reasons? I mean, two joints. *Really?* And tearing her away from her son when he was just six years old? Desiree being torn away from her kids about the same age with 11 years? Peru should truly be ashamed of itself. What has the justice system accomplished? Absolutely nothing. They're still a third-world country, second in the line for cocaine next to Columbia, and with more criminals than I can count, so their justice system, besides being disgusting, accomplishes absolutely nothing.

Melanie would come and bring in the new thermos and summer clothes that my sister got for me when Melanie was in the US, where I had to submit a solicitude for. I was originally told by the delegado that the stuff needed to be brought in that day only between 9 and 4 p.m. Melanie planned to drop them off at 3:30 along with the prescription medicine she had to pick up for me from the outside.

It was good that I spoke with another girl yesterday afternoon who said, "No, stuff can only come in today between 9 and 12. Anything after 12 would be another month and another solicitude before it would be allowed in." By the time I'd get the summer clothes, summer would be over. I ran to call Melanie to tell her, but she was in Santa Monica, so I asked my sister to relay the message for me so she could bring it there earlier so I could get it in a few days—after they inspected it all and whatever else they did with it.

I was still feeling like crap, just blah, really. All I wanted to do was sleep, yet I wasn't getting good sleep—just tossing and turning. I also feel nauseous for two days. Miraculously, Annie got to come in and visit Jenny and me yesterday with the two other women from the congregation. She was visiting Tania in pabellon B and was not allowed to see us in Pabellon D, but since Tania was home, they allowed her in to see us. She came in under Jenny's name, though, so I guess I'd never have her come to see "me." Since both she and Marge had come under Jenny's name, I could only have Clara D* ask for me. This was fine, but if Clara ever went away again (I know she did for one month in December), I'd be screwed in that neither of them would be allowed to call me. But as always, it was what it was. Grin and bear it was all I could do.

I was told that the director went to Pabellon A yesterday to tell them that you can only change their visitor list once every six months, and we were now there for six months. Sal originally told me that the law was every fifteen days, not every six months—but as I'd learned, who knew if Sal even knew Peru's laws? The director told Pabellon A that the list of ten names must be eight family and two friends. Again, what the fuck? US foreigners didn't have family there, so that was very prejudicial and discriminatory. But I wasn't planning to change my list anyway. This spread like wildfire, and all the Peruvians were curious about this rule. I asked a girl from the Philippines, and she said the director said the rule was final. It was amazing how, in six months of my being there so far, many new rules had surfaced.

She suggested that I make an appointment to talk to the director and she would translate for me, so we just asked the Llamadora to put us on a list. God only knows if/when they would call us, but honestly, they couldn't expect foreigners to only be allowed two friends to visit since all our families were in our countries. My list is all friends. And religious groups are all friends, plus Rosa and three of her friends who often take turns accompanying her to help her—plus Jenny and her mom. I had no family there, so my list was all friends, and she said I could only pick two people. Well, that was impossible. This, like always, would be interesting to see how it turned out.

Work stunk to the high end. Apparently, it's Tocosh and stinks, something about a potato in soup, but they put the potato in the dirt, stomped on it, and left it there for days, etc. They said it was good for you, but how? Your guess is as good as mine. I hate "venturing" in terms of food eating. I ate the same things every day when I'm home and didn't experiment with food. Too many times, I tried to order something different only to realize that I didn't like it, so I was stuck watching everyone else eat while I stared at a plate of food that I had to pay for and wouldn't eat. So, I avoided it.

One time a girl next to me in Taller was eating something. It looked like a big jet-black meatball and sweet potato chips. She was telling me to try it, and I honestly didn't want any, but she was so persistent and not taking no for an answer. Well, once I confirmed that it wasn't "carne," I took a tiny nibble of the black thing and didn't like it. I told her, "No me gusta," and started to drink it away with water. I asked what it was, and she said, "Sangre" (Blood?! What the fuck?). I chugged the whole water jug and couldn't believe that crap touched my lips. Blood of what? They claimed it was good for you. *No, thank you! I'll stick to eating what I know best here.*

Ironically, I went to the head of security with the Philippino translator to explain my situation and all foreigners' situations about the visit. She just said "No" to people. She said, "It's equal for everyone." I tried to say that this was far from equal. Peruvians had their families visit them, which was great for them. But who do we foreigners have? Our friends were our family while there, and we could only have two?! I protested and got nowhere, so I said I'd call my Embassy tomorrow. That always gets their attention, which is why it kills me that our Embassy doesn't help because they would listen to the US Embassy. Well, she got me in with the actual director. I tried to get the translator and got told no.

She sat me down and locked the door. Oh boy! But then she used her cell phone and used Google translator. She was saying this meeting was private and a secret and not to tell anyone about it because she didn't meet with people, but that she planned to talk to her superiors in the next few months to see if they could amend the rule to accept more people for foreigners, but for now, I must pick two. So much for thinking that she would help me, and so much for keeping it a secret. Funny how she said that she didn't meet all people because she'd met with the other Philippino girl yesterday and told her the exact same thing—word for word!

I told her that my contacts were religious groups and how they'd been visiting me since I was at Santa Monica but still got told to pick only two, so as always, what does Peru prison teach you? How to lie, cheat, steal, and use people. I was forced to pick the two that benefited me the most. This was *not* how I was at home, but there, I always carried the "survival of the fittest" mentality. The cop's daughter and mom, I had to exclude them. It sickened me to be this way, and it was beyond not right. I called my husband and asked him to go to Congress and have them demand that the Embassy get involved. All other country embassies would be, so it would be a universal team effort. My husband said he'd make the request, but I was sure it would be other embassies making demands instead. This idiotic place couldn't get any worse.

Melanie tried to bring in the clothes my sister sent her from the US—shorts, tank tops, and bras—and a new thermos. She rearranged her schedule to bring them in before noon one day, then spent an hour arguing to allow them in. First, she was told no to the shorts, saying they were men's shorts. What? She kept explaining how they were for women and not men. They were cotton, with cuffs. Men's wouldn't have cuffs. Then they still weren't agreeing, so she had to show that it was Hanes "Women" on the tag. After much back and forth, they said okay but stopped again and said no because they were too big—that I'm not a big person, so why would she be bringing in big clothes? What the fuck? They were a size "L" like I always wear. I don't wear tight clothes. I'd be 51 years old in a few weeks. There was a girl in my room who barely wore anything, her shorts were G-strings, and her top was barely around her boobs. She was barely dressed all the time, and *that* was okay, but size L shorts for me were a problem? What the fuck?

She kept trying to explain how I liked my clothes loose, etc. She said they kept going back and forth, and the INPE kept checking with other INPEs. Truly ridiculous, again—because I was a Gringo? They eventually said okay, but it was still ridiculous that she had to deal with their bullshit. I told my husband that this fucking nightmare was continuing to get worse! I was constantly saying, "How much worse could this get?" Yet, it somehow continued to grow worse every day.

Alberto came, but sadly, it was before I got this news or I would have told him, but he just kept assuring me to sit tight, that this would be over soon, that it would be fast, etc. I was sick of people saying "fast" when they were home and outside. Every single day there felt like one year. Words cannot explain what I mean, but it had been a torturous experience that didn't want to end or even try and end gracefully. It wanted to torture me every step of the way until the end. My patience was out, and I was running on zero resources. This was turning into hell.

My husband heard from Alberto that this new idiotic visitors rule was going to be across all the prisons. He said the foreigner issue had been raised, but the National Penitentiary Institute of Peru Committee said they'd consider it. Seeing how it was mostly Peruvians in the prisons, I didn't know the exact percentage of the foreigners, but I seriously doubted that they'd do anything to accommodate us, so it was what it was, *I guess.*

The director of Fatima came to each pabellon to tell us about the new visitor rule. Of course, everyone had questions about so many things—not just about the visitor rule, but how we were locked out of our rooms and forced to sit in the sun now every day from 12:30–1:30. We tried to say that was pure UV Index time but she whipped out her cell phone and said, "No, it's not. Next." Someone asked about the visitors and foreigners, and she just reiterated, "Only two," then a girl said (which I thought was funny) that since she (the director) had been recently arrested, she should have been a bit more compassionate. Well, that set her off. She felt that the girl was trying to make her look bad and told her that they had the right to write her up, and the girl was saying that her purpose for even bringing it up was to say how she should be more compassionate.

She cut the conversation short, told us, "Unlike all of *you,* I am innocent," and walked out. Well, that pissed me off. I was innocent, too, and it wasn't my fault that her country lacked true justice. Yes, I apparently brought drugs to the airport, but not intentionally. I had zero knowledge of it. The Nigerian's photo of me in the hands of the airport police proved how the corrupt police and cartels had set me up. The prosecutor was granted a nine-month investigation and did nothing, only to still be allowed to drag this on for two years! Then to say that they wouldn't look at any of the evidence that I had proving my innocence because they refused to set precedence, then gave me an ultimatum: "Say innocent once more, and we'll sentence you to a minimum of fifteen years. But plead guilty, and we'll go for less." So they forced me to plead guilty to something I wasn't guilty of. So yes, when she said, "We are all guilty, unlike her," it pissed me off. Well, anyway, I thought the whole exchange between her and the girl was funny.

I spoke with my husband and told him about it, but he cut me off and dissected pieces of the story, and we got into a fight. I literally had no more strength to fight. I told him I hung up and told him that I would talk later in the week. I just wanted to go to sleep and not wake up at that point. I was *so* over it.

I had not been sleeping because it'd been *so* hot with them locking the door every night. We were locked in all night with no water. I'd been getting massive headaches every day due to the lack of sleep. I knew my husband and family were all suffering back home. I got that, yet I couldn't say enough just *how different* we were suffering. I called my husband at 6 a.m., as I do every Wednesday and Saturday, and after getting into a fight on the phone on Friday, I just wanted to bring peace back. All I had time to do was think—all day and night. I realized how I needed help back then but couldn't see it at the time.

And maybe I would need help once I was back home. I could see how my brain was better than it was three years before at my arrest, and even how three years ago, it was better than the four-and-a-half years after the accident. It improved a bit every day, but would it ever be 100 percent? I had no clue.

I did not want to fight with him or anyone anymore. Words couldn't express how little strength I had left in me. I was sure the lack of sleep wasn't helping my mood or emotions anymore, and I hated to end the day with us hanging up after arguing. But what could I do? I tried to assure him that I was not picking a fight. We eventually were okay and ended the call when breakfast came (saved by the bell), but I still was an emotional wreck. I needed sleep. The oven we were sleeping in kept me awake all night. It was Saturday, so I had to sit and watch Spanish TV all freaking day (and that was after I waited at a gate in the morning for them to open it at 8:20, and I made a mad dash up the stairs where I damn near got trampled to try and get one of the 12 to 15 seats available). This went on until 4:30 when they did quenta again, so eight hours all day today and tomorrow, then back to work on Monday. Like I always said, trying to be positive was hard.

My husband said, "Tomorrow is March 10th, and only six months to go for filing for benefits." I tried to be positive about that but as had been shown to me for two to three years so far, the bad news continued to creep up and overshadow any positivity. This emotional roller coaster over the past two to three years had been so exhausting, and the ups and downs over emotions were sucking the life out of me. Again, I wanted to be happy and kept saying, "Six more months to go," but I guess I'd see what other nonsense surfaced in the coming six months.

Melanie and Rosa visited me, one in the morning and one in the afternoon. Rosa was so sad to hear that she could only visit me on Thursday morning but then no more after that. It broke my heart too. While she understood the situation, it still didn't make it okay at all. Not every visitor came every single week, so if we put four people on the list and they coordinated who was available and only two came in per week, that could be great, but the director said no, only two people on the list—nothing more. It was not right and not fair.

People at home did not understand what we went through. While I tried to explain, you just had to be there to understand fully. For example, as I already said, there were only twelve seats upstairs and eighty of us there. On Sunday, they cleaned each room more thoroughly than any other day. So, after quenta, when they let us upstairs, we needed to sit outside the room for two to three hours while it was cleaned. We couldn't go downstairs because it was a visitors' day. So, after quenta, the others and I crowded around the gate and patiently waited for them to open it. I was already being pushed and shoved in every direction for about 20–30 minutes while we waited for the INPEs to finish eating their breakfast in front of us and open the gate. Once we heard the buzz of the electronic gate, people pushed in all directions, and you were damn near trampled while people flew past me and scurried up the stairs to grab a seat. I would actually manage to get one, too. And then what? Here was where I'd sit for eight hours watching TV that I didn't even understand—all day long—waiting for the day to end, then quenta after the visitors left. This was a typical Sunday.

Others truly couldn't understand how we were forced to live in a Peru prison. I saved all bottles—yogurt bottles, water bottles, etc. I cleaned them and filled them with sink water. Why? To have water to brush my teeth, wash dishes and, wash me when we had no water—which was all the time. I caught one girl opening one of my yogurt bottles. I approached her and said what the fuck? She asked if it was mine. I said yes. (She knew it was.) And then she asked why I had so many. I just said, "Es mio – no toques," and walked out. It was none of her or anyone else's business why I had water bottles, and Marge could call me a hoarder all she wanted; I didn't care anymore. I had to do whatever I had to do to survive, and if it meant hoarding water to brush my teeth, wash my dishes, or wash myself, when we hardly ever had any water, then so be it. I would do whatever I had to do to survive this nightmare.

The water cut off, as usual, at 11 and never came back on. By 4, every bucket in our room was completely empty. No water to shower, wash dishes, flush the toilet, brush your teeth, etc. You can imagine how this was exactly the shit I planned for, yet the two above me thought it was funny and crazy to have all these water bottles. We were told that we probably wouldn't have any water until late tomorrow night, and their barrels were already empty. Now, who was the crazy one? Was I still the hoarder for being prepared for the crazy crap we endured? The next day, everyone would be crazy about showering and flushing the toilet, and I would be the only one with water. I just wrote and taped *No Toques* (Don't Touch) on it. But I wanted to see how fast they'd steal it. If I was at Taller, I obviously couldn't watch it, so it would be interesting. I didn't trust any of them, so yet another day in the shithole.

Marge and Annie came and talked about our lists. Marge believed I should put Rosa and her on my list. I wished to God/ Jehovah/Om, and whatever other name applies, that we could put three names, and that would make my life so much easier. At this point, I almost felt that putting Marge and Rosa was my only option. This was the type of crap we had to deal with.

CHAPTER 18

As usual, with the happenings in that shithole, they seemed to be changing the rules faster than I could count. It was always no pajamas at quenta. Then it was no shorts, too. Seriously? It was hell-hot, and no shorts? What did they want us to do, go to work in jackets, hats, and scarves in this hell-hot summer? Then certain INPEs wouldn't let us go to Taller in sleeveless shirts. They were insisting no shorts for work, too. What the fuck? It wasn't like we worked in a hospital! And pants? Plus, my shorts were just delivered to me. This nightmare truly couldn't end soon enough!

I had signed up for aerobics. It cost me S/5 (what else was new). When I went to it, it was one hour of aerobics and then an hour of dancing. I didn't know their dancing so I did the aerobics and then stood there and watched for the next hour. Once we were allowed to return to our pabellon, I was so hot, and of course, there was almost no water left in the buckets. I had quickly grabbed some and took a shower, and the two other girls did, too. Every man for himself, I learned.

The next dat at work, they were fumigating the prison again, so we had worked a half day and then had to sit outside in the heat until 5:00 p.m. I got to play dominos with other girls, so that was a nice change of pace.

I had tried to call the US Embassy at lunchtime to tell them about the visitor issue, the water issue, and needing cholesterol meds. Calling them was a horrendous ordeal. It cost me S/5 between being bounced around, and first, I was sent to a voicemail that didn't give me a name and said there was no space to leave a message. I called again and got sent to a man who only spoke Spanish. When he couldn't understand me, he hung up on me. Next, I was sent to a woman who spoke Spanish, who also hung up on me. On my fourth call, as I was again trying to explain what I needed to the operator, she patched me through to someone as I was still talking. I was sent to a woman, put on never-ending hold, then she picked up and wasn't saying anything, so I went off screaming about what a disgrace this was. She eventually asked my name and said she was not the person, but she'd take the message. *Un-fucking believable.* I told her all my issues, and she just said that she'd pass it along. I had zero faith that anything would come of it. It was a disgrace how little they did.

On a bright note, I had gotten a chance to call the girl, who was a Mexican and a US citizen, who went home two weeks before Christmas. She spent six months in prison, being innocent, so we had that in common. While she was there, she kept having stomach issues, and we had assumed it was the food. When she went home and got a full body exam, she was six months pregnant! She had no idea. She must've just gotten pregnant the night or so before getting arrested. She had a baby girl. I was so happy for her and so glad she was able to share the experience with her boyfriend and family. If she was still there and went into labor and didn't know she was pregnant, I'm afraid to know how that would have turned out. Plus, they would have booted her to Santa Monica after having the baby. But I was just happy she was home with her family and got a healthy baby after this mess.

By this time, there was a new virus going around—COVID-19. It sounded a lot like the SARS virus when it first came out. There was no cure for it yet, and it was passed around by germs—washing hands and covering your mouth was needed. They made an announcement that kids would no longer be permitted, nor pregnant women, nor people over age 65. This would not be good. Also, people who were traveling couldn't come in. Marge was off to Canada for two weeks during this announcement, and Melanie was off to the States for two months. So, unless there was a miraculous COVID-19 cure by then, they wouldn't be allowed back in. I knew Marge was in her fifties, but I didn't know how old Melanie or Rosa were. I also knew Rosa was retired, but if she was over 65, she wouldn't be allowed in.

Melanie had a fear that they'd not allow visitors to try and prevent someone from bringing the virus in, but I was more afraid that they wouldn't let us go. I needed to call Rosa the next day and ask her age because she was supposed to visit me that Sunday, but if she was over 65, they wouldn't let her in. I swear this nightmare just continued to grow. I understood, though—if one person brought this virus, the entire prison would be infected. But it didn't help to deal with any of this either. Plus, this would affect our visitor list, too. If we had been due to submit them on Tuesday, what would happem?

This ruling was temporary during COVID-19, but once there was a vaccine, then what? I was putting Marge and Rosa or Melanie on my list. Well, Marge and Melanie were traveling, and Rosa may have been over 65, and if that was the case, then what? If I put someone else on the list, then there was a cure for the virus, and the ban got lifted, would I not be allowed to change the lists again? The idiotic stuff that we had to deal with and that consumed us were things you'd never even think about unless you were there. I could just continue to pray.

As it turned out, Rosa was 71 years old, so they wouldn't allow her in. It sucked. They claimed it would just be for one month, but I didn't believe anything they said. Plus, with more people getting COVID and no cure, I couldn't see how it would only be for one month. A friend of Rosa's, who was on my list, planned to come and visit me that Sunday. That was great, but if I had to only put two people on my new list, this woman wouldn't be on it for April. And the people they wouldn't allow in were people the news said were the most susceptible to catching it. It seemed they didn't care if we got it in jail, but they didn't want us spreading it to someone outside who might be susceptible.

I tried to be a good person, a helpful person, yet it seemed this was not the place for it. I'd been robbed blind, lied to, used, etc., for so long. I had stopped lending money and items to certain people who borrowed so much and never paid me back, but then there would be someone who seemed genuine, and that woule bite me in the ass. The new girl in my room, who was crying the whole day, she worked constantly. She was in the bed next to mine and sat next to me in Taller. She asked to borrow S/20 one Tuesday and promised it back to me on Friday (the typical verbiage they all said). I figured while it was a lot, it was only three days, so I did it. She was always asking to borrow my radio, which was annoying. It wasn't like I could hide what I had; we all shared a small room, and we didn't have curtains on our beds, so they saw everything. I always kept my stuff on me so they didn't see how much I had, but they all assumed "the American has it," which was shitty.

I forgot about the loan and remembered one Saturday. I asked her where my money was and got told, "Manana." Sunday came (and she worked all day again), and I asked for it back and got told, "No, manana, at Taller." WTF? Plus, she'd been listening to my radio for four days straight now without the earplugs I had with it, so I was forced to listen to her blasting Spanish music on my radio. I asked her if she could put the volume down or the earbuds in it, and she seemed annoyed. *Unreal.* And when the battery died? I'd surely I'd get it back then.

The Bible teaches to give to those in need, and back home, that is totally who I am, but there, people obviously didn't have it. But if you borrowed from someone and said you'd give it back and didn't, that was just wrong. They didn't know if I needed it, too. Plus, with no visitors, I did need it, but as always, I was taken advantage of. She asked me for one of the bananas that she saw I had. I always got fruits and veggies for the week (one a day) because I needed them for stomach issues. She wanted one, but I needed one, and if I said no, I'd look like a jerk because I had five left. She'd also asked me for toilet paper, which I gave. The other girl last night asked me for some yogurt. That girl had money and things; she just didn't have yogurt. But our kiosko lady never had yogurt. I had to swindle and get this in Pabellon A via Taller but it was not easy for me to get stuff from there. Yet I became the go-to person all the time. My husband blamed me, saying it was because they all knew I had it. But I couldn't hide it; it was impossible. And it wasn't like I could just buy one a day because when a kiosko had something; it was gone if you didn't grab it fast. So, I had to buy a week's worth when she had it. I guess I'd be wrong as always, yet how did you work around all this?

Marge said to just say no but sharing a room and workspace with these people and being seen as the greedy jerk wouldn't work out too well. Sure, they may not ask again, but they'd probably just steal instead. Everyone knew everyone, and I didn't need any more potential trouble with only six months to go.

My husband had heard from Congress eventually. The Embassy told them, "We've actually spoken to Patricia. The visit is cut off due to the coronavirus. She just has to deal with it for a while, and we'll be visiting her and others on April 28." The visit issue had nothing to do with the temporary hold in visits due to COVID. I clearly explained that. The "only two friends and eight family" on your list was the issue we foreigners faced. We all had no family there, and our friends are more than two. The other issue was the cholesterol, which I could not get meds for, and it is was a problem that I'd been telling the Embassy for three years; as always, they do nothing about it. Plus, April 28th would be one week shy of eight months since their last visit. They truly were unreal and completely useless.

Annie had come and visited Jenny one Wednesday, but no one could visit *me*. She had brought me in some of my soles, and in the event they stopped allowing anyone in because of the virus spreading, she asked if I had enough to hold me over. I told her, "Marge can call me hoarder all she wants, but this is a perfect example of why I hoard. So yes, I have spare necessities if needed." Even the Dulce Sueno tea was no longer allowed in thanks to the idiots smoking it, so again, people can call me crazy or a hoarder but I had enough tea to get me through the next six months. So if it's not allowed in, I am still okay for six months.

No one there covers their mouths when they cough or sneeze. I sat in front of three elderly women one day. Every time they coughed or sneezed, I'd feel it on my back since they were leaning on my chair anyway to watch TV. So, then I got the dreaded flu. I went to Topico initially but had no fever, so they only gave me two pills (of what, as always, I had no clue). I lay in bed for a few hours. Eventually, I'd felt okay. I was getting cold the next day after eating, so I knew it was a fever. I went and laid down, and someone told the INPE, and they brought me to Topico. They had put a device on my finger that measured my bronchial or something, which was okay (no COVID!) But now I had a fever, so she gave me two more pills and an injection. I was told I'd sweat at night, but it would be good. I don't like sweating. It's so hot as it was, so I was constantly wetting my hair to cool off. I was constantly being yelled at by Peruvians to stop wetting my head and that I'd get sick, get bronchitis, pneumonia, etc. I never listened; it was just too hot. Well, of course, they were all saying I got the flu because I'm always wetting my hair. How stupid! You don't catch the flu from a wet head. It's a virus spread through the air, and all these people never cover their mouths when they cough or sneeze. Plus being locked in a room with a girl with the flu for over three weeks so far; that was why I got it, not from a wet head, but talking to these people was like talking to a wall. They all believe in their superstitions.

I was again running a super high fever, above 103. I was sent to Topico, where I got another injection. They use needles that are big enough for a horse, and I never have any idea what they injected me with. The injection helped me to sleep initially, but then Jenny came in and said I needed to go under the blanket. I sure did not want to; it was already hot. Well, I went under the blanket and sweat *so* much. My clothes and sheets were soaked. I got up and took a shower and changed my sheets. With no work that day, the laundry spot was obviously not open, so it was manually washing and hanging up the clothes to dry and then waiting two or three days for them to dry.

I felt a little better the next day, not 100 percent, but slightly better. The INPE took me to Topico again, and my fever was gone, so that was good. The one INPE was nice enough to give me a mask and, through a translator, told me that it was more for me than anyone else. She said that my fever is coming and going, which means my immune system is weak, and with everyone with the flu, it may keep me from getting it again and again. Aside from INPE and doctors, I was the only one in my pabellon wearing one, so of course, they are all panicking, thinking I am contagious. The delgado had to announce to everyone that I was only wearing it not to spread the flu. It's nuts, of course. I hear these idiots saying it's all because of wetting my head. I even lied and said in Spanish that my uncle is a doctor, and he says it's impossible to get the flu from a wet head; it's airborne, not a wet head virus. They all just believe their version and don't want to hear anything else. So I continued day four of nothing to do, but at least no fever; that was a bonus.

My fever came back again, so on that Monday, I saw the doctor. They set me up for five days of injections as well as Clorfeniramina and some other pills that I had no idea what they were. These were done in two separate injections, one more painful than the other. It's not so much the actual injection, it's whatever they were injecting me with. I can't describe it, but it hurt so bad I threw up for the first two days after it. The injections were moments before quenta. Luckily, my fever went away again, so then only one injection instead of two. Thank God! But even the one was so painful. Luckily that Sunday night, I got it fifteen minutes before quenta, so I got to lay down and let some of the pain subside so I didn't get lightheaded again. It's still so annoying how all I hear now is how this is all because I wet my head. I got into a small spat with one of the women I sit with for lunch because I was trying to explain how it's impossible to blame this on a wet head and how many people around us have been sick with the flu lately. The other woman we sit with at lunch even had the flu, and a few days prior, the girl in my room was still coughing and sick; it had been a month! So, when she didn't want to hear it, she just walked away and didn't talk to me for a day. Not that we could talk anyway—she knows zero English—but we all somehow get our messages across. They are so annoying.

Next I was up all night long coughing. There was no phlegm, only a dry cough, but it keept me up all night. I was exhausted. It had been two days of this. One girl had me buy a slice of ginger and orange, and she squeezed the orange and chopped up the ginger to make some nasty drink for me to drink. Will it do anything? Who knew, but I did it. Another girl made another concoction and told me to drink it fast. I did. It was nasty-tasting. Then she told me to gargle with vinegar, an orange, and salt. It's crazy the concoctions people make with the limited supplies we had. The kiosko hadnothing, and so people had been getting some stuff from the pabellon's kiosko across from us. Some INPEs allowed that, while others didn't.

But even things as simple as lime are nonexistent here. They were wiping out the shelves here just like on the outside.

I saw on the TV that there were 153 people with COVID in Peru at the time of writing this and only two deaths, but those deaths were Peruvians. But it's still nothing like the USA or Italy with hundreds. They had just arrested another fifty-plus people walking around and not obeying the quarantine in Peru. They were taking that very seriously. They showed the USA on the news there, where people were going about normal and were at the beaches and such, and they said that the USA wasn't taking it seriously enough. My question was, when was that video taken? It was March, and the USA is still in winter, not summer like Peru is. So, the USA would not be at the beaches now! It looked to me like a made-up story to say, "Peru is better than the USA because we take this seriously, have fewer infected, etc." While that may be true, the USA as a whole is way bigger than Peru, with people from all over the world in it. Peru does have foreigners, but nowhere as many as the USA does. But as always, apparently, what do I know? Sigh!

We were now on week two of not working. It was another long week—we still didn't know if they would end this after the first week or not, but we waited to see. The INPEs were at least letting the ladies watch TV during the day. On normal workdays, they don't let you until after work, around 4:30, but what else are eighty people supposed to do all day long? I'd been just in bed, reading, coloring, or resting. At 12:30, the INPE came and told everyone how they had to go downstairs and sit in the sun during lunch. As I said, this rule was new and truly ridiculous. Luckily, was sick, so I'd not had to go down for a few days so far. I've zero desire to sit in the heat unnecessarily for an hour, and if I am forced to, I would definitely wet my head to cool down, so for my sake, it's great that they hadn't made me go down. I just pretend to be sleeping in bed with my mask over my mouth when they came to put everyone out.

So, how did my time in Virgin de Fatima go during Covid? Let me take you through some diary notes....

Well, last night was a true shitshow. There are sixteen people in a room in each pabellon and five rooms. There is a Pabellon Delgado, but also a "room delgado" who keeps stuff in order in the room. Well, some rooms have a good delgado, where of course, I don't. Nine p.m. is evening quenta, where they lock us in the rooms for the night. You are supposed to go to sleep at that point, not stay up and hang out/party.

Most rooms have a ten-minute rule enforced by the delgado, where you have ten minutes to do what you need to, but no radios, talking, or other noise. Sadly, this is always an issue in my room—for me, anyway. People stay up, laughing, shouting, radios blasting, playing, etc. I am exhausted. Remember, I am up at 4:30 every morning to shower and fill the water buckets for the day. People normally make a request for noise for like an hour or so, and it is so annoying. Last night they were so loud that the INPEs came back in to ask what was going on; they were supposed to be sleeping. But this one woman (who I am not a huge fan of anyway), she's in her mid-forties, is Peruvian, a constant whiner, and a massive germaphobe. Still, anyway, she proceeded to talk to tell the INPEs that everyone was making noise and telling on everyone. I wear an eye mask and put earbuds in my ears every night, so I was not involved in this ordeal. I was in my bed with my eyes covered and earbuds in, sleeping facing the wall, but I heard it all. This went on for a bit, and I guess the INPE just said for everyone to go to sleep and left. About twenty minutes later, I heard the same woman yelling, "Technica…. Servicio," which was calling for the INPE. I had no idea what was going on; I rolled over and saw her running to the door screaming for the INPE. I saw a blanket on the floor and four women around one. I didn't know if someone fell, got hurt, what? I had no clue. Remember, they turn the lights off after the 9 pm quenta.

When the INPE finally came, I saw everyone scramble back to their beds. They fled as fast as cockroaches. Several INPEs came in now. From what I could understand, she was telling the INPEs that she got up to use the bathroom, and everyone tried to attack her. What? I was not part of anything, but I know that throwing a blanket over someone and beating them up (so they can't see "who" is doing it) is common in these prisons. I just lay in bed, eyes still covered. I moved the eye cover slightly to peek while pretending to be sleeping. Next thing I know, the girl who is always running around naked leaps out of bed, wearing nothing but a G-string (no bra or anything), and goes after this woman. There were about five INPEs in the room now. They held her back and calmed her down while the "target" was still yelling about how they wanted to kill her. They are all saying that she is nuts, they were all sleeping, and she's making it all up. I actually felt bad for her. I was not part of any of it, but I saw the blanket and four girls standing over it and then saw them scramble to their beds and say they were sleeping and she was just crazy. That wasn't right, but do *I* want to be their next target? Hell no. I feigned sleep through it all.

Another girl was now yelling at the woman. It was like a free-for-all; sadly, the INPEs didn't do anything. The woman asked if she could go to Waco because she felt unsafe there. The INPEs said no, to go to bed and deal with it tomorrow, then left. After they left, the girls pretty much saw how the INPEs weren't doing anything, and they saw it as their advantage and took it full throttle. I again just continued pretending to sleep. The INPEs left and turned the lights out. All the girls now proceeded to torment this woman like crazy. Any other time, I would jump in to help her, even though, to be honest, I can't stand this woman either, but in this situation, being here in another country, with zero US help and being a severe minority, I had to look out for me first. If I stood up for her, then I would be their target, and I don't need any more trouble than I already have.

She went to use the bathroom, and they snuck up and started pounding the door, scaring her. As she wanted to walk out, they were there staring right in her face like madmen. She ran to the door screaming for the INPEs again. I couldn't believe it, but no one came. She screamed for help, and not one soul came for her. The only response she got was the other rooms shouting out their doors for her to shut up, that she was keeping them awake. This woman stayed standing by the door for hours. I felt bad for her. She was a major troublemaker and a constant complainer and has even started trouble with me on numerous occasions, but I was not getting involved.

The girls continued to torment her. They would throw stuff at her, pretend to run toward her, point, laugh, etc. From what I saw, this went on until midnight, but then I fell asleep. I can't say how long it continued, but this poor woman stood at a door for hours, being tormented by these idiotic morons. Our delegado couldn't care less. She doesn't even like the woman either. When I got up at 4:30 to shower, I saw she was in bed but awake. I guess she saw the girls go to sleep and snuck into her bed. It's still insane what they put her through and only told the INPEs that she was nuts and they were sleeping.

At 6 a.m., quenta, the INPE, immediately called the "naked girl" to Alcaide, the head of security. They needed to follow up on what happened last night. As crazy as it was, everyone grouped and discussed "their story," they were all planning to say the woman was nuts, they were all sleeping, and she just made up the stories for attention. Apparently, Alcaide called several of them down, and they all told the same story, including our room delegado. No one called me, thank God. I can't speak and understand them anyway; I was not a part of it. By breakfast, the women were all telling everyone "their story" so that if this woman tried to tell her story, theirs outweighed hers. It truly wasn't right at all. I felt bad for her, but I got to see how these girls were. One was worse than the other, and they all stuck together. It's disgusting. Sadly, such is my life here, stuck in a Peru prison. I was surprised by some of the girls as I didn't expect that from some of them, but it just proves to me how they are all the same here.

I got a surprise note from my Fatima Lena today, which was nice. She had an INPE pass it on to me since we're in different pabellons. Not all INPEs would do that, but she had a connection with this INPE who did her this favor. It was just a short note saying hi and that she hoped I'm surviving. It's nice. I was hoping the same for her too. Ironically, on 3/29, I got another surprise from her. She somehow made a dish with cupcakes, peanut butter, jellybeans, cookies, and two balloons and sent them to me via another girl with a note wishing me *Happy Birthday*. She is a sweetheart. Everyone was asking me when my birthday was since I was not telling them.

It's just another day to me here, nothing else, but that was still so sweet of her.

Apparently, they were doing group aerobics by "Alcaide," and Desiree was doing it, too. The next thing I knew, I was called by an INPE; I had no idea why. I thought I was being brought to Topico. I assumed it was for my temperature again. So, I went and was brought to where the aerobics class was. I was told by Alcaide to sit, so I did. I had no idea why. I was wearing my face mask, and it was so hot, but I sat there watching the aerobics and not knowing why. I tried to motion a *thank you* to Desiree for the cake, and she smiled. After the aerobics, the Alcaide woman motioned for me to get up with the one woman leading the aerobics. They took the mic, and all started to sing "Happy Birthday" to me in Spanish. I looked straight at Desiree, and she was smiling—she is such a doll. I didn't know what to say or how to react. They couldn't see my facial expressions or smile due to the face masks, but it was still sweet of them. I didn't want anyone to know it was my birthday (well, it was still two days early), but it was too late anyway. Afterward, I hugged Desiree, my Fatima Lena, and told her she was crazy. She asked if I liked the "homemade cake" and then gave me chips and cookies. I felt bad because 4/1 was her birthday, and I had nothing for her, but I gave her a thank you note and S/50 for her birthday. I hope under these circumstances, with no visitors and no one having any money, that it would be helpful for her to get anything she might need.

We were told now that Thursday, we would be able to get "packages" sent to us. It's whatever a visitor would be allowed to bring to us. Annie said she'd have her taxi driver bring me and Jenny a packet. She's limited on what she could get as the stores outside are all still wiped out, but she'd put together a bag for each of us. Thank God for her. I've been getting whatever I can from the kiosko when she gets her stuff, but she's not getting a lot of stuff as it is, plus the prices are even higher now. Yesterday's bread was S/15, again four to five times higher. So, anything Annie can give us is extremely helpful. Not to mention, my S/ will only get me so far, so I hope they start allowing visitors back in after April 12th quarantine.

Of course, Marge is still in Canada, but at least Annie can bring me in my S/ to help. That's if they stop the quarantine and start allowing visitors again, but we shall see. In the meanwhile, allowing packets to come in after three weeks of nothing will be helpful for everyone. No one has money to get necessities, so it's been rough here.

Yesterday I sat for my birthday with Jenny, her girlfriend, and a woman from Russia. We played Dominos. I enjoyed it, and staying outside with people who speak English was good. All the girls put on the radio and started dancing for about two and a half hours. The INPEs were all gathered around, videoing it, watching, and laughing. All the INPEs and Peruvians were having the time of their lives. Yet, I, the woman from Russia, Jenny, and others from Spain, Africa, and her girlfriend from Columbia were just sitting there. We're all miserable and kept saying how we find nothing to be happy about here while the Peruvians always seem to find a reason to dance and be happy. We just don't get it. Even in the apartment, I'd see people with nothing, no job, etc., yet they were always partying with fireworks, drinking, and listening to music. It's such a different way of life. It's like they just accept how sucky the country is and the situation is and chalk it up as, "Oh well, it is what it is," and party. I just don't get it, and none of us foreigners can get it. How can you be happy and want to party constantly in this mess? I guess we'll just never get it.

Now they have extended the quarantine for two more weeks (to 4/26). The president decided this on 4/8. Why? Who freaking knows? This means still no work and doing nothing. At that point, it will be one-and-a-half months, and we are going crazy. If this isn't bad enough, we find out now that one of the men's prisons nearby has one INPE and four men infected now. I have been saying all along how the INPES should be quarantined here with us. They were told they must do a two-day shift now, but what's the point? They leave here and go outside in cabs, cars, etc. How do we know they are not bringing it in? Of course, they won't take any responsibility by saying the INPE gave it to the men's prison. Now they want to blame it on packages that we were finally allowed to get. So now they said no more packages could come in. We tried to say that the kiosko was getting her stuff from the outside, so what was the difference? They don't want to hear it, so no packages. Back to square 1.

The kiosko got a shipment of stuff on Tuesday. The doctor told her she must wash the fruits and veggies off. Well, if she was washing them in hot water or alcohol, I would totally get it. However, she was putting them in a wash basin with cold water. The fruits and veggies had dirt on them as if they were just freshly picked. Of course, it was dirty water after putting the first batch in the cold water. Did she change it? Nope, the next batch went in, and so on. How they felt that this was sterilizing or cleaning the stuff was beyond me, but this was their idea of wiping out any virus that may have been on any of it.

And this they feel is different or better than any of our friends/family bringing us what we need? It's unbelievable their form of thinking. The water, as always, has been non-consistent. This whole Corona Virus stresses washing your hands, etc. Yet you never constantly have water. Yesterday, ironically, we had water all day long. It just goes to show you how they could give us water 24/7, like we had in Santa Monica, but here they just choose not to and just don't care. The water stayed on an entire day, and they just turned it off at quenta at 6 p.m. That was when these girls decided to shower and do dishes, etc. Sometimes the INPE turns the water on for an hour at 8 p.m., and sometimes not; we just never know. Well, after the girls finished doing whatever they were doing, the water buckets were now empty. Of course, this happened to be a night where they didn't put the water on for an hour, so again, we had no water to pour in the toilets to flush them—another night of pure disgusting conditions, sixteen people using a toilet that we had no water to flush. It's so unhygienic and totally gross. We totally live like savages here. The Peruvians think nothing of it, yet we foreigners all live here in true disgust.

Apparently, with COVID being off-the-charts out of control back home, the US prisons started to let many people go. I'm told, right now, it's people over the age of 65 who will be the first to go, and pregnant women; over a thousand people were released in one day. The Peru prisons are off the charts and overcrowded. This has been the case since my first day here, but apparently, that is nothing new at all. Well, with COVID, they are now looking at other countries to get ideas on what they should do.

Desiree got a message to me through a window chain of communication asking how I was doing and to see if I needed anything. She wanted to make sure I had phone cards and anything else I might need. She's such a sweetheart, and I told her I had all I needed right now. She told her stepson Ben* that I was his "Madrina," and she had me write a note to him that she'd give the dad on his visits. Now, with no visits, she told me to call him. He's bored and always asks how his Madrina is. He's only eight years old but has a heart of gold. When she first told him about me, he was so concerned that I may have no shoes that he insisted she gets me a pair of sneakers—so sweet. She told me to call him today at 11 a.m. I called and asked Jenny to translate for me since I am limited in what I can say. She was translating and then heard a woman. It was Desiree saying, "Hello, my friend."

I was like, "OMG, you got your freedom?" Ha-ha. Since she knew I'd be calling at 11 a.m., she called too, and her boyfriend patched us through on a two-way call. That was so clever. Since we are in different pabellons and no Taller, we really can't see one another, so that was clever. She was again just saying hi and making sure I was okay.

On day 33 of the quarantine here in Peru, it was showing on the news how bad the USA is with COVID. Peru is way better with it, but I still remember when it was one person who was infected, then three, then seven, eleven, etc., and it is over 900 now. I'm told that the virus thrives in the cold and dies in the heat. This explains why the USA, currently in their winter, is way higher than us in Peru. But now the seasons will start changing. The USA is in spring, and Peru is in autumn. If the USA starts warming, the virus may be lessened, yet while Peru gets colder, it may start escalating. I'm not sure. But what will that mean for me now? God only knows. Right now, airports are cut off, and borders are closed. For how long? I have no clue. Of course, my fear is that it will just be delaying everyone's cases, on top of everything else, with the courts all closed so far for over one month, and we don't know yet if it will all reopen after 4/20 yet or not. I am terrified to spend any more time here. The poor 75-year-old man from New Jersey is still here, too. He was granted his freedom on 3/10, and then the quarantine started before they gave him the signed papers, so two weeks later, he still sits in prison. It is truly disgusting the situation we are both in.

People here are going nuts. Ancon II has been on the news with all the other issues going on in the prisons. Even here, people set mattresses on fire, people have been fighting left and right. Waco is full of people now. Two girls in my room got into fistfights just yesterday. They are in Waco now. It's crazy, with nothing to do all day, nothing to occupy yourself or pass the time. It is just driving everyone crazy. As I've been saying all along, every time I say, "How much worse can this situation get?" Then, lo and behold, it gets worse. My patience and strength are almost nonexistent. I've been on reserves now and am just done.

There are many people who have caught the virus and actually got better. The USA was saying that they may now have the antibodies and that doctors should take them to help people still infected. While that all sounds good, now there's a man from Korea who had the virus and got better, but then fifteen days later, he got it back again. This tells us that the virus must still be alive in you even after you beat it, and something triggers it to be active again. So, what now? Is this Armageddon? Population control? Who knows, but this mess so far is growing out of control while I sit helplessly stuck here in a country far away from my family. It kills me every day.

We are now on day 40 of the virus quarantine here in Peru. While the quarantine was due to be lifted today (4/26), the president extended it to May 10. That means no work still, no visitors, nothing to occupy us. People are going nuts, bored out of their minds, plus, with no visits, they have no money, making them even more nuts. Everywhere here we must pay to be in prison plus the pabellon always collected money from you for visitors (you had to pay for the table, chairs you sat on, and umbrella for the table) and that money was put into a "pot" to use for expenses the pabellon needed. Well, with no visitors to bring money into their people, everyone was now protesting that they wanted the S/1700 in the "pot" to be given back to everyone so that they could get things they may need.

Well, our delgado has a lot of money. I'm told she has everything she could ever need, and she doesn't care about anything else. She did not want to give everyone any money. Part of me can understand why. I've seen these prisoners for over two years so far and how they do not think beyond the here and now. We still must pay dues every Sunday, and if they allow her to give back the S/25 we'd each get, then they wouldn't pay their dues. Those dues also pay for some of the women who clean the pabellons, so they wouldn't be getting paid, and trust me, cleaning up after slobs in this place is not an easy or pleasant task. They truly are pigs, but I can also see their side.

The delegado is the same one who bought the entire pabellon food for Christmas (over S/1,000). I can't say for sure, but I've come to learn how many of the Peruvian prisoners function. Many of them take the fall for whatever crime they were accused of and take full blame and do not involve their family (even when they are guilty). They do so, and the family (and/or friends) take good care of them while they are in prison, in exchange for them not ratting them out and dragging them down, too. They get money and the best of everything. I can't say for sure that this is her story, but I can only make my guess and assumptions based on what I've learned so far while here.

Now with COVID still in full swing here and the prison so over-crowded, the president has started implementing things to lessen the number of people. The one thing was the removal of the Diaz Multa and Reparation Civil (the two fines we all must pay). If you don't pay, you can't leave. Many women, especially foreigners, have been here for so many years because they didn't have money for their fines. If you paid them, you could apply for benefits and be released. This would only remove 3,000 people, yet since they make money on all prisoners, they will never let more go; it's nuts.

There are people here for six, ten, fifteen years because they have no money to pay their fines. Jenny, for example, has been here for 6.2 years since she cannot pay her fines. My fines total S/10,500, which is about $3,000. I can afford that. Some other prisoners from other countries here just don't have it, so they must complete the full sentence. They have passed a law to eliminate these fines, which would allow a lot of people to go free who've already served a third of their time, but of course, Congress has yet to sign these bills. Until they do, the fines still need to be paid. Now with the quarantine, who knows if it will ever get passed? I seriously doubt it because prison is a business for Peru. Why would they take away money and employment for Peruvians for the sake of foreigners? I doubt we'll ever see that happen.

There's a new law that those who only have six months left of their sentence will be set free—fines or no fines. This is great for Jenny since she only has six months left, so she'll be allowed to go free when they do all the paperwork and such. It sucks because she's already served six years, and I'm happy she'll be going home, yet unfortunately for me, this house arrest issue screwed me. Even though I've been stuck here for three years, only twenty-two months count, and I'd still have five more months to complete what they see as one-third before I can file for benefits. Sal screwed me so badly with that house arrest. I'd have been home nine months ago if it weren't for that.

Another law is set to release pregnant women and women with children in prison, those 65 years or older, and those with illnesses such as HIV, TB, etc. None of these apply to me, so I just have to sit and wait my next five months to apply for benefits and hope this coronavirus doesn't skyrocket out of control more.

Another crazy thing, which was good for me, but the US should be ashamed of themselves, since we have no visitors and US foreigners have no family in Peru, we don't have much here. My older sister spoke with Melanie, who has a connection with the Thailand Embassy. Unlike my embassy, the Thai, Mexican, Spain, and Holland Embassies take care of their people. I received a care package from them that contained eight rolls of toilet paper, bars of soap, soap detergent for clothes, toothpaste, a toothbrush, a big bottle of shampoo, a big bottle of body lotion, a big bag of dried fruits and nuts, crackers, cookies, snacks, chips and a bag of fruits and veggies, plus they brought in my migraine and cholesterol medicine! I was amazed and beyond grateful. They brought the same in for all Thailand ladies, plus about seven more for other English women. I told my embassy about my need for migraine and cholesterol medicines three years ago in Santa Monica and then Ancon and always got the same generic replies, "We'll make a note of it," and did nothing. When they visit (I haven't seen them in almost eight months now), it's always the same: one sample-size bottle of one-use shampoo, conditioner, soap as you'd get in hotel bathrooms, one bottle of a three-month supply of calcium vitamins, vitamin C, and iron vitamins. That is all they ever bring. Can you see the difference? I got more from another country's embassy in one package than anything I've ever gotten from my US Embassy in three years. It's a disgrace.

My mom has been pretty sick—throwing up, fever, achy joints, etc. She refuses to go to a doctor (being stubborn as always), but it sounds to me like she has this coronavirus. She's got all the symptoms, unfortunately. It will crush me beyond words if she does have it and doesn't survive this. I truly just want out of this nightmare already. Whenever Jenny does go, I will have no other English translators in my pabellon anymore, so this will be quite interesting. Like I've been saying, every time I say, "How much worse can this get?" I get shown something worse. I must be as positive as possible and know that in five months, I can apply for benefits. That's all I can do, unfortunately. But another good thing, as I've said, INPEs work here two days now with the quarantine, and it's been a little easier to see routines and habits. Like the INPE we've had for the past two days is one that gives us water twenty hours a day. We get it all day and night, and it's only off from 1:00 to 4:00 a.m. Luckily, we have it all morning, afternoon, and night. This again proves that they *can* give us water if they want. They simply choose not to. I'm learning which INPEs withhold water now and can plan a little better that way. It's crazy. I just want to go home! Today's INPE is one that doesn't give water, so again, today, only water for one hour. It's insane how they are here.

With this quarantine, the prison has been rioting like crazy. They have been all over the news. Ancon II, Lurigancho, and Santa Monica have been rioting so badly that the INPEs don't want to go to work. They don't carry guns. They are (to me anyway) nothing more than Wal-Mart security. We thought that might convince the president to let us go, but nope. He said in the news, "Those are the same men that raped your daughters and the same people that robbed you, and you expect me to put them back on the street? No way." I learned this while in Santa Monica—Peru sees drug smuggling as worse than murderers. The president said he'd never let a drug trafficker go early. And for me, that is all I am looking at here. I can understand what he's saying, but it just sucks for me, too, but as always, there is nothing that I can do about it but wait. Only four-and-a-half more months to go.

While talking to Jenny's girlfriend (well, with Jenny translating), I learned that she comes from Ica, not Santa Monica. She was sent from Ica to Ancon, and now Fatima, too. She says Ica was worse than Fatima. I'm thanking God that I've no experience there, at least. She said it was a nine-hour drive from Ica to Ancon (I have no clue where any of these prisons are) and that they, too, rarely had water. She said the rooms were the same size as Ancon II's rooms, but where we had four bunk beds in Ancon II for eight people, Ica had ten beds for twenty-two people in a room. What did that mean? Ten people had to share a bed with two on the floor. It's insane how crowded their prisons are and how, like savages, they just expect you to suck it up and deal with it.

On a positive note, the New Jersey man's wife was finally able to take her husband home today, six months after he was allowed to file for benefits. Between his coma, several stints in the hospital, just about going blind from his diabetes, and Peru refusing to release him, it took another lawyer, coupled with him "accidentally" testing positive for COVID-19 for the Embassy, to work with her to get him released. Like every other foreigner, the courts and INPEs "accidentally" misplaced papers, causing delay after delay. She never thought they'd get out of here, but I'm happy for them that they finally got out of this mess once and for all. I can only pray and think positively that in four-and-a-half months, I can file for my benefits and that it all goes smoothly; that's all I can do.

We are now on day 51 of the quarantine. Sunday (Mother's Day), we shall see if they remove the quarantine, keep it, or semi-lift it. Who knows? We shall see. We've been out of work for about one-and-a-half months so far, and rumor has it that we won't be returning to work until July or August. Why? I have no idea. The only good thing is that the weather is changing, so it's not hell-hot all day now, so I don't have to keep showering and wetting my head and hair. When the sun is not out, it's comfortable, nice, and cool—a sweater works just fine. But if and when the sun comes out, it's still hot.

The bill for "no need to pay your fines" has not yet been signed, and it's been a few months. Seeing how Peru and its prisons are all about the money, it will be interesting to see if it ever gets signed. I'm not optimistic about that. With these new bills that the president needs to sign to release people with either six months or less left of their full sentence, anyone with a critical health issue, etc., it was calculated to remove only 200 women out of the 3,000 people expected to be removed. Sure, there are a lot more men than women in prison, but there are still 5,000 women incarcerated, and 200 won't do much in terms of clearing out some of these extremely crowded prisons. The prison sent a solicitude to the president asking him to add to the criteria—things such as those with sentences of six years or less (which doesn't help me) and other criteria—who knows if he'll acknowledge any of it or not, but none of it will help me anyway.

Alberto asked my husband and sister on Sunday to send him pictures of my skydiving accident and injuries, medical records, and Dr. Ladd's report. He physically brought it all to the Ministry of Justice today. He's trying to find loopholes or anything he can to try and get me out sooner. Melanie read the news article about my accident and said it all made sense now. She told Alberto that he must do whatever he can to get me out of here. He gave it to the Ministry of Justice and Humanitarian group for them to review. Sadly, this doesn't fall into the criteria to be released by these new rules, but he's trying, and that's more than Sal has ever done. I'm looking forward to four months to file and not expecting anything, but if it works and they allow it, that would be a wonderful surprise and bonus.

The Spanish Embassy came yesterday to see their people. I was surprised to learn that they bring their people S/300 every month. Wow, I couldn't even get my embassy to bring me stuff I already paid for, let alone give me something on their own, aside from a three-month supply of vitamin C and iron and a one-time-use tiny shampoo bottle. I'm told that two years ago, the Spanish Embassy also petitioned Peru to supply airplanes to remove Spaniards from Peru prisons and bring them back home to Spain, but out of three planes of people, Peru only released twenty-two. Peru does not make it easy to leave; that's for sure. They look for everything they can find to halt any effort. Even for people who apply to leave Peru and serve their sentences in their country, it customarily takes three to four years before they process them out. Is it because you are paying as long as you are in prison? I have no clue.

Same with this new law the president just signed, where people with six months or under, 65 years old, etc., can go. They are doing this in batches, not all at once. The first batch had 200 people. The prison director filters out who qualifies, and then it goes to the Ministry of Justice for them to sign off and/or accept or reject people. Out of the first 200 people, they denied 173! It's insane. If someone has a six-year-and-eight-months sentence and only has two or three more months, having already served six years and five months, why on earth would you not let them just go? Others have served anywhere from ten to twenty-five years so far. This country, with its crazy high sentences and lack of allowing anyone to leave is a disgrace. So, while it is nice that due to COVID and so many getting infected, they are allowing some to leave early, but if you say it and then do not allow it, how on earth is that sensible? Sadly, it's how they work here and what I've witnessed for the past three years.

Santa Monica, which is four times more crowded, we're told there are now eight confirmed cases of COVID-19 there now. Again, they will still not acknowledge how it's possible INPEs are the ones bringing it in. They will never admit to that. Now it will spread like wildfire there. We're told of how if one person gets it in here, *no one* will be leaving or be released—period. Well, of course, that makes me nervous with the temperature dropping now; what if someone here gets it? I'll never be out of here. It's like Peru has a semi-right idea, yet they didn't go about it right. They act like they are way better than other countries due to the fewer infections and deaths from COVID-19. Yes, the USA has tons more, but Peru is now up to 46,000 infected and 1,200 deaths, and the weather is changing to the prime weather for the virus, so will it worsen? We shall soon see.

Also, Peru is spread out, and not so many people. In the US, New York especially, there are millions of people all on top of each other with high risers and buildings. So many people are close, so yes, the numbers will be higher. Their "ideas" are semi–right here in Fatima, but I always scratch my head at their idiotic ways. For example, the "patio" is approximately half the size of the basketball court. Not very big. This patio is where the phones are, where Kiosko is, where we eat, sit at tables, wash clothes, go to the bathroom, play volleyball, do aerobics, etc. As you can see, a lot happens in the small spot. But we are, in essence, all around one another here. When we line up for the quenta (where they call your name and count you up for the night), we were told that we must wear a mask at quenta and also stand in line with five feet between us. Umm, okay. But from quenta, we go upstairs to our pabellon floor, which is about nine by twelve inches in space. The hall is where the TV and microwave are. The seats for the TV are side by side, elbow to elbow. No one keeps the mask on. It's only mandatory for quenta. So, we must wear it for quenta when we've been in the same space (patio) all day, only to go upstairs, enclosed, and in an even smaller space without a mask. What sense does this make?

Plus, now they say we must wear a mask while in line for food on the patio. Again, we've all been around each other in this space half the size of a basketball court, all day with no mask, we now must wear the mask now in line, with five feet of space (where this line wraps around everyone around us in their tables), to get our food, where we all then remove our masks to eat our food. It's the same space all around one another; what on earth sense does this even make? I don't get them. It's a start to a semi-good idea, but there's no real thought process. I was shaking my head, and one of the girls said something, and I just told her, "*Tu Paies es loca.*" She asked me in

Spanish why I was calling her country crazy. I truly didn't want to get into it with her. All I could say politely was how crazy I felt Peru was.

Today was a bit strange. The women here don't speak English (the Peruvians), yet if they know one or two words, they are so proud of themselves and always say them without knowing the actual meanings. Apparently, there was a commercial with Peter Pan and Tinker Bell. Well, I helped one girl today, and she thanked me and called me Tinker Bell. I was laughing. I honestly don't know whether to take it as a compliment or an insult. She meant it as a compliment and was so proud of herself for saying Tinker Bell. Crazy. If she understood that Tinker Bell is a small fly-like woman, and I am twice the size of most Peruvian women here, it's a bad comparison.

Then I saw a girl getting her head massaged by someone, and I told Jenny how I loved that and how it would put me to sleep. She told another woman who said today at 10:30 a.m. she'd do a head massage for me and read my vibes with an egg. What? Yep, I had to buy an egg (S/0.50), and she massaged my head and then rubbed the egg all over me (my head, arms, neck, shoulders, back, legs, and feet, all of me!). I thought I smelled something bad but thought it was the environment. When she was done, she just said, "Patricia, no Buena." Huh? Not good? Why? She smelled the egg, and the bad smell was from the egg! WTF? She was trying to tell me the bad smell was all the bad I was holding in—coming out. I had to find Jenny to translate for me. She said I have a lot of nervous energy and fear that was coming out and why the egg suddenly smelled. Wow, this was so bizarre. I thought all this crap was old wives' tales and superstitious, but I witnessed how the egg's smell totally changed after she rubbed me down with it. Of course, I have nervous energy and fear in me. I've been literally stuck here, for three years now, in a third-world country's prison—my third prison so far—where I don't speak the language and have no clue when this nightmare will end.

She said she would do this again in two days to try and draw it out. Hmmm. This will be interesting. This also explains to me what happened with Inga in SM. She was not feeling good one day (I thought she was teething; she was only eight months old), and her mom brought her to a woman. She did the same thing to the baby with an egg, then crumbled up a newspaper, rubbed her down with that, and then set the paper on fire until it was all ashes. Apparently, it was her way of pulling out the bad in the baby, so she'd be better. I had thought it was totally bizarre at the time, but now I see what she was doing. I'm definitely in a whole other world here. Welcome to my life in Peru's prisons.

Today was Mother's Day; we got more chicken donated to us for lunch, which was nice. The delgado also bought us each a soda (Inca Cola) out of the pabellon's money). The COVID number is up to 46,700 infected and 2,000 dead here in Peru. The quarantine is extended to two weeks to May 24, so we shall see, and the numbers are not going down, so who knows. I saw Switzerland on the news, and they were saying what they were doing. They are not quarantined, not wearing masks, and going about life like always, yet their number of infections is at a bare minimum. Why? Is it too cold there for the virus to survive? Do people not travel abroad to or from there much? I don't know. Fatima says if one person gets it, no one leaves, so I pray every day that over the next four or five months, no one here gets it, so I can get out of here once and for all.

I called my daughter for Mother's Day, and she told me that I'm the greatest mom and how strong I am, and she is who she is thanks to me and how she is strong and can handle so much because she's seen how much I've gone through and have always been a strong person. It melted my heart, and I wanted to cry. I have the two best kids in the world. She is so loving, sweet, kind, and awesome. I couldn't have asked for two better kids. They mean the world to me. My son wrote me a note, so I hope I get it soon. With no visitors still, it's impossible to get anything, but praying, as always, that this ends soon.

CHAPTER 19

It's been four years since my accident now, and I've always said I can't see anything wrong with me, so it's hard to know if I'm 100 percent back to normal. I was having a conversation with Jenny, and somehow, we were talking about people who've committed crimes before and how many are second- and third-time offenders and such, and about our circumstances. I was talking about my situation with Sal and the judges and how my husband said that the cops did their job by arresting me because I was caught at the airport with drugs. I noted how Sal claimed he gave the judges all the proof about my brain injury and how I did not even realize I was set up, but at the end of the day, we'll never know if he even gave them my defense or just told us that to keep dragging us along to make money. I told her how the brain injury got me into this mess and how I don't know if it would ever get better or if this was the best it would ever be.

She shocked me by saying, "You are actually better now than in Ancon." What? Could she see it too? She said I repeat myself a lot. She said the one story I told her today, I've told her about five times. She said that when I get aggravated, stressed, or nervous, I repeat a lot more, but when I seem calm, it is almost unnoticeable. I was shocked to hear this because I have heard my family repeat this exact same thing to me before. She said it seems to have gotten a bit better over the past years since we first met, so that is good to hear. This tells me that it's still improving.

She said Marge had given her a heads up before meeting me so that she and Tania were aware of the brain injury and were patient with me. So, Marge had seen it too. She said when I first got to Ancon, I was repeating myself constantly. She said, "I just was thinking, OMG. Is this what it's like going to be with her? Constantly saying the same shit over and over!" But then she caught on that it only seemed to be when I was stressed and nervous. Of course, this whole experience is stressful and makes me nervous. Anis* with the egg the other day even said that my body's vibes are all bad because of nervousness, so that is two confirming this. Four more months; that's all I can pray for, four more months to put this all behind me.

When I feel overwhelmed, I write stuff down. For example, while I have nothing else better to do if I'm not coloring in the coloring books my older sister got, I'm reading a book. I'm okay when it's only a handful of characters in the book, but when it's a lot, I write down who they are, their names, characters, association, and important details to keep me focused. I use the paper as my bookmark and refer to it throughout the book. Jenny thought I was nuts, but it kept me focused. I remember it was the same when I was home (post-accident). If I had a conference call or something and it involved a lot of things, I would record the call only as a means of referring to it to make sure I got it all and didn't miss anything. Apparently, I'm still following this routine, but I hadn't caught on to it until she just pointed it out to me.

Jenny feels that after studying me for a bit, it seems that, being an Aries and strong headed, when I don't understand something, it's when my brain seems to spaz out. I also am a person who has always gone out of my way to help people. Yet, now, and under these crazy circumstances, I can't. For example, my Fatima Lena, Desiree, has been here now for six years so far, all due to corrupt cops and corruption. I want to help her, yet I don't know how under these crazy circumstances. It's her country and their corrupt justice system, so what could I even do? Sadly, nothing. Jenny told me this story is one I've repeated several times to her without my realizing. She believes it plays like a music album, and if there's a scratch in the album, it will repeat repeatedly until you bump it. She feels that if my brain can't understand something or find a way to fix something, it just repeats. She may be right; I don't know. She said the one thing is for sure is that my stories never change. I'm not lying, so that is obvious, at least. I just had to tell her, like I have told my family, I don't know when I am repeating myself, so if I am doing it, to just nicely tell me, "Yes, you told me this before," and I can stop. That's all I can do.

At Santa Monica, the woman made a banner and hung it out the window screaming, "Help us! Help us! There's no doctor, no medicine, they are leaving us here to die!" and someone outside saw this and filmed it, and it made the news. People there are infected, and they just leave us all. Ironically, after that, we heard at least all babies and their moms in SM were removed and placed into an outside shelter. Well, I'm glad they at least did that much, but what about everyone else? All these new rules, over 65 years old, critical illness, etc. They said they could be released, yet it's been weeks, and not one single one has been released yet; it's ridiculous.

We're now at over 45,000 infected and 1,500 deaths so far. I saw China was getting fewer infections now and removed their quarantine, and the number's skyrocketed again. I can only pray that I go back home before this happens here. The director told us, "If one person here gets it, *no one* leaves. Freedom or no freedom, no one leaves." Today we were told now that if you were to be released and test positive for COVID, you'd have to be quarantined for forty days before ever being free. Who knows, as usual, they seem to make up the rules as they go along, changing them from day to day.

We are now on day 59, and we're told that the quarantine will go on for another five weeks, and then we will see if they'll extend it again. As the weather gets colder here, I know the numbers will keep rising, so this will be interesting. Just like back home, people can't not work forever. It's been two-and-a-half months so far. I know the people here are definitely feeling it. Normally there are many women, like myself, who pay the S/3 or S/5 not to clean the room biweekly or Ricojo, which is where you serve the meals. I think in my room alone, there were only three people who did it. The rest just paid the few soles to not have to do it. Well, now, with no work and no family coming to bring them money—not to mention with no one outside working—they don't have the money to send them anyway; it's been a problem. Now, almost everyone is cleaning and serving food. Only a few are not. I'm not a primadonna. To be honest, I clean and fill the water buckets and barrels every single day, so it's not that I don't want to get my hands dirty. I just 1) know that the delegado does this for money, so I am happy to pay her S/3–S/5 every two weeks to do it, and 2) it involves going downstairs and getting supplies every day, which is hard for me to do since I don't speak the language fluently.

When we first arrived in Fatima, our room light blew out and again, it was S/10 to change it. This went on for days, and no one cared, so they wouldn't put money on it. We were brand new here, too! I finally told the delgado that I'd pay the S/10 just to get light. Well, of course, as it seems typical of Peru, I'm now told that it's not just the bulb, but the whole light wiring needs to be fixed, which turned into S/30. Somehow, it didn't shock me anymore; I paid the S/30, and we got light. I told the delgado not to tell anyone I paid for it, so she agreed. Seeing how no one cared about light back then, I knew no one cared at all about the bathroom light that went out next. Plus, no one had money again. What did that mean? It was left to me again.

I agreed to pay S/10 for a new light but not S/30. Ironically, we were told that the maintenance man had to fix it, which still took four days to repair! We asked them initially if he had bulbs, and he said yes, that he'd be up that night to change it. That never happened. The next day, the same. On the third day, we said how it was disrupting everything and how we needed it, and he said, "Yeah, yeah, I'll be by later to change it." That never happened. By the fourth day, he came close to 5 p.m. to change it—ridiculous yet typical. At this point, everyone knew I paid for it since no one had any money, and the pabellon didn't have any either. Not that I wanted a pat on the back or anything because I did it more for me than anything; yet, as typical here, not a single thank you or anything.

I've learned here that while maneuvering in the dark sucks and they didn't like it, they would just make do with it and be okay. At night we are supposed to turn the light off after 9 p.m. quenta, and being locked in the room leaves it pitch black. Plus, Peru doesn't turn their clocks as we do back home for daylight saving time. It's now darker earlier and lighter later, so what was everyone doing? Leaving the room lights on late so they could talk and shower or whatever they do. Before even not showering, the room light went out, and they'd leave the bathroom light on and just keep the bathroom door open. That now wasn't an option. Plus, as I would be trying to shower at 4:30 a.m., in the pitch darkness and trying to fill up the buckets in the dark with the hose that kept popping off the faucet, where I couldn't see anything, it was nuts. Not to mention, one day, I got it going and couldn't see how high the water was in the bucket. I kept going in to check on it, and by the time I realized the water was to the top so, thank God I caught it in time.

It's the same with filling the buckets and stuff; I've been doing it for eight months so far. It's not because I enjoy filling them. The two girls even made a comment on how I'm addicted to it. Seriously? I learned so early on that people here care only about themselves. I lost count of how many times the buckets/barrels weren't filled with water when the water was on. What was the result? Sixteen women peeing and pooping in a toilet that you could not flush. Dirty Tupperware in the sink was stinking up the bathroom. They seem to just make do with whatever they have or don't have. Especially when it was hell-hot summer, I needed water to shower with. Yes, I had my bucket with water but having to sit and babysit it every day because no one else had water was just exhausting. I mean, they'd rather steal my water than put a hose to the bucket and fill the barrels.

My husband used to tell me not to fill anything and just to be dirty and smelly. I couldn't do that. I sweat a lot, especially in the summer and coupled with hot flashes from menopause. In Santa Monica, I took several showers a day. Here, the lack of water was a constant problem for me. Peruvians were used to this weather. They never sweat, from what I saw. I, on the other hand, had a different reaction to it. Either way, I just started filling the barrels myself because no one else was. Jenny used to say they don't do it because they know that I would. But that is not true; they just don't do it, period. Several people have gone home in my eight months of being here (completing their sentences). I believe one other girl was doing it, too, filling the buckets, washing everyone's Tupperware, but she went home seven months ago, and it just seems no one does it.

The weather now is getting cold. Unfortunately, the two warm sweatshirts I made myself in Ancon disappeared. In Ancon, we were allowed hoods. In Santa Monica and Fatima, we are not. The INPEs/

Alcaide tried to take my sweaters away from me a few months ago during a Requisa, and I fought them on it. They were mine. I paid for the material and made them myself! They could take the hoods but not the whole sweaters. They said okay. It was summer then, so I gave them to Marita* in Taller/costura. I asked her to cut the hoods off and sew them up nicely but told her there was no rush and that I wouldn't need them until autumn. Well, we never expected COVID-19, and now it's autumn and cold, and my sweaters are in Taller in a different space than mine. Marita is in a different pabellon, too, so I can't even ask her.

I had someone call Lena's dad for me to ask about Inga and Lena. He said they'd been worried sick over me. He hasn't heard from me since Ancon, and now Inga is home with him (since babies must leave the prison when they turn three, and she turned three two months ago), and Lena is on the list to be released, but when that happens is anyone's guess. Santa Monica has many people infected there, so they just hope it's soon so that she doesn't get COVID. I was happy to hear that they were okay and that she would be going home soon to the baby. Another woman here who was also the delgado of Topico was supposed to go home a month ago, and due to COVID-19, she's still here. We heard her screaming on the phone and crying. Someone in her family passed away yesterday, and she was upset not to have been there to say goodbye. And why wasn't she there? She should have gone home last month!

Alcaide tells us that everyone is still working but remotely now. Well, if they're still working, people who should have been released should be home!! It's truly sickening how they treat us here—like animals. My husband has said even with the Embassy, they see "just another criminal" and don't care one bit about your story. Just Google my name, for Pete's sake, and you'd see how I've been in business for decades. I've been on the cover of magazines, in newspapers, radio, etc. I'm not a nobody and definitely didn't need to fly to Peru to try and smuggle out 2.5 kilos of cocaine. But that's what I was arrested for, and that's all anyone seems to care about, unfortunately; three-and-a-half months, that's all I can focus on, and I just pray that the Big Guy upstairs sends me home and doesn't allow any more obstacles to stop me.

Well, we're now on June 1st, so we have three more months to go. This freaking nightmare can't end soon enough. The quarantine in this place is now set to continue until June 30th so far. We'll see if they extend it or not. It's been a little over two months of no work or anything for us here. I washed my clothes the other day and hung them out on the line to dry overnight. Due to the humidity in the air, they are almost dry but not 100 percent yet. I figured maybe another hour or two, and I'd bring them in. I happened to walk that way and didn't see any of my clothes on the line. *WTF? Did they steal my clothes again?* I ran down the stairs and went on a scavenger hunt. Well, as typical, they stole my clothes clips and moved them to a random spot. Not all in one spot; all over. I spent fifteen minutes searching for my workout clothes—socks, underwear, bra, shirt—all with no clips now and just randomly thrown all around on the line. I was furious. I had Jenny translate to the delgado of discipline about it. She said she'd say something at quenta, but I was livid.

Of course, she never said anything because why would she? It was obviously a Peruvian who did it, and they truly don't see anything wrong with it, and we all by now know whose clothes are who's, so fuck it, steal clips, and move the Gringo's shirt. It's truly ridiculous. I was not letting it go. The next day I mentioned to the delgado to say something, and I was adamant, so she did. She said that someone moved my clothes and to not touch other people's clothes. She never mentioned anything about them stealing my clips or how it is not allowed to move people's stuff. Unreal. People blew it off, and a few people commented that if clothes are dry, you need to take them off the line. Well, if they were dry, I would have, but they were still damp! So now, I put wet clothes out and spend all day preoccupied with checking on them all day to ensure they are not touched.

Jenny feels that since I put mine near the front, the others are too lazy to carry their wet clothes deeper in the line to hang them so they just take mine off and put theirs in that space and just move mine further down since it's not as heavy as a pile of wet clothes. I don't care what excuse they have. No one has a right to touch my shit, let alone steal my clips! This freaking nightmare can't end soon enough!

As it's getting cooler out, the sun isn't coming out as much as it did in the summer when we first started sitting. Outside, in the summer, Jenny and her girlfriend had a table against the wall, which was good because the sun didn't shine there at lunchtime. Well, one day, another two women took over that space, and all the Peruvians took over the whole wall, so she was then stuck putting her table away from the wall, where the sun hits prime at lunchtime. That's where the struggle for an umbrella at lunchtime came in. Every day was a fight to try and get one of the eight umbrellas. I started sitting with Jenny a few months back when the Peruvian woman I was originally sitting with booted me out of her table because she said she didn't want to get COVID-19 from anyone. That was stupid, but I am tired of trying to expect common sense from anyone here. I'd now sit with Jenny and her girlfriend. There are only so many tables and chairs. I needed a table and chair to sit on. So, I joined hers and participated every day in a scavenger hunt for an umbrella. Now that the sun isn't out much, many of the people who were originally against the wall all summer have moved their tables back to the sides where they originally were. We didn't care.

So, we moved our table by the wall, and everyone else moved theirs around, so we put ours back where we originally had it. No one owns the space. Well, stupid us for thinking they would ever be okay with a foreigner doing what the Peruvians do. They complained that the space belonged to another three girls (2 of whom are in my room). We were saying how it's not her *space*. They did not want to hear it and pushed their table over directly on top of ours, causing Jenny's girlfriend to have to move. Were they fucking kidding? It's unbelievable. We literally had to move. I was furious. If not for the fact that I only have three more months to file for benefits, I'd have raised all hell over this, but I just moved and now completely ignore the two girls in my room. I truly don't need them for anything. They always ask *me* for stuff, not the other way around, so screw them! They can kiss my ass!

It's funny because they won't mess with me personally because they don't know how I'd react. I'm way taller than they are, for starters, and since I usually keep to myself and when I *do* speak up, they don't understand me anyway so they tread carefully. They haven't a clue, especially when I don't back down from any of them. I stand tall and speak back in English, so since I'm not afraid of them, they don't know how to read me.

On July 28th, yet another Peru national holiday, the entire popliteal cabinet resigned as a gesture of goodwill and generosity to the president. The president then appoints a new cabinet (usually the same people against his friends). If someone is to be fired, it happens during this resignation. So as not to cause anyone to lose face, they all approve of this method. As crazy as it is, where did this attitude come from? The loss of face is an aging issue with Arabs. The Moors from North Africa invaded and settled in southern Spain. Several generations later, this characteristic became consolidated in the personality of those in the land. That is also a part of Spain that Pizarro, the Conquistadores, and the original Spanish settlers came from. The trait was a gift from Spain.

So, now that I have nothing but time on my hands here, I study everything around me and try as best I can to understand them. What have I learned so far? First and foremost, guilty until proven innocent, personally known, and trusted. I don't even know if they realize what that even means here. No one, to them, is innocent. You are guilty and thrown into the revenue pot, end of the story.

Being in Lima, Peru, I learned about Lima time. Funerals start on time at the given time, yet anything else, like parties, meals, games, plays, weddings, etc. fall under "Lima-time," which is about a three-hour difference from the expected or announced time. For example, noon in Lima is approximately between 12:00 and 3:00 p.m. and is time to sit down, relax, visit and enjoy the sobremesa (dessert). Sobremesa is the time spent at the table long after the food is gone, socializing. It's a time to relax and enjoy one another's company. They envy our way of thinking and how we function with our head ahead of us. In terms of "what's next" and preparing ahead, yet as with everything else, they do nothing at all about it.

Pride is another huge factor in Peruvians. They will always agree to help and never say that they can't or don't know how. For example, if I was walking and was lost and asked directions, if they didn't know or couldn't understand me, they would never say that. Instead, they would direct me *somewhere,* knowing I'd be gone and could never return, and say it was wrong. That, to them, doesn't matter. It is more of a pride thing to have an answer to my question. Whether it was right or wrong didn't matter.

Regarding ethics, we stop at stop signs. They see no cars and think it's stupid to stop and don't. They determine right from wrong based on whether the result of the action is positive or negative. Right and proper moves and behaviors lend to that which is good; stopping your car at an intersection at 11:00 p.m. when there are no other cars is crazy to them.

It seems that Peruvians will also never lose face. "*No me hagas quedar mal*" means, "Do not make me look foolish." If you ask for a favor or directions, they will never say, "I can't," so they will always say yes to not lose face. Yet their directions may be wrong or the favor not done. To them, it looks better to say yes and not to do the favor than to say no. It's crazy.

Family is very important to them. The majority stay home until they are married. You leave the nest only when the wedding bells sound, and even then, you will most likely move in with one of the parents. The elderly, if not already living at home, will most likely move in when they get too old to care for themselves. They would never put their family into a nursing home. I don't even know if they exist in Peru. They also have many kids. They know the kids will take care of you when you are older.

Here in Peru, they see Holy Week as a pungent to death, and the highlight is Food Friday, with mournful crowds following a dead Christ and a weeping virgin. I saw this firsthand when I was made to carry a cross of Jesus across Santa Monica.

Peruvians don't trust Gringos or anyone not directly introduced by a trusted Peruvian. Why? They've been deceived by foreigners over the centuries. I've read stories about how Lima came to be. Ri-mac in Quechua means "the one who speaks," but Spanish people couldn't understand how to pronounce it and changed it to Limac as it was the name of the valley in which the Spanish were to found the capital of the Spanish Empire in South America. The city was then called a more Spanish-sounding name Lima, six million people in Rimac (Lima).

Today's people from Lima are a mix of descendants of Atahualpa and Pizarro. After the events of Cajamarca, today, people from Lima only trust a few. Any outsider, including all other people from Lima not personally known and proven, will not be trusted period. This is why friends and recommendations are so important. Here you are guilty until proven innocent, totally the opposite of how it is in the USA. When someone wants to talk to a judge or someone of power, if they are not Peruvian or recommended by a Peruvian, it is a waste of time.

Sadly, it's three more months to start the process, and we've already learned that Peru is not fast. Same with the new laws. While it all sounds good, no one has been released. It's a new "law" that people over sixty years, people with less than six months of their sentence, and people with a terminal illness or aids or diabetes, etc., are to be released. They've put together a list of all the people to be released, and that's as far as it went. This was one month ago. The director had a meeting and just said, "It's all a process, and it takes time," so sadly, nothing Peru does is ever done fast.

In my case, once the judge says that I can go, I'm technically the property of the US Embassy. Still in prison, yes, but it's the Embassy who can get me home fast or not, paperwork, immigration, etc. They handle it all. They can get it done in two weeks to six months, depending on how they choose to handle it. Unfortunately for me, having the US Congress breathe down their necks has made a bad name for me with them. Their flaws were shown back home how they do nothing. Apparently, for me, that's pissed them off.

We are on day 91 of the quarantine here, and so far, 167,400 have been infected here in Peru. Now my mom has had symptoms of this COVID-19 for some time yet has refused to go to the doctor. I only have her word since I'm not there, but from what I hear from her and my sister, she's been sick as a dog for a few weeks. Today, she finally slipped and admitted that she has COVID-19. Of course, this breaks my heart. When I confronted her on her slip, she again denied it and said she was fine, but now, it's been confirmed. I guess she didn't want me to know so as not to upset me under these circumstances, but she's my mom. I need to know and can only pray she beats this and is home whenever this nightmare ends.

Day 94 now, and 187,400 are infected. New law where people under eight-year sentences who've completed a third fine of their fine will get released, so they say. Again, thanks to Sal, this doesn't help me. I've technically completed a few small months shy of a third of my sentence, yet due to Sal's lie of "house arrest definitely counts" when it doesn't, I now still have three months left to complete what they feel is a third of my time. They also made a few new laws that will help Peruvians, yet won't help us foreigners. People can get released with ankle bracelets but must have a Peruvian address. Of course, I could go to Rosa's or Marge's or Melanie's, which would put me in some place, but this new law wasn't meant to help foreigners—such discrimination. Their attitude is, "Then you shouldn't have come to our country to commit a crime." And yet again, not everyone is guilty of their accused crime, but it is what it is.

We're told now that the quarantine will be extended partially for three more months. Well, I assume that means no work for me for three more months, no visitors, etc. I can only pray that in three more months, I will have court (delahencia) and that the Embassy and all are semi-working to enable me to get out of here once and for all!

I saw there are 199,696 infected today. This nightmare just does not want to end. We now have COVID-19 inside *this* prison, so here comes even more suffering! We're told that people with health issues are very susceptible to catching this. That being said, they want to move all the people with illness (not COVID-19) to one area, so they keep them separated, but ironically my pabellon is the only one so far with zero illness—no flu, COVID-19, etc. Our pabellon was protesting moving anyone in or out of our pabellon. If they moved sick people to one pabellon, they would then be moving others from Pabellons A, B, C, and E to our pabellon to fill up space. Since they'd have to shuffle everyone around to make room to put all those with illness into one area, people were saying, "We have no way of knowing if people would then be bringing COVID-19 *into* our pabellon."

The director said they'd give everyone a COVID-19 test before moving them here. Still, everyone said, "No, it stays in your system for ten days before showing on a test, so if they test negative today and you move them here, they could still be positive, and by the time it would show, it would already have infected countless others." We were told in the morning that there were three infected (of course, blaming it on bags brought in from the outside). By midday, the three grew to twelve, and by evening, people said thirty-two. Wow! It apparently spreads like wildfire.

Well, everyone said "No." They told the delegado that they want no one in or out of our pabellon. The INPE at the 6 p.m. quenta ran over a list of about six to eight names of people in our Pabellon who had illnesses (diabetes, high blood pressure, asthma, etc.). that they planned to move out of our pabellon to Pabellon E. Everyone said, "No, we are not moving. We don't know if where you are sending us is infected with COVID-19. We all are healthy now and want to stay that way."

Two people agreed to go through, packed up their stuff, and moved to Pabellon E. That put the INPEs in a bad position. They were given orders to move six to eight people, yet only two were willing to go. The INPEs kept coming and returning to Alcaide, trying to figure out what to do. The INPE then said everyone who refused to go needed to write and sign their names on a blank sheet of paper. Of course, they refused because no one trusted this prison. They could all sign this blank paper, and the prison could then write something like, "I wish to stay in prison for ten more years" or "I agree I murdered someone, give me ten more." Who knows? No one trusted them, so they refused to sign anything.

Now the INPEs were in a rougher spot. They then tried to move the two women to Pabellon E, who were willing to go, only to have Pabellon E start protesting the same thing. They did not want outsiders coming in and potentially bringing illness to them either. As this was happening, the girls in my pabellon were creating banners. *Ayúdame - Penal de Fátima, llegó el COVID-19, 32 contagia-dos, ayúdennos, estamos atrapados,* which meant: "Help. Fatima penal, COVID-19 is here, 32 infected, help us. We're trapped." As Pabellon E was protesting, Pabellon D (my pabellon) started rioting. They were yelling, screaming, hanging out their signs, and banging stuff. They even moved beds into the hallway and piled chairs all on top of it, so the INPEs couldn't come in. I stayed in my bed, not that it mattered. The whole pabellon went berserk, and sadly this country would just treat Pabellon D as a whole.

The INPEs then turned off the lights from outside. I guess thinking that it would stop everyone, but it just made it worse. The two women trying to get moved into Pabellon E were never able to get in, so the INPEs brought them back to our Pabellon. Well, now they were looked at as traitors for going against what they were all trying to say. Honestly, I would have gone, too. I only have three more months and would not want more trouble. I understood their position, but it didn't help them having to come back here after all.

The INPEs eventually turned the lights back on, but it didn't stop the rioting. They were hoping that somehow it would catch the media's attention as with other prisons. It would just take someone outside to catch it on film with their cell phone. I can't say how loud or visible any of this is on the outside. We don't see much of anything outside from here. I don't believe anyone outside saw or heard anything because it never aired anywhere, and it definitely would have. This mess went on for hours. I tried to stay in bed and rest, but it was so noisy and chaotic.

Apparently, all the pabellons were yelling, "Ayúdame!" (Help me!) The INPEs didn't know what to do. Unlike back home, the INPEs don't carry guns or anything. They are just like security guards, really. They did come up (although they couldn't get in if they tried) and talked to the woman through the gate. It seemed to calm some of them down, but while the rioting lessened, it never completely stopped. I tried my best to sleep, but it was near impossible. Quenta is usually at 9 p.m., but it didn't happen until almost midnight. The INPEs managed to squeeze their way through the gate by pushing everything out of the way (beds, chairs, etc.,) and everyone was still chatting until God only knew what time. I didn't wake up until I heard the INPEs opening the doors this morning. I'm normally the first one up between 4:30 and 5:00 a.m. and filling up buckets and barrels and stuff. I slept through it all. All night, girls were trying to get me involved because I'm tall, trying to get me to hang up banners, but I kept refusing. I only had three months left to start my papers, and I was not about to get an *Informe* or any more trouble that would tack on an additional nine months of time here, so I refused and just stayed in my bed. Unfortunately for me, they just see us as a whole, and it doesn't matter.

In the morning, I got up and called my sister to tell her what was happening. I told her to let the lawyer know because I don't want additional time here, especially over stuff I was not involved in. He needs to also be aware that I'm told here that the director is the one who is holding everything up. She doesn't want to let anyone go, even if your papers say, "She is deadly ill. She gets freedom." I'm told that the director then says, "Nah, she looks fine to me," and keeps you, so I wanted him to be aware of any obstacles that may be in our path.

The Alclide came this morning with the INPEs after quenta to reprimand everyone for last night's fiasco. She's saying that COVID has been difficult and that we are all trying to work through this. Then they said we must start social distancing on the quenta line. It's so hard for people as we are all on top of each other in the small spaces of pabellon. As I always say, "What fucking sense does this even make?" I truly cannot believe the stupidity. I guess I've been saying, "Peru, Peru, Peru" so much lately that others now all look at me shaking my head and just say, "Yes, we know, Peru, Peru, Peru." I don't mean to be a jerk, but the stupidity leaves me speechless. At quenta the INPE, standing with Alcaide, says, "The spacing isn't only for quenta. You must continue spacing upstairs, too." Super!

They've probably seen it on TV, social distancing, but come on. They've been upstairs, and they see the limited space we are in. How could they even say that or think that? I can only shake my head. Peru, Peru, Peru; the land of actions I will never ever understand.

Day 97, now their solution is to take one of the five rooms in my pabellon and make it the quarantine room. This room is to be used not for COVID folks but for the elderly or people with some illness who may be considered to have a lower immune system and are at higher risk of getting it. Well, while that sounds great, it's still a joke. First, people are all scattered in various rooms. Now, older people (above 60 years) don't want to move into the quarantine room. That room is to now be cut off from everyone else. No one goes in or out, someone is to bring them their food every day, and they cannot come and join us for TV in the hallway now.

It's so hard for the people outside to comprehend, like when I told my husband and sister how they want to mix us now, that they are spoon-feeding us this virus, and how we will all wind up getting it. My husband feels, "Eh, you're healthy; you'll be okay. Even if you get it, you'll just pass it through and be okay." I don't feel that way at all. Everyone reacts differently. Four people can all get it, and each will have a totally different reaction.

Today, I guess the Alcaide is punishing us by making us stay upstairs all day due to last night's chaos. Well, it's not so much as a punishment. Plus, everyone is so tired. Most are sleeping now, anyway. This is a perfect example of the lack of intelligence I deal with here. At quenta, two rooms had to go downstairs and line up with spacing only to then come upstairs, right past us, all for the next three rooms to go down for quenta, and then all of us come back up and are all on the top of each other in the small spaces of the pabellon to watch TV. As I say all the time, "What fucking sense does this even make?" I truly cannot believe the stupidity. Plus, the people from room 1 got moved to rooms 2, 3, and 4, making the rooms crowded again. They can't come out for TV, phones, kiosko, or anything, so no one wants to go in it. Well, except for three people. The funny thing is, none of the three people are even sick or anything. I think they made up some crap to hope that it will be their fast ticket out of here by being in this room now. Ha, good luck with that. I doubt it will work the way they want. They are now cut off from everything, and let's see how that works out for them.

I'm told that we are now up to over thirty-two people infected now in this prison, but I have no way of knowing how true that is. Today, this INPE, who's a hard-ass, is withholding the water on us. The Pabellon Delegado was moved into my room with this whole room seclusion. You think she'd say something about it! It's so unhygienic and goes against all the COVID-19 precautions—washing up and cleaning constantly. Well, we can't live without water, and now, with even more people in our rooms, our barrels run out faster.

CHAPTER 20

My lawyer seems to feel that his petition for me for humanitarian release is going well. He said by next month, July, I will be released. I'm tired of the emotional roller coaster of getting my hopes up and having them shot down, but I hope he's right. One of the girls here was humming, "Happy New Year" the other day, and I mentioned to Jenny how I would not do another New Year's here. She tells me there's nothing that I can do about it.

It's true, but it's still difficult watching my life passing me by, and now with COVID, who knows what will happen. My sister tells me my mom is still suffering from COVID. She's having trouble breathing, and as stubborn as she is, she won't go to the doctor to get oxygen.

I spoke to my son for about an hour yesterday. He's dealing with a lot right now, and it breaks my heart to not be there for him or my daughter. My husband is struggling with it all. Still, it's just been crazy, so I just told Jenny my heart, mind, and soul cannot do another New Year's here. I have done nothing to deserve this at all, and I've paid dearly for this crime that I had no clue I was set up to commit. She told me that there was nothing that I could do about it. I just told Jenny, as I always say, "We can agree to disagree."

I just pray that this humanitarian thing goes through and that I can get out of this mess once and for all. This would be a dream come true, yet I'm not sure how positive I want to be due to me having had my hopes squashed so many times over the past three years, but I will be positive and wish for good vibes and positivity to ripple effect me the hell out of here, fingers and toes all crossed.

Today, doctors came in and tested us all for COVID-19. We had been saying all along how we were the only pabellon with zero illnesses. Well, that ended today with the test. We were told that there are several in my pabellon infected (three of which are in my room). I'm guessing that we will all get it at this rate. We all touch the same stuff—the doors, the faucets, the buckets for the bathroom, etc.—so now they will be back in ten more days to retest everyone. I have no doubt that the number of infections will just keep rising. And who knows if I even had it before when we thought I had the flu or not. Either way, I'm sure I'll be testing positive soon. Even Jenny is starting with the symptoms, and I sit with her every day, and she hands me my thermos every day. It's just a matter of time. There is no cure for this yet. It's a shame because I can't even quarantine myself throughout all of it because I'm stuck here surrounded by it. As always, there is nothing at all that I can do about this. It's a crying shame.

I had a conversation with Melanie, who spoke to Alberto, and the consensus was he felt he'd submitted a good report to the courts, and now it's just a waiting game. We still don't know if they will accept it, and if they don't, then two-and-a-half more months for me to file for benefits. Plus, I'm told on the news that there's a new form of COVID-19, stronger than the first. Like I've been saying all along, every time I believe the situation can't get any worse, it truly surprises me and does get worse. I honestly don't know how much more of this I can take. My most recent grandbaby is having her first birthday at my home back home. It sickens me to keep missing all of this. Plus, with COVID-19 now all around and me being unable to hide from it, this is swallowing me whole. I literally am at my wit's end.

My room is now full of everyone sick with fevers, coughing, sneezing, etc. I can't even hide and self-quarantine because I'm literally stuck here surrounded by this. More people have tested positive for COVID here too, so we're all just marinating in illness here, and as always, there's nothing at all that I can do about it. They came out with a new law thing again mid-week, saying that they will pick up a copy of our sentences on Monday, and it is for the early release of people who fall into certain categories. I fall into it, but I am honestly not even thinking about it because they never do what they say.

Alberto said he went yesterday and met with the Embassy and still says my papers are being processed well and that he's hoping to get good news soon. For whatever that is worth, he said to apply for whatever this thing is on Monday, believing that we should just apply for everything and anything and see which sticks. Well, today is Friday, and we just got told to bring down the copy of our sentence now. WTF? Today is not Monday! Jenny asked us not to bother because it's only for "Redention" now, nothing else. That wouldn't apply to me, despite my being here for three years and three months. They only count two years and two months due to them not counting the house arrest. From a 6.10-year sentence, they only saw me here for 2.2 out of it. Redention doesn't really help me. It's for people who've been here just shy of one year of completing their sentence and where they use work (Taller) to lessen their sentence. The law was originally 5:1. For every five days of work, you'd get one day knocked off your sentence, then it went to 2:1. As of late, we're told it's now 1:1. While that all sounds great, people getting released are still only being counted 5:1. It's typical of this country, what they say and do never match and just because they claim new laws, they don't do anything.

Melanie told me to submit it anyway. Of course, by the time I went to submit it, they'd already left, and I couldn't submit mine. I mentioned it to the delegado, and they, as always, just blew it off. Sure, it all benefits her and other Peruvians, but "Oh well" if the Gringo didn't get it. It's so ridiculous and discriminatory. I can't take much more of this here; two-and-a-half more months is like my last breath. This must end soon.

As I've always said, I am not a drug trafficker, nor did I know that's what I was set up to come here for, so to mess with my life like this is just inhumane, and so many countless others who were set up as targets, these scammers truly have no heart or soul. I'm told by someone here who's dealt with the Nigerian Drug cartels for a few years before getting caught that they literally have no heart and how they'd sell their mothers to make money. It's a crying shame. You see these things in movies and books that you'd believe to be fiction.

But to literally be living in it now just blows my mind. I'd never have believed this if I wasn't living in it.

Since eleven people tested positive for COVID-19 in our pabellon two weeks ago, they waited another day or two and then decided to move the three people that were quarantined in room 1 out of room 1 back into the regular population (since honestly, they were never sick to start with) and moved all the other people who tested positive into room 1. Well, except for one of the three people from my room, the one who showed symptoms with the flu, fever, sneezing, and aches, they moved to prevention for two weeks. When they did the test, they said myself and the other elderly women were at high risk and that they needed to do another test on us (swabbing our throats), and that we'd get those results in four to five days. I have no idea what the test was, but as always, that was two weeks ago and we are yet to get any results either way.

For two weeks now, several others in my room and other rooms and I have had no sense of taste or smell. I felt okay, but several other girls, besides no smell or taste, were suffering from more symptoms, including fevers, aches, cough, and sneezing. Another one of them has been throwing up for a few days so far. Do any of us now have COVID? Who knows? They never came back to test us again. They don't want to see the high numbers because the prison looks bad.

One of the girls in my room has been burning eucalyptus leaves, claiming that it kills the germs in the air, and making us some concoction of hot water, orange juice, ginger, garlic, and lime. She makes it for each of us twice a day. I'm glad I could not smell or taste it, but now that two weeks have passed, I'm getting my smell and taste back. While that is good, I can actually taste the concoction now, and it is nasty. Who knows if any of this helps. They all swear by all these concoctions. I've seen so many strange concoctions and ceremonies and stuff. I've been wiped down with pee, given dozens of horse-size shots of God only knows what, had eggs rolled all over my body to remove the bad vibes, had garlic taped to my head, and more. You literally cannot make this stuff up.

They lifted the quarantine here finally after three-and-a-half months. The lawyer said now he'd go to the courts and find out about mine and other cases. He told my family that the Embassy was actually working with him on my case, which he liked. I don't believe that. My guess is that, as always, they're just saying what they think we want to hear, but I doubt that they are doing anything as always.

I received a second package this week from the Thailand Embassy. That's the second package I've gotten from another country's embassy since this COVID came out over three months ago. Has my Embassy brought us anything? Nope. It's truly a disgrace. They gave two packages of 4pk of toilet paper, deodorant, four bars of soap, clothes detergent, dish detergent, shampoo, fruits and vegetables, snacks such as peanuts and raisins, face masks, baby wipes, and more. It's so beautiful how another embassy thinks of us, yet so disgraceful how my embassy doesn't even acknowledge us. Like I said, they always say, "We have no budget." Yet, at the very least, the vitamins are donations not paid for by the Embassy. You'd think they'd at least drop them off for us, but nope, nothing.

As a matter of fact, one of the religious groups here had been so helpful. Even in my case, for my cholesterol, they gave me tons of medicines and vitamins, all of which I had to buy myself or have someone buy for me on the outside and drop them off! As a foreigner, what if I didn't have anyone to get them for me? Or if I didn't have the money to get them? This was the case for many other foreigners, and they were screwed. There was nothing that they could do about it. Fortunately for me, I could pay for it and thank God the religious groups were kind enough to pick them up and drop them off for me. If not, I'd be screwed because I already know from experience that the US Embassy won't do it for me.

They allowed packages in last week, which is a start. Would it be a one-time thing, or would they start allowing this again like pre-COVID? Who knows? Annie would be bringing us a package of basic supplies and munchies to hold us over for a little. Every little bit helps under these circumstances. Even Jenna, the cop's daughter, sent me a note through the one INPE sending their love, and she said she sent me a package of eucalyptus (which was supposed to help me with breathing, plus some toilet paper and basic supplies), but I hadn't gotten the package yet. That was still so nice of them.

They wish they could do more, but I was grateful for all they've done already.

The lawyer said he's ready to start gathering all the paperwork to have on hand to be able to start my papers in two months. I truly hope it all goes fast. He had hoped that all he's petitioned for me would have taken, but as always, nope. Peru truly could care less about foreigners and had no desire to see us go, especially drug traffickers, whom they consider worse than murderers. I just had to think positively that two months would go by fast, that the process would go even faster, and that I would be home quickly. I'd be missing yet another summer back home, taking the grandbabies to the beach, on the boat, to the amusement parks, birthdays, etc., but this must be my last summer missing this. That's all I could pray and hope for.

Since they lifted the quarantine, Peru has had over 500 new COVID cases and over 32 deaths in the last 24 hours. I just want to go home. The director here didn't want to ever look bad, so she was telling the media that there were not many infected here and no deaths. When they asked about the one death that they had heard of, she said, "No, they died in the hospital of natural causes." That was a lie. There were many here infected, and one woman died in her bed in the prison because she couldn't breathe, and the INPEs wouldn't rush her to Topico for oxygen. It was just lie after lie. In the past week, they came and retested only the positive COVID people again, but no one else. That was insane. I had no doubt that a lot more of us had it, and yet we'll never know. Plus, she won't look bad if there were no new cases.

The one religious group had gotten letters from other countries' embassies granting them permission to drop stuff off for people at the various prisons. The same things, fruits, veggies, toilet paper, wipes, soap, etc. Other countries had provided them with notes where they'd dropped off packages for people in those countries. The woman told me that she asked the US Embassy one-and-a-half months ago for a letter from the US Embassy to enable them to drop off a package for me. So far, one and a half months later, they haven't received a reply. They were not even asking them to pay for this stuff.

The religious groups were sending it on their own. They did not care about us here at all, and it was crazy because here they view the USA as such a powerful country with tons of money, yet, I could attest to how other countries help their people here and how the USA does absolutely nothing at all. I know that once I am home, I would not want to relive any of this experience again, but I did feel that people need to be aware, aware how un-protected we all were back home from these scams, even Lisa Parker, who was only a three-hour drive from me in the USA, who scammed me out of $150k.

When I contacted the police back home, I was given an attitude of "Well, you fell for it; shame on you." I was aware of how, once you fell victim to this all, how screwed and unprotected you were. God forbid if you were like me and countless other US citizens who had fallen victim to these scams and wound up imprisoned in South America or other countries. I know firsthand how abandoned you were and how the USA wouldn't do anything at all to assist you. I was speaking on my behalf as well as what I witnessed from countless USA citizens I met through three and a half years here. Unless you are someone with a name, or power – they don't even acknowledge you. It's the mentality of "What's in it for me? How can us helping *you* help us?"

Flyer Beware! That was what I wanted to name my book. Once you flew out of the US, you needed to know how unprotected you truly were. It may help open ones eyes to this so that people are more cautious. As I've said before, once I am back home, I want to burn my passport, and it was not because I now see the US as the greatest in the world, and I don't want to leave. No, it was because I've learned that once you cross the border, God forbid something like this happens to you (and it does happen; there were over 290 Americans here in Peru alone who had fallen for this scam like me). You were on your own with zero help from the US. I never knew this, nor would I have believed it if I wasn't living through it myself.

We've had two deaths now here in Fatima from COVID. Both women were Peruvians; one was 50 and the other 53. I am 51 now, so, of course, this worries me. One woman died en-route to the hospital, the other here in prison. All the doctors here now had COVID, so we had no doctors for several days, and while there was no cure yet for COVID, there were no medicines here in Fatima: no aspirin or anything. Room 1 had not been released, and more and more people were positive, yet they were no longer being separated, and they weren't doing any more testing for it unless you asked for it (which was how we know about newer positives). I had no doubt we all had it by now, yet I was not requesting a test. I didn't want any hold-up for me to be released. I'd deal with it when I was back home. I was told lack of taste and lack of smell, along with very bad headaches, were a big sign of COVID.

Well, all of us in our room (the room with three positive COVID women initially) had suffered these symptoms for over two weeks, and now it had passed. A few of us suffered fever, chills, aches, and pains, and one even vomited for oer a week, yet they wouldn't retest us because, by this time, it would have passed. We were on our three-plus weeks now since the initial test and exposure. I literally just want to be home with my family. My first grandbaby would be celebrating her fourth birthday in two weeks. I missed the newest grandbaby's first birthday two months ago and would miss this one again. I just had to hope that my new lawyer would get me home fast since Sal fucked everything up.

We received donations from the Peru Red Cross this week: soap, masks, toothbrushes, toothpaste, Kotex, and a sachet packet of Suavitel fabric softener. That was very nice of them. I was an avid blood donor for the red cross back home. Today we got chicken donated for lunch, too, because today is yet another holiday here, the de Delincuente fiesta (no joke).

I asked my sister to send money (S/65) to my Fatima Lena. She didn't ask for it, but I knew she needed it. She didn't have any money, and her boyfriend had been without work and had his mom and two kids to support back home. Now Desiree had diabetes and high blood pressure, and they were trying to have her lawyer try and use that for her freedom. This new law said people with diabetes and other critical illnesses could go free, but what they said and did was never the same. The director said, "No, she was not sick enough. She could do another year."

What? Peruvians had no "embassy," so all she could do was see if her lawyer could try and fight this. Their justice was sickening. I know her boyfriend was working with a new lawyer online and fighting for her freedom (six years so far), but money was a problem. So, I donated the S/65 and told her we'd be sending her S/65 and her boyfriend S/65 a month after to help her get necessities that she needs here (toilet paper, milk, shampoo, Kotex, etc.) and for him to put whatever was left towards their legal bill and her medicine. With our money being about four times their money, it was not too much for me, and I truly knew it would help her immensely. She had been nothing but good to me. So, it was the least that I could do to help her.

It was funny, but again, they had been separating lovers here, yet they kept missing some. They moved the girls to other pabellons yet kept the "man in the relationship" here in my pabellon. There were still many here. Our delegado had two of her girlfriends move before, and one got her freedom yesterday, so she was sad. She had money, so girls flocked to her for that because she bought the best of everything and food and stuff, so they catered to her like a princess, and she took care of them. I, for one, didn't need her money, so she couldn't buy me, obviously, but it didn't stop her from trying. She showed me pictures from her wallet one day, and in it included a sexy photo portrait of her. I was surprised that she was showing me this, but I just said, "Oh, nice photos," and gave it all back to her and left the room. She tried to chat with me despite the language barrier; it was obviously not very successful. I spent my days saying to everyone, "No *entiendo*" (I don't understand) no matter how much I did understand. It just makes my life easier.

The other day, she wanted to go up to the top bed to talk with someone from the other pabellon and asked me to give her a boost up (as opposed to just using a chair like everyone else; she asked me to push her up via pushing her butt up). Ironic? I think not. They truly were funny here to me. I just went along with the "No entiendo" all day and night. I understood more than I spoke. She technically had two years more to go, but with the work benefits, she was hoping to leave in the next few months with money and pull. I was sure she'd pull it off. A lot of people should have been able to leave soon with the new work benefits (they were now offering 1:1 as opposed to the original 5:1 and then 2:1, meaning for every month you worked, you'd get one month off your sentence), but it all didn't really help me. This was what they refer to as Redention. But while it all sounded good, of course, nothing had even happened yet. One Peruvian here, she should have been released over one month ago on Redention, but as usual, they misspelled her name (which was typical of them here to just drag your situation on longer). They apparently corrected it, and she was supposed to be released on a Monday, yet it was now Thursday, and she was still here.

She was released two weeks later (yet one and a half months since she should have been released). Like, I said, they were just used to me always saying, "Peru, Peru, Peru" while shaking my head. The girl in my room tried to tell me today, "It's not the country; it's the justice," so I answered in Spanish, "Justice? In Peru? Your country has zero justice! None at all," and with her having been here for seven years so far, she agreed with me. I tried to tell them all, "I'm sure your country is great in its own way, but my experience with Peru is far from good."

Between coming here for what I believed to be a business trip, staying in hotels with no air conditioning or elevators, and being surrounded by people robbing, stealing, mugging, etc. Then, how their corrupt police apparently worked with these Nigerian cartels and set me up and arrested me only to have their judges do absolutely nothing at all, the police robbing me of my money and all of my belongings and then taken advantage of by the only English speaking lawyer we found and being bounced around for the past four years through Peru was prisons, I really did not have anything good to report from my experience. I wish that weren't the case, but it was what it was.

A few people were released yesterday, which was good, yet countless others who should have been released were not. From the original list (those over 60 years, those with illnesses, and those with less than six months left of completing their entire sentence), the director just submitted their paperwork for processing yesterday (three months after the list was put up). Ironically, several of those women had already been released for having completed their entire sentence now. It was ridiculous. Like I said, they didn't care about prisoners at all. While I could somewhat understand, we were all human beings at the end of the day. Repeat offenders, okay! I get it. But many were first-time offenders and given crazy high sentences for the most idiotic reasons. The girl above my bed should be going home this week. She was already here seven years so far. For what? I didn't know, but seven years with two months to go, first-time offense, and she didn't kill anyone or rob a bank.

Her boyfriend was arrested, too. It seems excessive to me, but what did I know? She should be getting released on this Redention. She was expecting to go home two days ago, but nothing happened. I asked her today, "What is going on?"

She said, "There was a problem with my papers."

The prisons here did that on purpose, to keep you here longer. Like I said, with me, my first name was perfect, and my second name was misspelled. I caught it and asked for it to be corrected. What did they do? Correct the second name and then went in and misspelled the first name, which was perfect before! It was something like that could keep me here another six months while they "work on fixing it." My sentence papers had my name misspelled throughout the whole entire thirty-plus page document, and not just the same error; it varies throughout the whole document. Sloppy, idiotic, and true games they play with people's lives. As a foreigner, it sickens me. As a Peruvian, they just shrug their shoulders and assume it would get fixed when they get to it. It was a whole other world to me.

We were now five months since this quarantine/COVID-19 started. Like I said, the quarantine had been somewhat lifted here, but we still couldn't have visitors or work (Taller) because then the pabellons were mixing. They did allow us to get packages last week (food, the same stuff we'd also get if it were a visit). I was told that we should be allowed packages every two weeks. We shall see. The funny thing was we tried reaching out to many people who normally offer to drop us off packages with food (unlike prison food, home cooked food would be like heaven right now), and while they all wanted to drop off food, most were still afraid of COVID and wouldn't go to the prison. Annie did, though. She dropped off snacks, toilet paper, soap, etc., for Jenny and me. No home-cooked food, but she said if they accepted packages again in two weeks, she'd bring us food. It was still a blessing that she and these other volunteers came here from other countries and helped us out. They were saints.

Today, eleven months after our arrival in Fatima, I've tried my best to gauge some sort of routine and gauge, at the very least, when the water turns off in the morning. It changed again. There is no consistency here. Sometimes the water is turned on at 5:00 a.m. Sometimes, it's 4:30, 4:40, 4:50, 5:15, 5:30, 5:40, 6:00, etc. Sometimes not at all. Sometimes it was full force where you could plug in the hose to the sink, fill up the barrels, and take a shower simultaneously. Other times, there was not enough water pressure to do both. It all depends on the INPE and whether they put it on and whether they pushed the lever to give us full pressure or not. If it came on, it usually stayed on until 7:30.

Since we were woken up and let out of our cages at 6 a.m., it stayed on until 7:30 for people to take showers, sweep the floor, eat breakfast, and wash their Tupperware bowls. I tried to exercise in the morning and showered at 6:40 a.m. Usually, it was plain and simple—except today. As I was in the outside shower, freezing, showering in the ice-cold water, halfway through my shower, the water was turned off. Were they fucking kidding me here? This place was insane.

Of course, almost everyone was upstairs now eating, cleaning, still sleeping, etc., and no one was even in the downstairs shower. I had to stand there freezing for fifteen minutes until I heard someone around who I could ask in Spanish to get me a small bucket of water from near the toilets so I could wash the soap off me. By the time I rinsed off, dressed, and went upstairs to eat my breakfast, about fifteen minutes later, the water was back on. Why they did this idiotic nonsense was beyond me.

I was also told by the lawyer now that I need to pay "Tupa" and request papers for him to start my papers this coming month. What was Tupa? It was another money game they played here. They should have all our information in a file, yet you had to request and pay them to pull your records of work, psychology, and behavior. To get these records would run with me about S/60, which many didn't have, but I need it for my application for expulsion. With my being in three different prisons and house arrest and each prison rule was different, this should be interesting. Would they have it all? Would they play games with this? We shall see. I was supposed to be able to do this today, but of course, I was told, "No, not today, maybe tomorrow."

Let the games begin.

I missed my granddaughter's fourth birthday this past weekend (I've missed all other birthdays so far), and my son's birthday was yesterday. Friday was my wedding anniversary. I was sick over constantly missing so much of my life due to something I had no idea I was scammed into. It was sickening just how heartless these scammers were in this world. It was equally sickening how we, victims, were left to deal with the consequences of these scams with no help at all. I couldn't speak for other countries, but I know the US was aware of these scams and how these scammers purchase medical records of people with brain injuries, dementia, senility, etc.

I was sure it was hard to stop all scammers, but if the USA knew this was happening, then why weren't they doing *anything* to help us once we've fallen victim? Even my scammer—again, it took someone (a lawyer from another country, Australia, who works for stopmulevictims.org) who investigated it, pro bono, to tell me this—a Nigerian man, had a number that was actually a landline in the UK.

So, unlike a throwaway phone or computer number, he was traceable. Also, I didn't buy my airline tickets. They were purchased by him. The charges were on someone else's credit card, not mine, so again, they were traceable. Why was the USA not investigating this to help me? Their attitude was, "You committed the crime in another country, so we wouldn't waste our money and manpower on it."

True, but I was victimized in the US repeatedly, and even as such, the USA hasn't done anything at all to assist me or track down these perpetrators to try and prevent this from happening to more people.

I was no child, and I've seen other Americans here, over 74 years old, who had fallen victim to these scams and were stuck in these prisons here, same as me, awaiting their release.

It was not right and very sad that this was the world we lived in, and these were the demons we were subject to with little to no help. Like I said, I physically saw two elderly Americans go through the same as me, and Lord only knows how many more I hadn't seen. Back home, the attitude I received was, "You were dumb enough to fall for it," yet, prior to my accident, I never would have fallen for it. Same with the elderly and those with dementia and senility, they didn't know that they were doing this, and yet where was our help? It was not right. That was all I could say anymore.

I finally got to pay my Tupa, just shy of S/60, and then we were supposed to submit a solicitude requesting all that I just paid for, which was explained in each application. How stupid was that? I was told that if I requested it, it would take months (and these Tupa were only valid for three months), yet if a lawyer requested it, they would get it in days. Once I paid and applied for each, we called my lawyer, and he said that he would submit the solicitudes to obtain the necessary documents. It was all needed for my expulsion application, and he'd ensure he got them fast. Thank God he was on top of this all. I was beyond grateful that we finally tossed that asshole scamming lawyer Sal Monty and went with Alberto. He was way more on top of things and was doing what was in my best interest, not his own.

I threw out my back again today. These crappy beds were horrible to start with, and I broke my mid-back in the sky diving accident. I also had bulging discs in my lower back from car accidents years ago. Normally that was okay, but if I slept or moved the wrong way, it acted up, and I would be in agony for about one or two weeks. It happened to me a few months ago, and I had to have Topico inject muscle relaxers.

The injection helped, yet getting it was not easy. The INPE was initially refusing to let me go to Topico, telling the translator, "She is fine; she just wants the injection."

What? These needles were like horse-sized needles and were not painless. What the hell was it about me that made her think that I wanted that? Finally, the delegado for Topico had convinced her to let me go that day.

Now my back is thrown out again. How did it happen? My typical morning routine was waking up at 4:30 am and showering with water from buckets, and then if the water came on at 5:00 or so, I filled up the barrels and buckets for all of us. The same as the last time, my back blew out as I bent down to pick up the one spackle-sized bucket of water to move it to the shower.

No one cares here as long as the buckets are full. When Jenny and Ruth told me to stop doing it because they were all just spoiled now, I agreed, but the problem was that it was not only them that I did it for. It was for me, too. I had my own bucket of water, so yes, I could say, "To hell with them, I'd take care of me and only me."

But there had been a few times when I didn't fill the buckets, and neither did they. Well, sixteen people in a room sharing one toilet with no water to flush the toilet and sixteen people's dirty Tupperware from breakfast, lunch, and dinner with no water to wash them, you could understand just how dirty and nasty it was. The bathroom smelled horrific from the dirty toilet and Tupperware. So, for my sanity, if I was there, I ensured the buckets were always full when the water eventually came on to fill them. I just could no longer lift them to move them; my back couldn't take much more of it.

A girl in my room had also thrown her back out (a Peruvian) and was getting muscle relaxer injections herself. She explained to Jenny how she needed to request the same for me (since Jenny speaks Spanish and English). I eventually got called to Topico, yet I had to wait while several positive-COVID women were being tended to.

After I finally got in, I was told, "No injections, we have none left. We will give you two *Ibuprufeno* (Ibuprofen) and two parac-etamol to take one of each now and one of each tonight," like that would actually do anything for me—and only today and tonight. It was what it was. It was crazy how they told me they had no injec-tions, yet the Peruvian in my room was getting injections.

I was complaining to the Russian woman I was playing cards with, and she told me the same happened to her. She was COVID-positive several weeks ago, as were others in her room. She was suffering from major flu symptoms and asked for an injection of pain meds. She got told the same, "We had no injections," yet when two Peruvians from her room came in talking about how they had just got their injections, she blew a fit. It was crazy how discriminating they were here. It seems that they had tons of stuff for Peruvians, yet nothing for extranjeras (foreigners). I could only pray that my lawyer got all the necessary paperwork, that I get a court date within this month, and that I get out of this country once and for all.

We paid my fines (dias multa and Reparation Civil) which came to S/10,000. Of course, they made new rules months ago that one didn't have to pay them, yet as always, this law has yet to be signed and implemented. I didn't want any more holdups, so we just paid it. That was usually the first question the judges asked at a Delehencia, "Did you pay your fines?" A typical money game here.

Sadly, most people, Peruvians and foreigners alike, were all here completing their full sentences because they didn't have money for their fines. If you couldn't pay them, you couldn't apply for expulsion. I've seen people from all over the world, all completing over size to eight years due to not paying the fines. Thank God my business could afford to pay the fines for me so I could get out of there. Due to the exchange rate right now, it was only $2,800, which was not terrible. Every day was one day closer, so moving forward was all I could do.

I know for me to apply for expulsion, aside from paying your fines, you had to obtain various documents that my lawyer submitted solicitudes for from Santa Monica, Ancon II, and Fatima. These consisted of psychology reports, behavior reports, and work reports. I saw our psychologist the day before and grabbed her to tell her I'd be filing my papers in two or three weeks. I know they didn't do anything fast here; if I just sat back and waited for them to do things, I would be waiting forever. So, I took the opportunity to jump on her now. Good thing I did. She called me this afternoon, filled out some forms, and told me she'd be filing my forms Friday and Monday. That was a good start, so I was happy to hear that (since her papers were needed for this process to move forward). Now, if Santa Monica and Ancon follow suit, I'd be in good shape.

Today was a day I will never forget. As with this whole entire experience, they moved people around the rooms for whatever their reasoning. Quite often, usually, it was troublemakers being moved due to problems. Fortunately for me, I've been in the same room for one and a half months so far, but I've seen various people leave for freedom and various others circulate through my room and other rooms.

One girl was so loud and big, but she had been in my room for several months now, having moved about from other rooms prior. She was always creating issues, usually fighting or girlfriend issues, or what have you. It was always something. She was on another girl in my bed (they're good friends) and crying. Why? I had no idea. But she was with her friend, and I let it be; it's not my business. She then took a shower, and everyone was doing their own thing. I was sitting in my bed reading a book like I did every night.

The way the beds were set up, I couldn't see the windows because they were behind me. I was reading like always, and suddenly, one girl screamed. I didn't know what she was screaming at, so I turned to look, and the crying big girl hung herself with a rope from the window. From where I was sitting, all I could see when I turned to look was her face, with the rope around her neck hanging from the window. Everyone was screaming and running to the INPE for help. Some tried to cut her down, but she was a big girl, so it wasn't easy.

I ran out with everyone else for help. They seemed to get her down and dragged her on a blanket to the gate, where someone carried her down with the INPE to the doctor's office. I'm shaking as I write this. Was she okay? Was she dead? I had no idea. I would find out tomorrow, I guess. All I knew was that was not a vision that would result in me getting sleep tonight, that was for sure. Literally seeing someone hanging from a window by their neck was not a pretty sight.

Nothing here should have surprised me now, but it did. About an hour after this girl was taken down to Topico, she was brought back up, alive, crying, but okay. I didn't know what to make of this place. The INPEs had no idea what to do with her; the doctors were not real doctors, and there was no psych during the night. If it were me, I'd keep her quarantined all night, so I could watch her and keep her safe until the psych comes the next day, but that would make too much common sense for this place. So, what did they do? They sent her back to the room like nothing had happened.

I was shaking and didn't know what to do or react. Did she really try and kill herself? Was she doing it for attention? I had no idea. All I knew was either way, it was not normal. And she was in our room again for the night. I was concerned. What if she tried it again or tried something else? What if I got up to pee, and she was on the floor dead? What if she hung herself again? What if she snapped and started killing us all in here? Would they lock the door for the night?

Obviously, we're not allowed knives, scissors, etc., here, but that means nothing. They all had them in my room and others, so who was to say when we tried and sleep that she didn't go on a tear and try killing everyone? One of her friends was in another room from me, so the INPE let her come and sleep in our room last night to keep her company. This was truly nuts! I didn't know this girl, really. I knew her from Santa Monica but didn't really know her. Was she a deep sleeper? Would she hear this girl if she snapped? Who knows? Needless to say, I got zero sleep last night. Every time I heard a sound, my eyes flew open. I didn't know what to think or expect.

Apparently, that was the case for all others in the room, too; that, coupled with the fact that the INPEs came into the room four times, were turning on the lights throughout the night and checking on her. Obviously, the light and noise of the metal bolts on the door woke all of us regardless. I was a wreck all night long.

In the morning, I got up at 4:45 a.m., filled the buckets as usual, and waited until 6 a.m. to leave the room once the INPE unlocked us. She and her friend stayed sleeping throughout breakfast and quenta. The psych came today and said nothing to any of us traumatized by this ordeal last night. Shocking? Sadly, no. She supposedly talked to the girl and felt that "Everything's fine, she doesn't need to go anywhere; she's fine where she's at."

I didn't know whether to laugh or cry. I was just dumbfounded by the stupidity of this place, truly. Does the psych not see how, whether intentionally or for attention, how unusual it was? Or how all of us were traumatized by it. That vision was still flowing through my head. Sure, I've seen similar on TV and in movies, but to see it ten feet away from me was nerve-racking.

I couldn't get out of here soon enough. And to think this psych's report of me had the power to keep me here and not let me go. How crazy was that? She got that power but couldn't help someone who needed it. You could only shake your head at it.

I swear, this nightmare truly must end soon. I was told that since courts were all being done remotely, they were behind. I truly hoped and prayed that my lawyer could get me a court date fast so that this nightmare would end quickly. Three and a half years of my life wasted here had taken its toll on me.

CHAPTER 21

We had three days of no sleep with this girl's friend staying with her and people popping in and out throughout the day to keep an eye on her, leaving the door open if anyone stepped out so people outside could see her. It was truly ridiculous. This was not the solution; she needed help! But now, on the fourth night, the friend from another room didn't sleep in our room last night. Of course, I didn't sleep again for fear that she'd do something due to feeling neglected. I was told all of this was because her girlfriend had left her. She was in another pabellon. Either way, INPEs only checked on her three times that night. Did she care? Despite the doctors giving her medicines and injections to cause her to sleep all the time, it didn't stop her from trying to slice her wrists. This was what we endured *that night.*

We had all mentioned to INPEs, the psychiatrist, and the delegado how we were all affected by this. We couldn't sleep, were constantly nervous, and were traumatized by what we all saw and what we feared would come next. Apparently, no one cared. They still locked us in the room with her every night. The psych came and did a house call with her in the room for about half an hour.

Again, they felt she was fine and left. How fine was she? She again tried to hang herself with a tighter strap. Everyone was yelling and screaming for help. The effect this was having on all of us was horrific. To witness someone hanging by a rope around their neck, not once but twice, was something that stayed with you. I tried to sleep but kept seeing those visions in my head.

Finally, it seemed they realized that she needed help. They sent her to a hospital that night. I prayed they would keep her there until I was gone, but we shall see. Since the government would pay for this, I was sure they would make a quick diagnosis and send her back. Back in my room, we were all still on pins and needles. It was insane.

The psychiatrist had me do my papers: Proyecto de vida. It was six pages of tons of questions—all in Spanish. Then I had to draw a picture of me at work. Why? I have no idea. Then, I had to write my story before, during, and after this ordeal. I learned here that less was more. You had to keep it short and sweet because the more you wrote, the more they tried to dissect it to make it worse. I paid someone S/20 to translate it in Castellano for me, drew (and even colored) my picture of me at work, and had three different translators help me with the six pages of questions. The psychiatrist was supposed to call me that day and complete this process.

Did she call me? Nope. She was here because I saw her, but she never called for me, which was typical here. I couldn't say enough about how horrible it was. What happened to, "Say what you mean and mean what you say"? They had no concept of that.

Someone said, "Oh, she's probably busy." Then she shouldn't have told me Monday the 24th!

Wednesday, the assistant social worker came and took my papers for psych. That was good because at least the process was moving. She had to review them all and give her "diagnosis" or opinion of me. So ridiculous. I guarantee I was more educated than her, but sadly, my fate lied in her diagnosis, so fingers crossed. One and a half more weeks and my lawyer could file for a court date. He told my family, "She'll be home before the holidays," meaning Christmas and Thanksgiving. Thanksgiving was a US holiday, not Peru. That was three months away, so I hoped so.

The girl who tried to kill herself, as I expected, was back from the hospital in less than twenty-four hours. She spent three days in Topico where they reviewed her, and they felt that she was totally fine, not crazy, just needed attention. Were they freaking kidding me? Sure, she may not technically have been crazy, but it was not normal to pretend to kill yourself and traumatize other people. So, of course, they sent her back to my room. I guess we would all be back to not sleeping again.

Well, my lawyer came back on Labor Day to try to get the additional papers he needed to be able to file for a court date for me. Sadly, they just told him that he was not allowed to file yet. They also said the one paper you needed, that said I didn't have any additional cases on me, you must request online due to quarantine.

So now, who knew how long they would take to get this paper since it was all an online request and not a face-to-face? Also, my sentence said that my fines were dias multa e Inhabilitacion 240 days, and Reparacion Civil Debera' Abonar S/8,009. How convenient this corrupt and shady country was. They listed days but not an amount on my sentence. My lawyer tried to pay my fines that day since that was one of the first questions they asked at the trial. He based the 240 days on whatever the norm was.

Well, conveniently, they told him, "We haven't calculated it, so you couldn't pay it yet. We didn't have the amount yet."

Unbelievable. They had sixteen months since they sentenced me; this was so typical. They'll play games now to drag this out longer and then come up with an amount to rob me blind. Part of the psych evaluation they asked about your work, your husband's salary, kid's salary, etc., then they gave astronomical fines to take as much from you as they could.

This was why so many foreigners stayed to complete their full sentences because they didn't have the S/$ to pay these fines. Sure, they made a new law when COVID came about, saying we didn't have to pay the fines anymore, but as typical with Peru, the law still hasn't been signed. It could very well take them ten years to sign it. And until it was signed, you still had to pay, and they would take as much as they could from all they could.

They had taken, so far, over three years of my life, taken me away from family, kids, husband, grandkids, my business, traumatized me beyond words with all I went through, and witnessed and endured everything they threw at me. Despite it, they couldn't care one bit. And my country just looked the other way. Sure, many were truly guilty and deserve what they got, but I couldn't stress enough how not all of us were guilty. And here I sat, in a world where justice either didn't exist or was a complete joke.

I truly thought we'd have a court date this week and that this nightmare would be over soon, but as has been my case all along, every time I think this mess would end, it just keeps continuing on and on. I truly couldn't take much more. The only one good thing was that I now had a lawyer who would keep on top of this.

Yet again, I ask, if there truly was a God, why on Earth was he doing this to me? Why has he completely ignored my cries for help for over three years? Why was he allowing this? I was a good person! I have tried to understand yet have zero answers. I begged, cried, pleaded, prayed, talked to God and have been sincere as possible, yet here I sat, zero answers and a situation that just continued.

I was tired of hearing, "There are answers we just don't know, and we must have faith."

Why? Because I had seen it here with myself and countless others. In my situation, I fell for a scam, and this had ruined me horrendously. It hurt me beyond words, as well as my husband, kids, grandkids, mom, dad, sisters, and business. Absolutely nothing good has come out of this. My family have all been so stressed over this and lashing out between them; my business has suffered. I had two new grandbabies that I had not met yet, my son and daughter didn't have their mom to talk to on a whim when they needed me, my husband got instantly thrown out into paying for every bill in the house.

The only one who seemed to have benefitted from this scam was the scammer (the Nigerian drug cartel in Peru) as well as the corrupt police here in Peru at the airport who robbed me of all of my stuff, as well as the corrupt country who plays games with people's lives, keeping them locked away for years and years so they could milk as much as they can from us as they could. So, who was listening to my prayers and cries for help? Apparently, no one. And who wins in the end here? Not the good guys from what I saw. Having absolutely nothing to do all day but think caused me to doubt a lot. I spent two-and-a-half years believing so much, but this past year as things just continued to get worse and worse, it was hard to have faith. This nightmare had to end soon. My strength was truly gone.

Plus, here, you were allowed a razor to shave with. Well, that depended on the INPE on duty. When someone brought it for you,

90 percent of the INPEs allowed it in, but then there were 10 percent that didn't. Now, since the psycho in my room had tried to slice her wrists last time (the one they felt was totally fine), my blade was missing from my razor. With 10–16 people in the room, unless you were sitting on your bed all day, every day, you couldn't know who was touching your stuff. But, with over a year here now, this was the first time this has happened and, of course, now I think it was the girl. So here I go again, no sleep now because who knew if she would pull more nonsense. This place sickens me beyond words.

I got no sleep last night, of course, and today the girl who tried to kill herself has been crying (for reasons, as usual, I have no idea). Of course, her friends were all coming and talking to her, calming her down, etc. This whole situation was nuts. She was so unstable. Either fix her meds or send her away for mental help. Acting this way every day was *not* normal!

I had my sister sending money online to our kiosko lady's son. I used to have Marge and Annie bring me some money that I left with them weekly on their visits, but with the quarantine and no visits, getting money was a problem. The kiosko lady told me that I could send money to her son, and he'd give it to her for me. I thought that was perfect, yet every time I asked my sister to send my money to him, the kiosko lady would say that she didn't have any money on hand since everyone else was buying with credit. The way the plan was, if my sister sent S/100, the kiosko lady would give me S/100 until her son brought it to her with the kiosko groceries. Since she was now conveniently telling me she had no money, I wound up just saying to keep it as credit for me, and I could buy what I needed and not have to exchange money.

I had her send $200 twice a month, which was S/660-S/750 each time. Every week, I'd buy toilet paper, fruits, veggies, milk, peanuts, and bread—nothing crazy since there was no money changing hands and my sister was doing it automatically. I lost track of where we were in terms of money.

My sister said, "I'll send money again tomorrow." I told her to wait, as it was actually S/1,320 a month, and I knew I was not spending that much. In money, she'd basically gotten S/5,000. I asked her where we were at with credit, as I felt I should now have an abundance of credit with her. Of course, as the dumb Gringo who's been robbed blind here in Peru prisons since day one, she told me, "No, I owe her S/110."

I told her how that was impossible! Then she said, "No, okay, we are even. You don't owe me, and I don't owe you. It's a zero now." Unreal. First, if she even *thought* I owed her S/1, she'd hunt me down until she got it. Now, she went from me owing her S/110 to "No, it's okay. We're even." And I know it was impossible. I should have at least S/2,000 credit.

The kiosko lady always claimed to not have change, so I was limited with how I could get S/ now without visits. I hated how I needed her. I just said, "No more credit." If I spent S/50, I'd have my sister send S/50. I can't trust a single person here. That had already been proven to me since day one, trying to survive under these circumstances. It was so ridiculous, but as always, what could I do? Nothing, unfortunately. I just hoped this would end soon.

Another week went by, and on Tuesday (when I should have had a zero balance with the kiosko), I got my usual hand full of fruits, veggies, toilet paper, yogurt, tea, and she had a hand cream she wanted to sell me. So assuming it couldn't be more than S/15, I got that too. As usual, she wouldn't give me the balance. She kept telling me, "Later, I'm busy." That turned into 11 days, and after I continued to pester her, she said I owed her S/601. That was fucking impossible!

I even demanded the book where she wrote it all down and sat with a calculator. First, for the S/15 small tube of hand cream, she charged me S/45. This was as bad as the last time she charged me S/30 for a S/10 bottle of baby powder. On top of it all, the prices were all over the place. One day something was S/5, and the next, it was S/12. This went on throughout the list. She also double-charged me repeatedly on many things. When I challenged it, she'd tell me that I was wrong (when I knew damn well what I got). Plus, using a calculator, I got to know she was off on her price, which she manually calculated. Again, she said that I was wrong. There was no surprise at all that she was here for robbery, but as always, what could I do about it? Absolutely nothing.

A new person is supposed to take over the kiosko in one and a half weeks, so we would see. Plus, Desiree's husband had been sending me food (fruits, veggies, yogurt, etc.), and I just asked my sister to wire him the money for it. Sadly, it was only every two weeks that we could get packages now, not weekly, but he was bringing me in three times as much as I ever got from this kiosko, with much bigger products, for a third of what she was scamming from me.

My lawyer had been waiting to go to the courts to get a court date for me to file my benefits, yet as always, we were short one paper still, "Ojo penalagica," which showed that you have no other cases against and that you've not been arrested before. I requested this paper and paid Tupa "and" did a solicitude for this over one-and a-half months ago, yet we were still waiting. I was told they had to provide the stuff within 15–30 days, but as always, they made their own rules and disagreed about what should happen. They were too busy working on letting most Peruvians go on "redention," where, as long as you had no strikes against you, you could go home if you worked and had time credit. Sure, that works for all of them, but what about me? They obviously didn't care at all. It's nuts how they let people go, people who've murdered others, etc. It was crazy how Peru views drug smugglers worse than murderers. When I was in Santa Monica, there was a Peruvian who killed her two kids and chopped them into pieces. She was sentenced to five years and could get out sooner with benefits, whereas someone with .5 kilos of drugs got five to eight years. How did that make sense? Sadly, this is Peru's insane logic. As a matter of fact, I was told by our delegado that a girl who was in my room this past year had just gotten released on Saturday. I didn't know why she was in jail, but our new delgado said that she was arrested for killing someone by stabbing them twenty-three times! She was sentenced to five years, only spent just over three years, and was just released with redention. Yet, I was still here for three-and-a-half years so far with a six-year ten-month sentence and was still waiting for papers for my lawyer to even ask for a court date then, hoping and praying that the judges allow my release. And even that was a whole process.

After waiting seven weeks for this "Ojo Penalogico" and still nothing, as a desperate measure, I asked my mom to reach out to the cop to see if he, by chance, knew who did this paper. I was told it was by the INPEs. Since he was a cop and knew INPEs, I thought it harmless to ask. As expected, the INPE he knew said, "Oh yes, the person who did that is my friend. It was going to cost though, S/50–S/100 to do it, and then she will bring it to my lawyer." It was just a typical example of the corruption that goes on here. Another person was waiting for the OTT to do papers for her, and the OTT told her, "I don't have a phone or internet. I can't do them right now." As a witness to the corruption here, I take that to mean, "It'll cost you if you want them now." Most people didn't have money, so all they could do was wait, unfortunately. Many finish their complete sentences before these folks do the work needed for them to go sooner. It was insanely corrupt. One woman from Russia had no money and was using the free prison lawyer. She should have been out of here over a year ago on a medical condition. But it was just another example of how since she couldn't pay her way out, she was still here and would probably be here another four years until her sentence was done.

I was surprised and shocked last week when I got called down for a package. It was from the Embassy. It was now over a year since I had last seen them, and I guess, since they couldn't see us due to COVID, they at least sent a package. It was the usual three-month supply of vitamins and sample packets of soap, shampoo, and lotion. I can only assume, due to COVID, that they got donations because, for the first time ever, we also got two (used) sweaters and a box of Kotex and tampons. What a shock that was.

With me now in my second month of still waiting for this paper, I got a call to see the director. This was a first. I didn't know what was going on. I went and sat down, and she asked me if I had called my Embassy. I said no because I had not. She asked, "Not this month, last month?" I said no. I last called them seven months ago, and that was a waste of a call, so I had no idea what she was talking about.

She said the Embassy was calling to talk to me and Jill (the only two Americans here). Well, when she mentioned the other person, I realized that this was just their annual review. I had to wait almost ten minutes for them to phone back for me, so in the meantime, the director asked me how things were going. I figured I could use this to my advantage since I had the floor, and she was concerned about the Embassy calling me. I told her how I was waiting to go home, how I was still waiting for this one paper, how I was tired of still being here. I didn't deserve this; my patience was gone, etc. I just wanted to be back home with my family.

I was all choked up and wanted her to see my frustration with their procedures. I wasn't sure if it was just my being upset. It wouldn't mean anything, but since I was about to be speaking to the Embassy, she excused herself for a moment and then came back and said, "We'll have your paper ready on Friday." It was Wednesday.

I was shocked. They truly *could* do it fast; they just always choose not to. Like I had always been saying, my embassy truly hadn't done anything to help me thus far, but as useless as I felt they were, their calling just worked to my advantage. They called, and I was escorted next door to talk to them. It was the typical stuff like, "Any issues, problems, or concerns? Do you need to add anyone to your privacy waiver?"

I told them about the paper. I gave them my current lawyer's info (since I haven't seen them in over a year). I told them about how in Santa Monica, I was on a vegetarian diet as well as Ancon, yet here in Fatima, they didn't give me vegetarian food until I saw the nutritionist, and I was on a list to be him for over a year now. She said she'd make a note (their typical reply). I told her how it didn't matter now. I had been eating the prison slop for over a year now due to the lack of function in Fatima. I told her, "You asked, and I answered. Doing something about it now is pointless. I'm working on going home now."

I also told her about my genetically high cholesterol. I told her how I had told the Embassy for over three years how it was genetic, and back home, I take 40 mg of Lipitor. They've not done anything at all about it. About eight months ago, a Thai woman told me that if I paid for blood work, the prison would at least investigate it. After I did, they confirmed that my cholesterol was very high, and their solution was vitamin B, Acetic salicylic and Atorvastatin 20 mg plus Collagen powder. None of these are prescription, like I'd get at home. It was crazy. I told this to the Embassy, and as usual, "I'll make a note of it." But again, she asked, and I answered. She made a note of the paper I was missing. I went back next door to the director and said, "To confirm, it was *this week you'll do the paper for me, yes?*"

I did mention this to the Embassy. As you can imagine, my lawyer had the paper that afternoon! Crazy, right? It was crazy.

I obviously didn't need to pay the corrupt INPE now since I got it done myself, but this was yet another example of how they jumped at the sound or thought of the US Embassy, yet sadly, the Embassy did not take advantage of this. I was not asking them to do anything illegal, just help us when needed, yet sadly, they didn't. We'd see what would happen when I really needed their help with the expulsion. So, Alberto had the paper, but now it gets sent to another division and then back to the prison for them to sign off and then Alberto can take it, along with everything else, to the judge and ask for a court date. They said, "If everyone did their job, you should have the paper back in a week so you can go to the judge." We shall see how long it takes from here now and pray he gets a fast court date.

I was also told they would open the airports for more flights. It was a window of opportunity. I was afraid that with opening the airlines now, COVID would obviously spike a little. I was scared that then they'll shut them down again. It was an open window that I must get through. This would be interesting, to say at least.

I was shocked that the Embassy came this week and asked another American and me in different pabellons to sign a paper giving them permission to see our medical records. I said, "No problem. I have nothing to hide."

The other girl said no. I was surprised and wondered if, by chance, she knew something that I didn't and that maybe I should be saying no, too. She spoke to them in Spanish and refused, but I said okay and signed the paper. I just didn't want anything at all to keep me one more minute longer. I have no clue what their files say.

In Santa Monica, they put me on clonazepam and Fluoxetine, neither of which I should ever have been put on, nor what their reason was in my file. I have no idea what they wrote. I was not put on anything in Ancon or Fatima. While I believe everyone here has had COVID, fortunately for me, my file would not show it since they only tested us once in the very beginning and never tested us again, so my file should be good.

It took two weeks, but thanks to Alberto pressuring them, he finally got the paper yesterday afternoon. He'd go to court today and get me a court date. I hope and pray he can get one fast. He confirmed that my reports were all positive and that I was a model prisoner (gee, thanks). My reviews were all good, my psych reports were favorable, and my fines are paid, so there should be no reason for them to disallow my request for expulsion. He mentioned how I was now in court number five, and Jenny said that this was good. She's seen many others go to court number four and get denied eight times, her ex-girlfriend included. She said she was denied eight times in court number four, so thank God I was in number five, and with everything in place, we just needed a date and positive energy on my side. Fingers, toes, and everything else crossed. I had to call him Friday, and we hoped to have a court date set by then.

So Jenny completed her 6.8 years on Nov 8th. They couldn't keep her here a day more. My lawyer was trying to see if he could get her out sooner using various methods, but sadly, Peru just didn't care about releasing foreigners easily. She had three weeks more to go. Alberto tried his best and just told her, "Enjoy the rest of your vacation. It will be over very soon."

I was shocked by the use of the word "vacation." Apparently, most Peruvians view prison as a vacation. No work, no cooking, no keeping a roof over your head, no babies, etc. I was told this was still better than many people's home life. I guess that's where the third-world country comes in. This couldn't be further from my real life back home. I guess that explains why most Peruvians here were always happy, cheerful, singing, and dancing with not a care in the world, whereas I missed my family dearly and just wanted to be back home with them. I was truly in a foreign world here.

Alberto managed to pull some strings and got me a court date (Delegencia) for November 6, two days before Jenny's release. At least she'll still be here to translate instructions from Alberto for me. He's going to send me a list of questions and answers for me to be prepared when the judge asks me whatever questions he asks me. I truly need to be prepared so they can't deny my release. I've paid my fines, got excellent reviews, but I don't put anything past Peru. I'm also told that it looks good if I can answer in Castellano, as it looks like I've put an effort into learning their language to fit in. I know some Spanish, but not everything. I'll study the question and answers once he sends them. He is ensuring that the court will have a translator, but Jenny said it will look good for me to answer a few in Castellano just the same. It's sucks because they want to hear how sorry I am for coming to Peru to smuggle drugs and how Peru is a beautiful country and doesn't deserve the embarrassment. Yet, I did not come here to smuggle drugs, and I have no clue about Peru's so-called beauty. Yet, I must answer with whatever they want to hear so I can get out of here once and for all.

I've always said, "I seem to have a black cloud over my head that follows me everywhere." You think I don't have a reason to say that? How's this? When I got to Fatima, Alberto told me that he'd start gathering my papers in July so that we could file for my benefits and that I'd be home end of September. I still have a note where he wrote that, and that was pre-COVID-19, and everything's now been delayed. But, at that time, I mentioned how my first lawyer filed a habeas corpus on the judges and how I was told that I was the first American to get house arrest, and they weren't happy. Alberto told me, "Don't worry, you're no longer in the Supreme Court; all new judges for you are back in the regular court." I was relieved. Well, after Alberto pulled some strings and got me a court date for November 6, he happened to see that it was the exact same judge who sentenced me. My typical black cloud. You can't make this stuff up. What are the odds of a Supreme Court judge who happened to sentence me being demoted to regular court and assigned to my case again?

Alberto quickly yanked me out of that court schedule. As he said that, thanks to Sal, he left a bad taste in their mouths about me, and he'd deny me and leave me to rot here and finish my sentence, despite my having been here for three-and-a-half years. Thanks to Sal's house arrest lie, they only counted two years, and with a 6.10-year sentence, he'd leave me here to rot for another four years. Thank God Alberto caught that and yanked it. So now, I was in courtroom number 6 (which is new, and no one seems to know much about it), and trying to "fit me in" was another deal. With COVID, they said only forty judges were working, and there are plenty of cases ahead of me, so Alberto spent the day at the court trying to pull strings to honor the November 6 date but had no luck yet. He was going to see the judges on Monday and hopes to have a definite update for me then. I was so upset. Jenny's translation was that my first lawyer made me look bad in the courts, and it was hurting me. The judges didn't like him. Was I stuck paying the price? I mean, if anyone hated the first lawyer, it was me. All he managed to accomplish for me was charge us a small fortune and make my situation worse. If it wasn't for him, I'd have been home fourteen months ago, before Fatima and COVID-19. Yet, here I sat, trying to get the hell out of Peru once and for all.

This has been a learning experience for all of us. I keep getting so angry and frustrated, and all I ever hear is, "Tranquila, paciencia." I want to strangle someone. Relax and have patience. Really? I didn't blame Alberto at all; it was sad how Peru worked, and I was stuck dealing with it. It was not right, but if I had learned anything, it was that the US wouldn't help, and there was nothing at all I could do about it. Alberto is trying his best and doing way more than Sal ever would, so I just have to wait and call on Monday and hope he gets a court date this year.

Alberto also sent the questions he predicted the judge would ask. It was comical. Questions like, "What will you do when you get back home?"

Answer: Ask for forgiveness from society and those around me.

Seriously? I must ask for forgiveness? Yet I had to answer in a way that would please the judges, or they would deny me. I had to stress how sorry I was and how wrong it was. I had to say what I did to appease them so I could go home.

The emotional roller coaster that I had been on for the past three-and-a-half years was slowly dragging the life from me.

Finally, Alberto and that call with my embassy managed to get the missing paper, but then I was told, "There are other cases ahead of hers. We are busy but can schedule a court date on February." February was almost four months away, and that meant another Christmas here. Alberto did all he could to get me a court date in three weeks, but it didn't work

And the black cloud over my head just continued to go on. Alberto tried to go to the courts that day to find out if they could see me before Christmas, and, of course, "They're busy." All he could do was request a court date via paper and wait for them to reply. On top of that, they did another transfer in Fatima, and I was moved to Pabellon C.

This made things worse because there were no English-speaking people there, and the one crazy woman who was in my room in Pabellon D got moved with me, along with a few other people, but the crazy one was right next to my bed. She and I did not get along to start with, and with her being right next to me, this was proving to be a continuous nightmare. She already started pissing me off, but as always, what can I do about it? Nothing.

Jenny was leaving in two weeks after completing her 6.8, so I wouldn't have a translator there anymore either, but I was used to Pabellon D. I had been there one week shy of fourteen months. Now I was in a new pabellon and had to relearn all their rules and procedures. This nightmare did not want to end. All I could do now was wait and hear what court date Alberto gets, and hopefully, they'd tell him soon.

This psychiatrist said the moves were part of progression, where you start new at Pabellon E, then move to D, then C, B, A. Apparently, I had been out of trouble and good, so I got moved since I had been here a while. People who have been here for several years are now in A and B. I truly pray that I wouldn't be here long enough for that.

Well, my first day in Pabellon C is already proving to piss me off. As I had mentioned, one of my biggest issues here in Fatima was the water when it was not on. I was a huge sweater, but couple that with menopause, and it was ten times worse. That's been my fight all along. With me wetting my hair or head, I try and explain to people that with hot and cold flashes constant, all day and all night, no matter how hot someone felt, it was ten times hotter for me. They didn't get it. Well, in Pabellon D, we had barrels that we used to flush the toilet and wash our Tupperware when there was no water, plus we had a bucket (like a spackle bucket) that we could fill up also and use to shower if needed.

That's why I also had my private spackle bucket in case I needed it since no one ever refilled the buckets in the room except me. It turns out that in Pabellon C, they only have the big barrels and not the buckets. If you want to take a shower and there's no water, you are supposed to use your own water, whether it be a water bottle, jug, or whatever. I immediately got my bucket back from Pabellon D and put it in the bathroom with my name and "Do not touch" written in Spanish. One would think that this was sufficient, but of course not.

In Pabellon D, I was showering from 3 a.m. to 5 a.m. every day. Here, in Pabellon C, you couldn't enter the bathroom until 5 am because the "cleaning prisoner" had to clean it. I entered the bathroom at 5:30 my first morning, and my bucket wasn't there.

I was looking around, and it was nowhere to be found. Eventually, a woman came out of the shower and told me in Spanish that she had borrowed it and would refill it. To me, that is not the point; it was mine. It clearly says, "No TOQUE." As my luck would have it, she was also the delgado of the pabellon, so there was nothing I could do about it. Then, as I mentioned, the woman I didn't get along with from my room in Pabellon D was now next to my bed in Pabellon C, and she took over the whole space where we kept our belongings. I complained about how only half the space is hers—not the whole space. I complained to the delgado and to the INPEs, but as I had already witnessed here, they never wanted to bother with the "crazies," so instead, they just gave them their way.

So, I put my stuff on the other side, and then the girl from that side said she wanted that space. So where am I supposed to put my stuff? She told me to put it on the top bed since it was vacant. Okay, fair enough. I put it all up there, and then another girl told me that it all depended on the INPE. Some INPEs didn't care; others didn't allow you to take over the whole bed. I was so livid at this point. Then they said, "Put it under the bed." While that would be okay, these beds are closer to the ground than the beds in Pabellon D, and there's not much room to squeeze bags under, not to mention my "canastas." I was just a mess. In only twenty-four hours here, this was my experience.

Jenny saw me in the "rotunda" that morning and asked how I was. Of course, I was livid and a mess, so I just started to cry. I said how I literally couldn't take much more of this. It was not right and not fair. Plus, I heard Christmas music on the radio, and the thought of spending another Christmas here ripped me apart. The psych just happened to be passing by at that time, and Jenny grabbed her and asked her why I was moved and how now I was not with anyone who spoke English. The psych just says it was a progression and for me to just relax; I'll be going home soon.

Sure, she still has November 6 on her computer, but that was before when it would have been the same judge who sentenced me. Since we had now moved it, I was in limbo now while we just waited for them to give me a new court date. She just kept saying to relax, that it would be soon. Sure, if there's one thing that I learned here, it was that Peru's idea of "soon" could be eight months. That wasn't not soon to me at all!

It was just about a week since Alberto asked for a new court date, and we had received no reply. This is totally typical of this country and is one of my biggest fears. Plus, the airlines have opened, and I was told overnight the US had 83,000 new COVID cases. My fear was that they would start shutting it down again. I had this window of opportunity to get out of here, and I needed to get out before they shut the window again.

I was told that Ireland and Europe had shut their airlines again due to COVID. So, we shall see if the US follows suit soon. Alberto got me a court date finally—December 9. While that is still five weeks away and near Christmas, he said the court was giving him a date of January 20! Yikes! He managed to get them to squeeze me for December 9 so that was better than the end of January, but still, three months after, I was able to start my papers for expulsion. It was typical of this shitshow place. I just pray I was back home for Christmas. Even after the court, it was not an instant "Go, leave," like back home.

It was still a process here. I had seen people go anywhere from three weeks after court to four months later. I'd only have two weeks before Christmas, so I prayed Alberto could pull whatever strings he could to get me home for Christmas. And this is only if the airlines are still flying normally. If not, then I was at the mercy of humane flights, schedule, and availability. I'd think positively that I would be home for Christmas. That's all I could do.

Jenny officially left today, having completed her 6.8-year sentence. A few of the Thai and Philippino girls left yesterday on "redention," where their time was cut abut short due to work. Of course, there's always a fee. The one girl was denied, yet she was released yesterday once she paid S/700 for some convenient paper. It was so typical here; they move to the sound of money.

Jenny was sad to leave (while overjoyed to be leaving at the same time). I told her to be happy; her nightmare was finally over. But I understand, having spent 6.8 years of your life on the inside, it was scary and overwhelming to start again on the outside, not to mention the friends you made inside.

Here, the Asian girls and Jenny would be staying in a convent. The Christian ladies help us all as best they could, and they had a connection with a convent that would put people up until they could get money to fly home. It was very nice of them to open their doors to folks like that. Tomorrow, I have one month until my court date, so I could only think positive.

The folks here and in Peru in general eat so much. Back home, we have three meals a day, breakfast, lunch, and dinner, with two snacks in between. Here, they eat breakfast (Quaker, two rolls, and something else that can be ham, cheese, jelly, butter, or three olives) at 7 a.m. Then around 8:30 am, they had more food (which I'd eat for lunch), then lunch. Then another big meal around 2:30/3 and then dinner, and then they continued to eat big meals. It always amazed me (yet explains why most are so big). Even if I say I'm full, they continue to tell me, "Comer, comer, comer." (Eat, eat, eat.)

They don't take no for an answer. I literally can't eat so much. Besides the weight that I've put on from the crap they put in the food they feed us, this pushing food on me isn't the best. I kept saying today, "I have no more space," pointing to my stomach. No more space. But again, "Comer." Well, I reached my limit. I felt so full and not good. I couldn't even sit without being uncomfortable. I literally threw up. Not on purpose. I was just over capacity in my stomach, and it apparently needed release. I still have a fruit salad I haven't eaten and two "plantains" (big) for dinner that I haven't touched. That will have to wait until tomorrow.

After I eat the Quaker, orange, and banana, the girl then gives me three sandwiches, usually cheese, lettuce, tomato, and chips on a roll, and sometimes there's even an egg. Three of these! I managed to get her down to two sandwiches, but I've literally just had the Quaker, banana, and orange! I keep telling her how I'm too full and how she's turning me into two to three more "Pattys". She just laughs and tells me to eat. As I write this, I am so uncomfortably full it's not even funny. I swear, I just want to go home—back to my normal life. And for the record, they aren't feeding me out of the goodness of their hearts. I buy the food for the week, and they prepare it for us. It is a win-win for them. They don't have to pay for the food; they just prepare it and get to eat as well. That would all be great, but I physically cannot eat as much as they all do here.

As it turned out, I was so nauseous from all that food I literally was sick. Lunch was potato and beans in gravy, plus rice, plus a potato, plus I had a huge salad that kiosko makes for me every day for S/3 per day, plus the girl I sit with at lunch made a beetroot salad, plus the tea they serve at lunch, which I usually get a pitcher full. I literally kept pointing to my stomach saying, "No mas espacio" (no more space) to fit in anything more, yet they just kept saying, "Comer comer."

I had soup for dinner, but I was still so full from the day that I was nauseous all night. The next morning, I kept saying that I was still nauseous, and we had to start lessening what I ate, which lasted three days and then they started with the food again. Ugh!

Yesterday was Friday the thirteenth so the animals were in full force. There was also a soccer game. They did quenta at 5:30 so everyone could go up and watch the game. I've never been a soccer fan. When my son was little, he was on a soccer team for a few years, as was my daughter. *That* soccer I went to and watched weekly, but professional soccer, I have no interest.

In this pabellon, I'm in room number 1. In this room 1 is three rooms. Think of a capital letter E, but backwards. It's technically three rooms separated by a wall in between each but with no doors in between each (like E). I'm in the middle. Well, the rooms have three windows along the walls where in the spring, summer, and fall weather, they open the windows to let air and light in. As my luck is, my room in the middle (2) has the windows locked and painted black. Apparently, there is a big wall on the other side, but beyond that is the street (the outside world), and this paranoid place is afraid that people would put up signs and banners and yell to the outside world, so instead they block it so we have no access to it. While that would be fine, it's hotter than it normally is and constantly dark. I can see rooms with the windows when I walk to the door, all bright, and I can feel the cross breeze. Yet in my section, it's a sauna and constantly dark.

I'm told that President Trump did not win the reelection this year, and now it's President Biden. I've been here pretty much all of Trump's office, so I can't say much about it, and I really don't know anything about Biden as I've been dealing with my situation the past 3.8 years. I hear COVID-19 is spiking high again, and they are canceling flights in the States and closing many places again. With one month left for my hearing and then however long it takes after that, I only hope and pray that there are still flights to take me home. I don't want to stay in this shithole place a second more than I have to.

My sister bought me several unicorn coloring books since I absolutely love unicorns, but also a few other types of coloring books.

Manta craft, stress relieving designs for adult relaxation. I have all animals, hummingbirds, inspirational quotes, words to color by, etc. They are all quite relaxing, especially since I have nothing at all but time on my hands here. I've colored more than 250 pages so far. All I have dedicated to my family, some for my mom, stepdad, dad, stepmom, sisters, son, daughter, grandbabies, husband, etc. I've put so much time and energy into them that I said they could laminate them and use them as placemats. I thought this was a good idea anyway. It seems many of the women here have fallen in love with my colored pages, which they've all asked to "borrow" them so that they can copy them. As expected, the books then circulate. I started out with 250+, I'm now down to about 110. Of course, everyone says, "It's not me, I didn't take anything." But someone did!

This reminds me of high school. I was going through my teenage hormones, first love, etc. I was very good at poetry and wrote many in a book—so many poems from the heart about my emotions, first love, first breakup, first kiss, first heartbreak, etc. They were quite good since they were original and from my heart. Just like now, girls in school kept borrowing my poem book, saying that they wanted to copy a poem. After weeks of this, my book suddenly disappeared, and no one claimed to be the last one who had it. It was infuriating. To this day, whenever I read a greeting card, I can't help but wonder, "Was this one of my poems that was stolen from me?" I guess the signs have been all along on how cruel people could be in this world. I just never noticed it since I always tried to see the best in people. However, my experience in Peru has taken much of that away from me.

Peru is a country that I can never understand. They've ousted countless presidents in the past and even arrested some. They've been trying to oust their current president for the past few months. They got him to stand down on Friday (which is crazy because he'd only remain in office until March anyway when it's time to reelect a president). Yesterday they put in a new president in the interim. Last night, there were riots like crazy, and two people were killed. This afternoon this president was forced out. It hasn't ever been twenty-four hours! This country is truly just off the charts insane from what I see. As always, I'll never figure them out. I just will sit tight and wait twenty-four more days until my court date. That's all I can do.

This morning was funny. Well, not really but it just goes along with all that I've been saying all along. The water is unpredictable, and today it didn't come on until 5:40. I'd been standing in the bathroom since 5:15, since in this pabellon, you can't shower until 5:30. In the meantime, I brushed my teeth and drank my fiber drink and then had a bottle of water to wash my stuff out. I have this bottle of water for these exact situations. Whenever there is no water, I have my bottles to do what I need to do. It's crazy what this place teaches you. It doesn't teach people how to be better people on the outside or teach people employment skills or educate people. Nope. They teach us nothing more than to prepare for the constant occasion of no water. How ridiculous is that? Yet this is my every day, unfortunately. Sadly, this country has nothing but opportunities to better themselves and change and not be a third-world country. Yet their priorities are nothing more than music and partying. They are why they will never advance. And it's not just prison; I saw the same on the outside, too. Eighteen more days until my court, I just pray this ends once and for all—for good!

One of the women I met in Santa Monica is here with me in Fatima. I feel bad for her. She just found out that her husband passed away. She's a mess. I met her almost four years ago in Santa Monica. I'm told that her son killed his girlfriend, and they arrested the whole family—her husband and son. And, like drug cases, since it's considered "a group" now, her sentence is ten years, unlike the typical five with benefits. She's 76 years old! This country just never ceases to amaze me. This poor woman can't read or write, has no education at all, and I'm sure she had no idea about what happened with her son, yet she's now in prison at 73 years old with a ten-year sentence. She'll most likely die here also, like her husband in another jail and her son in another jail. Yet, others go free after three years at younger ages—who clearly knew what they were doing. It's crazy.

Today they allowed us to do a solicitude to enable us to see our lawyers. But they give you a date and a twenty-minute time slot. If you say, "My lawyer is in court that day/time," or if he is out of town, they don't care. That's the twenty minutes they'll allow for you, and that's it. Too bad if it doesn't accommodate you or your lawyer. I submitted the solicitude and will now wait and see when they tell me he can come. Who knows if it will even be before my court date, but we shall see. I just must have faith that, regardless, I'll be home for Christmas. That will be the greatest Christmas ever!

One girl, who is only 29 years old, has been here now for eight years and was supposed to go home yesterday after completing her sentence, but as usual, due to a misspelling in her papers, she is still here. It's ridiculous. I mean, she was a baby when she came here and eight years? I asked, "Did she shoot the president?" Nope. She dealt a few grams of marijuana. I mean, it's a disgrace how they decide their prison sentences and how they tear families apart and just don't care. All my family says is, "Be thankful that you didn't go to Hong Kong because they have the death penalty." They don't understand what it's been like for me. The thought has crossed my mind repeatedly: *At least then this nightmare would have ended quicker.* I know my family is dealing with this in their way, but I've said repeatedly, "Unless you are in my shoes, you truly don't have a clue what I'm dealing with." You could read a book, see a movie, talk to someone else, but as I've witnessed myself, no two prisons are the same, no two people are the same, and no two situations are the same.

For example, I read a book about a prisoner who happened to be in two of the prisons I have been in. Others here read the book too and were saying, "Oh, she lied. Oh, she exaggerated, etc." Yet, when I asked what she said that was a lie or exaggerated, they'd say things she wrote that happened to *me,* too. So, I tried to tell them just because *you* didn't experience it doesn't mean that it didn't happen. No two people's experiences are the exact same. It's literally living a nightmare every single day. Not to mention that tomorrow's Thanksgiving Day and is yet another Thanksgiving that I'm missing. This saddens me so much. I remember back in the apartment, with the house arrest, Sal came with the wife of the other American he was representing. He bought some turkey, potatoes, salads, wine. etc. and had a tiny "Thanksgiving" for us and said, "This will be your last Thanksgiving here in Peru." Well, this is now my second Thanksgiving *since then* in a prison. So much for more of his false promises.

People can assume or guess what it's like for us, but unless you are in my shoes, you just don't know. So yes, my family is dealing in their way and helping me as best they can, and I am truly grateful for all their help and patience. I can only guarantee that as hard as it may be on them, it's worse for me. And to keep hearing Christmas on the radio and TV just truly sickens my stomach. I've already spent three Christmases here in prison. Christmas is one month away. I just pray that my Delahencia in two weeks goes smoothly.

They are allowing my lawyer in to see me tomorrow for twenty minutes. Not much notice, but I'm just shocked that they even set it up before my court date, but I'm happy just the same. I had to do a solicitude to have someone translate for me, so hopefully they allow it because I won't understand him and vice versa. Otherwise, I'll jot down my questions so that we get it all covered since we only have twenty minutes to chat, not a minute more.

I got to see my lawyer, for fifteen minutes instead of twenty, but either way, at least I got to see him. He tells me to tell the judge at the end of the hearing, "*Te pido perdón y espero que me perdones por este horrible error que cometí en tu hermoso país. He aprendido mi lección y me arrepentiré por el resto de mi vida en casa.*" (I ask for forgiveness and hope that you will pardon me for this horrible mistake that I made in your beautiful country. I have learned my lesson and will repent for the rest of my life back home.) At this point, I'll say whatever to get me the hell out of this country once and for all. I'll be crossing my fingers, toes, and all I can for this hearing to go well in two weeks. It's only two weeks away, but I'll think positively.

I've said all along how Peru's priority seems to be music and parties—nothing more. I even saw it in the condo on house arrest. They have no S/ for food or rent but they blast fireworks and party almost every day. Even the school's band practice and shows were every day. Instead of preparing kids to not be like adults, focusing on things that will help bring them out of a third-world country, they just continue the pattern. In prison, I mentioned how they create holidays out of thin air, anything to take a day off—holiday for the chicken, for the first day of spring, etc. They also party and create shows out of thin air. I saw it in Santa Monica too but was too pre-occupied with being new try to acclimate myself and was busying myself playing with the babies.

In Ancones 2, I immediately saw the same. As crazy as it is, your participation in this nonsense helps your case. It's the most idiotic nonsense, but sadly this is my life here. Today they were practicing for another show this week. Again, the director, psychiatrist, etc. will all come to watch each pabellon perform. I've only been in this pabellon three weeks, and this is the third performance. For what? I have no idea. Again, it'll be making costumes out of crap, people performing/dancing to some idiotic music, etc. God forbid they actually teach prisoners something useful to better their lives. Yes, I'm inserting sar-casm. Anyway, as they are practicing this, I just colored more pictures and listened to the radio. English music, which isn't any new music, but it's still good either way to hear English, which I never hear oth-erwise. Nine more days to go for court. It can't come soon enough.

Another thing that amazes me is that, aside from partying and music as a constant, cosmetic surgery is huge here. I'm told through-out South America it's a big thing. So many women here (they're not shy about admitting it) have silicone in their butts and boobs. Yet again, they have no money for anything else, but they are quick to spend on silicone. Back home, sure, I have known women who got boob jobs, but I'd never met anyone who had gotten a butt job. I've met six people throughout my three-and-a-half years that have had both. They also shave their eyebrows and pencil then in every day. It's strange to me. Even in Santa Monica, this woman would spend forty-five minutes every day putting on makeup, doing her hair all fancy, washing her sneakers so they sparkle, etc. They think I'm crazy because I do none of that. I truly don't care at all what any of them think of me, and I'm not about to get dolled up to appease any of them. Sure, back home I dress nice and wear limited makeup, but here, for what? My clothes are majority hand-me-downs from oth-ers—too small, don't match, etc. I look like a walking box of colored crayons, and I don't care at all.

CHAPTER 22

Desiree has been a sweetheart, and she, too, always feels that I should dress and do my hair, etc. It must be a Latin-American thing. She's had her family send me sandals, sneakers, slacks, body cream, a light windbreaker, natural soap, socks, bras, and panties. I appreciate it so much but keep telling her to stop sending me clothes. I'm going home soon and will not be taking all my things with me. She says that I need to dress nice, like a lady, when I go home and that she wants to see a photo of me at the airport wearing these things for when I go home to my husband. She's such a funny lady, but I said okay. She truly means well. Her husband is the one who's been bringing me packages every two weeks. She tells him what to bring, and he sends in packages to both of us with home-cooked food and other things. I am grateful that she is a nice lady who does not see me like most other Peruvians do, as an intruder in her country. She, as well as the baby's mom in Santa Monica, have been nothing but great to me, and if anything, I will miss them both once I leave. I'll continue to try and help them as much as I can once I am home. It's the least I can do for as nice as they were to me while inside.

It's amazing how Peruvians assume all Gringos are rich. Today a girl was coming around taking names of people who wanted or needed to see the new "prison lawyer" (aka free lawyer). She asked every single person *except me*. I asked why not me. "Because it's for the free lawyer" was the reply. Um, yes, so why not ask me? They all just assume I don't need it, that I can pay for my lawyer. Yes, that's true, but she didn't know that for a fact. It's so prejudiced.

Well, as always, I go two steps forward and then three steps back. Today was my Delahencia. It was also the day they were doing flu shots, so it was a bit chaotic. My paper said my court was for 10 a.m. and to arrive at 9:40. I obviously can't go anywhere until the INPEs tell me. They didn't call me until 10:20. I was terrified that the judge would already have moved on. They don't care about my situation or why I was late. Well, either way, instead of in the auditorium, I was put in a side room of the prison director, which was odd, but at least I got in, or so I thought. I spent an hour and a half trying to get the internet to work but to no avail. Unfucking-believable. The internet kept popping off, the audio wasn't working, the video wasn't working. My lawyer kept WhatsApping the director and calling her but she was saying the internet was just iffy. He asked for her to do the video on her cellular, which is glued to her hand/ear all day, but she didn't want to do it. She kept making excuses and then said that it's not allowed. He kept pressing, and eventually, she gave the number but then said that if he called and she didn't answer, it's because she's busy. Unreal! They tried another laptop to no avail. Apparently, my lawyer paid for an interpreter also, but none of us could get online.

The psychiatrist was with me, and she was saying (in Spanish) how she gave a great report on me—all is good, I've never been a problem—and that my fines were paid in full (so much for their stupid new law stating that fines don't need to be paid) and all my paperwork is there. So she said, "Maybe the judge will just sign off on it with you." Of course, in a perfect world, that would have happened, but this is me we are talking about with my black cloud over my head. As stupid as this country's joke of justice system is, apparently the prosecutor had said they had no problem letting me go. Yet, they won't sign off on anything until he sees my face and hears me express my sorrow for coming here and committing a crime. All I can think is, *Are you fucking kidding me?* I have to say how sorry I am and beg forgiveness? They should apologize to *me* for having zero justice. For never once looking at any of the evidence my first lawyer gave them. For robbing me of all of my belongings, including my wedding rings. For bouncing me from prison to prison—one worse than the other. For licensing lawyers, like my first one, who had done nothing but lie to my family and me. For causing me to be here three months shy of four years so far—an additional thirteen more months than I should have been. For truly robbing me of so much of my life, all for something they know takes place in their country.

These Nigerian drug cartels were scamming people, yet they truly don't care. Yet, I am supposed to apologize and beg forgiveness. The only thing I am sorry for is stepping foot in Peru. This entire experience is sickening. Yet, whenever they get around to rescheduling this Delahencia, I will say whatever they want to hear just to get me the fuck out here and end this nightmare once and for all.

And as if that wasn't enough, Christmas is only two weeks away. I said to the psychiatrist and director, "Oh great, so now another Christmas I have to spend here," and the director says, "Oh, yes. Of course. It's fifteen days for immigration alone. I'm holding a paper here for someone's release, which had her Delahencia two months ago." They say it like it's no big deal. This is people's lives they mess with. I replied, "Well, my compatriota was sent home two weeks after his Delahencia," and they just looked at me like I had two heads. I feel like I am stuck in the Bermuda Triangle. My husband didn't even go to work today because he knew he'd be a nervous wreck waiting to hear how this went today. So much for that. Even my lawyer was devastated. We're now told the internet has been down since Friday (and today is Wednesday). Five days? Their excuse was Movistar couldn't come and fix it because yesterday was a federal holiday. Okay, but what about Saturday? Sunday? Monday? Plus, if we can't physically go to court due to COVID-19 and are solely only able to attend a Delahencia via the internet, you would think that they'd make sure there is working internet. But as always, they truly don't care. They just see all of us as waste-of-life criminals and won't do anything to assist us.

I thought that I'd leave the Delahencia with positive news. Knowing that here, it's not an instant release. But still, I would have known that I'd be leaving soon. Yet again, here I sit, not having a clue when they'll reschedule this or when this nightmare will end. I'd love to know what on earth I ever did to deserve this; it's so not right or fair.

I'm now told that my new Delahencia is on December 21, four days before Christmas. The director told me on December ninth, "It'll be done on Monday," and yet Alberto said, "I don't have confirmation of that." And after hunting him down all weekend, he finally confirmed December 21 in the afternoon. All I could do was crouch and cry. Another Christmas stuck in this shithole, where I don't belong, away from my family.

The Peruvian girl who's been translating for me is in because she had a few grams of weed in her pocket, for personal use. Grams! Enough to hold in one palm. She and her sister got eight-year sentences. They've been here seven so far. Her son was six years old when she got arrested. He's 13 now. She tells me (in Spanish), "Look at me, I feel your pain. This country's justice system is horrific. I couldn't agree more. You're upset, but I'm here seven years so far, and all because of a few small grams of weed."

I must bite my tongue. I know what she's saying. I get it, and I feel horrible for her (and countless others) who are stuck going through these experiences because of this country's complete and utter disgrace of a so-called justice system. But at the same time, I want to shout, "But it's your freaking country!" I mean. I don't get it. Countless people are here for so many years for the stupidest things.

And it's funny how part of this "Delahencia" they want to hear how the psychiatrist has taught me and others to be better. Obviously, we say whatever they want to hear to go home. But what exactly do they teach? The whole psych evaluation, which is once a year, is less than two minutes. It's three checkpoints. Did she ever get sent to Waco? Does she have any complaints against her? Does she work Taller, pay for Taller, etc.? Yes, yes, yes! Okay, check. That's it.

I started in superior court with three judges. Every time I had a Delahencia, the men would either be on their cell phones or talking and laughing amongst one another, not paying an ounce of attention to us (prosecutor and defense) at all. I couldn't believe my eyes. That would never ever happen back home in the US. There, the judge gives his/her undivided attention to the entire process. Here, in Peru, they don't care at all. After several Delahencia with zero attention from any of the three judges, I got told point blank, "We don't care. We have zero interest in your defense or evidence. If you plead innocent one more time, we'll go for fifteen years. If you plead guilty, we'll go for less," leaving me no other choice but to plead guilty.

Today I had my Delahencia. I was nervous because today was also a day where (again) they had some type of festivities, another competition between pabellons, judging on performances and decorations, etc. I know the director and psychiatrist go with all the INPEs and workers to each pabellon to watch and judge them. I was nervous that they'd be busy with this stuff and not be available to attend my video conference Delahencia. Shockingly, we had internet that time. But they tried to jerk me around again as usual.

Not only did the judge and prosecutor want to talk to the psychiatrist (which is normal), they also demanded to speak to the assistent social worker, plus the director, plus the prison lawyer, whom I've never even met before. Truly ridiculous. Normally, all of them would not have all been here at the same day and time. But fortunately, due to these festivities today, they were. The judge and prosecution didn't know this, so ha! Because if they weren't here, they'd say, "Oh, we'll need to reschedule," dragging this on and on more. It was a miracle that they were all here, but still it's a typical means of them jerking me around. I'd never ever met this prison lawyer so what was the point of needing to talk to him? Just pure BS. Plus, they were grilling the psychiatrist. All four had positive reviews for me based on my records, but I felt like they were looking for a means to deny me. The judge and prosecutor were asking her, "How can you tell she's good and rehabilitated? You've only seen her for a year. You see her as a group, so how can you really tell? She doesn't speak Spanish, so how can we know?" She (and I) explained I understand Spanish, but just because I don't speak it fluently doesn't mean I don't understand.

Then, they asked me, "What did you learn while here?" Wow, where to begin? I learned what a horrible place this is, how their justice system is nonexistent, how music and dance are priorities in life, how corrupt everyone here is, etc. I obviously couldn't tell them how I really feel, so I had to make up some lie that they'd like. Then they asked what I planned to do if they grant me freedom. Where will I live? How do they know that I won't fall for this again? It's truly crazy. I had to express how sorry I was and then ask for forgiveness. As if all of that wasn't bad enough (this took over one hour), you'd think that they'd say yes or no. Nope! They say, "We'll let you know" and send me on my way. I was shocked.

So I go back to my pabellon and call my husband; him and my sisters were texting the lawyer. He said the judge has eight to ten days to make their decision. But at the holidays it could be little more. Christmas is four days away (although here, they celebrate it December 24; New Year's is the week after.) So, when they'll get around to giving me an answer, who knows. Alberto feels positive and says all is good. While that all sounds good, the one thing Peru has taught me is to expect the unexpected because the unexpected always happens.

I said, "Until you hold a paper in your hand that says I'm free, I won't get my hope up yet." Besides, once the judge gives their answer, it's still a process. Papers need to come to the prison, immigration needs to do their part, then my family can purchase the plane ticket, and then I'm escorted to the plane home. I'm obviously missing my fourth Christmas from home now, but I pray this nightmare ends soon and that I can start 2021 off at home in the USA, where I belong. Hope and pray, hope and pray. That's all I'll be doing for the next few weeks.

My husband also feels that I should leave all my suitcases behind now, too. I didn't wish to do that originally because it is *my* stuff. But like he said, "What if?" I'm here in prison because of a suitcase that was given to me. My suitcases have been out of my hands for years. While I know they've been locked away in the Christian woman's storage, they are still away. And with not trusting the police here one bit, my husband said, "Leave it all. We'll replace whatever you need when you are home. Don't take any chances with Peru anymore." So, I'll leave all my stuff behind for donation, I guess.

Alberto has pulled off a miracle! It's two days after my Delahencia, and he's managed to get the judge to sign off on my freedom. Now I can have a good Christmas. While I'll still be in prison, at least I now know that I'm leaving soon. The judge signed and stamped the paper, so it's just a matter of days now. Now, the INPEs, Immigration, and the Embassy do their part, but with the holidays, it will obviously be delayed. But I'm almost there now.

Alberto said that while he's sorry that he couldn't get me home for Christmas, he worked hard and pushed and pushed to at least get me an official verdict for Christmas. I said it's the best Christmas present that I could have asked for, aside from being home. It's funny too because today I saw the Asistenta social worker, who even told me how strange it was that they wanted to talk to her about me. She knows that she doesn't really know me, so even she thought it was an odd request, but it was just another stunt they played to drag this out. I'm glad we stopped that game by everyone being present. Now, I cross my fingers and toes that I leave this nightmare once and for all soon. In the meantime, I'll celebrate Christmas here happy now knowing that it's almost over—finally!

Christmas dinner (the 24th as Peru celebrates it), we ate dinner donated by the Switzerland Embassy. That was very nice of them. It was rice, turkey veggies, and panatone for everyone. In my almost four years here, I've seen more donations by other countries' embassies and none from the US. Crazy! Desiree's husband brought me homecooked food, another huge panatone, fruits, veggies, etc. Even the cop and wife and daughter brought me chicken and tumuli. They truly are so sweet. I can say that not all Peruvians are mean. There are a handful of people here that are genuinely good-hearted people but not because they want something in return. My Santa Monica friend and her dad, Rosa, and the cop and family are among these genuinely great people. While it has sucked being here for Christmas, I am at least happy to know that it is my last Christmas here and that I am going home soon.

It's crazy. I was talking to a girl here today. She's Peruvian. She's been here so far seven years on an eight-year sentence. She has one more year to go. I asked if she had any kids. She said yes, a seven-year-old daughter. I was afraid to ask, but asked if she had the baby in prison. She said no. Her baby was two weeks old when she got arrested. Why was she arrested? Because the person she was with had a half gram of marijuana on her pocket. Not the girl but her friend. And since they were together, they both got arrested and got an eight-year sentence. It's totally insane! Her baby was two weeks old. Peru doesn't care. I've had nothing but time here and totally figured out how prisons are a business that employs people (police, INPEs, judges, staff, secretaries, food vendors, telephones, etc.) So regardless of how they ruin people lives by throwing everyone and anyone into prison for insanely large sentences, they really don't care. It's just the way it is here in Peru. Another girl I met has been here for eight years so far on a fifteen-year sentence. For what? For stealing, and robbing a bank at gun point? Nope. For stealing from a neighbor (a few dollars and a cell phone). Again, it's a business here. The craziest part of it all is that it seems the only low sentences here are murder. Can you believe it? You murder someone and walk out in three years, but do anything else and the sentences are off the charts.

I think it's human nature to always have (or look for) an answer as to why things happen. At least, it is for me. When we don't have an answer, we either search for one or go with the old saying, "We may never know until after we die." What kind of answer is that? It's just something to appease us with a semi-answer when one doesn't really exist. I've been through them all! Why is God doing this to me? Or why is God allowing this to happen/continue? What did I do in a past life to be enduring all this now? But while here, I've studied with various religions and even they all contradict each other. Yet each religion believes that their religion is the right one and others are wrong, so what are we supposed to believe?

The new year is here, 2021. I have only one reason to smile. It's my last New Year's in this shithole place! Last night they partied in the rooms until 2:30 a.m. Just like last year, they all get all dolled up, hair all done, dress nice, makeup, etc. I even saw Desiree for a moment while she went to Topico, and she was shaking her head telling me how I need to dress up and be a lady. I could care less what any of these people think of me here. In fact, I had pajamas on by 7:30 p.m. It was impossible to sleep with them with the TV blasting music and them using the space as a dance floor, but what could I do? Just lay and try to sleep. By 12:45 the INPEs locked us in and turned off the lights, including the bathroom light. People then screamed until 1:00 a.m., asking the INPEs to turn back on the bathroom light (which got ignored). By 1:00 a.m. I was out cold, I was so exhausted. By 5:30 I was up as always taking a shower in the dark. It's now January 1 and a whole new year where I will smile because soon, I will be back home where I belong with my family.

I didn't think I'd ever see the day, but I am beyond grateful and happy that I'm now at the finish line. It's a matter of Immigration, the Embassy, and INPEs to finalize the paperwork, and I'll be escorted to the airport and put on a plane. I can hardly wait.

It's now January 5, 2021, four months after I was able to start my paper for expulsion, and I'm still here, as always, waiting for Peru to get their shit together and get me home. I know it's finally official in that the judge has signed off, and now it's up to the Embassy, Immigration, and INPEs to do the paperwork to go. Today is two weeks since my Delahencia, and I know Christmas and New Year's hasn't helped. My only concern is that there is a new strand of COVID-19, and it's back in the prison, where we were one of the only prisons without COVID originally; once they actually started testing us, we all had it. They had stopped testing us, but we all had it. Now it's back. I hear outside countries are all spiking again and closing boarders. My fear has been that once I can leave, due to COVID, I'm going to be stuck here, and I've been saying for two months that I have a window of opportunity to get out as planes are flying. But as they drag their asses, I sit, nervous. I only hope and pray that they don't close boarders again or stop fights due to COVID and leave me stuck here.

I saw the lawyer yesterday, and he told me, "Maybe Monday or Tuesday," hoping everyone does their job and gets the paperwork done. That's another week away, but I will remain positive in that I'm at the finish line and just need to cross it. Another issue is that there's only one nonstop flight to JFK, and it's a midnight flight. All others are connections but in South America. And as bad as this sounds, I do not trust South America anymore. I've already seen how Americans are seen as nothing more than ATM machines, and how back home, one needs evidence to convict someone. Here, they don't. So even if I had a connecting flight in South America and never stepped foot out of the airport, I don't trust them to claim that I'm guilty of something else since they don't need proof of anything. I can't bear the thought of reliving this nightmare. That being said, there's an 11 p.m. curfew now and all cars must be off the road, so yet another bump in my road to freedom—two-and-a-half weeks so far and still waiting. I hate this place.

After two-and-a-half weeks from the date of my Delahencia, we are finally moving forward. I got a date of January 13 to leave on my flight home. As happy as I am, if there's one thing this whole experience has taught me, it's to expect the unexpected. I'm happy but won't breathe easy until the plane wheels are off the ground and in the air. I had to fingerprint a ton of papers on Friday and didn't have my glasses on since I was sent there unexpectedly.

Thank God the woman caught it because I had to go again since she noticed a typo in my name (typical). It's shit like that that would keep me here longer, so thank God she caught it. It's a midnight flight, but I'm sure I'll sleep like baby once out of here. Desiree had gotten permission from Alcaide today to say her goodbye to me. Since we're in different pabellons, they let us have a few minutes to chat. She was crying and hugging me, calling me her angel and best friend and saying how grateful she is to me. Of course, that got me crying. I feel the same. She's truly been a blessing to me, helpful in so many ways. I told her how I would continue helping her after I am home. It's the least I could do. As always, I know many people will think I'm stupid, but unless they were physically here with me, they'll never understand. It's as simple as that. I'm beyond grateful to her friendship and Lena's from Santa Monica. Both women were my angels, and I'll forever be grateful.

Now I've gone through my stuff and have started to give away much of it. I really don't have much left at this point, but whatever I have, I know others can use. I won't be taking any of it home. So, I'll give it all away to those still here when I go. It's tough because I know many Peruvians don't have while some do. But most of the foreigners are also stuck and have no family to bring them stuff. I'll mix it up and share whatever I have left.

And if Peru's sloppy work hasn't been abundantly clear already, I had to go again today to re-fingerprint and sign all the papers. They will never get their shit together. I'm glad they fixed whatever issues now and not after I'm supposed to leave, but here's to hoping that this was the last error.

I was talking to another Peruvian girl here today. She's been here seven years so far with an eight-year sentence. Her mom left when she was a baby. Her dad and family are currently in prison or have been in prison. It's a shame. Not that I can predict the future, but seriously, with all this happening to her family, Peru making a business out of constantly throwing people in jails for crazy sentences, what will happen to her kids? They will most likely wind up in prison tours like I was. It's all they know and all they have seen. And Peru doesn't care; it's all business for them. Instead of teaching people to be better educated, trained in a field that they could make money. Instead, they do nothing. They will never ever get out of third-world-country status at this rate. It's crazy.

My day has finally arrived, January 13. The INPEs were supposed to pick me up at 6 p.m., but of course nothing is ever fast or on time in Peru. They came at 7 p.m. It was the usual routine, tearing apart all my bags before I left Fatima, stuffing me in the ambulance where I got car sick by the time we arrived at the airport. It was embarrassing, as usual. They had the handcuffs on so tight, and I got escorted into the airport. I don't know what made me more nauseous, the ambulance ride, riding in the back of the dark ambulance with no window or lights being bounced all over—or being back in the airport where this whole nightmare started. It all made me so sick.

Once the handcuffs were removed, I was escorted by a male and female INPE holding my elbow to make sure I was totally guarded so as not to escape. It's crazy and beyond embarrassing. Then on top of being escorted with the two INPEs, we had the airport police with their bright yellow police vests also guard me. It's insane. You'd think that I was Jeffery Dahmer or something. My flight is at 12:05, and it's now 10:15 p.m. as I write this, so about another hour of sitting here being surrounded by police like I'm some sort of maniac. But once I am on the plane, I'm officially free.

I'm exhausted and just want this nightmare over with once and for all. I'm waiting for my plane to arrive. Once I'm on it, my nightmare officially ends. Thank God!! Plus, it couldn't have happened at a better time. Our director of the prison resigned today (so good luck with a new one being trained) and with COVID-19 running rampant again, the president of Peru just slapped on new quarantines and is cracking down on them, so it's great that I'm leaving now before they close their borders again.

I was babysat the entire time at the airport. One thing that was odd, even though I was given back my passport when I was in the apartment, either Immigration or the Embassy canceled my passport and reissued a new one with the exact photo that was on the previous one. It caused a lot of issues during the entire airport process because it had no prior stamps or information about when I arrived in Peru, how long I was there, etc., so for every process and transition at the airport, the minute they would view my passport, the cop had to go into detail about everything. With most people speaking Spanish, everyone knew my situation. It never ends.

I eventually made it onto the plane. I know the lawyer had greased the palms of the male INPE at the airport originally, telling him to treat me nice. The female INPE assumed that I would be doing the same with her. Ha! Fat chance. Peru has taken enough from me already, and at the end of the day, she's doing her job!

Once on the plane, I refused to breathe easy until the plane wheels were off the ground. Planes usually take a while during the time they are preparing for takeoff. Plus, with COVID, we had to wear masks and the plastic shields over our faces. I was sandwiched in the middle of people but didn't care one bit. I was no longer in prison, and that's all that mattered to me. After a while, the doors were shut, and we were off. Finally—I was free.

The flight attendants served us dinner, which I ate happily. I could not sleep because I was too excited to be going home. My husband, daughter, and my husband's friend planned to pick me up at the airport. Thank God for that. I had some soles left and had planned to exchange them at the airport in Lima, Peru. But of course, as my luck always is, they were no longer open. That being said, I had no money at all on my arrival back to the USA so thank God they would be there to get me.

Upon landing at JFK Airport (it is now winter in the US, where it was summer in Peru), I quickly changed from shorts and a tank top to pants and the one sweater I had in the airplane bathroom before exiting the plane. I did not check any luggage since I did not have that much. Everything I had fit into one plastic bag that I carried on the plane. When I was walking back towards immigration, obviously my passport must have been flagged as a drug trafficker. I was conveniently escorted to another section, where no one explained to me why. I was met with a group of police from immigration who proceeded to grill me with tons of questions from where I was, why was I there so long, etc. and then tore apart my bag. It didn't take too long for me to realize what was going on. This was an interrogation to see if I was bringing drugs back. How on earth could I have accomplished that when I was escorted from a prison to an airplane?

I had all the drawings and coloring papers I did, as well as one or two books, and notes from my family. I had one of the notes from the Bible study, and I thought it was funny that in the note were Bible quotes and passages. Apparently, they must have thought this was code for drugs, so the one cop kept taking the page and leaving with it to bring it to other cops for their thoughts. It was the most idiotic thing. I finally snapped at the cop. He told me that they can do whatever they want: interrogate me, search me, etc. I threw my hands up in the air. I told him that if they did their job in the first place I would never have been in that situation! Well, that turned into me being escorted into another room where two female officers searched me inside and out. Eventually they found nothing and sent me on my way.

This apparently went on for quite some time. Due to COVID, the airport was not allowing people inside if they were not on a flight. So, my husband, friend, and my daughter were waiting outside in the freezing cold since 6:30 a.m. They saw so many people from my flight leave, including the pilot, but I was not coming out. They had no idea that I was being interrogated. They thought maybe I was sent back or something. They didn't know what to think. Eventually they saw me through the glass walking, and the person at the door let them come in and get me. I was anxious and just wanted to go home.

My Peru nightmare was officially over. For the most part. The US police or immigration or whatever it is *now* wanted to finally step up and act, instead of when I was begging for their help after the first few scams I fell for before Peru. I was done. The passport they gave me to come home was only good for ten days. I have no intention of ever getting another passport to leave the USA again. I repeat, it's not because I feel that the USA is the greatest in the whole wide world and I just don't want to leave it. I used to think that, but I also wanted to tour around the world and see all the beauty in it. But if this whole experience has taught me anything, it's that once you cross the US border and go out of the country, if you are ever in trouble, you are on your own. The US won't do anything to help you. I witnessed that myself, along with many other Americans in foreign prisons who can attest to this.

I am now back home, trying to pick up the pieces of my life, trying to salvage my business, which just about fell apart, meeting my new grandbabies and bonding with them, seeing my family, starting over, and destroying the passport just out of principle. If I don't fly out of the country, I believe I will never be bothered again. Not to mention, I have nothing to hide anyway. Now I just must pick up the pieces of my life and move forward.

What is the purpose of this book? To tell my story and let the world know what can happen to you and what *does* happen to many others, and at the end of the day, **beware if you fly out of the country!** Not every country has a valid justice system. There is corruption all over the place, and it doesn't take much to get caught up in it. Beware! And don't assume this is only a fictional thing that happens to stupid people. I, myself, met many intelligent people along my journey who fell for a scam and were in the same situation as me. Never say never. It happens, so be aware.

PHOTO OF ME IN DRIVING HOME
FROM THE AIRPORT – TIRED BUT HAPPY

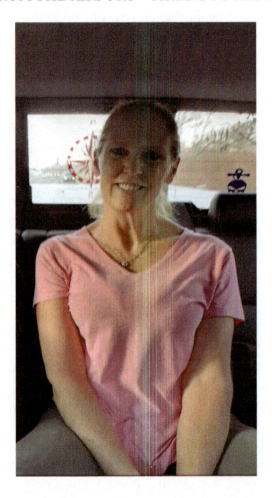

As you can see, I am *not* a stupid person. I am very educated. (I graduated high school as valedictorian and obtained my master's degree in college Suma Cum Laude with a 4.0 GPA.) I am a constant learner and strive for perfection. Sadly, my accident caused a hiccup in my brain for a while, but don't assume everyone who falls for these types of things is stupid or an idiot. It can happen to anyone. I am living proof.

EPILOGUE

TRIUMPH AMIDST TRIALS

As I penned down the last sentence of my memoir, I felt a whirlwind of emotions envelop me. The shadows of my past mingled with the promise of a new dawn. My journey through an unimaginable labyrinth, which began with a naïve fall into a scam that dragged me to a foreign land where I was ensnared for four long years, was a test of my soul.

I must confess that there was trepidation in my heart about sharing this story. The thoughts crossed my mind: *What would the world think? Would this narrative somehow cast shadows upon my character and my business?*

But something shifted within me as I looked through the pages of my life. There, in the ink, lay resilience, determination, and courage. There was a spirit that refused to be crushed and a voice that yearned to rise above the tumultuous waves.

My publisher, with a reassuring voice, said something that stilled my stormy heart. He said that in sharing this odyssey, people would see not the shadows but the strength that emerged from it. They would see a person who faced fears, battled unfamiliarity, and navigated through an unknown language and culture—all while forging an inner steel that now is a part of who I am.

This tale is not just mine; it is the story of countless souls who find themselves entangled in situations beyond their making. It is a story that needed to be told.

So, to you, dear reader, who has followed me through these pages, know this: We are, at times, a product of circumstances, but always the shapers of our destinies. The road may be rough, the night may seem endless, but the strength within us is boundless.

I hope that by opening these chapters of my life to you, I have not just shared a story, but I have extended a hand—a hand that says, "You are not alone."

My hope is that my tale inspires you to embrace your challenges, stand tall, and always forge forward. Let us all be the lanterns in the dark and the heralds of our victories.

Let this book be a testament not just to my journey, but to the indomitable human spirit that resides within each of us.

Thank you for walking this path with me.

Printed in Great Britain
by Amazon

41439696R00208